EP Fifth Reader
Days 91-180

EP Reader Series

Volume 5

CONTENTS

ACKNOWLEDGEMENTS

Thank you to Abigail Baia for her beautiful cover art.

Welcome to Easy Peasy All-in-One Homeschool's Fifth Reader

We hope you enjoy curling up with this book of books.

This is Easy Peasy's offline version of its assignments for the second half of Reading 5. The novels and poetry included are found in the public domain and have been gathered here along with each lesson's assignment directions. There are differences between this course and the online version because some reading assignments are not found in the public domain and had to be replaced.

Online activities from Easy Peasy's website, apart from reading, have been replaced with offline readings and activities found in this book.

This is only the second half of the course, Lessons 91-180. The rest of the course is in EP Fifth Reader Lessons 1-90.

Lesson 91

1. Put the words (below) in alphabetical order. Look at the first letter of the word and write the word that begins with the letter that comes first in the alphabet. If words begin with the same letter, look at the second letter of the words to compare them to see which comes first. If the second letter is the same, look at the third letters and so on. (Answers)

    *   polite, conflagration, alphabetize, congregate, congratulations, political

Lesson 92

Vocabulary

1. Label each set of words as synonyms (words that mean the same thing), antonyms (words that have opposite meanings) or homonyms (words that sound alike). (Answers)

    1. slow – languid
    2. coax – persuade
    3. contradict – agree
    4. threw – through
    5. provoke – soothe
    6. forth – fourth
    7. earnest – sincere
    8. contemptuous – honoring

Lesson 93

Vocabulary

1. Write as many synonyms as you can think of for the words given below. (Answers)

    *   big, small, loud
    *   vigilant, subside, venerable

Lesson 94

1. Read the first half of "Lost in the Fog" (A Tale of Adventure) by Irving Bacheller.

IT'S odd how some people take to geese. As a boy I never could understand, for the life of me, how one could ever have any love of a goose in him. When I came out in the glory of my first trousers a whole flock of geese came after me, the sacred garment with their bills, and hissing me

1

to shame of my new dignity, and screaming in derision as they pulled me down. After that and for long I treasured a most unrighteous hatred of the whole goose family. They were to me a low, waddling tribe with the evil spirit of envy in them. The worst thing about Mother Tipton was her geese, I used to think. She lived in a shanty by herself—a lonely man-hater—and the bit of land that climbed to the ridges on either side of it was known as Mother Tipton's Hollow. Every day skirmishers, sentinels, and reserves of geese covered the green slopes of the Hollow, and a white squadron of them was always sailing the black waters of the pond in its center. I came betimes, of a summer day, and peered over the circling ridge in a tremble of fear, whereupon a stir of white wings and a yell of defiance greeted me. Mother Tipton herself was a kindly creature who rescued me whenever I was captured by that noisy rabble of boy-haters. She was an Englishwoman, the daughter of a rich man, I believe, in the city of Bristol, and turned out of her home for some reason—we never knew why. I know she had in her shanty wonderful trinkets of gold and silver, the relics of a better day, and more than once I had the inestimable pleasure of holding them in my hands. The Hollow was half a mile from the shore of the broad Sound, and Mother Tipton took her geese and feathers to market in a rowboat. There was a big town across the bay, and she went always from the end of Shirley Point when the weather was fine, rowing as strong an oar as any man of all the many that made their living on those waters.

One morning—I was then a boy of eight years—I got permission to go with her in the boat. I remember she had a cargo of ten young geese, that were towed away, their legs tied together, in the bow of the boat.

It was a mile and a half across the bay, and the water lay like a mill-pond, with scarcely a ripple showing. A thin mist hovered about the farther shore as we pulled away, but we could see the dock clearly and the building that lay beyond it.

"Land o' Goshen!" Mother Tipton cried, after rowing a few minutes, "it's foggin'"; then she sat a long time, as it seemed to me, looking over the water at a misty wall that lay not far ahead of us. Of a sudden she began to pull vigorously on the right oar.

"It's the ebb-tide," said she, "and we must get back as quick as we can or we'll be in trouble."

Evidently she saw it coming, for she began to pull with redoubled energy. I could just see the dim outline of rocks on Shirley Point as we turned about.

"The tide has taken us half over," she muttered. "It runs like a mill-race."

Now I could see mist rising on the water under the side, as if it had turned hot suddenly. The fog thickened fast, and presently the boat had seemed to lengthen, and we to go far apart, so that I could see but dimly the face of Mother Tipton. Then I could hear her groan and breathe heavily as she put all her strength to the oars. She was lifting the bow from the water every stroke now, but suddenly I heard the snap of an oar, and the boat turned in the tide; then a splash of water hit my face.

Mother Tipton rose in the boat and shouted a long halloo. We listened for some answer, but, hearing none, she called "Help!" a dozen times, at the top of her voice. Between her cries we could hear nothing but the tide rippling under the boat.

I felt a fine thrill then, having little sense at best, and none of our danger. I remember growing very manly and chivalrous when I saw Mother Tipton crying in her seat, and did my best to comfort her.

She was up to shouting for help again presently, but not a sound came back to us. We drifted of course, with the tide, and could see nothing. She kept calling all the time, and when my tongue was dry for the need of water, and the thought of cake and cookies kept crowding on me, I lost a bit of my bravery. It was time to be getting home—there was no longer any doubt of that.

"Mother Tipton," I said, "where do you suppose we are?"

"The Lord only knows, child," was her answer. "I'm afraid we're out in the deep water half over to Long Island. But the tide has turned, and it may take us back before night comes. We'll just sit still and keep calling."

I was lying on my back in the stern, resting my head on the seat behind me, and was feeling very miserable indeed, when I heard a great disturbance among the geese.

"Willie, come here," said Mother Tipton. Two of the geese were lying in her lap, and she was unwinding a long fish-line.

"Tie it tightly," said she, "just above the big joint of the leg. Wait—let's cut it first into even lengths. That's right—now cut it."

She measured for me, and I cut the line, as she held it into ten pieces, with probably as many feet in each. Then we tied them securely to the geese, above the big joint of the legs, and fastened the loose ends together, winding them with a bit of string. We tied another fish-line to this ten-stranded cable, cut the geese apart, and let them all go at once. They flew for a little distance, and, being not all of a mind, came down in a rather bad tangle. I had hold of the line, and if I had not paid it out quickly we would surely have lost them. They ducked their heads in the water, and shook their wings, and screamed as if delighted with their liberty. Meanwhile they had begun to pull like a team of horses, and I could feel the stretch of the line. It had parted in a minute—and a thick, strong line it was at that—and I had gone overboard and was clutching for the loose end. There was a thunder of wings when they saw me coming upon them, and when I got my hand on the cord they began to pull me through the water at a great rate. I was a good swimmer, but was glad to lie over on my back and rest a little after the violence of my exertion. Then, suddenly, I heard the voice of Mother Tipton calling me, and it seemed far away. I looked in the direction it came from, and then I got a scare I hope never to have again. I could see nothing of the boat. The geese were swimming with the tide, and over all, the fog lay on the sea as thick as darkness. I was breathing hard, and lay for a long time floating on my back, my fingers clutching the tight strings.

When I turned over and got a little of the water out of my eyes, I could hear faintly in the distance the voice of Mother Tipton calling the geese just as I had heard her many a time over there in the Hollow. I could see them turn and listen, and then the whole flock veered about, cackling together as if they knew the meaning of it. The ten of them were now swimming comfortably. Every moment I could hear more distinctly the voice of Mother Tipton, and after a little I could hear the water on the boat. Suddenly its end broke through the wall of fog, and I saw my companion looming above me in the thick air, her head showing first. She answered with a cheery "Thank Heaven!" as I called to her, and the whole flock rose out of the water and tried to fly.

The geese came up to the boat-side, and she touched their beaks fondly with her hand as she came to help me in. The water had chilled me through, and I was glad enough to set my feet on the boat-bottom, and to take off my coat and wrap my shoulders in the warm shawl that Mother Tipton offered. You may be sure I kept a good hold of the strings, and before I sat down we made them fast to some ten feet of the small anchor-rope and tied it at the bow. Then those that had got their feet over the traces were carefully attended to. They lay quietly under the gunwale as Mother Tipton fussed with them, sometimes lifting one above another. She shooed them off in a moment, and they made away, turning their heads knowingly as she began to paddle.

"I believe those creatures will have sense enough to go ashore. They know more than we do about a good many things," said she. "That old gray gander of mine goes a mile away sometimes, but he'll get home, if it is foggy, every night of his life."

Lesson 95

1. Read the second half of "Lost in the Fog."

It was growing dark, and in five minutes we couldn't see our team. I was kneeling in the bow, my hand on the rope, peering to get a view of the geese, when I heard a loud quacking and a big ripple in the water just ahead. I was about to speak, when I saw a drift of dark objects on either side of the boat. I made out what they were, and caught one of them by the neck just as Mother Tipton shouted, "Ducks!" Then there was a roar of wings that made me jump back, and that set the geese in a panic. I hung on to my captive, and brought him in flapping and drenching my sleeve with spray.

"Bring him here," said Mother Tipton, as I crept to the middle seat, the poor creature fighting me desperately all the way.

"We shall need him for our supper, my dear child," said she, as she took him. "I think we're coming to shore somewhere, and I know you're hungry."

It was not long before we heard our boat-bottom grinding on the sand, but it was very dark. Mother Tipton went to the bow of the boat, and I was near the middle seat.

"Thank Heaven, we're somewhere!" I heard her say; and then she stood up, and I heard her paddle strike in the sand, and felt the boat lift forward and go up on the dry beach. I was out pulling in a moment, and I tell you the firm earth had never so good a feeling. I felt my way up the beach, and Mother Tipton came after me. It was so dark and foggy we could see nothing. After a little I felt the grass under me, and my companion lit a match and touched it to a bit of paper she had taken off of a bundle in the boat.

"Make haste, now," she said, "and pick up all the bits of small wood you see around."

The dry drift lay all around us, and in half a minute a good bit of it was crackling on that flaming wad of paper. Then we brought sticks as thick as a man's leg, and fed the flames until they leaped higher than our heads and lit the misty reaches of the shore a good distance.

"Lawsy me!" said she, presently, "I think we're on Charles Island." Then she took a brand out of the fire, and walked away in the thick grass, waving it above her head. She was calling me in a moment.

"Bring the fish-line and the tin pail!" she shouted.

I went to the boat for them, and was shortly groping through the tall grass in the direction of that flickering torch. She was not nearly so far away as I thought, the fog had such a trick of deepening the perspective in every scene. I found her by an old ruin of a house, peering into a deep well, the cover of which had mostly rotted away. We were not long tying that line to the pail and dropping it down the well-hole. The line raced through my fingers, and the pail bounded as it struck, and rang like a bell on the splashing water. When I had hauled it up, we sat looking at the slopping cylinder of cold, clear water, the golden flare of the torch shining in it, each insisting that the other must drink first, until I was quite out of patience.

She took the pail at last, and buried her mouth at the rim, and nearly smothered herself with the water. I thanked her with a good heart when I got my hands on it, for I had a mighty fever of thirst in me. When my dry tongue was soaking in the sweet, pure water, I could feel my heart lighten, and soon it was floating off its rock of despair.

"Now let's take a pailful with us, and get supper," said Mother Tipton. "We're on Charles Island, five miles from home, but it isn't more than half a mile from Milford. We'd better stop here for the night, and maybe it'll be clear before morning."

I took the torch, and she dragged behind her a bit of the fallen roof that had once covered the old house. By the light of the fire we began to dig clams with the oar and paddle. In ten minutes we had enough for a fine bake, and laid them out on a rock, and raked the hot coals over them. Mother Tipton had killed and dressed the duck, and while I tended the clams she was cutting turf and shaking the clay off it into a hollow she scooped out of the sand. She wet the clay then with salt water, and, when it was thick and sticky, rolled the duck in it until the bare skin was coated. Then she poked it into the ashes under the hot fire, and came to help me uncover the clams. We ate them with sharpened sticks, and, while some butter would have helped a bit, they went with a fine relish. The duck came out of the fire looking like a boulder of gray granite. Mother Tipton broke the hard clay with a stone, and the duck came out clean and smoking hot, leaving its skin in the shell. A more tender and delicious bit of fowl I have never eaten, the salt clay having given it the right savor.

After supper we untied the flock and set it free, and dragged the boat above tidewater. Then we drove two stakes in front of a rock near the fire, and set our strip of roofing over all. Under it we threw a good layer of hot sand from near the fire, and built high ridges on either side of our shelter. There were sacks of down for pillows, and my overcoat and the big woolen shawl as covering. Though it is so long ago—I was, as I said, only eight years old—I remember still when Mother Tipton told me to creep in and draw up the wraps around me. The warm sand gave me a grateful sense of comfort. I lay for a time and looked at the dying firelight, but before very long I fell asleep.

As I awoke, next day, I could hear the bellow of a great fog-siren, away in the distance, that sent its echoes crashing through the dungeon of mist. Next I noticed the sound of the noisy water on the rocks near by. It was growing light, and somebody was poking the fire. When I lifted my head I felt a warm breeze and saw that the fog had gone. A man with a wooden leg and a patch of gray whiskers on his chin was standing by the fire. I crept out and greeted him, rubbing my eyes with drowsiness.

"Ketched in the fog, I suppose," said he, kicking the fire.

"Yes, sir," I answered; "we were caught by the tide and lost, yesterday."

"Hum!" he muttered, as he glanced under the lean-to roof of our shanty and took a good look at Mother Tipton. "Rather a tidy bit of a woman—stout as an ox an' a good-looker."

"I'd thank you not to disturb her," I said with indignation.

"Not for the world," he answered, returning and shying another bit of wood at the fire. "I like t' see 'em sleep—it's good for 'em. Got anything for breakfus'?"

"I'm going to dig some clams," I answered.

"You jes' wait," he said, winking at me, "an' I'll go off to the tug an' bring ye some coffee an' fish an' bread an' butter. Got loads of it aboard there. No trouble at all."

He made off for his boat, that lay on the beach near by, and rowed around the point. I walked down the shore a few rods, and from a high rock saw the tug lying at anchor a little way off the shore. He came back in a short time, bringing a basket of provisions. Mother Tipton was up, and by that time I had a good fire going.

"Madam," he said, laying down the basket, "may I be so bold as to offer you su'thin' for your breakfus'? Here's a snack o' coffee an' fish an' a tidy bit o' bread an' butter."

She thanked him politely, and while we were getting breakfast, he told us that he was a menhaden-fisherman "—as owned his own tug." Then we told him our story. Afterward he insisted on taking us home. We were glad to accept his kindness, and the sun was shining brightly when we put off for the tug, with all our geese in the boat; I made Mother Tipton promise me that not one of them would ever be sold. The captain brought a big armchair and made her very comfortable in the bow of the boat. We were home in an hour, and I was as glad to get there as all were to see me. The adventure resulted in great good, for it gave me some respect for geese, and gave Mother Tipton a greater regard for men. It was not long after that she added to her museum in the Hollow a man with a wooden leg; and you may be sure I went to the wedding.

Lesson 96

1. During your reading of the next book, you are going to be practicing strategies that will help you to be actively involved in your reading. You will make predictions and ask questions before you read, you will try to figure out things that confuse you, you will connect what you read with things that you already know (your Background Knowledge), and you will reflect after you have read before going on to the next assignment. Active reading is much more than knowing words; it is bringing all that you are and know to interact with a text to make it more meaningful and fun for you — and more useful. Don't skip any steps.

2. Our new book is called *Little Men* by Louisa May Alcott.

3. Look at the cover page of the book. (following page)

4. Make some guesses. What is the book going to be about? What do you think is Plumfield? Who do you think is Jo?

5. The author is Louisa Mae Alcott. Do you know anything about her? What would you like to find out?

6. Louisa Mae Alcott was born in 1932 in Pennsylvania and was educated by her father. Her first book was published when she was 22 and before that she had writings published in magazines. She was very similar to the main character of her most famous novel, *Little Women*.

   ... young Louisa was a tomboy. "No boy could be my friend till I had beaten him in a race," she claimed, "and no girl if she refused to climb trees, leap fences ..." For Louisa, writing was an early passion. She had a rich imagination and often her stories became melodramas that she and her sisters would act out for friends... . At age 15, troubled by the poverty that plagued her family, she vowed: "I will do something by and by. Don't care what, teach, sew, act, write, anything to help the family; and I'll be rich and famous and happy before I die, see if I won't!" (from http://www.louisamayalcott.org/louisamaytext.html)

7. What surprised you about her? What are you thinking about the book or about her?

Vocabulary

1. Read through the vocabulary list carefully and try and learn the definitions.
2. Write a sentence OR draw a picture for each one.
3. If you are confused about any word, ask for clarification.

detriment : a cause of harm

recumbent: lying down

amiable: having a friendly attitude

insinuate: hint something negative in an indirect and unpleasant way

aquatic: relating to water

precocious: having abilities at an earlier age than usual

cultivate: try to develop a quality or skill

menagerie: like a zoo

Lesson 97

1. Look at the title of the first chapter. What would you like to find out?
2. Read the first part of chapter 1, "Nat."
3. What have you learned about Nat?
4. What have you learned about Plumfield?
5. About Jo?
6. Who do you think Mr. Laurence is?
7. What are you thinking?
8. Create a character sketch for Nat. Draw a picture of him and use quotes from the book to describe him. Use "" quotation marks around the words from the book and write the page number (p. 15) after the quote. You don't have to use full sentences.
9. Complete the vocabulary activity at the end of the reading. (Answers)

Chapter I. Nat

"Please, sir, is this Plumfield?" asked a ragged boy of the man who opened the great gate at which the omnibus left him.

"Yes. Who sent you?"

"Mr. Laurence. I have got a letter for the lady."

"All right; go up to the house, and give it to her; she'll see to you, little chap."

The man spoke pleasantly, and the boy went on, feeling much cheered by the words. Through the soft spring rain that fell on sprouting grass and budding trees, Nat saw a large square house before him a hospitable-looking house, with an old-fashioned porch, wide steps, and lights shining in many windows. Neither curtains nor shutters hid the cheerful glimmer; and, pausing a moment before he rang, Nat saw many little shadows dancing on the walls, heard the pleasant hum of young voices, and felt that it was hardly possible that the light and warmth and comfort within could be for a homeless "little chap" like him.

"I hope the lady will see to me," he thought, and gave a timid rap with the great bronze knocker, which was a jovial griffin's head.

A rosy-faced servant-maid opened the door, and smiled as she took the letter which he silently offered. She seemed used to receiving strange boys, for she pointed to a seat in the hall, and said, with a nod:

"Sit there and drip on the mat a bit, while I take this in to missis."

Nat found plenty to amuse him while he waited, and stared about him curiously, enjoying the view, yet glad to do so unobserved in the dusky recess by the door.

The house seemed swarming with boys, who were beguiling the rainy twilight with all sorts of amusements. There were boys everywhere, "up-stairs and down-stairs and in the lady's chamber," apparently, for various open doors showed pleasant groups of big boys, little boys, and middle-sized boys in all stages of evening relaxation, not to say effervescence. Two large rooms on the right were evidently schoolrooms, for desks, maps, blackboards, and books were scattered about. An open fire burned on the hearth, and several indolent lads lay on their backs before it, discussing a new cricket-ground, with such animation that their boots waved in the air. A tall youth was practising on the flute in one corner, quite undisturbed by the racket all about him. Two or three others were jumping over the desks, pausing, now and then, to get their breath and laugh at the droll sketches of a little wag who was caricaturing the whole household on a blackboard.

In the room on the left a long supper-table was seen, set forth with great pitchers of new milk, piles of brown and white bread, and perfect stacks of the shiny gingerbread so dear to boyish souls. A flavor of toast was in the air, also suggestions of baked apples, very tantalizing to one hungry little nose and stomach.

The hall, however, presented the most inviting prospect of all, for a brisk game of tag was going on in the upper entry. One landing was devoted to marbles, the other to checkers, while the stairs were occupied by a boy reading, a girl singing a lullaby to her doll, two puppies, a kitten, and a constant succession of small boys sliding down the banisters, to the great detriment of their clothes and danger to their limbs.

So absorbed did Nat become in this exciting race, that he ventured farther and farther out of his corner; and when one very lively boy came down so swiftly that he could not stop himself, but fell off the banisters, with a crash that would have broken any head but one rendered nearly as hard as a cannon-ball by eleven years of constant bumping, Nat forgot himself, and ran up to the fallen rider, expecting to find him half-dead. The boy, however, only winked rapidly for a second, then lay calmly looking up at the new face with a surprised, "Hullo!"

"Hullo!" returned Nat, not knowing what else to say, and thinking that form of reply both brief and easy.

"Are you a new boy?" asked the recumbent youth, without stirring.

"Don't know yet."

"What's your name?"

"Nat Blake."

"Mine's Tommy Bangs. Come up and have a go, will you?" and Tommy got upon his legs like one suddenly remembering the duties of hospitality.

"Guess I won't, till I see whether I'm going to stay or not," returned Nat, feeling the desire to stay increase every moment.

"I say, Demi, here's a new one. Come and see to him;" and the lively Thomas returned to his sport with unabated relish.

At his call, the boy reading on the stairs looked up with a pair of big brown eyes, and after an instant's pause, as if a little shy, he put the book under his arm, and came soberly down to greet the new-comer, who found something very attractive in the pleasant face of this slender, mild-eyed boy.

"Have you seen Aunt Jo?" he asked, as if that was some sort of important ceremony.

"I haven't seen anybody yet but you boys; I'm waiting," answered Nat.

"Did Uncle Laurie send you?" proceeded Demi, politely, but gravely.

"Mr. Laurence did."

"He is Uncle Laurie; and he always sends nice boys."

Nat looked gratified at the remark, and smiled, in a way that made his thin face very pleasant. He did not know what to say next, so the two stood staring at one another in friendly silence, till the little girl came up with her doll in her arms. She was very like Demi, only not so tall, and had a rounder, rosier face, and blue eyes.

"This is my sister, Daisy," announced Demi, as if presenting a rare and precious creature.

The children nodded to one another; and the little girl's face dimpled with pleasure, as she said affably:

"I hope you'll stay. We have such good times here; don't we, Demi?"

"Of course, we do: that's what Aunt Jo has Plumfield for."

"It seems a very nice place indeed," observed Nat, feeling that he must respond to these amiable young persons.

11

"It's the nicest place in the world, isn't it, Demi?" said Daisy, who evidently regarded her brother as authority on all subjects.

"No, I think Greenland, where the icebergs and seals are, is more interesting. But I'm fond of Plumfield, and it is a very nice place to be in," returned Demi, who was interested just now in a book on Greenland. He was about to offer to show Nat the pictures and explain them, when the servant returned, saying with a nod toward the parlor-door:

"All right; you are to stop."

"I'm glad; now come to Aunt Jo." And Daisy took him by the hand with a pretty protecting air, which made Nat feel at home at once.

Demi returned to his beloved book, while his sister led the new-comer into a back room, where a stout gentleman was frolicking with two little boys on the sofa, and a thin lady was just finishing the letter which she seemed to have been re-reading.

"Here he is, aunty!" cried Daisy.

"So this is my new boy? I am glad to see you, my dear, and hope you'll be happy here," said the lady, drawing him to her, and stroking back the hair from his forehead with a kind hand and a motherly look, which made Nat's lonely little heart yearn toward her.

She was not at all handsome, but she had a merry sort of face that never seemed to have forgotten certain childish ways and looks, any more than her voice and manner had; and these things, hard to describe but very plain to see and feel, made her a genial, comfortable kind of person, easy to get on with, and generally "jolly," as boys would say. She saw the little tremble of Nat's lips as she smoothed his hair, and her keen eyes grew softer, but she only drew the shabby figure nearer and said, laughing:

"I am Mother Bhaer, that gentleman is Father Bhaer, and these are the two little Bhaers. Come here, boys, and see Nat."

The three wrestlers obeyed at once; and the stout man, with a chubby child on each shoulder, came up to welcome the new boy. Rob and Teddy merely grinned at him, but Mr. Bhaer shook hands, and pointing to a low chair near the fire, said, in a cordial voice:

"There is a place all ready for thee, my son; sit down and dry thy wet feet at once."

"Wet? So they are! My dear, off with your shoes this minute, and I'll have some dry things ready for you in a jiffy," cried Mrs. Bhaer, bustling about so energetically that Nat found himself in the cosy little chair, with dry socks and warm slippers on his feet, before he would have had time to say Jack Robinson, if he had wanted to try. He said "Thank you, ma'am," instead; and said it so gratefully that Mrs. Bhaer's eyes grew soft again, and she said something merry, because she felt so tender, which was a way she had.

"There are Tommy Bangs' slippers; but he never will remember to put them on in the house; so he shall not have them. They are too big; but that's all the better; you can't run away from us so fast as if they fitted."

"I don't want to run away, ma'am." And Nat spread his grimy little hands before the comfortable blaze, with a long sigh of satisfaction.

"That's good! Now I am going to toast you well, and try to get rid of that ugly cough. How long have you had it, dear?" asked Mrs. Bhaer, as she rummaged in her big basket for a strip of flannel.

"All winter. I got cold, and it wouldn't get better, somehow."

"No wonder, living in that damp cellar with hardly a rag to his poor dear back!" said Mrs. Bhaer, in a low tone to her husband, who was looking at the boy with a skillful pair of eyes that marked the thin temples and feverish lips, as well as the hoarse voice and frequent fits of coughing that shook the bent shoulders under the patched jacket.

"Robin, my man, trot up to Nursey, and tell her to give thee the cough-bottle and the liniment," said Mr. Bhaer, after his eyes had exchanged telegrams with his wife's.

Nat looked a little anxious at the preparations, but forgot his fears in a hearty laugh, when Mrs. Bhaer whispered to him, with a droll look:

"Hear my rogue Teddy try to cough. The syrup I'm going to give you has honey in it; and he wants some."

Little Ted was red in the face with his exertions by the time the bottle came, and was allowed to suck the spoon after Nat had manfully taken a dose and had the bit of flannel put about his throat.

These first steps toward a cure were hardly completed when a great bell rang, and a loud tramping through the hall announced supper. Bashful Nat quaked at the thought of meeting many strange boys, but Mrs. Bhaer held out her hand to him, and Rob said, patronizingly, "Don't be 'fraid; I'll take care of you."

Twelve boys, six on a side, stood behind their chairs, prancing with impatience to begin, while the tall flute-playing youth was trying to curb their ardor. But no one sat down till Mrs. Bhaer was in her place behind the teapot, with Teddy on her left, and Nat on her right.

"This is our new boy, Nat Blake. After supper you can say how do you do? Gently, boys, gently."

As she spoke every one stared at Nat, and then whisked into their seats, trying to be orderly and failing utterly. The Bhaers did their best to have the lads behave well at meal times, and generally succeeded pretty well, for their rules were few and sensible, and the boys, knowing that they tried to make things easy and happy, did their best to obey. But there are times when hungry boys cannot be repressed without real cruelty, and Saturday evening, after a half-holiday, was one of those times.

"Dear little souls, do let them have one day in which they can howl and racket and frolic to their hearts' content. A holiday isn't a holiday without plenty of freedom and fun; and they shall have full swing once a week," Mrs. Bhaer used to say, when prim people wondered why banister-sliding, pillow-fights, and all manner of jovial games were allowed under the once decorous roof of Plumfield.

It did seem at times as if the aforesaid roof was in danger of flying off, but it never did, for a word from Father Bhaer could at any time produce a lull, and the lads had learned that liberty must not be abused. So, in spite of many dark predictions, the school flourished, and manners and morals were insinuated, without the pupils exactly knowing how it was done.

Nat found himself very well off behind the tall pitchers, with Tommy Bangs just around the corner, and Mrs. Bhaer close by to fill up plate and mug as fast as he could empty them.

"Who is that boy next the girl down at the other end?" whispered Nat to his young neighbor under cover of a general laugh.

"That's Demi Brooke. Mr. Bhaer is his uncle."

"What a queer name!"

"His real name is John, but they call him Demi-John, because his father is John too. That's a joke, don't you see?" said Tommy, kindly explaining. Nat did not see, but politely smiled, and asked, with interest:

"Isn't he a very nice boy?"

"I bet you he is; knows lots and reads like any thing."

"Who is the fat one next him?"

"Oh, that's Stuffy Cole. His name is George, but we call him Stuffy 'cause he eats so much. The little fellow next Father Bhaer is his boy Rob, and then there's big Franz his nephew; he teaches some, and kind of sees to us."

"He plays the flute, doesn't he?" asked Nat as Tommy rendered himself speechless by putting a whole baked apple into his mouth at one blow.

Tommy nodded, and said, sooner than one would have imagined possible under the circumstances, "Oh, don't he, though? And we dance sometimes, and do gymnastics to music. I like a drum myself, and mean to learn as soon as ever I can."

"I like a fiddle best; I can play one too," said Nat, getting confidential on this attractive subject.

"Can you?" and Tommy stared over the rim of his mug with round eyes, full of interest. "Mr. Bhaer's got an old fiddle, and he'll let you play on it if you want to."

"Could I? Oh, I would like it ever so much. You see, I used to go round fiddling with my father, and another man, till he died."

"Wasn't that fun?" cried Tommy, much impressed.

"No, it was horrid; so cold in winter, and hot in summer. And I got tired; and they were cross sometimes; and I didn't get enough to eat." Nat paused to take a generous bite of gingerbread, as if to assure himself that the hard times were over; and then he added regretfully: "But I did love my little fiddle, and I miss it. Nicolo took it away when father died, and wouldn't have me any longer, 'cause I was sick."

"You'll belong to the band if you play good. See if you don't."

"Do you have a band here?" Nat's eyes sparkled.

"Guess we do; a jolly band, all boys; and they have concerts and things. You just see what happens to-morrow night."

After this pleasantly exciting remark, Tommy returned to his supper, and Nat sank into a blissful reverie over his full plate.

Mrs. Bhaer had heard all they said, while apparently absorbed in filling mugs, and overseeing little Ted, who was so sleepy that he put his spoon in his eye, nodded like a rosy poppy, and finally fell fast asleep, with his cheek pillowed on a soft bun. Mrs. Bhaer had put Nat next to Tommy, because that roly-poly boy had a frank and social way with him, very attractive to shy persons. Nat felt this, and had made several small confidences during supper, which gave Mrs. Bhaer the key to the new boy's character, better than if she had talked to him herself.

In the letter which Mr. Laurence had sent with Nat, he had said:

> DEAR JO: Here is a case after your own heart. This poor lad is an orphan now, sick and friendless. He has been a street-musician; and I found him in a cellar, mourning for his dead father, and his lost violin. I think there is something in him, and have a fancy that between us we may give this little man a lift. You cure his overtasked body, Fritz help his neglected mind, and when he is ready I'll see if he is a genius or only a boy with a talent which may earn his bread for him. Give him a trial, for the sake of your own boy,
>
> TEDDY.

Vocabulary

1. Review your words from Lesson 96 by matching the words to their definitions. Write the numbers and matching letters on a separate piece of paper.

   1. hint something negative in an indirect way   A. menagerie

   2. having abilities at an earlier age than usual   B. amiable

   3. try to develop a quality or skill   C. recumbent

   4. having a friendly attitude   D. insinuate

   5. relating to water   E. cultivate

   6. a cause of harm   F. precocious

   7. like a zoo   G. aquatic

   8. lying down   H. detriment

Lesson 98

1. What would you like to find out as you read the rest of the chapter?
2. Finish reading chapter 1.
3. Now what are you thinking? Does anything surprise you? Does anything confuse you?
4. Create a setting sketch for Plumfield. Draw a picture of some part of it and use quotes from the book to describe it.
5. Who is Jo and what is Plumfield? (Answers)
6. What kind of place is Plumfield? Is it a strict? Fun? Why? (Answers)
7. What are you thinking about this school? There's no wrong answer to this question as long as you think something!

Chapter I. continued

"Of course we will!" cried Mrs. Bhaer, as she read the letter; and when she saw Nat she felt at once that, whether he was a genius or not, here was a lonely, sick boy who needed just what she loved to give, a home and motherly care. Both she and Mr. Bhaer observed him quietly; and in spite of ragged clothes, awkward manners, and a dirty face, they saw much about Nat that pleased them. He was a thin, pale boy, of twelve, with blue eyes, and a good forehead under the rough, neglected hair; an anxious, scared face, at times, as if he expected hard words, or blows; and a sensitive mouth that trembled when a kind glance fell on him; while a gentle speech called up a look of gratitude, very sweet to see. "Bless the poor dear, he shall fiddle all day long if he likes," said Mrs. Bhaer to herself, as she saw the eager, happy expression on his face when Tommy talked of the band.

So, after supper, when the lads flocked into the schoolroom for more "high jinks," Mrs. Jo appeared with a violin in her hand, and after a word with her husband, went to Nat, who sat in a corner watching the scene with intense interest.

"Now, my lad, give us a little tune. We want a violin in our band, and I think you will do it nicely."

She expected that he would hesitate; but he seized the old fiddle at once, and handled it with such loving care, it was plain to see that music was his passion.

"I'll do the best I can, ma'am," was all he said; and then drew the bow across the strings, as if eager to hear the dear notes again.

There was a great clatter in the room, but as if deaf to any sounds but those he made, Nat played softly to himself, forgetting every thing in his delight. It was only a simple melody, such as street-musicians play, but it caught the ears of the boys at once, and silenced them, till they stood listening with surprise and pleasure. Gradually they got nearer and nearer, and Mr. Bhaer came up to watch the boy; for, as if he was in his element now, Nat played away and never minded any one, while his eyes shone, his cheeks reddened, and his thin fingers flew, as he hugged the old fiddle and made it speak to all their hearts the language that he loved.

A hearty round of applause rewarded him better than a shower of pennies, when he stopped and glanced about him, as if to say:

"I've done my best; please like it."

"I say, you do that first rate," cried Tommy, who considered Nat his protege.

"You shall be the first fiddle in my band," added Franz, with an approving smile.

Mrs. Bhaer whispered to her husband:

"Teddy is right: there's something in the child." And Mr. Bhaer nodded his head emphatically, as he clapped Nat on the shoulder, saying, heartily:

"You play well, my son. Come now and play something which we can sing."

It was the proudest, happiest minute of the poor boy's life when he was led to the place of honor by the piano, and the lads gathered round, never heeding his poor clothes, but eying him respectfully and waiting eagerly to hear him play again.

They chose a song he knew; and after one or two false starts they got going, and violin, flute, and piano led a chorus of boyish voices that made the old roof ring again. It was too much for Nat, more feeble than he knew; and as the final shout died away, his face began to work, he dropped the fiddle, and turning to the wall sobbed like a little child.

"My dear, what is it?" asked Mrs. Bhaer, who had been singing with all her might, and trying to keep little Rob from beating time with his boots.

"You are all so kind and it's so beautiful I can't help it," sobbed Nat, coughing till he was breathless.

"Come with me, dear; you must go to bed and rest; you are worn out, and this is too noisy a place for you," whispered Mrs. Bhaer; and took him away to her own parlor, where she let him cry himself quiet.

Then she won him to tell her all his troubles, and listened to the little story with tears in her own eyes, though it was not a new one to her.

"My child, you have got a father and a mother now, and this is home. Don't think of those sad times any more, but get well and happy; and be sure you shall never suffer again, if we can help it. This place is made for all sorts of boys to have a good time in, and to learn how to help themselves and be useful men, I hope. You shall have as much music as you want, only you must get strong first. Now come up to Nursey and have a bath, and then go to bed, and to-morrow we will lay some nice little plans together."

Nat held her hand fast in his, but had not a word to say, and let his grateful eyes speak for him, as Mrs. Bhaer led him up to a big room, where they found a stout German woman with a face so round and cheery that it looked like a sort of sun, with the wide frill of her cap for rays.

"This is Nursey Hummel, and she will give you a nice bath, and cut your hair, and make you all 'comfy,' as Rob says. That's the bath-room in there; and on Saturday nights we scrub all the little lads first, and pack them away in bed before the big ones get through singing. Now then, Rob, in with you."

As she talked, Mrs. Bhaer had whipped off Rob's clothes and popped him into a long bath-tub in the little room opening into the nursery.

There were two tubs, besides foot-baths, basins, douche-pipes, and all manner of contrivances for cleanliness. Nat was soon luxuriating in the other bath; and while simmering there, he watched the performances of the two women, who scrubbed, clean night-gowned, and bundled into bed four or five small boys, who, of course, cut up all sorts of capers during the operation, and kept every one in a gale of merriment till they were extinguished in their beds.

By the time Nat was washed and done up in a blanket by the fire, while Nursey cut his hair, a new detachment of boys arrived and were shut into the bath-room, where they made as much splashing and noise as a school of young whales at play.

"Nat had better sleep here, so that if his cough troubles him in the night you can see that he takes a good draught of flax-seed tea," said Mrs. Bhaer, who was flying about like a distracted hen with a large brood of lively ducklings.

Nursey approved the plan, finished Nat off with a flannel night-gown, a drink of something warm and sweet, and then tucked him into one of the three little beds standing in the room, where he lay looking like a contented mummy and feeling that nothing more in the way of luxury could be offered him. Cleanliness in itself was a new and delightful sensation; flannel gowns were unknown comforts in his world; sips of "good stuff" soothed his cough as pleasantly as kind words did his lonely heart; and the feeling that somebody cared for him made that plain room seem a sort of heaven to the homeless child. It was like a cosy dream; and he often shut his eyes to see if it would not vanish when he opened them again. It was too pleasant to let him sleep, and he could not have done so if he had tried, for in a few minutes one of the peculiar institutions of Plumfield was revealed to his astonished but appreciative eyes.

A momentary lull in the aquatic exercises was followed by the sudden appearance of pillows flying in all directions, hurled by white goblins, who came rioting out of their beds. The battle raged in several rooms, all down the upper hall, and even surged at intervals into the nursery, when some hard-pressed warrior took refuge there. No one seemed to mind this explosion in the least; no one forbade it, or even looked surprised. Nursey went on hanging up towels, and Mrs. Bhaer laid out clean clothes, as calmly as if the most perfect order reigned. Nay, she even chased one daring boy out of the room, and fired after him the pillow he had slyly thrown at her.

"Won't they hurt 'em?" asked Nat, who lay laughing with all his might.

"Oh dear, no! We always allow one pillow-fight Saturday night. The cases are changed to-morrow; and it gets up a glow after the boys' baths; so I rather like it myself," said Mrs. Bhaer, busy again among her dozen pairs of socks.

"What a very nice school this is!" observed Nat, in a burst of admiration.

"It's an odd one," laughed Mrs. Bhaer, "but you see we don't believe in making children miserable by too many rules, and too much study. I forbade night-gown parties at first; but, bless you, it was of no use. I could no more keep those boys in their beds than so many jacks in the box. So I made an agreement with them: I was to allow a fifteen-minute pillow-fight every Saturday night; and they promised to go properly to bed every other night. I tried it, and it worked well. If they don't keep their word, no frolic; if they do, I just turn the glasses round, put the lamps in safe places, and let them rampage as much as they like."

"It's a beautiful plan," said Nat, feeling that he should like to join in the fray, but not venturing to propose it the first night. So he lay enjoying the spectacle, which certainly was a lively one.

Tommy Bangs led the assailing party, and Demi defended his own room with a dogged courage fine to see, collecting pillows behind him as fast as they were thrown, till the besiegers were out of ammunition, when they would charge upon him in a body, and recover their arms. A few slight accidents occurred, but nobody minded, and gave and took sounding thwacks with perfect good humor, while pillows flew like big snowflakes, till Mrs. Bhaer looked at her watch, and called out:

"Time is up, boys. Into bed, every man jack, or pay the forfeit!"

"What is the forfeit?" asked Nat, sitting up in his eagerness to know what happened to those wretches who disobeyed this most peculiar, but public-spirited school-ma'am.

"Lose their fun next time," answered Mrs. Bhaer. "I give them five minutes to settle down, then put out the lights, and expect order. They are honorable lads, and they keep their word."

That was evident, for the battle ended as abruptly as it began a parting shot or two, a final cheer, as Demi fired the seventh pillow at the retiring foe, a few challenges for next time, then order prevailed. And nothing but an occasional giggle or a suppressed whisper broke the quiet which followed the Saturday-night frolic, as Mother Bhaer kissed her new boy and left him to happy dreams of life at Plumfield.

Lesson 99

1. The title of the next chapter is "The Boys." Predict what you might find out in Chapter 2.
2. Read chapter 2.
3. Tell someone about the chapter.
4. What kind of animal is a dromedary? Have you ever seen one? If so, where?

5. After reading chapter 2, which boy is your favorite? Why? Which is your least favorite? Why? Is there one like you? Which one?

6. Each of the boys is at Plumfield school for a different reason. Explain two of the reasons.

7. What are you thinking?

8. Create a character page for one of "the boys."

Chapter II. The Boys

While Nat takes a good long sleep, I will tell my little readers something about the boys, among whom he found himself when he woke up.

To begin with our old friends. Franz was a tall lad, of sixteen now, a regular German, big, blond, and bookish, also very domestic, amiable, and musical. His uncle was fitting him for college, and his aunt for a happy home of his own hereafter, because she carefully fostered in him gentle manners, love of children, respect for women, old and young, and helpful ways about the house. He was her right-hand man on all occasions, steady, kind, and patient; and he loved his merry aunt like a mother, for such she had tried to be to him.

Emil was quite different, being quick-tempered, restless, and enterprising, bent on going to sea, for the blood of the old vikings stirred in his veins, and could not be tamed. His uncle promised that he should go when he was sixteen, and set him to studying navigation, gave him stories of good and famous admirals and heroes to read, and let him lead the life of a frog in river, pond, and brook, when lessons were done. His room looked like the cabin of a man-of-war, for every thing was nautical, military, and shipshape. Captain Kyd was his delight, and his favorite amusement was to rig up like that piratical gentleman, and roar out sanguinary sea-songs at the top of his voice. He would dance nothing but sailors' hornpipes, rolled in his gait, and was as nautical in conversation to his uncle would permit. The boys called him "Commodore," and took great pride in his fleet, which whitened the pond and suffered disasters that would have daunted any commander but a sea-struck boy.

Demi was one of the children who show plainly the effect of intelligent love and care, for soul and body worked harmoniously together. The natural refinement which nothing but home influence can teach, gave him sweet and simple manners: his mother had cherished an innocent and loving heart in him; his father had watched over the physical growth of his boy, and kept the little body straight and strong on wholesome food and exercise and sleep, while Grandpa March cultivated the little mind with the tender wisdom of a modern Pythagoras, not tasking it with long, hard lessons, parrot-learned, but helping it to unfold as naturally and beautifully as sun and dew help roses bloom. He was not a perfect child, by any means, but his faults were of the better sort; and being early taught the secret of self-control, he was not left at the mercy of appetites and passions, as some poor little mortals are, and then punished for yielding to the temptations against which they have no armor. A quiet, quaint boy was Demi, serious, yet cheery, quite unconscious that he was unusually bright and beautiful, yet quick to see and love intelligence or beauty in other children. Very fond of books, and full of lively fancies, born of a strong imagination and a spiritual nature, these traits made his parents anxious to balance them with useful knowledge and healthful society, lest they should make him one of those pale precocious children who amaze and delight a family sometimes, and fade away like hot-house flowers, because the young soul blooms too soon, and has not a hearty body to root it firmly in the wholesome soil of this world.

So Demi was transplanted to Plumfield, and took so kindly to the life there, that Meg and John and Grandpa felt satisfied that they had done well. Mixing with other boys brought out the practical side of him, roused his spirit, and brushed away the pretty cobwebs he was so fond of spinning in that little brain of his. To be sure, he rather shocked his mother when he came home, by banging doors, saying "by George" emphatically, and demanding tall thick boots "that clumped like papa's." But John rejoiced over him, laughed at his explosive remarks, got the boots, and said contentedly,

"He is doing well; so let him clump. I want my son to be a manly boy, and this temporary roughness won't hurt him. We can polish him up by and by; and as for learning, he will pick that up as pigeons do peas. So don't hurry him."

Daisy was as sunshiny and charming as ever, with all sorts of womanlinesses budding in her, for she was like her gentle mother, and delighted in domestic things. She had a family of dolls, whom she brought up in the most exemplary manner; she could not get on without her little work-basket and bits of sewing, which she did so nicely, that Demi frequently pulled out his handkerchief display her neat stitches, and Baby Josy had a flannel petticoat beautifully made by Sister Daisy. She like to quiddle about the china-closet, prepare the salt-cellars, put the spoons straight on the table; and every day went round the parlor with her brush, dusting chairs and tables. Demi called her a "Betty," but was very glad to have her keep his things in order, lend him her nimble fingers in all sorts of work, and help him with his lessons, for they kept abreast there, and had no thought of rivalry.

The love between them was as strong as ever; and no one could laugh Demi out of his affectionate ways with Daisy. He fought her battles valiantly, and never could understand why boys should be ashamed to say "right out," that they loved their sisters. Daisy adored her twin, thought "my brother" the most remarkable boy in the world, and every morning, in her little wrapper, trotted to tap at his door with a motherly "Get up, my dear, it's 'most breakfast time; and here's your clean collar."

Rob was an energetic morsel of a boy, who seemed to have discovered the secret of perpetual motion, for he never was still. Fortunately, he was not mischievous, nor very brave; so he kept out of trouble pretty well, and vibrated between father and mother like an affectionate little pendulum with a lively tick, for Rob was a chatterbox.

Teddy was too young to play a very important part in the affairs of Plumfield, yet he had his little sphere, and filled it beautifully. Every one felt the need of a pet at times, and Baby was always ready to accommodate, for kissing and cuddling suited him excellently. Mrs. Jo seldom stirred without him; so he had his little finger in all the domestic pies, and every one found them all the better for it, for they believed in babies at Plumfield.

Dick Brown, and Adolphus or Dolly Pettingill, were two eight year-olds. Dolly stuttered badly, but was gradually getting over it, for no one was allowed to mock him and Mr. Bhaer tried to cure it, by making him talk slowly. Dolly was a good little lad, quite uninteresting and ordinary, but he flourished here, and went through his daily duties and pleasures with placid content and propriety.

Dick Brown's affliction was a crooked back, yet he bore his burden so cheerfully, that Demi once asked in his queer way, "Do humps make people good-natured? I'd like one if they do." Dick was always merry, and did his best to be like other boys, for a plucky spirit lived in the feeble little body. When he first came, he was very sensitive about his misfortune, but soon learned to forget it, for no one dared remind him of it, after Mr. Bhaer had punished one boy for laughing at him.

"God don't care; for my soul is straight if my back isn't," sobbed Dick to his tormentor on that occasion; and, by cherishing this idea, the Bhaers soon led him to believe that people also loved his soul, and did not mind his body, except to pity and help him to bear it.

Playing menagerie once with the others, some one said, "What animal will you be, Dick?"

"Oh, I'm the dromedary; don't you see the hump on my back?" was the laughing answer.

"So you are, my nice little one that don't carry loads, but marches by the elephant first in the procession," said Demi, who was arranging the spectacle.

"I hope others will be as kind to the poor dear as my boys have learned to be," said Mrs. Jo, quite satisfied with the success of her teaching, as Dick ambled past her, looking like a very happy, but a very feeble little dromedary, beside stout Stuffy, who did the elephant with ponderous propriety.

Jack Ford was a sharp, rather a sly lad, who was sent to this school, because it was cheap. Many men would have thought him a smart boy, but Mr. Bhaer did not like his way of illustrating that Yankee word, and thought his unboyish keenness and money-loving as much of an affliction as Dolly's stutter, or Dick's hump.

Ned Barker was like a thousand other boys of fourteen, all legs, blunder, and bluster. Indeed the family called him the "Blunderbuss," and always expected to see him tumble over the chairs, bump against the tables, and knock down any small articles near him. He bragged a good deal about what he could do, but seldom did any thing to prove it, was not brave, and a little given to tale-telling. He was apt to bully the small boys, and flatter the big ones, and without being at all bad, was just the sort of fellow who could very easily be led astray.

George Cole had been spoilt by an over-indulgent mother, who stuffed him with sweetmeats till he was sick, and then thought him too delicate to study, so that at twelve years old, he was a pale, puffy boy, dull, fretful, and lazy. A friend persuaded her to send him to Plumfield, and there he soon got waked up, for sweet things were seldom allowed, much exercise required, and study made so pleasant, that Stuffy was gently lured along, till he quite amazed his anxious mamma by his improvement, and convinced her that there was really something remarkable in Plumfield air.

Billy Ward was what the Scotch tenderly call an "innocent," for though thirteen years old, he was like a child of six. He had been an unusually intelligent boy, and his father had hurried him on too fast, giving him all sorts of hard lessons, keeping at his books six hours a day, and expecting him to absorb knowledge as a Strasburg goose does the food crammed down its throat. He thought he was doing his duty, but he nearly killed the boy, for a fever gave the poor child a sad holiday, and when he recovered, the overtasked brain gave out, and Billy's mind was like a slate over which a sponge has passed, leaving it blank.

It was a terrible lesson to his ambitious father; he could not bear the sight of his promising child, changed to a feeble idiot, and he sent him away to Plumfield, scarcely hoping that he could be helped, but sure that he would be kindly treated. Quite docile and harmless was Billy, and it was pitiful to see how hard he tried to learn, as if groping dimly after the lost knowledge which had cost him so much.

Day after day, he pored over the alphabet, proudly said A and B, and thought that he knew them, but on the morrow they were gone, and all the work was to be done over again. Mr. Bhaer had infinite patience with him, and kept on in spite of the apparent hopelessness of the task, not caring for book lessons, but trying gently to clear away the mists from the darkened mind, and give it back intelligence enough to make the boy less a burden and an affliction.

Mrs. Bhaer strengthened his health by every aid she could invent, and the boys all pitied and were kind to him. He did not like their active plays, but would sit for hours watching the doves, would dig holes for Teddy till even that ardent grubber was satisfied, or follow Silas, the man, from place to place seeing him work, for honest Si was very good to him, and though he forgot his letters Billy remembered friendly faces.

Tommy Bangs was the scapegrace of the school, and the most trying scapegrace that ever lived. As full of mischief as a monkey, yet so good-hearted that one could not help forgiving his tricks; so scatter-brained that words went by him like the wind, yet so penitent for every misdeed, that it was impossible to keep sober when he vowed tremendous vows of reformation, or proposed all sorts of queer punishments to be inflicted upon himself. Mr. and Mrs. Bhaer lived in a state of preparation for any mishap, from the breaking of Tommy's own neck, to the blowing up of the entire family with gunpowder; and Nursey had a particular drawer in which she kept bandages, plasters, and salves for his especial use, for Tommy was always being brought in half dead; but nothing ever killed him, and he arose from every downfall with redoubled vigor.

The first day he came, he chopped the top off one finger in the hay-cutter, and during the week, fell from the shed roof, was chased by an angry hen who tried to pick his out because he examined her chickens, got run away with, and had his ears boxed violent by Asia, who caught him luxuriously skimming a pan of cream with half a stolen pie. Undaunted, however, by any failures or rebuffs, this indomitable youth went on amusing himself with all sorts of tricks till no one felt safe. If he did not know his lessons, he always had some droll excuse to offer, and as he was usually clever at his books, and as bright as a button in composing answers when he did not know them, he go on pretty well at school. But out of school, Ye gods and little fishes! how Tommy did carouse!

He wound fat Asia up in her own clothes line against the post, and left here there to fume and scold for half an hour one busy Monday morning. He dropped a hot cent down Mary Ann's back as that pretty maid was waiting at table one day when there were gentlemen to dinner, whereat the poor girl upset the soup and rushed out of the room in dismay, leaving the family to think that she had gone mad. He fixed a pail of water up in a tree, with a bit of ribbon fastened to the handle, and when Daisy, attracted by the gay streamer, tried to pull it down, she got a douche bath that spoiled her clean frock and hurt her little feelings very much. He put rough white pebbles in the sugar-bowl when his grandmother came to tea, and the poor old lady wondered why they didn't melt in her cup, but was too polite to say anything. He passed around snuff in church so that five of the boys sneezed with such violence they had to go out. He dug paths in winter time, and then privately watered them so that people should tumble down. He drove poor Silas nearly wild by hanging his big boots in conspicuous places, for his feet were enormous, and he was very much ashamed of them. He persuaded confiding little Dolly to tie a thread to one of his loose teeth, and leave the string hanging from his mouth when he went to sleep, so that Tommy could pull it out without his feeling the dreaded operation. But the tooth wouldn't come at the first tweak, and poor Dolly woke up in great anguish of spirit, and lost all faith in Tommy from that day forth.

The last prank had been to give the hens bread soaked in rum, which made them tipsy and scandalized all the other fowls, for the respectable old biddies went staggering about, pecking and clucking in the most maudlin manner, while the family were convulsed with laughter at their antics, till Daisy took pity on them and shut them up in the hen-house to sleep off their intoxication.

These were the boys and they lived together as happy as twelve lads could, studying and playing, working and squabbling, fighting faults and cultivating virtues in the good old-fashioned way. Boys at other schools probably learned more from books, but less of that better wisdom which makes good men. Latin, Greek, and mathematics were all very well, but in Professor Bhaer's opinion, self knowledge, self-help, and self-control were more important, and he tried to teach them carefully. People shook their heads sometimes at his ideas, even while they owned that the boys improved wonderfully in manners and morals. But then, as Mrs. Jo said to Nat, "it was an odd school."

Lesson 100

1. Read the chapter title. What do you predict will happen on Sundays at Plumfield? Explain your thinking.
2. Read the first part of chapter 3.
3. Squab just refers to pigeon.
4. It talks about the family going on walks. What did they learn on walks? What do you think it means that there are "sermons in stones." (Answers)
5. Think about a time when you were in a totally new environment and wondered how to fit in. Who or what helped you to get adjusted? Who or what is helping Nat? How?
6. Fill in a setting sketch for Demi and Tommy's "private place."

Vocabulary

1. Review your words from Lesson 96.

Chapter III. Sunday

The moment the bell rang next morning Nat flew out of bed, and dressed himself with great satisfaction in the suit of clothes he found on the chair. They were not new, being half-worn garments of one of the well-to-do boys; but Mrs. Bhaer kept all such cast-off feathers for the picked robins who strayed into her nest. They were hardly on when Tommy appeared in a high state of clean collar, and escorted Nat down to breakfast.

The sun was shining into the dining-room on the well-spread table, and the flock of hungry, hearty lads who gathered round it. Nat observed that they were much more orderly than they had been the night before, and every one stood silently behind his chair while little Rob, standing beside his father at the head of the table, folded his hands, reverently bent his curly head, and softly repeated a short grace in the devout German fashion, which Mr. Bhaer loved and taught his little son to honor. Then they all sat down to enjoy the Sunday-morning breakfast of coffee, steak, and baked potatoes, instead of the bread and milk fare with which they usually satisfied their young appetites. There was much pleasant talk while the knives and forks rattled briskly, for certain Sunday lessons were to be learned, the Sunday walk settled, and plans for the week discussed. As he listened, Nat thought it seemed as if this day must be a very pleasant one, for he loved quiet, and there was a cheerful sort of hush over every thing that pleased him very much; because, in spite of his rough life, the boy possessed the sensitive nerves which belong to a music-loving nature.

"Now, my lads, get your morning jobs done, and let me find you ready for church when the 'bus comes round," said Father Bhaer, and set the example by going into the school-room to get books ready for the morrow.

Every one scattered to his or her task, for each had some little daily duty, and was expected to perform it faithfully. Some brought wood and water, brushed the steps, or ran errands for Mrs. Bhaer. Others fed the pet animals, and did chores about the barn with Franz. Daisy washed the cups, and Demi wiped them, for the twins liked to work together, and Demi had been taught to make himself useful in the little house at home. Even Baby Teddy had his small job to do, and trotted to and fro, putting napkins away, and pushing chairs into their places. For half and hour the lads buzzed about like a hive of bees, then the 'bus drove round, Father Bhaer and Franz with the eight older boys piled in, and away they went for a three-mile drive to church in town.

Because of the troublesome cough Nat preferred to stay at home with the four small boys, and spent a happy morning in Mrs. Bhaer's room, listening to the stories she read them, learning the hymns she taught them, and then quietly employing himself pasting pictures into an old ledger.

"This is my Sunday closet," she said, showing him shelves filled with picture-books, paint-boxes, architectural blocks, little diaries, and materials for letter-writing. "I want my boys to love Sunday, to find it a peaceful, pleasant day, when they can rest from common study and play, yet enjoy quiet pleasures, and learn, in simple ways, lessons more important than any taught in school. Do you understand me?" she asked, watching Nat's attentive face.

"You mean to be good?" he said, after hesitating a minute.

"Yes; to be good, and to love to be good. It is hard work sometimes, I know very well; but we all help one another, and so we get on. This is one of the ways in which I try to help my boys," and she took down a thick book, which seemed half-full of writing, and opened at a page on which there was one word at the top.

"Why, that's my name!" cried Nat, looking both surprised and interested.

"Yes; I have a page for each boy. I keep a little account of how he gets on through the week, and Sunday night I show him the record. If it is bad I am sorry and disappointed, if it is good I am glad and proud; but, whichever it is, the boys know I want to help them, and they try to do their best for love of me and Father Bhaer."

"I should think they would," said Nat, catching a glimpse of Tommy's name opposite his own, and wondering what was written under it.

Mrs. Bhaer saw his eye on the words, and shook her head, saying, as she turned a leaf

"No, I don't show my records to any but the one to whom each belongs. I call this my conscience book; and only you and I will ever know what is to be written on the page below your name. Whether you will be pleased or ashamed to read it next Sunday depends on yourself. I think it will be a good report; at any rate, I shall try to make things easy for you in this new place, and shall be quite contented if you keep our few rules, live happily with the boys, and learn something."

"I'll try ma'am;" and Nat's thin face flushed up with the earnestness of his desire to make Mrs. Bhaer "glad and proud," not "sorry and disappointed." "It must be a great deal of trouble to write about so many," he added, as she shut her book with an encouraging pat on the shoulder.

"Not to me, for I really don't know which I like best, writing or boys," she said, laughing to see Nat stare with astonishment at the last item. "Yes, I know many people think boys are a nuisance, but that is because they don't understand them. I do; and I never saw the boy yet whom I could not get on capitally with after I had once found the soft spot in his heart. Bless me, I couldn't get on at all without my flock of dear, noisy, naughty, harum-scarum little lads, could I, my Teddy?" and Mrs. Bhaer hugged the young rogue, just in time to save the big inkstand from going into his pocket.

Nat, who had never heard anything like this before, really did not know whether Mother Bhaer was a trifle crazy, or the most delightful woman he had ever met. He rather inclined to the latter opinion, in spite of her peculiar tastes, for she had a way of filling up a fellow's plate before he asked, of laughing at his jokes, gently tweaking him by the ear, or clapping him on the shoulder, that Nat found very engaging.

"Now, I think you would like to go into the school-room and practise some of the hymns we are to sing to-night," she said, rightly guessing the thing of all others that he wanted to do.

Alone with the beloved violin and the music-book propped up before him in the sunny window, while Spring beauty filled the world outside, and Sabbath silence reigned within, Nat enjoyed an hour or two of genuine happiness, learning the sweet old tunes, and forgetting the hard past in the cheerful present.

When the church-goers came back and dinner was over, every one read, wrote letters home, said their Sunday lessons, or talked quietly to one another, sitting here and there about the house. At three o'clock the entire family turned out to walk, for all the active young bodies must have exercise; and in these walks the active young minds were taught to see and love the providence of God in the beautiful miracles which Nature was working before their eyes. Mr. Bhaer always went with them, and in his simple, fatherly way, found for his flock, "Sermons in stones, books in the running brooks, and good in everything."

Mrs. Bhaer with Daisy and her own two boys drove into town, to pay the weekly visit to Grandma, which was busy Mother Bhaer's one holiday and greatest pleasure. Nat was not strong enough for the long walk, and asked to stay at home with Tommy, who kindly offered to do the honors of Plumfield. "You've seen the house, so come out and have a look at the garden, and the barn, and the menagerie," said Tommy, when they were left alone with Asia, to see that they didn't get into mischief; for, though Tommy was one of the best-meaning boys who ever adorned knickerbockers, accidents of the most direful nature were always happening to him, no one could exactly tell how.

"What is your menagerie?" asked Nat, as they trotted along the drive that encircled the house.

"We all have pets, you see, and we keep 'em in the corn-barn, and call it the menagerie. Here you are. Isn't my guinea-pig a beauty?" and Tommy proudly presented one of the ugliest specimens of that pleasing animal that Nat ever saw.

"I know a boy with a dozen of 'em, and he said he'd give me one, only I hadn't any place to keep it, so I couldn't have it. It was white, with black spots, a regular rouser, and maybe I could get it for you if you'd like it," said Nat, feeling it would be a delicate return for Tommy's attentions.

"I'd like it ever so much, and I'll give you this one, and they can live together if they don't fight. Those white mice are Rob's, Franz gave 'em to him. The rabbits are Ned's, and the bantams outside are Stuffy's. That box thing is Demi's turtle-tank, only he hasn't begun to get 'em yet. Last year he had sixty-two, whackers some of 'em. He stamped one of 'em with his name and the year, and let it go; and he says maybe he will find it ever so long after and know it. He read about a turtle being found that had a mark on it that showed it must be hundreds of years old. Demi's such a funny chap."

"What is in this box?" asked Nat, stopping before a large deep one, half-full of earth.

"Oh, that's Jack Ford's worm-shop. He digs heaps of 'em and keeps 'em here, and when we want any to go afishing with, we buy some of him. It saves lots of trouble, only he charged too much for 'em. Why, last time we traded I had to pay two cents a dozen, and then got little ones. Jack's mean sometimes, and I told him I'd dig for myself if he didn't lower his prices. Now, I own two hens, those gray ones with top knots, first-rate ones they are too, and I sell Mrs. Bhaer the eggs, but I never ask her more than twenty-five cents a dozen, never! I'd be ashamed to do it," cried Tommy, with a glance of scorn at the worm-shop.

"Who owns the dogs?" asked Nat, much interested in these commercial transactions, and feeling that T. Bangs was a man whom it would be a privilege and a pleasure to patronize.

"The big dog is Emil's. His name is Christopher Columbus. Mrs. Bhaer named him because she likes to say Christopher Columbus, and no one minds it if she means the dog," answered Tommy, in the tone of a show-man displaying his menagerie. "The white pup is Rob's, and the yellow one is Teddy's. A man was going to drown them in our pond, and Pa Bhaer wouldn't let him. They do well enough for the little chaps, I don't think much of 'em myself. Their names are Castor and Pollux."

"I'd like Toby the donkey best, if I could have anything, it's so nice to ride, and he's so little and good," said Nat, remembering the weary tramps he had taken on his own tired feet.

"Mr. Laurie sent him out to Mrs. Bhaer, so she shouldn't carry Teddy on her back when we go to walk. We're all fond of Toby, and he's a first-rate donkey, sir. Those pigeons belong to the whole lot of us, we each have our pet one, and go shares in all the little ones as they come along. Squabs are great fun; there ain't any now, but you can go up and take a look at the old fellows, while I see if Cockletop and Granny have laid any eggs."

Nat climbed up a ladder, put his head through a trap door and took a long look at the pretty doves billing and cooing in their spacious loft. Some on their nests, some bustling in and out, and some sitting at their doors, while many went flying from the sunny housetop to the straw-strewn farmyard, where six sleek cows were placidly ruminating.

"Everybody has got something but me. I wish I had a dove, or a hen, or even a turtle, all my own," thought Nat, feeling very poor as he saw the interesting treasures of the other boys. "How do you get these things?" he asked, when he joined Tommy in the barn.

"We find 'em or buy 'em, or folks give 'em to us. My father sends me mine; but as soon as I get egg money enough, I'm going to buy a pair of ducks. There's a nice little pond for 'em behind the barn, and people pay well for duck-eggs, and the little duckies are pretty, and it's fun to see 'em swim," said Tommy, with the air of a millionaire.

Nat sighed, for he had neither father nor money, nothing in the wide world but an old empty pocketbook, and the skill that lay in his ten finger tips. Tommy seemed to understand the question and the sigh which followed his answer, for after a moment of deep thought, he suddenly broke out,

"Look here, I'll tell you what I'll do. If you will hunt eggs for me, I hate it, I'll give you one egg out of every dozen. You keep account, and when you've had twelve, Mother Bhaer will give you twenty-five cents for 'em, and then you can buy what you like, don't you see?"

"I'll do it! What a kind feller you are, Tommy!" cried Nat, quite dazzled by this brilliant offer.

"Pooh! that is not anything. You begin now and rummage the barn, and I'll wait here for you. Granny is cackling, so you're sure to find one somewhere," and Tommy threw himself down on the hay with a luxurious sense of having made a good bargain, and done a friendly thing.

Nat joyfully began his search, and went rustling from loft to loft till he found two fine eggs, one hidden under a beam, and the other in an old peck measure, which Mrs. Cockletop had appropriated.

"You may have one and I'll have the other, that will just make up my last dozen, and to-morrow we'll start fresh.

"Here, you chalk your accounts up near mine, and then we'll be all straight," said Tommy, showing a row of mysterious figures on the side of an old winnowing machine.

With a delightful sense of importance, the proud possessor of one egg opened his account with his friend, who laughingly wrote above the figures these imposing words,

"T. Bangs & Co."

Poor Nat found them so fascinating that he was with difficulty persuaded to go and deposit his first piece of portable property in Asia's store-room. Then they went on again, and having made the acquaintance of the two horses, six cows, three pigs, and one Alderney "Bossy," as calves are called in New England, Tommy took Nat to a certain old willow-tree that overhung a noisy little brook. From the fence it was an easy scramble into a wide niche between the three big branches, which had been cut off to send out from year to year a crowd of slender twigs, till a green canopy rustled overhead. Here little seats had been fixed, and a hollow place a closet made big enough to hold a book or two, a dismantled boat, and several half-finished whistles.

"This is Demi's and my private place; we made it, and nobody can come up unless we let 'em, except Daisy, we don't mind her," said Tommy, as Nat looked with delight from the babbling brown water below to the green arch above, where bees were making a musical murmur as they feasted on the long yellow blossoms that filled the air with sweetness.

"Oh, it's just beautiful!" cried Nat. "I do hope you'll let me up sometimes. I never saw such a nice place in all my life. I'd like to be a bird, and live here always."

"It is pretty nice. You can come if Demi don't mind, and I guess he won't, because he said last night that he liked you."

"Did he?" and Nat smiled with pleasure, for Demi's regard seemed to be valued by all the boys, partly because he was Father Bhaer's nephew, and partly because he was such a sober, conscientious little fellow.

"Yes; Demi likes quiet chaps, and I guess he and you will get on if you care about reading as he does."

Poor Nat's flush of pleasure deepened to a painful scarlet at those last words, and he stammered out,

"I can't read very well; I never had any time; I was always fiddling round, you know."

"I don't love it myself, but I can do it well enough when I want to," said Tommy, after a surprised look, which said as plainly as words, "A boy twelve years old and can't read!"

"I can read music, anyway," added Nat, rather ruffled at having to confess his ignorance.

"I can't;" and Tommy spoke in a respectful tone, which emboldened Nat to say firmly,

"I mean to study real hard and learn every thing I can, for I never had a chance before. Does Mr. Bhaer give hard lessons?"

"No; he isn't a bit cross; he sort of explains and gives you a boost over the hard places. Some folks don't; my other master didn't. If we missed a word, didn't we get raps on the head!" and Tommy rubbed his own pate as if it tingled yet with the liberal supply of raps, the memory of which was the only thing he brought away after a year with his "other master."

"I think I could read this," said Nat, who had been examining the books.

"Read a bit, then; I'll help you," resumed Tommy, with a patronizing air.

So Nat did his best, and floundered through a page with may friendly "boosts" from Tommy, who told him he would soon "go it" as well as anybody. Then they sat and talked boy-fashion about all sorts of things, among others, gardening; for Nat, looking down from his perch, asked what was planted in the many little patches lying below them on the other side of the brook.

"These are our farms," said Tommy. "We each have our own patch, and raise what we like in it, only have to choose different things, and can't change till the crop is in, and we must keep it in order all summer."

"What are you going to raise this year?"

"Wal, I cattleated to hev beans, as they are about the easiest crop a-goin'."

Nat could not help laughing, for Tommy had pushed back his hat, put his hands in his pockets, and drawled out his words in unconscious imitation of Silas, the man who managed the place for Mr. Bhaer.

"Come, you needn't laugh; beans are ever so much easier than corn or potatoes. I tried melons last year, but the bugs were a bother, and the old things wouldn't get ripe before the frost, so I didn't have but one good water and two little 'mush mellions,' " said Tommy, relapsing into a "Silasism" with the last word.

"Corn looks pretty growing," said Nat, politely, to atone for his laugh.

"Yes, but you have to hoe it over and over again. Now, six weeks' beans only have to be done once or so, and they get ripe soon. I'm going to try 'em, for I spoke first. Stuffy wanted 'em, but he's got to take peas; they only have to be picked, and he ought to do it, he eats such a lot."

Lesson 101

1. Finish reading chapter 3.
2. "We will plant self-denial, and hoe it and water it, and make it grow so well that next Christmas no one will get ill by eating too much dinner." What does this mean? (Answers)
3. What makes Sundays special at your house? Would you have enjoyed Sundays at Plumfield? Why or why not?

Chapter III. continued

"I wonder if I shall have a garden?" said Nat, thinking that even corn-hoeing must be pleasant work.

"Of course you will," said a voice from below, and there was Mr. Bhaer returned from his walk, and come to find them, for he managed to have a little talk with every one of the lads some time during the day, and found that these chats gave them a good start for the coming week.

Sympathy is a sweet thing, and it worked wonders here, for each boy knew that Father Bhaer was interested in him, and some were readier to open their hearts to him than to a woman, especially the older ones, who liked to talk over their hopes and plans, man to man. When sick or in trouble they instinctively turned to Mrs. Jo, while the little ones made her their mother-confessor on all occasions.

In descending from their nest, Tommy fell into the brook; being used to it, he calmly picked himself out and retired to the house to be dried. This left Nat to Mr. Bhaer, which was just what he wished, and, during the stroll they took among the garden plots, he won the lad's heart by giving him a little "farm," and discussing crops with him as gravely as if the food for the family depended on the harvest. From this pleasant topic they went to others, and Nat had many new and helpful thoughts put into a mind that received them as gratefully as the thirsty earth had received the warm spring rain. All supper time he brooded over them, often fixing his eyes on Mr. Bhaer with an inquiring look, that seemed to say, "I like that, do it again, sir." I don't know whether the man understood the child's mute language or not, but when the boys were all gathered together in Mrs. Bhaer's parlor for the Sunday evening talk, he chose a subject which might have been suggested by the walk in the garden.

As he looked about him Nat thought it seemed more like a great family than a school, for the lads were sitting in a wide half-circle round the fire, some on chairs, some on the rug, Daisy and Demi on the knees of Uncle Fritz, and Rob snugly stowed away in the back of his mother's easy-chair, where he could nod unseen if the talk got beyond his depth.

Every one looked quite comfortable, and listened attentively, for the long walk made rest agreeable, and as every boy there knew that he would be called upon for his views, he kept his wits awake to be ready with an answer.

"Once upon a time," began Mr. Bhaer, in the dear old-fashioned way, "there was a great and wise gardener who had the largest garden ever seen. A wonderful and lovely place it was, and he watched over it with the greatest skill and care, and raised all manner of excellent and useful things. But weeds would grow even in this fine garden; often the ground was bad and the good seeds sown in it would not spring up. He had many under gardeners to help him. Some did their duty and earned the rich wages he gave them; but others neglected their parts and let them run to waste, which displeased him very much. But he was very patient, and for thousands and thousands of years he worked and waited for his great harvest."

"He must have been pretty old," said Demi, who was looking straight into Uncle Fritz's face, as if to catch every word.

"Hush, Demi, it's a fairy story," whispered Daisy.

"No, I think it's an arrygory," said Demi.

"What is a arrygory?" called out Tommy, who was of an inquiring turn.

"Tell him, Demi, if you can, and don't use words unless you are quite sure you know what they mean," said Mr. Bhaer.

"I do know, Grandpa told me! A fable is a arrygory; it's a story that means something. My 'Story without an end' is one, because the child in it means a soul; don't it, Aunty?" cried Demi, eager to prove himself right.

"That's it, dear; and Uncle's story is an allegory, I am quite sure; so listen and see what it means," returned Mrs. Jo, who always took part in whatever was going on, and enjoyed it as much as any boy among them.

Demi composed himself, and Mr. Bhaer went on in his best English, for he had improved much in the last five years, and said the boys did it.

"This great gardener gave a dozen or so of little plots to one of his servants, and told him to do his best and see what he could raise. Now this servant was not rich, nor wise, nor very good, but he wanted to help because the gardener had been very kind to him in many ways. So he gladly took the little plots and fell to work. They were all sorts of shapes and sizes, and some were very good soil, some rather stony, and all of them needed much care, for in the rich soil the weeds grew fast, and in the poor soil there were many stones."

"What was growing in them besides the weeds, and stones?" asked Nat; so interested, he forgot his shyness and spoke before them all.

"Flowers," said Mr. Bhaer, with a kind look. "Even the roughest, most neglected little bed had a bit of heart's-ease or a sprig of mignonette in it. One had roses, sweet peas, and daisies in it," here he pinched the plump cheek of the little girl leaning on his arm. "Another had all sorts of curious plants in it, bright pebbles, a vine that went climbing up like Jack's beanstalk, and many good seeds just beginning to sprout; for, you see, this bed had been taken fine care of by a wise old man, who had worked in gardens of this sort all his life."

At this part of the "arrygory," Demi put his head on one side like an inquisitive bird, and fixed his bright eye on his uncle's face, as if he suspected something and was on the watch. But Mr. Bhaer looked perfectly innocent, and went on glancing from one young face to another, with a grave, wistful look, that said much to his wife, who knew how earnestly he desired to do his duty in these little garden plots.

"As I tell you, some of these beds were easy to cultivate, that means to take care of Daisy, and others were very hard. There was one particularly sunshiny little bed that might have been full of fruits and vegetables as well as flowers, only it wouldn't take any pains, and when the man sowed, well, we'll say melons in this bed, they came to nothing, because the little bed neglected them. The man was sorry, and kept on trying, though every time the crop failed, all the bed said, was, 'I forgot.'"

Here a general laugh broke out, and every one looked at Tommy, who had pricked up his ears at the word "melons," and hung down his head at the sound of his favorite excuse.

"I knew he meant us!" cried Demi, clapping his hands. "You are the man, and we are the little gardens; aren't we, Uncle Fritz?"

"You have guessed it. Now each of you tell me what crop I shall try to sow in you this spring, so that next autumn I may get a good harvest out of my twelve, no, thirteen, plots," said Mr. Bhaer, nodding at Nat as he corrected himself.

"You can't sow corn and beans and peas in us. Unless you mean we are to eat a great many and get fat," said Stuffy, with a sudden brightening of his round, dull face as the pleasing idea occurred to him.

"He don't mean that kind of seeds. He means things to make us good; and the weeds are faults," cried Demi, who usually took the lead in these talks, because he was used to this sort of thing, and liked it very much.

"Yes, each of you think what you need most, and tell me, and I will help you to grow it; only you must do your best, or you will turn out like Tommy's melons, all leaves and no fruit. I will begin with the oldest, and ask the mother what she will have in her plot, for we are all parts of the beautiful garden, and may have rich harvests for our Master if we love Him enough," said Father Bhaer.

"I shall devote the whole of my plot to the largest crop of patience I can get, for that is what I need most," said Mrs. Jo, so soberly that the lads fell to thinking in good earnest what they should say when their turns came, and some among them felt a twinge of remorse, that they had helped to use up Mother Bhaer's stock of patience so fast.

Franz wanted perseverance, Tommy steadiness, Ned went in for good temper, Daisy for industry, Demi for "as much wiseness as Grandpa," and Nat timidly said he wanted so many things he would let Mr. Bhaer choose for him. The others chose much the same things, and patience, good temper, and generosity seemed the favorite crops. One boy wished to like to get up early, but did not know what name to give that sort of seed; and poor Stuffy sighed out,

"I wish I loved my lessons as much as I do my dinner, but I can't."

"We will plant self-denial, and hoe it and water it, and make it grow so well that next Christmas no one will get ill by eating too much dinner. If you exercise your mind, George, it will get hungry just as your body does, and you will love books almost as much as my philosopher here," said Mr. Bhaer; adding, as he stroked the hair off Demi's fine forehead, "You are greedy also, my son, and you like to stuff your little mind full of fairy tales and fancies, as well as George likes to fill his little stomach with cake and candy. Both are bad, and I want you to try something better. Arithmetic is not half so pleasant as 'Arabian Nights,' I know, but it is a very useful thing, and now is the time to learn it, else you will be ashamed and sorry by and by."

"But, 'Harry and Lucy,' and 'Frank,' are not fairy books, and they are all full of barometers, and bricks, and shoeing horses, and useful things, and I'm fond of them; ain't I, Daisy?" said Demi, anxious to defend himself.

"So they are; but I find you reading 'Roland and Maybird,' a great deal oftener than 'Harry and Lucy,' and I think you are not half so fond of 'Frank' as you are of 'Sinbad.' Come, I shall make a little bargain with you both, George shall eat but three times a day, and you shall read but one story-book a week, and I will give you the new cricket-ground; only, you must promise to play in it," said Uncle Fritz, in his persuasive way, for Stuffy hated to run about, and Demi was always reading in play hours.

"But we don't like cricket," said Demi.

"Perhaps not now, but you will when you know it. Besides, you do like to be generous, and the other boys want to play, and you can give them the new ground if you choose."

This was taken them both on the right side, and they agreed to the bargain, to the great satisfaction of the rest.

There was a little more talk about the gardens, and then they all sang together. The band delighted Nat, for Mrs. Bhaer played the piano, Franz the flute, Mr. Bhaer a bass viol, and he himself the violin. A very simple little concert, but all seemed to enjoy it, and old Asia, sitting in the corner, joined at times with the sweetest voice of any, for in this family, master and servant, old and young, black and white, shared in the Sunday song, which went up to the Father of them all. After this they each shook hands with Father Bhaer; Mother Bhaer kissed them every one from sixteen-year-old Franz to little Rob, how kept the tip of her nose for his own particular kisses, and then they trooped up to bed.

The light of the shaded lamp that burned in the nursery shone softly on a picture hanging at the foot of Nat's bed. There were several others on the walls, but the boy thought there must be something peculiar about this one, for it had a graceful frame of moss and cones about it, and on a little bracket underneath stood a vase of wild flowers freshly gathered from the spring woods. It was the most beautiful picture of them all, and Nat lay looking at it, dimly feeling what it meant, and wishing he knew all about it.

"That's my picture," said a little voice in the room. Nat popped up his head, and there was Demi in his night-gown pausing on his way back from Aunt Jo's chamber, whither he had gone to get a cot for a cut finger.

"What is he doing to the children?" asked Nat.

"That is Christ, the Good Man, and He is blessing the children. Don't you know about Him?" said Demi, wondering.

"Not much, but I'd like to, He looks so kind," answered Nat, whose chief knowledge of the Good Man consisted in hearing His name taken in vain.

"I know all about it, and I like it very much, because it is true," said Demi.

"Who told you?"

"My Grandpa, he knows every thing, and tells the best stories in the world. I used to play with his big books, and make bridges, and railroads, and houses, when I was a little boy," began Demi.

"How old are you now?" asked Nat, respectfully.

"'Most ten."

"You know a lot of things, don't you?"

"Yes; you see my head is pretty big, and Grandpa says it will take a good deal to fill it, so I keep putting pieces of wisdom into it as fast as I can," returned Demi, in his quaint way.

Nat laughed, and then said soberly,

"Tell on, please."

And Demi gladly told on without pause or punctuation. "I found a very pretty book one day and wanted to play with it, but Grandpa said I mustn't, and showed me the pictures, and told me about them, and I liked the stories very much, all about Joseph and his bad brothers, and the frogs that came up out of the sea, and dear little Moses in the water, and ever so many more lovely ones, but I liked about the Good Man best of all, and Grandpa told it to me so many times that I learned it by heart, and he gave me this picture so I shouldn't forget, and it was put up here once when I was sick, and I left it for other sick boys to see."

"What makes Him bless the children?" asked Nat, who found something very attractive in the chief figure of the group.

"Because He loved them."

"Were they poor children?" asked Nat, wistfully.

"Yes, I think so; you see some haven't got hardly any clothes on, and the mothers don't look like rich ladies. He liked poor people, and was very good to them. He made them well, and helped them, and told rich people they must not be cross to them, and they loved Him dearly, dearly," cried Demi, with enthusiasm.

"Was He rich?"

"Oh no! He was born in a barn, and was so poor He hadn't any house to live in when He grew up, and nothing to eat sometimes, but what people gave Him, and He went round preaching to everybody, and trying to make them good, till the bad men killed Him."

"What for?" and Nat sat up in his bed to look and listen, so interested was he in this man who cared for the poor so much.

"I'll tell you all about it; Aunt Jo won't mind;" and Demi settled himself on the opposite bed, glad to tell his favorite story to so good a listener.

Nursey peeped in to see if Nat was asleep, but when she saw what was going on, she slipped away again, and went to Mrs. Bhaer, saying with her kind face full of motherly emotion,

"Will the dear lady come and see a pretty sight? It's Nat listening with all his heart to Demi telling the story of the Christ-child, like a little white angel as he is."

Mrs. Bhaer had meant to go and talk with Nat a moment before he slept, for she had found that a serious word spoken at this time often did much good. But when she stole to the nursery door, and saw Nat eagerly drinking in the words of his little friends, while Demi told the sweet and solemn story as it had been taught him, speaking softly as he sat with his beautiful eyes fixed on the tender face above them, her own filled with tears, and she went silently away, thinking to herself,

"Demi is unconsciously helping the poor boy better than I can; I will not spoil it by a single word."

The murmur of the childish voice went on for a long time, as one innocent heart preached that great sermon to another, and no one hushed it. When it ceased at last, and Mrs. Bhaer went to take away the lamp, Demi was gone and Nat fast asleep, lying with his face toward the picture, as if he had already learned to love the Good Man who loved little children, and was a faithful friend to the poor. The boy's face was very placid, and as she looked at it she felt that if a single day of care and kindness had done so much, a year of patient cultivation would surely bring a grateful harvest from this neglected garden, which was already sown with the best of all seed by the little missionary in the night-gown.

Lesson 102

1.   What do you picture when you read the title to chapter 4, "Stepping-stones?" What would you like to find out?

2.   Read chapter 4.

3.   Summarize the chapter for someone.

4.   What are you thinking?

Vocabulary

1.   Review your vocabulary from Lesson 96.

Chapter IV. Stepping-Stones

When Nat went into school on Monday morning, he quaked inwardly, for now he thought he should have to display his ignorance before them all. But Mr. Bhaer gave him a seat in the deep window, where he could turn his back on the others, and Franz heard him say his lessons there, so no one could hear his blunders or see how he blotted his copybook. He was truly grateful for this, and toiled away so diligently that Mr. Bhaer said, smiling, when he saw his hot face and inky fingers:

"Don't work so hard, my boy; you will tire yourself out, and there is time enough."

"But I must work hard, or I can't catch up with the others. They know heaps, and I don't know anything," said Nat, who had been reduced to a state of despair by hearing the boys recite their grammar, history, and geography with what he thought amazing ease and accuracy.

"You know a good many things which they don't," said Mr. Bhaer, sitting down beside him, while Franz led a class of small students through the intricacies of the multiplication table.

"Do I?" and Nat looked utterly incredulous.

"Yes; for one thing, you can keep your temper, and Jack, who is quick at numbers, cannot; that is an excellent lesson, and I think you have learned it well. Then, you can play the violin, and not one of the lads can, though they want to do it very much. But, best of all, Nat, you really care to learn something, and that is half the battle. It seems hard at first, and you will feel discouraged, but plod away, and things will get easier and easier as you go on."

Nat's face had brightened more and more as he listened, for, small as the list of his learning was, it cheered him immensely to feel that he had anything to fall back upon. "Yes, I can keep my temper father's beating taught me that; and I can fiddle, though I don't know where the Bay of Biscay is,"

41

he thought, with a sense of comfort impossible to express. Then he said aloud, and so earnestly that Demi heard him:

"I do want to learn, and I will try. I never went to school, but I couldn't help it; and if the fellows don't laugh at me, I guess I'll get on first rate you and the lady are so good to me."

"They shan't laugh at you; if they do, I'll I'll tell them not to," cried Demi, quite forgetting where he was.

The class stopped in the middle of 7 times 9, and everyone looked up to see what was going on.

Thinking that a lesson in learning to help one another was better than arithmetic just then, Mr. Bhaer told them about Nat, making such an interesting and touching little story out of it that the good-hearted lads all promised to lend him a hand, and felt quite honored to be called upon to impart their stores of wisdom to the chap who fiddled so capitally. This appeal established the right feeling among them, and Nat had few hindrances to struggle against, for every one was glad to give him a "boost" up the ladder of learning.

Till he was stronger, much study was not good for him, however, and Mrs. Jo found various amusements in the house for him while others were at their books. But his garden was his best medicine, and he worked away like a beaver, preparing his little farm, sowing his beans, watching eagerly to see them grow, and rejoicing over each green leaf and slender stock that shot up and flourished in the warm spring weather. Never was a garden more faithfully hoed; Mr. Bhaer really feared that nothing would find time to grow, Nat kept up such a stirring of the soil; so he gave him easy jobs in the flower garden or among the strawberries, where he worked and hummed as busily as the bees booming all about him.

"This is the crop I like best," Mrs. Bhaer used to say, as she pinched the once thin cheeks, now getting plump and ruddy, or stroked the bent shoulders that were slowly straightening up with healthful work, good food, and the absence of that heavy burden, poverty.

Demi was his little friend, Tommy his patron, and Daisy the comforter of all his woes; for, though the children were younger than he, his timid spirit found a pleasure in their innocent society, and rather shrunk from the rough sports of the elder lads. Mr. Laurence did not forget him, but sent clothes and books, music and kind messages, and now and then came out to see how his boy was getting on, or took him into town to a concert; on which occasions Nat felt himself translated into the seventh heaven of bliss, for he went to Mr. Laurence's great house, saw his pretty wife and little fairy of a daughter, had a good dinner, and was made so comfortable, that he talked and dreamed of it for days and nights afterward.

It takes so little to make a child happy that it is a pity, in a world so full of sunshine and pleasant things, that there should be any wistful faces, empty hands, or lonely little hearts. Feeling this, the Bhaers gathered up all the crumbs they could find to feed their flock of hungry sparrows, for they were not rich, except in charity. Many of Mrs. Jo's friends who had nurseries sent her they toys of which their children so soon tired, and in mending these Nat found an employment that just suited him. He was very neat and skillful with those slender fingers of his, and passed many a rainy afternoon with his gum-bottle, paint-box, and knife, repairing furniture, animals, and games, while Daisy was dressmaker to the dilapidated dolls. As fast as the toys were mended, they were put carefully away in a certain drawer which was to furnish forth a Christmas-tree for all the poor children of the neighborhood, that being the way the Plumfield boys celebrated the birthday of Him who loved the poor and blessed the little ones.

Demi was never tired of reading and explaining his favorite books, and many a pleasant hour did they spend in the old willow, revelling over "Robinson Crusoe," "Arabian Nights," "Edgeworth's Tales," and the other dear immortal stories that will delight children for centuries to come. This opened a new world to Nat, and his eagerness to see what came next in the story helped him on till he could read as well as anybody, and felt so rich and proud with his new accomplishment, that there was danger of his being as much of a bookworm as Demi.

Another helpful thing happened in a most unexpected and agreeable manner. Several of the boys were "in business," as they called it, for most of them were poor, and knowing that they would have their own way to make by and by, the Bhaers encouraged any efforts at independence. Tommy sold his eggs; Jack speculated in live stock; Franz helped in the teaching, and was paid for it; Ned had a taste for carpentry, and a turning-lathe was set up for him in which he turned all sorts of useful or pretty things, and sold them; while Demi constructed water-mills, whirligigs, and unknown machines of an intricate and useless nature, and disposed of them to the boys.

"Let him be a mechanic if he likes," said Mr. Bhaer. "Give a boy a trade, and he is independent. Work is wholesome, and whatever talent these lads possess, be it for poetry or ploughing, it shall be cultivated and made useful to them if possible."

So, when Nat came running to him one day to ask with an excited face:

"Can I go and fiddle for some people who are to have a picnic in our woods? They will pay me, and I'd like to earn some money as the other boys do, and fiddling is the only way I know how to do it."

Mr. Bhaer answered readily:

"Go, and welcome. It is an easy and a pleasant way to work, and I am glad it is offered you."

Nat went, and did so well that when he came home he had two dollars in his pocket, which he displayed with intense satisfaction, as he told how much he had enjoyed the afternoon, how kind the young people were, and how they had praised his dance music, and promised to have him again.

"It is so much nicer than fiddling in the street, for then I got none of the money, and now I have it all, and a good time besides. I'm in business now as well as Tommy and Jack, and I like it ever so much," said Nat, proudly patting the old pocketbook, and feeling like a millionaire already.

He was in business truly, for picnics were plenty as summer opened, and Nat's skill was in great demand. He was always at liberty to go if lessons were not neglected, and if the picnickers were respectable young people. For Mr. Bhaer explained to him that a good plain education is necessary for everyone, and that no amount of money should hire him to go where he might be tempted to do wrong. Nat quite agreed to this, and it was a pleasant sight to see the innocent-hearted lad go driving away in the gay wagons that stopped at the gate for him, or to hear him come fiddling home tired but happy, with his well-earned money in one pocket, and some "goodies" from the feast for Daisy or little Ted, whom he never forgot.

"I'm going to save up till I get enough to buy a violin for myself, and then I can earn my own living, can't I?" he used to say, as he brought his dollars to Mr. Bhaer to keep.

"I hope so, Nat; but we must get you strong and hearty first, and put a little more knowledge into this musical head of yours. Then Mr. Laurie will find you a place somewhere, and in a few years we will all come to hear you play in public."

With much congenial work, encouragement, and hope, Nat found life getting easier and happier every day, and made such progress in his music lessons that his teacher forgave his slowness in some other things, knowing very well that where the heart is the mind works best. The only punishment the boy ever needed for neglect of more important lessons was to hang up the fiddle and the bow for a day. The fear of losing his bosom friend entirely made him go at his books with a will; and having proved that he could master the lessons, what was the use of saying "I can't?"

Daisy had a great love of music, and a great reverence for any one who could make it, and she was often found sitting on the stairs outside Nat's door while he was practising. This pleased him very much, and he played his best for that one quiet little listener; for she never would come in, but preferred to sit sewing her gay patchwork, or tending one of her many dolls, with an expression of dreamy pleasure on her face that made Aunt Jo say, with tears in her eyes: "So like my Beth," and go softly by, lest even her familiar presence mar the child's sweet satisfaction.

Nat was very fond of Mrs. Bhaer, but found something even more attractive in the good professor, who took fatherly care of the shy feeble boy, who had barely escaped with his life from the rough sea on which his little boat had been tossing rudderless for twelve years. Some good angel must have been watching over him, for, though his body had suffered, his soul seemed to have taken little harm, and came ashore as innocent as a shipwrecked baby. Perhaps his love of music kept it sweet in spite of the discord all about him; Mr. Laurie said so, and he ought to know. However that might be, Father Bhaer took pleasure in fostering poor Nat's virtues, and in curing his faults, finding his new pupil as docile and affectionate as a girl. He often called Nat his "daughter" when speaking of him to Mrs. Jo, and she used to laugh at his fancy, for Madame liked manly boys, and thought Nat amiable but weak, though you never would have guessed it, for she petted him as she did Daisy, and he thought her a very delightful woman.

One fault of Nat's gave the Bhaers much anxiety, although they saw how it had been strengthened by fear and ignorance. I regret to say that Nat sometimes told lies. Not very black ones, seldom getting deeper than gray, and often the mildest of white fibs; but that did not matter, a lie is a lie, and though we all tell many polite untruths in this queer world of ours, it is not right, and everybody knows it.

"You cannot be too careful; watch your tongue, and eyes, and hands, for it is easy to tell, and look, and act untruth," said Mr. Bhaer, in one of the talks he had with Nat about his chief temptation.

"I know it, and I don't mean to, but it's so much easier to get along if you ain't very fussy about being exactly true. I used to tell 'em because I was afraid of father and Nicolo, and now I do sometimes because the boys laugh at me. I know it's bad, but I forget," and Nat looked much depressed by his sins.

"When I was a little lad I used to tell lies! Ach! what fibs they were, and my old grandmother cured me of it how, do you think? My parents had talked, and cried, and punished, but still did I forget as you. Then said the dear old grandmother, 'I shall help you to remember, and put a check on this unruly part,' with that she drew out my tongue and snipped the end with her scissors till the blood ran. That was terrible, you may believe, but it did me much good, because it was sore for days, and every word I said came so slowly that I had time to think. After that I was more careful, and got on better, for I feared the big scissors. Yet the dear grandmother was most kind to me in all things, and when she lay dying far away in Nuremberg, she prayed that little Fritz might love God and tell the truth."

"I never had any grandmothers, but if you think it will cure me, I'll let you snip my tongue," said Nat, heroically, for he dreaded pain, yet did wish to stop fibbing.

Mr. Bhaer smiled, but shook his head.

"I have a better way than that, I tried it once before and it worked well. See now, when you tell a lie I will not punish you, but you shall punish me."

"How?" asked Nat, startled at the idea.

"You shall ferule me in the good old-fashioned way; I seldom do it myself, but it may make you remember better to give me pain than to feel it yourself."

"Strike you? Oh, I couldn't!" cried Nat.

"Then mind that tripping tongue of thine. I have no wish to be hurt, but I would gladly bear much pain to cure this fault."

This suggestion made such an impression on Nat, that for a long time he set a watch upon his lips, and was desperately accurate, for Mr. Bhaer judged rightly, that love of him would be more powerful with Nat that fear for himself. But alas! one sad day Nat was off his guard, and when peppery Emil threatened to thrash him, if it was he who had run over his garden and broken down his best hills of corn, Nat declared he didn't, and then was ashamed to own up that he did do it, when Jack was chasing him the night before.

He thought no one would find it out, but Tommy happened to see him, and when Emil spoke of it a day or two later, Tommy gave his evidence, and Mr. Bhaer heard it. School was over, and they were all standing about in the hall, and Mr. Bhaer had just set down on the straw settee to enjoy his frolic with Teddy; but when he heard Tommy and saw Nat turn scarlet, and look at him with a frightened face, he put the little boy down, saying, "Go to thy mother, bebchen, I will come soon," and taking Nat by the hand led him into the school and shut the door.

The boys looked at one another in silence for a minute, then Tommy slipped out and peeping in at the half-closed blinds, beheld a sight that quite bewildered him. Mr. Bhaer had just taken down the long rule that hung over his desk, so seldom used that it was covered with dust.

"My eye! He's going to come down heavy on Nat this time. Wish I hadn't told," thought good-natured Tommy, for to be feruled was the deepest disgrace at this school.

"You remember what I told you last time?" said Mr. Bhaer, sorrowfully, not angrily.

"Yes; but please don't make me, I can't bear it," cried Nat, backing up against the door with both hands behind him, and a face full of distress.

"Why don't he up and take it like a man? I would," thought Tommy, though his heart beat fast at the sight.

"I shall keep my word, and you must remember to tell the truth. Obey me, Nat, take this and give me six good strokes."

Tommy was so staggered by this last speech that he nearly tumbled down the bank, but saved himself, and hung onto the window ledge, staring in with eyes as round as the stuffed owl's on the chimney-piece.

Nat took the rule, for when Mr. Bhaer spoke in that tone everyone obeyed him, and, looking as scared and guilty as if about to stab his master, he gave two feeble blows on the broad hand held out to him. Then he stopped and looked up half-blind with tears, but Mr. Bhaer said steadily:

"Go on, and strike harder."

As if seeing that it must be done, and eager to have the hard task soon over, Nat drew his sleeve across his eyes and gave two more quick hard strokes that reddened the hand, yet hurt the giver more.

"Isn't that enough?" he asked in a breathless sort of tone.

"Two more," was all the answer, and he gave them, hardly seeing where they fell, then threw the rule all across the room, and hugging the kind hand in both his own, laid his face down on it sobbing out in a passion of love, and shame, and penitence:

"I will remember! Oh! I will!"

Then Mr. Bhaer put an arm about him, and said in a tone as compassionate as it had just now been firm:

"I think you will. Ask the dear God to help you, and try to spare us both another scene like this."

Tommy saw no more, for he crept back to the hall, looking so excited and sober that the boys crowded round him to ask what was being done to Nat.

In a most impressive whisper Tommy told them, and they looked as if the sky was about to fall, for this reversing the order of things almost took their breath away.

"He made me do the same thing once," said Emil, as if confessing a crime of the deepest dye.

"And you hit him? dear old Father Bhaer? By thunder, I'd just like to see you do it now!" said Ned, collaring Emil in a fit of righteous wrath.

"It was ever so long ago. I'd rather have my head cut off than do it now," and Emil mildly laid Ned on his back instead of cuffing him, as he would have felt it his duty to do on any less solemn occasion.

"How could you?" said Demi, appalled at the idea.

"I was hopping mad at the time, and thought I shouldn't mind a bit, rather like it perhaps. But when I'd hit uncle one good crack, everything he had ever done for me came into my head all at once somehow, and I couldn't go on. No sir! If he'd laid me down and walked on me, I wouldn't have minded, I felt so mean," and Emil gave himself a good thump in the chest to express his sense of remorse for the past.

"Nat's crying like anything, and feels no end sorry, so don't let's say a word about it; will we?" said tender-hearted Tommy.

"Of course we won't, but it's awful to tell lies," and Demi looked as if he found the awfulness much increased when the punishment fell not upon the sinner, but his best Uncle Fritz.

"Suppose we all clear out, so Nat can cut upstairs if he wants to," proposed Franz, and led the way to the barn, their refuge in troublous times.

Nat did not come to dinner, but Mrs. Jo took some up to him, and said a tender word, which did him good, though he could not look at her. By and by the lads playing outside heard the violin, and said among themselves: "He's all right now." He was all right, but felt shy about going down, till opening his door to slip away into the woods, he found Daisy sitting on the stairs with neither work nor doll, only her little handkerchief in her hand, as if she had been mourning for her captive friend.

"I'm going to walk; want to come?" asked Nat, trying to look as if nothing was the matter, yet feeling very grateful for her silent sympathy, because he fancied everyone must look upon him as a wretch.

"Oh yes!" and Daisy ran for her hat, proud to be chosen as a companion by one of the big boys.

The others saw them go, but no one followed, for boys have a great deal more delicacy than they get credit for, and the lads instinctively felt that, when in disgrace, gentle little Daisy was their most congenial friend.

The walk did Nat good, and he came home quieter than usual, but looking cheerful again, and hung all over with daisy-chains made by his little playmate while he lay on the grass and told her stories.

No one said a word about the scene of the morning, but its effect was all the more lasting for that reason, perhaps. Nat tried his very best, and found much help, not only from the earnest little prayers he prayed to his Friend in heaven, but also in the patient care of the earthly friend whose kind hand he never touched without remembering that it had willingly borne pain for his sake.

Lesson 103

1. What is the title of Chapter 5? What do you think it means?
2. Read the first part of chapter 5.
3. Draw a picture of the kitchen.
4. Does her description make it easy to draw? When you describe things, you have to think about making it so that the people reading it "see" what you see when you are describing it.

Chapter V. Pattypans
"What's the matter, Daisy?"

"The boys won't let me play with them."

"Why not?"

"They say girls can't play football."

"They can, for I've done it!" and Mrs. Bhaer laughed at the remembrance of certain youthful frolics.

"I know I can play; Demi and I used to, and have nice times, but he won't let me now because the other boys laugh at him," and Daisy looked deeply grieved at her brother's hardness of heart.

"On the whole, I think he is right, deary. It's all very well when you two are alone, but it is too rough a game for you with a dozen boys; so I'd find some nice little play for myself."

"I'm tired of playing alone!" and Daisy's tone was very mournful.

"I'll play with you by and by, but just now I must fly about and get things ready for a trip into town. You shall go with me and see mamma, and if you like you can stay with her."

"I should like to go and see her and Baby Josy, but I'd rather come back, please. Demi would miss me, and I love to be here, Aunty."

"You can't get on without your Demi, can you?" and Aunt Jo looked as if she quite understood the love of the little girl for her only brother.

"'Course I can't; we're twins, and so we love each other more than other people," answered Daisy, with a brightening face, for she considered being a twin one of the highest honors she could ever receive.

"Now, what will you do with your little self while I fly around?" asked Mrs. Bhaer, who was whisking piles of linen into a wardrobe with great rapidity.

"I don't know, I'm tired of dolls and things; I wish you'd make up a new play for me, Aunty Jo," said Daisy, swinging listlessly on the door.

"I shall have to think of a brand new one, and it will take me some time; so suppose you go down and see what Asia has got for your lunch," suggested Mrs. Bhaer, thinking that would be a good way in which to dispose of the little hindrance for a time.

"Yes, I think I'd like that, if she isn't cross," and Daisy slowly departed to the kitchen, where Asia, the black cook, reigned undisturbed.

In five minutes, Daisy was back again, with a wide-awake face, a bit of dough in her hand and a dab of flour on her little nose.

"Oh aunty! Please could I go and make gingersnaps and things? Asia isn't cross, and she says I may, and it would be such fun, please do," cried Daisy, all in one breath.

"Just the thing, go and welcome, make what you like, and stay as long as you please," answered Mrs. Bhaer, much relieved, for sometimes the one little girl was harder to amuse than the dozen boys.

Daisy ran off, and while she worked, Aunt Jo racked her brain for a new play. All of a sudden she seemed to have an idea, for she smiled to herself, slammed the doors of the wardrobe, and walked briskly away, saying, "I'll do it, if it's a possible thing!"

What it was no one found out that day, but Aunt Jo's eyes twinkled so when she told Daisy she had thought of a new play, and was going to buy it, that Daisy was much excited and asked questions all the way into town, without getting answers that told her anything. She was left at home to play with the new baby, and delight her mother's eyes, while Aunt Jo went off shopping. When she came back with all sorts of queer parcels in corners of the carry-all, Daisy was so full of curiosity that she wanted to go back to Plumfield at once. But her aunt would not be hurried, and made a long call in mamma's room, sitting on the floor with baby in her lap, making Mrs. Brooke laugh at the pranks of the boys, and all sorts of droll nonsense.

How her aunt told the secret Daisy could not imagine, but her mother evidently knew it, for she said, as she tied on the little bonnet and kissed the rosy little face inside, "Be a good child, my Daisy, and learn the nice new play aunty has got for you. It's a most useful and interesting one, and it is very kind of her to play it with you, because she does not like it very well herself."

This last speech made the two ladies laugh heartily, and increased Daisy's bewilderment. As they drove away something rattled in the back of the carriage.

"What's that?" asked Daisy, pricking up her ears.

"The new play," answered Mrs. Jo, solemnly.

"What is it made of?" cried Daisy.

"Iron, tin, wood, brass, sugar, salt, coal, and a hundred other things."

"How strange! What color is it?"

"All sorts of colors."

"Is it large?"

"Part of it is, and a part isn't."

"Did I ever see one?"

"Ever so many, but never one so nice as this."

"Oh! what can it be? I can't wait. When shall I see it?" and Daisy bounced up and down with impatience.

"Tomorrow morning, after lessons."

"Is it for the boys, too?"

"No, all for you and Bess. The boys will like to see it, and want to play one part of it. But you can do as you like about letting them."

"I'll let Demi, if he wants to."

"No fear that they won't all want to, especially Stuffy," and Mrs. Bhaer's eyes twinkled more than ever as she patted a queer knobby bundle in her lap.

"Let me feel just once," prayed Daisy.

"Not a feel; you'd guess in a minute and spoil the fun."

Daisy groaned and then smiled all over her face, for through a little hole in the paper she caught a glimpse of something bright.

"How can I wait so long? Couldn't I see it today?"

"Oh dear, no! It has got to be arranged, and ever so many parts fixed in their places. I promised Uncle Teddy that you shouldn't see it till it was all in apple-pie order."

"If uncle knows about it then it must be splendid!" cried Daisy, clapping her hands; for this kind, rich, jolly uncle of hers was as good as a fairy godmother to the children, and was always planning merry surprises, pretty gifts, and droll amusements for them.

"Yes; Teddy went and bought it with me, and we had such fun in the shop choosing the different parts. He would have everything fine and large, and my little plan got regularly splendid when he took hold. You must give him your very best kiss when he comes, for he is the kindest uncle that ever went and bought a charming little coo Bless me! I nearly told you what it was!" and Mrs. Bhaer cut that most interesting word short off in the middle, and began to look over her bills, as if afraid she would let the cat out of the bag if she talked any more. Daisy folded her hands with an air of resignation, and sat quite still trying to think what play had a "coo" in it.

When they got home she eyed every bundle that was taken out, and one large heavy one, which Franz took straight upstairs and hid in the nursery, filled her with amazement and curiosity. Something very mysterious went on up there that afternoon, for Franz was hammering, and Asia trotting up and down, and Aunt Jo flying around like a will-o'-the-wisp, with all sort of things under her apron, while little Ted, who was the only child admitted, because he couldn't talk plain, babbled and laughed, and tried to tell what the "sumpin pitty" was.

All this made Daisy half-wild, and her excitement spread among the boys, who quite overwhelmed Mother Bhaer with offers of assistance, which she declined by quoting their own words to Daisy:

"Girls can't play with boys. This is for Daisy, and Bess, and me, so we don't want you." Whereupon the young gentlemen meekly retired, and invited Daisy to a game of marbles, horse, football, anything she liked, with a sudden warmth and politeness which astonished her innocent little soul.

Thanks to these attentions, she got through the afternoon, went early to bed, and next morning did her lessons with an energy which made Uncle Fritz wish that a new game could be invented every day. Quite a thrill pervaded the school-room when Daisy was dismissed at eleven o'clock, for everyone knew that now she was going to have the new and mysterious play.

Many eyes followed her as she ran away, and Demi's mind was so distracted by this event that when Franz asked him where the desert of Sahara was, he mournfully replied, "In the nursery," and the whole school laughed at him.

"Aunt Jo, I've done all my lessons, and I can't wait one single minute more!" cried Daisy, flying into Mrs. Bhaer's room.

"It's all ready, come on;" and tucking Ted under one arm, and her workbasket under the other, Aunt Jo promptly led the way upstairs.

"I don't see anything," said Daisy, staring about her as she got inside the nursery door.

"Do you hear anything?" asked Aunt Jo, catching Ted back by his little frock as he was making straight for one side of the room.

Daisy did hear an odd crackling, and then a purry little sound as of a kettle singing. These noises came from behind a curtain drawn before a deep bay window. Daisy snatched it back, gave one joyful, "Oh!" and then stood gazing with delight at what do you think?

A wide seat ran round the three sides of the window; on one side hung and stood all sorts of little pots and pans, gridirons and skillets; on the other side a small dinner and tea set; and on the middle part a cooking-stove. Not a tin one, that was of no use, but a real iron stove, big enough to cook for a large family of very hungry dolls. But the best of it was that a real fire burned in it, real steam came out of the nose of the little tea-kettle, and the lid of the little boiler actually danced a jig, the water inside bubbled so hard. A pane of glass had been taken out and replaced by a sheet of tin, with a hole for the small funnel, and real smoke went sailing away outside so naturally, that it did one's heart good to see it. The box of wood with a hod of charcoal stood near by; just above hung dust-pan, brush and broom; a little market basket was on the low table at which Daisy used to play, and over the back of her little chair hung a white apron with a bib, and a droll mob cap. The sun shone in as if he enjoyed the fun, the little stove roared beautifully, the kettle steamed, the new tins sparkled on the walls, the pretty china stood in tempting rows, and it was altogether as cheery and complete a kitchen as any child could desire.

Daisy stood quite still after the first glad "Oh!" but her eyes went quickly from one charming object to another, brightening as they looked, till they came to Aunt Jo's merry face; there they stopped as the happy little girl hugged her, saying gratefully:

"Oh aunty, it's a splendid new play! Can I really cook at the dear stove, and have parties and mess, and sweep, and make fires that truly burn? I like it so much! What made you think of it?"

"Your liking to make gingersnaps with Asia made me think of it," said Mrs. Bhaer, holding Daisy, who frisked as if she would fly. "I knew Asia wouldn't let you mess in her kitchen very often, and it wouldn't be safe at this fire up here, so I thought I'd see if I could find a little stove for you, and teach you to cook; that would be fun, and useful too. So I travelled round among the toy shops, but everything large cost too much and I was thinking I should have to give it up, when I met Uncle Teddy. As soon as he knew what I was about, he said he wanted to help, and insisted on buying the biggest toy stove we could find. I scolded, but he only laughed, and teased me about my cooking when we were young, and said I must teach Bess as well as you, and went on buying all sorts of nice little things for my 'cooking class' as he called it."

"I'm so glad you met him!" said Daisy, as Mrs. Jo stopped to laugh at the memory of the funny time she had with Uncle Teddy.

"You must study hard and learn to make all kinds of things, for he says he shall come out to tea very often, and expects something uncommonly nice."

"It's the sweetest, dearest kitchen in the world, and I'd rather study with it than do anything else. Can't I learn pies, and cake, and macaroni, and everything?" cried Daisy, dancing round the room with a new saucepan in one hand and the tiny poker in the other.

"All in good time. This is to be a useful play, I am to help you, and you are to be my cook, so I shall tell you what to do, and show you how. Then we shall have things fit to eat, and you will be really learning how to cook on a small scale. I'll call you Sally, and say you are a new girl just come," added Mrs. Jo, settling down to work, while Teddy sat on the floor sucking his thumb, and staring at the stove as if it was a live thing, whose appearance deeply interested him.

"That will be so lovely! What shall I do first?" asked Sally, with such a happy face and willing air that Aunt Jo wished all new cooks were half as pretty and pleasant.

"First of all, put on this clean cap and apron. I am rather old-fashioned, and I like my cook to be very tidy."

Sally tucked her curly hair into the round cap, and put on the apron without a murmur, though usually she rebelled against bibs.

"Now, you can put things in order, and wash up the new china. The old set needs washing also, for my last girl was apt to leave it in a sad state after a party."

Aunt Jo spoke quite soberly, but Sally laughed, for she knew who the untidy girl was who had left the cups sticky. Then she turned up her cuffs, and with a sigh of satisfaction began to stir about her kitchen, having little raptures now and then over the "sweet rolling pin," the "darling dish-tub," or the "cunning pepper-pot."

"Now, Sally, take your basket and go to market; here is the list of things I want for dinner," said Mrs. Jo, giving her a bit of paper when the dishes were all in order.

"Where is the market?" asked Daisy, thinking that the new play got more and more interesting every minute.

"Asia is the market."

Away went Sally, causing another stir in the schoolroom as she passed the door in her new costume, and whispered to Demi, with a face full of delight, "It's a perfectly splendid play!"

Old Asia enjoyed the joke as much as Daisy, and laughed jollily as the little girl came flying into the room with her cap all on one side, the lids of her basket rattling like castanets and looking like a very crazy little cook.

"Mrs. Aunt Jo wants these things, and I must have them right away," said Daisy, importantly.

'Let's see, honey; here's two pounds of steak, potatoes, squash, apples, bread, and butter. The meat ain't come yet; when it does I'll send it up. The other things are all handy."

Then Asia packed one potato, one apple, a bit of squash, a little pat of butter, and a roll, into the basket, telling Sally to be on the watch for the butcher's boy, because he sometimes played tricks.

"Who is he?" and Daisy hoped it would be Demi.

"You'll see," was all Asia would say; and Sally went off in great spirits, singing a verse from dear Mary Howitt's sweet story in rhyme:

> Away went little Mabel,
> With the wheaten cake so fine,
> The new-made pot of butter,
> And the little flask of wine.

"Put everything but the apple into the store-closet for the present," said Mrs. Jo, when the cook got home.

There was a cupboard under the middle shelf, and on opening the door fresh delights appeared. One half was evidently the cellar, for wood, coal, and kindlings were piled there. The other half was full of little jars, boxes, and all sorts of droll contrivances for holding small quantities of flour, meal, sugar, salt, and other household stores. A pot of jam was there, a little tin box of gingerbread, a cologne bottle full of currant wine, and a tiny canister of tea. But the crowning charm was two doll's pans of new milk, with cream actually rising on it, and a wee skimmer all ready to skim it with. Daisy clasped her hands at this delicious spectacle, and wanted to skim it immediately. But Aunt Jo said:

"Not yet; you will want the cream to eat on your apple pie at dinner, and must not disturb it till then."

"Am I going to have pie?" cried Daisy, hardly believing that such bliss could be in store for her.

"Yes; if your oven does well we will have two pies, one apple and one strawberry," said Mrs. Jo, who was nearly as much interested in the new play as Daisy herself.

"Oh, what next?" asked Sally, all impatience to begin.

"Shut the lower draught of the stove, so that the oven may heat. Then wash your hands and get out the flour, sugar, salt, butter, and cinnamon. See if the pie-board is clean, and pare your apple ready to put in."

Daisy got things together with as little noise and spilling as could be expected, from so young a cook.

"I really don't know how to measure for such tiny pies; I must guess at it, and if these don't succeed, we must try again," said Mrs. Jo, looking rather perplexed, and very much amused with the small concern before her. "Take that little pan full of flour, put in a pinch of salt, and then rub in as much butter as will go on that plate. Always remember to put your dry things together first, and then the wet. It mixes better so."

"I know how; I saw Asia do it. Don't I butter the pie plates too? She did, the first thing," said Daisy, whisking the flour about at a great rate.

Lesson 104

1. What would you still like to find out in chapter 5?
2. Finish reading chapter 5.
3. Summarize the chapter for someone.
4. Do you understand the meaning of the chapter title now? If not, how could you figure it out?
5. Recall a special toy that you enjoyed as Daisy enjoyed her kitchen. Describe it. Why did you like it?
6. Do a character sketch of Aunt Jo.

Chapter V. continued

"Quite right! I do believe you have a gift for cooking, you take to it so cleverly," said Aunt Jo, approvingly. "Now a dash of cold water, just enough to wet it; then scatter some flour on the board, work in a little, and roll the paste out; yes, that's the way. Now put dabs of butter all over it, and roll it out again. We won't have our pastry very rich, or the dolls will get dyspeptic."

Daisy laughed at the idea, and scattered the dabs with a liberal hand. Then she rolled and rolled with her delightful little pin, and having got her paste ready proceeded to cover the plates with it. Next the apple was sliced in, sugar and cinnamon lavishly sprinkled over it, and then the top crust put on with breathless care.

"I always wanted to cut them round, and Asia never would let me. How nice it is to do it all my ownty donty self!" said Daisy, as the little knife went clipping round the doll's plate poised on her hand.

All cooks, even the best, meet with mishaps sometimes, and Sally's first one occurred then, for the knife went so fast that the plate slipped, turned a somersault in the air, and landed the dear little pie upside down on the floor. Sally screamed, Mrs. Jo laughed, Teddy scrambled to get it, and for a moment confusion reigned in the new kitchen.

"It didn't spill or break, because I pinched the edges together so hard; it isn't hurt a bit, so I'll prick holes in it, and then it will be ready," said Sally, picking up the capsized treasure and putting it into shape with a child-like disregard of the dust it had gathered in its fall.

"My new cook has a good temper, I see, and that is such a comfort," said Mrs. Jo. "Now open the jar of strawberry jam, fill the uncovered pie, and put some strips of paste over the top as Asia does."

"I'll make a D in the middle, and have zigzags all round, that will be so interesting when I come to eat it," said Sally, loading the pie with quirls and flourishes that would have driven a real pastry cook wild. "Now I put them in!" she exclaimed; when the last grimy knob had been carefully planted in the red field of jam, and with an air of triumph she shut them into the little oven.

"Clear up your things; a good cook never lets her utensils collect. Then pare your squash and potatoes."

"There is only one potato," giggled Sally.

"Cut it in four pieces, so it will go into the little kettle, and put the bits into cold water till it is time to cook them."

"Do I soak the squash too?"

"No, indeed! Just pare it and cut it up, and put in into the steamer over the pot. It is drier so, though it takes longer to cook."

Here a scratching at the door caused Sally to run and open it, when Kit appeared with a covered basket in his mouth.

"Here's the butcher boy!" cried Daisy, much tickled at the idea, as she relieved him of his load, whereat he licked his lips and began to beg, evidently thinking that it was his own dinner, for he often carried it to his master in that way. Being undeceived, he departed in great wrath and barked all the way downstairs, to ease his wounded feelings.

In the basket were two bits of steak (doll's pounds), a baked pear, a small cake, and paper with them on which Asia had scrawled, "For Missy's lunch, if her cookin' don't turn out well."

"I don't want any of her old pears and things; my cooking will turn out well, and I'll have a splendid dinner; see if I don't!" cried Daisy, indignantly.

"We may like them if company should come. It is always well to have something in the storeroom," said Aunt Jo, who had been taught this valuable fact by a series of domestic panics.

"Me is hundry," announced Teddy, who began to think what with so much cooking going on it was about time for somebody to eat something. His mother gave him her workbasket to rummage, hoping to keep him quiet till dinner was ready, and returned to her housekeeping.

"Put on your vegetables, set the table, and then have some coals kindling ready for the steak."

What a thing it was to see the potatoes bobbing about in the little pot; to peep at the squash getting soft so fast in the tiny steamer; to whisk open the oven door every five minutes to see how the pies got on, and at last when the coals were red and glowing, to put two real steaks on a finger-long gridiron and proudly turn them with a fork. The potatoes were done first, and no wonder, for they had boiled frantically all the while. The were pounded up with a little pestle, had much butter and no salt put in (cook forgot it in the excitement of the moment), then it was made into a mound in a gay red dish, smoothed over with a knife dipped in milk, and put in the oven to brown.

So absorbed in these last performances had Sally been, that she forgot her pastry till she opened the door to put in the potato, then a wail arose, for alas! alas! the little pies were burnt black!

"Oh, my pies! My darling pies! They are all spoilt!" cried poor Sally, wringing her dirty little hands as she surveyed the ruin of her work. The tart was especially pathetic, for the quirls and zigzags stuck up in all directions from the blackened jelly, like the walls and chimney of a house after a fire.

"Dear, dear, I forgot to remind you to take them out; it's just my luck," said Aunt Jo, remorsefully. "Don't cry, darling, it was my fault; we'll try again after dinner," she added, as a great tear dropped from Sally's eyes and sizzled on the hot ruins of the tart.

More would have followed, if the steak had not blazed up just then, and so occupied the attention of cook, that she quickly forgot the lost pastry.

"Put the meat-dish and your own plates down to warm, while you mash the squash with butter, salt, and a little pepper on the top," said Mrs. Jo, devoutly hoping that the dinner would meet with no further disasters.

The "cunning pepper-pot" soothed Sally's feelings, and she dished up her squash in fine style. The dinner was safely put upon the table; the six dolls were seated three on a side; Teddy took the bottom, and Sally the top. When all were settled, it was a most imposing spectacle, for one doll was in full ball costume, another in her night-gown; Jerry, the worsted boy, wore his red winter suit, while Annabella, the noseless darling, was airily attired in nothing but her own kid skin. Teddy, as father of the family, behaved with great propriety, for he smilingly devoured everything offered him, and did not find a single fault. Daisy beamed upon her company like the weary, warm, but hospitable hostess so often to be seen at larger tables than this, and did the honors with an air of innocent satisfaction, which we do not often see elsewhere.

The steak was so tough that the little carving-knife would not cut it; the potato did not go round, and the squash was very lumpy; but the guests appeared politely unconscious of these trifles; and the master and mistress of the house cleared the table with appetites that anyone might envy them. The joy of skimming a jug-full of cream mitigated the anguish felt for the loss of the pies, and Asia's despised cake proved a treasure in the way of dessert.

"That is the nicest lunch I ever had; can't I do it every day?" asked Daisy as she scraped up and ate the leavings all round.

"You can cook things every day after lessons, but I prefer that you should eat your dishes at your regular meals, and only have a bit of gingerbread for lunch. To-day, being the first time, I don't mind, but we must keep our rules. This afternoon you can make something for tea if you like," said Mrs. Jo, who had enjoyed the dinner-party very much, though no one had invited her to partake.

"Do let me make flapjacks for Demi, he loves them so, and it's such fun to turn them and put sugar in between," cried Daisy, tenderly wiping a yellow stain off Annabella's broken nose, for Bella had refused to eat squash when it was pressed upon her as good for "lumatism," a complaint which it is no wonder she suffered from, considering the lightness of her attire.

"But if you give Demi goodies, all the others will expect some also, and then you will have your hands full."

"Couldn't I have Demi come up to tea alone just this one time? And after that I could cook things for the others if they were good," proposed Daisy, with a sudden inspiration.

"That is a capital idea, Posy! We will make your little messes rewards for the good boys, and I don't know one among them who would not like something nice to eat more than almost anything else. If little men are like big ones, good cooking will touch their hearts and soothe their tempers delightfully," added Aunt Jo, with a merry nod toward the door, where stood Papa Bhaer, surveying the scene with a face full of amusement.

"That last hit was for me, sharp woman. I accept it, for it is true; but if I had married thee for thy cooking, heart's dearest, I should have fared badly all these years," answered the professor, laughing as he tossed Teddy, who became quite apoplectic in his endeavors to describe the feast he had just enjoyed.

Daisy proudly showed her kitchen, and rashly promised Uncle Fritz as many flapjacks as he could eat. She was just telling about the new rewards when the boys, headed by Demi, burst into the room snuffing the air like a pack of hungry hounds, for school was out, dinner was not ready, and the fragrance of Daisy's steak led them straight to the spot.

A prouder little damsel was never seen than Sally as she displayed her treasures and told the lads what was in store for them. Several rather scoffed at the idea of her cooking anything fit to eat, but Stuffy's heart was won at once. Nat and Demi had firm faith in her skill, and the others said they would wait and see. All admired the kitchen, however, and examined the stove with deep interest. Demi offered to buy the boiler on the spot, to be used in a steam-engine which he was constructing; and Ned declared that the best and biggest saucepan was just the thing to melt his lead in when he ran bullets, hatchets, and such trifles.

Daisy looked so alarmed at these proposals, that Mrs. Jo then and there made and proclaimed a law that no boy should touch, use, or even approach the sacred stove without a special permit from the owner thereof. This increased its value immensely in the eyes of the gentlemen, especially as any infringement of the law would be punished by forfeiture of all right to partake of the delicacies promised to the virtuous.

At this point the bell rang, and the entire population went down to dinner, which meal was enlivened by each of the boys giving Daisy a list of things he would like to have cooked for him as fast as he earned them. Daisy, whose faith in her stove was unlimited, promised everything, if Aunt Jo would tell her how to make them. This suggestion rather alarmed Mrs. Jo, for some of the dishes were quite beyond her skill wedding-cake, for instance, bull's-eye candy; and cabbage soup with herrings and cherries in it, which Mr. Bhaer proposed as his favorite, and immediately reduced his wife to despair, for German cookery was beyond her.

Daisy wanted to begin again the minute dinner was done, but she was only allowed to clear up, fill the kettle ready for tea, and wash out her apron, which looked as if she had a Christmas feast. She was then sent out to play till five o'clock, for Uncle Fritz said that too much study, even at cooking stoves, was bad for little minds and bodies, and Aunt Jo knew by long experience how soon new toys lose their charm if they are not prudently used.

Everyone was very kind to Daisy that afternoon. Tommy promised her the first fruits of his garden, though the only visible crop just then was pigweed; Nat offered to supply her with wood, free of charge; Stuffy quite worshipped her; Ned immediately fell to work on a little refrigerator for her kitchen; and Demi, with a punctuality beautiful to see in one so young, escorted her to the nursery just as the clock struck five. It was not time for the party to begin, but he begged so hard to come in and help that he was allowed privileges few visitors enjoy, for he kindled the fire, ran errands, and watched the progress of his supper with intense interest. Mrs. Jo directed the affair as she came and went, being very busy putting up clean curtains all over the house.

"Ask Asia for a cup of sour cream, then your cakes will be light without much soda, which I don't like," was the first order.

Demi tore downstairs, and returned with the cream, also a puckered-up face, for he had tasted it on his way, and found it so sour that he predicted the cakes would be uneatable. Mrs. Jo took this occasion to deliver a short lecture from the step-ladder on the chemical properties of soda, to which Daisy did not listen, but Demi did, and understood it, as he proved by the brief but comprehensive reply:

"Yes, I see, soda turns sour things sweet, and the fizzling up makes them light. Let's see you do it, Daisy."

"Fill that bowl nearly full of flour and add a little salt to it," continued Mrs. Jo.

"Oh dear, everything has to have salt in it, seems to me," said Sally, who was tired of opening the pill-box in which it was kept.

"Salt is like good-humor, and nearly every thing is better for a pinch of it, Posy," and Uncle Fritz stopped as he passed, hammer in hand, to drive up two or three nails for Sally's little pans to hang on.

"You are not invited to tea, but I'll give you some cakes, and I won't be cross," said Daisy, putting up her floury little face to thank him with a kiss.

"Fritz, you must not interrupt my cooking class, or I'll come in and moralize when you are teaching Latin. How would you like that?" said Mrs. Jo, throwing a great chintz curtain down on his head.

"Very much, try it and see," and the amiable Father Bhaer went singing and tapping about the house like a mammoth woodpecker.

"Put the soda into the cream, and when it 'fizzles,' as Demi says, stir it into the flour, and beat it up as hard as ever you can. Have your griddle hot, butter it well, and then fry away till I come back," and Aunt Jo vanished also.

Such a clatter as the little spoon made, and such a beating as the batter got, it quite foamed, I assure you; and when Daisy poured some on to the griddle, it rose like magic into a puffy flapjack that made Demi's mouth water. To be sure, the first one stuck and scorched, because she forgot the butter, but after that first failure all went well, and six capital little cakes were safely landed in a dish.

"I think I like maple-syrup better than sugar," said Demi, from his arm-chair where he had settled himself after setting the table in a new and peculiar manner.

"Then go and ask Asia for some," answered Daisy, going into the bath-room to wash her hands.

While the nursery was empty something dreadful happened. You see, Kit had been feeling hurt all day because he had carried meat safely and yet got none to pay him. He was not a bad dog, but he had his little faults like the rest of us, and could not always resist temptation. Happening to stroll into the nursery at that moment, he smelt the cakes, saw them unguarded on the low table, and never stopping to think of consequences, swallowed all six at one mouthful. I am glad to say that they were very hot, and burned him so badly that he could not repress a surprised yelp. Daisy heard it, ran in, saw the empty dish, also the end of a yellow tail disappearing under the bed. Without a word she seized that tail, pulled out the thief, and shook him till his ears flapped wildly, then bundled him down-stairs to the shed, where he spent a lonely evening in the coal-bin.

Cheered by the sympathy which Demi gave her, Daisy made another bowlful of batter, and fried a dozen cakes, which were even better than the others. Indeed, Uncle Fritz after eating two sent up word that he had never tasted any so nice, and every boy at the table below envied Demi at the flapjack party above.

It was a truly delightful supper, for the little teapot lid only fell off three times and the milk jug upset but once; the cakes floated in syrup, and the toast had a delicious beef-steak flavor, owing to cook's using the gridiron to make it on. Demi forgot philosophy, and stuffed like any carnal boy, while Daisy planned sumptuous banquets, and the dolls looked on smiling affably.

"Well, dearies, have you had a good time?" asked Mrs. Jo, coming up with Teddy on her shoulder.

"A very good time. I shall come again soon," answered Demi, with emphasis.

"I'm afraid you have eaten too much, by the look of that table."

"No, I haven't; I only ate fifteen cakes, and they were very little ones," protested Demi, who had kept his sister busy supplying his plate.

"They won't hurt him, they are so nice," said Daisy, with such a funny mixture of maternal fondness and housewifely pride that Aunt Jo could only smile and say:

"Well, on the whole, the new game is a success then?"

"I like it," said Demi, as if his approval was all that was necessary.

"It is the dearest play ever made!" cried Daisy, hugging her little dish-tub as she proposed to wash up the cups. "I just wish everybody had a sweet cooking stove like mine," she added, regarding it with affection.

"This play out to have a name," said Demi, gravely removing the syrup from his countenance with his tongue.

"It has."

"Oh, what?" asked both children eagerly.

"Well, I think we will call it Pattypans," and Aunt Jo retired, satisfied with the success of her last trap to catch a sunbeam.

Lesson 105

1. Read the title to chapter 6. What do you think might be going to happen in this chapter?
2. Read the first part of chapter 6.
3. How are you feeling about Dan? Why?
4. What do you think is going to happen next? (The only wrong answer is no answer.)

Chapter VI. A Fire Brand

"Please, ma'am, could I speak to you? It is something very important," said Nat, popping his head in at the door of Mrs. Bhaer's room.

It was the fifth head which had popped in during the last half-hour; but Mrs. Jo was used to it, so she looked up, and said, briskly,

"What is it, my lad?"

Nat came in, shut the door carefully behind him, and said in an eager, anxious tone,

"Dan has come."

"Who is Dan?"

"He's a boy I used to know when I fiddled round the streets. He sold papers, and he was kind to me, and I saw him the other day in town, and told him how nice it was here, and he's come."

"But, my dear boy, that is rather a sudden way to pay a visit."

"Oh, it isn't a visit; he wants to stay if you will let him!" said Nat innocently.

"Well, I don't know about that," began Mrs. Bhaer, rather startled by the coolness of the proposition.

"Why, I thought you liked to have poor boys come and live with you, and be kind to 'em as you were to me," said Nat, looking surprised and alarmed.

"So I do, but I like to know something about them first. I have to choose them, because there are so many. I have not room for all. I wish I had."

"I told him to come because I thought you'd like it, but if there isn't room he can go away again," said Nat, sorrowfully.

The boy's confidence in her hospitality touched Mrs. Bhaer, and she could not find the heart to disappoint his hope, and spoil his kind little plan, so she said, "Tell me about this Dan."

"I don't know any thing, only he hasn't got any folks, and he's poor, and he was good to me, so I'd like to be good to him if I could."

"Excellent reasons every one; but really, Nat, the house is full, and I don't know where I could put him," said Mrs. Bhaer, more and more inclined to prove herself the haven of refuge he seemed to think her.

"He could have my bed, and I could sleep in the barn. It isn't cold now, and I don't mind, I used to sleep anywhere with father," said Nat, eagerly.

Something in his speech and face made Mrs. Jo put her hand on his shoulder, and say in her kindest tone:

"Bring in your friend, Nat; I think we must find room for him without giving him your place."

Nat joyfully ran off, and soon returned followed by a most unprepossessing boy, who slouched in and stood looking about him, with a half bold, half sullen look, which made Mrs. Bhaer say to herself, after one glance,

"A bad specimen, I am afraid."

"This is Dan," said Nat, presenting him as if sure of his welcome.

"Nat tells me you would like to come and stay with us," began Mrs. Jo, in a friendly tone.

"Yes," was the gruff reply.

"Have you no friends to take care of you?"

"No."

"Say, 'No, ma'am,' " whispered Nat.

"Shan't neither," muttered Dan.

"How old are you?"

"About fourteen."

"You look older. What can you do?"

"'Most anything."

"If you stay here we shall want you to do as the others do, work and study as well as play. Are you willing to agree to that?"

"Don't mind trying."

"Well, you can stay a few days, and we will see how we get on together. Take him out, Nat, and amuse him till Mr. Bhaer comes home, when we will settle about the matter," said Mrs. Jo, finding it rather difficult to get on with this cool young person, who fixed his big black eyes on her with a hard, suspicious expression, sorrowfully unboyish.

"Come on, Nat," he said, and slouched out again.

"Thank you, ma'am," added Nat, as he followed him, feeling without quite understanding the difference in the welcome given to him and to his ungracious friend.

"The fellows are having a circus out in the barn; don't you want to come and see it?" he asked, as they came down the wide steps on to the lawn.

"Are they big fellows?" said Dan.

"No; the big ones are gone fishing."

"Fire away, then," said Dan.

Nat led him to the great barn and introduced him to his set, who were disporting themselves among the half-empty lofts. A large circle was marked out with hay on the wide floor, and in the middle stood Demi with a long whip, while Tommy, mounted on the much-enduring Toby, pranced about the circle playing being a monkey.

"You must pay a pin apiece, or you can't see the show," said Stuffy, who stood by the wheelbarrow in which sat the band, consisting of a pocket-comb blown upon by Ned, and a toy drum beaten spasmodically by Rob.

"He's company, so I'll pay for both," said Nat, handsomely, as he stuck two crooked pins in the dried mushroom which served as money-box.

With a nod to the company they seated themselves on a couple of boards, and the performance went on. After the monkey act, Ned gave them a fine specimen of his agility by jumping over an old chair, and running up and down ladders, sailor fashion. Then Demi danced a jig with a gravity beautiful to behold. Nat was called upon to wrestle with Stuffy, and speedily laid that stout youth upon the ground. After this, Tommy proudly advanced to turn a somersault, an accomplishment which he had acquired by painful perseverance, practising in private till every joint of his little frame was black and blue. His feats were received with great applause, and he was about to retire, flushed with pride and a rush of blood to the head, when a scornful voice in the audience was heard to say,

"Ho! that ain't any thing!"

"Say that again, will you?" and Tommy bristled up like an angry turkey-cock.

"Do you want to fight?" said Dan, promptly descending from the barrel and doubling up his fists in a business-like manner.

"No, I don't;" and the candid Thomas retired a step, rather taken aback by the proposition.

"Fighting isn't allowed!" cried the others, much excited.

"You're a nice lot," sneered Dan.

"Come, if you don't behave, you shan't stay," said Nat, firing up at that insult to his friends.

"I'd like to see him do better than I did, that's all," observed Tommy, with a swagger.

"Clear the way, then," and without the slightest preparation Dan turned three somersaults one after the other and came up on his feet.

"You can't beat that, Tom; you always hit your head and tumble flat," said Nat, pleased at his friend's success.

Before he could say any more the audience were electrified by three more somersaults backwards, and a short promenade on the hands, head down, feet up. This brought down the house, and Tommy joined in the admiring cries which greeted the accomplished gymnast as he righted himself, and looked at them with an air of calm superiority.

"Do you think I could learn to do it without its hurting me very much?" Tom meekly asked, as he rubbed the elbows which still smarted after the last attempt.

"What will you give me if I'll teach you?" said Dan.

"My new jack-knife; it's got five blades, and only one is broken."

"Give it here, then."

Tommy handed it over with an affectionate look at its smooth handle. Dan examined it carefully, then putting it into his pocket, walked off, saying with a wink,

"Keep it up till you learn, that's all."

A howl of wrath from Tommy was followed by a general uproar, which did not subside till Dan, finding himself in a minority, proposed that they should play stick-knife, and whichever won should have the treasure. Tommy agreed, and the game was played in a circle of excited faces, which all wore an expression of satisfaction, when Tommy won and secured the knife in the depth of his safest pocket.

"You come off with me, and I'll show you round," said Nat, feeling that he must have a little serious conversation with his friend in private.

What passed between them no one knew, but when they appeared again, Dan was more respectful to every one, though still gruff in his speech, and rough in his manner; and what else could be expected of the poor lad who had been knocking about the world all his short life with no one to teach him any better?

The boys had decided that they did not like him, and so they left him to Nat, who soon felt rather oppressed by the responsibility, but too kind-hearted to desert him.

Tommy, however, felt that in spite of the jack-knife transaction, there was a bond of sympathy between them, and longed to return to the interesting subject of somersaults. He soon found an opportunity, for Dan, seeing how much he admired him, grew more amiable, and by the end of the first week was quite intimate with the lively Tom.

Mr. Bhaer, when he heard the story and saw Dan, shook his head, but only said quietly,

"The experiment may cost us something, but we will try it."

If Dan felt any gratitude for his protection, he did not show it, and took without thanks all that was give him. He was ignorant, but very quick to learn when he chose; had sharp eyes to watch what went on about him; a saucy tongue, rough manners, and a temper that was fierce and sullen by turns. He played with all his might, and played well at almost all the games. He was silent and gruff before grown people, and only now and then was thoroughly sociable among the lads. Few of them really liked him, but few could help admiring his courage and strength, for nothing daunted him, and he knocked tall Franz flat on one occasion with an ease that caused all the others to keep at a respectful distance from his fists. Mr. Bhaer watched him silently, and did his best to tame the "Wild Boy," as they called him, but in private the worthy man shook his head, and said soberly, "I hope the experiment will turn out well, but I am a little afraid it may cost too much."

Mrs. Bhaer lost her patience with him half a dozen times a day, yet never gave him up, and always insisted that there was something good in the lad, after all; for he was kinder to animals than to people, he liked to rove about in the woods, and, best of all, little Ted was fond of him. What the secret was no one could discover, but Baby took to him at once gabbled and crowed whenever he saw him preferred his strong back to ride on to any of the others and called him "My Danny" out of his own little head. Teddy was the only creature to whom Dan showed an affection, and this was only manifested when he thought no one else would see it; but mothers' eyes are quick, and motherly hearts instinctively divine who love their babies. So Mrs. Jo soon saw and felt that there was a soft spot in rough Dan, and bided her time to touch and win him.

But an unexpected and decidedly alarming event upset all their plans, and banished Dan from Plumfield.

Tommy, Nat, and Demi began by patronizing Dan, because the other lads rather slighted him; but soon they each felt there was a certain fascination about the bad boy, and from looking down upon him they came to looking up, each for a different reason. Tommy admired his skill and courage;

Nat was grateful for past kindness; and Demi regarded him as a sort of animated story book, for when he chose Dan could tell his adventures in a most interesting way. It pleased Dan to have the three favorites like him, and he exerted himself to be agreeable, which was the secret of his success.

The Bhaers were surprised, but hoped the lads would have a good influence over Dan, and waited with some anxiety, trusting that no harm would come of it.

Dan felt they did not quite trust him, and never showed them his best side, but took a wilful pleasure in trying their patience and thwarting their hopes as far as he dared.

Mr. Bhaer did not approve of fighting, and did not think it a proof of either manliness or courage for two lads to pommel one another for the amusement of the rest. All sorts of hardy games and exercises were encouraged, and the boys were expected to take hard knocks and tumbles without whining; but black eyes and bloody noses given for the fun of it were forbidden as a foolish and a brutal play.

Dan laughed at this rule, and told such exciting tales of his own valor, and the many frays that he had been in, that some of the lads were fired with a desire to have a regular good "mill."

"Don't tell, and I'll show you how," said Dan; and, getting half a dozen of the lads together behind the barn, he gave them a lesson in boxing, which quite satisfied the ardor of most of them. Emil, however, could not submit to be beaten by a fellow younger than himself, for Emil was past fourteen and a plucky fellow, so he challenged Dan to a fight. Dan accepted at once, and the others looked on with intense interest.

What little bird carried the news to head-quarters no one ever knew, but, in the very hottest of the fray, when Dan and Emil were fighting like a pair of young bulldogs, and the others with fierce, excited faces were cheering them on, Mr. Bhaer walked into the ring, plucked the combatants apart with a strong hand, and said, in the voice they seldom heard,

"I can't allow this, boys! Stop it at once; and never let me see it again. I keep a school for boys, not for wild beasts. Look at each other and be ashamed of yourselves."

"You let me go, and I'll knock him down again," shouted Dan, sparring away in spite of the grip on his collar.

"Come on, come on, I ain't thrashed yet!" cried Emil, who had been down five times, but did not know when he was beaten.

"They are playing be gladdy what-you-call-'ems, like the Romans, Uncle Fritz," called out Demi, whose eyes were bigger than ever with the excitement of this new pastime.

"They were a fine set of brutes; but we have learned something since then, I hope, and I cannot have you make my barn a Colosseum. Who proposed this?" asked Mr. Bhaer.

"Dan," answered several voices.

"Don't you know that it is forbidden?"

"Yes," growled Dan, sullenly.

"Then why break the rule?"

"They'll all be molly-coddles, if they don't know how to fight."

"Have you found Emil a molly-coddle? He doesn't look much like one," and Mr. Bhaer brought the two face to face. Dan had a black eye, and his jacket was torn to rags, but Emil's face was covered with blood from a cut lip and a bruised nose, while a bump on his forehead was already as purple as a plum. In spite of his wounds however, he still glared upon his foe, and evidently panted to renew the fight.

"He'd make a first-rater if he was taught," said Dan, unable to withhold the praise from the boy who made it necessary for him to do his best.

"He'll be taught to fence and box by and by, and till then I think he will do very well without any lessons in mauling. Go and wash your faces; and remember, Dan, if you break any more of the rules again, you will be sent away. That was the bargain; do your part and we will do ours."

The lads went off, and after a few more words to the spectators, Mr. Bhaer followed to bind up the wounds of the young gladiators. Emil went to bed sick, and Dan was an unpleasant spectacle for a week.

But the lawless lad had no thought of obeying, and soon transgressed again.

One Saturday afternoon as a party of the boys went out to play, Tommy said,

"Let's go down to the river, and cut a lot of new fish-poles."

"Take Toby to drag them back, and one of us can ride him down," proposed Stuffy, who hated to walk.

"That means you, I suppose; well, hurry up, lazy-bones," said Dan.

Away they went, and having got the poles were about to go home, when Demi unluckily said to Tommy, who was on Toby with a long rod in his hand,

"You look like the picture of the man in the bull-fight, only you haven't got a red cloth, or pretty clothes on."

"I'd like to see one; there's old Buttercup in the big meadow, ride at her, Tom, and see her run," proposed Dan, bent on mischief.

"No, you mustn't," began Demi, who was learning to distrust Dan's propositions.

"Why not, little fuss-button?" demanded Dan.

"I don't think Uncle Fritz would like it."

"Did he ever say we must not have a bull-fight?"

"No, I don't think he ever did," admitted Demi.

"Then hold your tongue. Drive on, Tom, and here's a red rag to flap at the old thing. I'll help you to stir her up," and over the wall went Dan, full of the new game, and the rest followed like a flock of sheep; even Demi, who sat upon the bars, and watched the fun with interest.

Lesson 106

1. Finish reading chapter 6.
2. What are you thinking? Are you surprised that Dan could not or would not give up his wild ways? Why or why not?

3. Why do you think Dan had so much influence on the other boys even though they knew that what he was doing was not right?

4. How is Dan a "firebrand?"

5. Complete a character sketch of Dan.

Chapter VI. continued

Poor Buttercup was not in a very good mood, for she had been lately bereft of her calf, and mourned for the little thing most dismally. Just now she regarded all mankind as her enemies (and I do not blame her), so when the matadore came prancing towards her with the red handkerchief flying at the end of his long lance, she threw up her head, and gave a most appropriate "Moo!" Tommy rode gallantly at her, and Toby recognizing an old friend, was quite willing to approach; but when the lance came down on her back with a loud whack, both cow and donkey were surprised and disgusted. Toby back with a bray of remonstrance, and Buttercup lowered her horns angrily.

"At her again, Tom; she's jolly cross, and will do it capitally!" called Dan, coming up behind with another rod, while Jack and Ned followed his example.

Seeing herself thus beset, and treated with such disrespect, Buttercup trotted round the field, getting more and more bewildered and excited every moment, for whichever way she turned, there was a dreadful boy, yelling and brandishing a new and very disagreeable sort of whip. It was great fun for them, but real misery for her, till she lost patience and turned the tables in the most unexpected manner. All at once she wheeled short round, and charged full at her old friend Toby, whose conduct cut her to the heart. Poor slow Toby backed so precipitately that he tripped over a stone, and down went horse, matadore, and all, in one ignominious heap, while distracted Buttercup took a surprising leap over the wall, and galloped wildly out of sight down the road.

"Catch her, stop her, head her off! run, boys, run!" shouted Dan, tearing after her at his best pace, for she was Mr. Bhaer's pet Alderney, and if anything happened to her, Dan feared it would be all over with him. Such a running and racing and bawling and puffing as there was before she was caught! The fish-poles were left behind; Toby was trotted nearly off his legs in the chase; and every boy was red, breathless, and scared. They found poor Buttercup at last in a flower garden, where she had taken refuge, worn out with the long run. Borrowing a rope for a halter, Dan led her home, followed by a party of very sober young gentlemen, for the cow was in a sad state, having strained her shoulder jumping, so that she limped, her eyes looked wild, and her glossy coat was wet and muddy.

"You'll catch it this time, Dan," said Tommy, as he led the wheezing donkey beside the maltreated cow.

"So will you, for you helped."

"We all did, but Demi," added Jack.

"He put it into our heads," said Ned.

"I told you not to do it," cried Demi, who was most broken-hearted at poor Buttercup's state.

"Old Bhaer will send me off, I guess. Don't care if he does," muttered Dan, looking worried in spite of his words.

"We'll ask him not to, all of us," said Demi, and the others assented with the exception of Stuffy, who cherished the hope that all the punishment might fall on one guilty head. Dan only said, "Don't bother about me;" but he never forgot it, even though he led the lads astray again, as soon as the temptation came.

When Mr. Bhaer saw the animal, and heard the story, he said very little, evidently fearing that he should say too much in the first moments of impatience. Buttercup was made comfortable in her stall, and the boys sent to their rooms till supper-time. This brief respite gave them time to think the matter over, to wonder what the penalty would be, and to try to imagine where Dan would be sent. He whistled briskly in his room, so that no one should think he cared a bit; but while he waited to know his fate, the longing to stay grew stronger and stronger, the more he recalled the comfort and kindness he had known here, the hardship and neglect he had felt elsewhere. He knew they tried to help him, and at the bottom of his heart he was grateful, but his rough life had made him hard and careless, suspicious and wilful. He hated restraint of any sort, and fought against it like an untamed creature, even while he knew it was kindly meant, and dimly felt that he would be the better for it. He made up his mind to be turned adrift again, to knock about the city as he had done nearly all his life; a prospect that made him knit his black brows, and look about the cosy little room with a wistful expression that would have touched a much harder heart than Mr. Bhaer's if he had seen it. It vanished instantly, however, when the good man came in, and said in his accustomed grave way,

"I have heard all about it, Dan, and though you have broken the rules again, I am going to give you one more trial, to please Mother Bhaer."

Dan flushed up to his forehead at this unexpected reprieve, but he only said in his gruff way,

"I didn't know there was any rule about bull-fighting."

"As I never expected to have any at Plumfield, I never did make such a rule," answered Mr. Bhaer, smiling in spite of himself at the boy's excuse. Then he added gravely, "But one of the first and most important of our few laws is the law of kindness to every dumb creature on the place. I want everybody and everything to be happy here, to love and trust, and serve us, as we try to love and trust and serve them faithfully and willingly. I have often said that you were kinder to the animals than any of the other boys, and Mrs. Bhaer liked that trait in you very much, because she thought it showed a good heart. But you have disappointed us in that, and we are sorry, for we hoped to make you quite one of us. Shall we try again?"

Dan's eyes had been on the floor, and his hands nervously picking at the bit of wood he had been whittling as Mr. Bhaer came in, but when he heard the kind voice ask that question, he looked up quickly, and said in a more respectful tone than he had ever used before,

"Yes, please."

"Very well, then, we will say no more, only you will stay at home from the walk to-morrow, as the other boys will and all of you must wait on poor Buttercup till she is well again."

"I will."

"Now, go down to supper, and do your best, my boy, more for your own sake than for ours." Then Mr. Bhaer shook hands with him, and Dan went down more tamed by kindness than he would have been by the good whipping which Asia had strongly recommended.

Dan did try for a day or two, but not being used to it, he soon tired and relapsed into his old wilful ways. Mr. Bhaer was called from home on business one day, and the boys had no lessons. They liked this, and played hard till bedtime, when most of them turned in and slept like dormice. Dan, however, had a plan in his head, and when he and Nat were alone, he unfolded it.

"Look here!" he said, taking from under his bed a bottle, a cigar, and a pack of cards, "I'm going to have some fun, and do as I used to with the fellows in town. Here's some beer, I got if of the old man at the station, and this cigar; you can pay for 'em or Tommy will, he's got heaps of money and I haven't a cent. I'm going to ask him in; no, you go, they won't mind you."

"The folks won't like it," began Nat.

"They won't know. Daddy Bhaer is away, and Mrs. Bhaer's busy with Ted; he's got croup or something, and she can't leave him. We shan't sit up late or make any noise, so where's the harm?"

"Asia will know if we burn the lamp long, she always does."

"No, she won't, I've got a dark lantern on purpose; it don't give much light, and we can shut it quick if we hear anyone coming," said Dan.

This idea struck Nat as a fine one, and lent an air of romance to the thing. He started off to tell Tommy, but put his head in again to say,

"You want Demi, too, don't you?"

"No, I don't; the Deacon will rollup eyes and preach if you tell him. He will be asleep, so just tip the wink to Tom and cut back again."

Nat obeyed, and returned in a minute with Tommy half dressed, rather tousled about the head and very sleepy, but quite ready for fun as usual.

"Now, keep quiet, and I'll show you how to play a first-rate game called 'Poker,' " said Dan, as the three revellers gathered round the table, on which were set forth the bottle, the cigar, and the cards. "First we'll all have a drink, then we'll take a go at the 'weed,' and then we'll play. That's the way men do, and it's jolly fun."

The beer circulated in a mug, and all three smacked their lips over it, though Nat and Tommy did not like the bitter stuff. The cigar was worse still, but they dared not say so, and each puffed away till he was dizzy or choked, when he passed the "weed" on to his neighbor. Dan liked it, for it seemed like old times when he now and then had a chance to imitate the low men who surrounded him. He drank, and smoked, and swaggered as much like them as he could, and, getting into the spirit of the part he assumed, he soon began to swear under his breath for fear some one should hear him. "You mustn't; it's wicked to [curse]!" cried Tommy, who had followed his leader so far.

"Oh, hang! don't you preach, but play away; it's part of the fun to swear."

"I'd rather say 'thunder turtles,' " said Tommy, who had composed this interesting exclamation and was very proud of it.

"And I'll say 'The Devil;' that sounds well," added Nat, much impressed by Dan's manly ways.

Dan scoffed at their "nonsense," and swore stoutly as he tried to teach them the new game.

But Tommy was very sleepy, and Nat's head began to ache with the beer and the smoke, so neither of them was very quick to learn, and the game dragged. The room was nearly dark, for the lantern burned badly; they could not laugh loud nor move about much, for Silas slept next door in the shed-chamber, and altogether the party was dull. In the middle of a deal Dan stopped suddenly, and called out, "Who's that?" in a startled tone, and at the same moment drew the slide over the light. A voice in the darkness said tremulously, "I can't find Tommy," and then there was the quick patter of bare feet running away down the entry that led from the wing to the main house.

"It's Demi! he's gone to call some one; cut into bed, Tom, and don't tell!" cried Dan, whisking all signs of the revel out of sight, and beginning to tear off his clothes, while Nat did the same.

Tommy flew to his room and dived into bed, where he lay, laughing till something burned his hand, when he discovered that he was still clutching the stump of the festive cigar, which he happened to be smoking when the revel broke up.

It was nearly out, and he was about to extinguish it carefully when Nursey's voice was heard, and fearing it would betray him if he hid it in the bed, he threw it underneath, after a final pinch which he thought finished it.

Nursey came in with Demi, who looked much amazed to see the red face of Tommy reposing peacefully upon his pillow.

"He wasn't there just now, because I woke up and could not find him anywhere," said Demi, pouncing on him.

"What mischief are you at now, bad child?" asked Nursey, with a good-natured shake, which made the sleeper open his eyes to say meekly,

"I only ran into Nat's room to see him about something. Go away, and let me alone; I'm awful sleepy."

Nursey tucked Demi in, and went off to reconnoitre, but only found two boys slumbering peacefully in Dan's room. "Some little frolic," she thought, and as there was no harm done she said nothing to Mrs. Bhaer, who was busy and worried over little Teddy.

Tommy was sleepy, and telling Demi to mind his own business and not ask questions, he was snoring in ten minutes, little dreaming what was going on under his bed. The cigar did not go out, but smouldered away on the straw carpet till it was nicely on fire, and a hungry little flame went creeping along till the dimity bedcover caught, then the sheets, and then the bed itself. The beer made Tommy sleep heavily, and the smoke stupified Demi, so they slept on till the fire began to scorch them, and they were in danger of being burned to death.

Franz was sitting up to study, and as he left the school-room he smelt the smoke, dashed up-stairs and saw it coming in a cloud from the left wing of the house. Without stopping to call any one, he ran into the room, dragged the boys from the blazing bed, and splashed all the water he could find at hand on to the flames. It checked but did not quench the fire, and the children wakened on being tumbled topsy-turvy into a cold hall, began to roar at the top of their voices. Mrs. Bhaer instantly appeared, and a minute after Silas burst out of his room shouting, "Fire!" in a tone that raised the whole house. A flock of white goblins with scared faces crowded into the hall, and for a minute every one was panic-stricken.

Then Mrs. Bhaer found her wits, bade Nursey see to the burnt boys, and sent Franz and Silas down-stairs for some tubs of wet clothes which she flung on the bed, over the carpet, and up against the curtains, now burning finely, and threatening to kindle the walls.

Most of the boys stood dumbly looking on, but Dan and Emil worked bravely, running to and fro with water from the bath-room, and helping to pull down the dangerous curtains.

The peril was soon over, and ordering the boys all back to bed, and leaving Silas to watch lest the fire broke out again, Mrs. Bhaer and Franz went to see how the poor boys got on. Demi had escaped with one burn and a grand scare, but Tommy had not only most of his hair scorched off his head, but a great burn on his arm, that made him half crazy with the pain. Demi was soon made cosy, and Franz took him away to his own bed, where the kind lad soothed his fright and hummed him to sleep as cosily as a woman. Nursey watched over poor Tommy all night, trying to ease his misery, and Mrs. Bhaer vibrated between him and little Teddy with oil and cotton, paregoric and squills, saying to herself from time to time, as if she found great amusement in the thought, "I always knew Tommy would set the house on fire, and now he has done it!"

When Mr. Bhaer got home next morning he found a nice state of things. Tommy in bed, Teddy wheezing like a little grampus, Mrs. Jo quite used up, and the whole flock of boys so excited that they all talked at once, and almost dragged him by main force to view the ruins. Under his quiet management things soon fell into order, for every one felt that he was equal to a dozen conflagrations, and worked with a will at whatever task he gave them.

There was no school that morning, but by afternoon the damaged room was put to rights, the invalids were better, and there was time to hear and judge the little culprits quietly. Nat and Tommy told their parts in the mischief, and were honestly sorry for the danger they had brought to the dear old house and all in it. But Dan put on his devil-may-care look, and would not own that there was much harm done.

Now, of all things, Mr. Bhaer hated drinking, gambling, and swearing; smoking he had given up that the lads might not be tempted to try it, and it grieved and angered him deeply to find that the boy, with whom he had tried to be most forbearing, should take advantage of his absence to introduce these forbidden vices, and teach his innocent little lads to think it manly and pleasant to indulge in them. He talked long and earnestly to the assembled boys, and ended by saying, with an air of mingled firmness and regret,

"I think Tommy is punished enough, and that scar on his arm will remind him for a long time to let these things alone. Nat's fright will do for him, for he is really sorry, and does try to obey me. But you, Dan, have been many times forgiven, and yet it does no good. I cannot have my boys hurt by your bad example, nor my time wasted in talking to deaf ears, so you can say good-bye to them all, and tell Nursey to put up your things in my little black bag."

"Oh! sir, where is he going?" cried Nat.

"To a pleasant place up in the country, where I sometimes send boys when they don't do well here. Mr. Page is a kind man, and Dan will be happy there if he chooses to do his best."

"Will he ever come back?" asked Demi.

"That will depend on himself; I hope so."

As he spoke, Mr. Bhaer left the room to write his letter to Mr. Page, and the boys crowded round Dan very much as people do about a man who is going on a long and perilous journey to unknown regions.

"I wonder if you'll like it," began Jack.

"Shan't stay if I don't," said Dan coolly.

"Where will you go?" asked Nat.

"I may go to sea, or out west, or take a look at California," answered Dan, with a reckless air that quite took away the breath of the little boys.

"Oh, don't! stay with Mr. Page awhile and then come back here; do, Dan," pleaded Nat, much affected at the whole affair.

"I don't care where I go, or how long I stay, and I'll be hanged if I ever come back here," with which wrathful speech Dan went away to put up his things, every one of which Mr. Bhaer had given him.

That was the only good-bye he gave the boys, for they were all talking the matter over in the barn when he came down, and he told Nat not to call them. The wagon stood at the door, and Mrs. Bhaer came out to speak to Dan, looking so sad that his heart smote him, and he said in a low tone,

"May I say good-bye to Teddy?"

"Yes, dear; go in and kiss him, he will miss his Danny very much."

No one saw the look in Dan's eyes as he stooped over the crib, and saw the little face light up at first sight of him, but he heard Mrs. Bhaer say pleadingly,

"Can't we give the poor lad one more trial, Fritz?" and Mr. Bhaer answer in his steady way,

"My dear, it is not best, so let him go where he can do no harm to others, while they do good to him, and by and by he shall come back, I promise you."
"He's the only boy we ever failed with, and I am so grieved, for I thought there was the making of a fine man in him, spite of his faults."

Dan heard Mrs. Bhaer sigh, and he wanted to ask for one more trial himself, but his pride would not let him, and he came out with the hard look on his face, shook hands without a word, and drove away with Mr. Bhaer, leaving Nat and Mrs. Jo to look after him with tears in their eyes.

A few days afterwards they received a letter from Mr. Page, saying that Dan was doing well, whereat they all rejoiced. But three weeks later came another letter, saying that Dan had run away, and nothing had been heard of him, whereat they all looked sober, and Mr. Bhaer said,

"Perhaps I ought to have given him another chance."

Mrs. Bhaer, however, nodded wisely and answered, "Don't be troubled, Fritz; the boy will come back to us, I'm sure of it."

But time went on and no Dan came.

Lesson 107

1. Read the title to Chapter 7. What would you like to find out?
2. Read chapter 7.
3. Write a one-sentence summary of the chapter.
4. What are you thinking about Nan after finishing the chapter? Do you like her? Why or why not?

Chapter VII. Naughty Nan

"Fritz, I've got a new idea," cried Mrs. Bhaer, as she met her husband one day after school.

"Well, my dear, what is it?" and he waited willingly to hear the new plan, for some of Mrs. Jo's ideas were so droll, it was impossible to help laughing at them, though usually they were quite sensible, and he was glad to carry them out.

"Daisy needs a companion, and the boys would be all the better for another girl among them; you know we believe in bringing up little men and women together, and it is high time we acted up to our belief. They pet and tyrannize over Daisy by turns, and she is getting spoilt. Then they must learn gentle ways, and improve their manners, and having girls about will do it better than any thing else."

"You are right, as usual. Now, who shall we have?" asked Mr. Bhaer, seeing by the look in her eye that Mrs. Jo had some one all ready to propose.

"Little Annie Harding."

"What! Naughty Nan, as the lads call her?" cried Mr. Bhaer, looking very much amused.

"Yes, she is running wild at home since her mother died, and is too bright a child to be spoilt by servants. I have had my eye on her for some time, and when I met her father in town the other day I asked him why he did not send her to school. He said he would gladly if he could find as good a school for girls as ours was for boys. I know he would rejoice to have her come; so suppose we drive over this afternoon and see about it."

"Have not you cares enough now, my Jo, without this little gypsy to torment you?" asked Mr. Bhaer, patting the hand that lay on his arm.

"Oh dear, no," said Mother Bhaer, briskly. "I like it, and never was happier than since I had my wilderness of boys. You see, Fritz, I feel a great sympathy for Nan, because I was such a naughty child myself that I know all about it. She is full of spirits, and only needs to be taught what to do with them to be as nice a little girl as Daisy. Those quick wits of hers would enjoy lessons if they were rightly directed, and what is now a tricksy midget would soon become a busy, happy child. I know how to manage her, for I remember how my blessed mother managed me, and-"

"And if you succeed half as well as she did, you will have done a magnificent work," interrupted Mr. Bhaer, who labored under the delusion that Mrs. B. was the best and most charming woman alive.

"Now, if you make fun of my plan I'll give you bad coffee for a week, and then where are you, sir?" cried Mrs. Jo, tweaking him by the ear just as if he was one of the boys.

"Won't Daisy's hair stand erect with horror at Nan's wild ways?" asked Mr. Bhaer, presently, when Teddy had swarmed up his waistcoat, and Rob up his back, for they always flew at their father the minute school was done.

"At first, perhaps, but it will do Posy good. She is getting prim and Bettyish, and needs stirring up a bit. She always has a good time when Nan comes over to play, and the two will help each other without knowing it. Dear me, half the science of teaching is knowing how much children do for one another, and when to mix them."

"I only hope she won't turn out another firebrand."

"My poor Dan! I never can quite forgive myself for letting him go," sighed Mrs. Bhaer.

At the sound of the name, little Teddy, who had never forgotten his friend, struggled down from his father's arms, and trotted to the door, looked out over the sunny lawn with a wistful face, and then trotted back again, saying, as he always did when disappointed of the longed-for sight,

"My Danny's tummin' soon."

"I really think we ought to have kept him, if only for Teddy's sake, he was so fond of him, and perhaps baby's love would have done for him what we failed to do."

"I've sometimes felt that myself; but after keeping the boys in a ferment, and nearly burning up the whole family, I thought it safer to remove the firebrand, for a time at least," said Mr. Bhaer.

"Dinner's ready, let me ring the bell," and Rob began a solo upon that instrument which made it impossible to hear one's self speak.

"Then I may have Nan, may I?" asked Mrs. Jo.

"A dozen Nans if you want them, my dear," answered Mr. Bhaer, who had room in his fatherly heart for all the naughty neglected children in the world.

When Mrs. Bhaer returned from her drive that afternoon, before she could unpack the load of little boys, without whom she seldom moved, a small girl of ten skipped out at the back of the carry-all and ran into the house, shouting,

"Hi, Daisy! where are you?"

Daisy came, and looked pleased to see her guest, but also a trifle alarmed, when Nan said, still prancing, as if it was impossible to keep still,

"I'm going to stay here always, papa says I may, and my box is coming tomorrow, all my things had to be washed and mended, and your aunt came and carried me off. Isn't it great fun?"

"Why, yes. Did you bring your big doll?" asked Daisy, hoping she had, for on the last visit Nan had ravaged the baby house, and insisted on washing Blanche Matilda's plaster face, which spoilt the poor dear's complexion for ever.

"Yes, she's somewhere round," returned Nan, with most unmaternal carelessness. "I made you a ring coming along, and pulled the hairs out of Dobbin's tail. Don't you want it?" and Nan presented a horse-hair ring in token of friendship, as they had both vowed they would never speak to one another again when they last parted.

Won by the beauty of the offering, Daisy grew more cordial, and proposed retiring to the nursery, but Nan said, "No, I want to see the boys, and the barn," and ran off, swinging her hat by one string till it broke, when she left it to its fate on the grass.

"Hullo! Nan!" cried the boys as she bounced in among them with the announcement,

"I'm going to stay."

"Hooray!" bawled Tommy from the wall on which he was perched, for Nan was a kindred spirit, and he foresaw "larks" in the future.

"I can bat; let me play," said Nan, who could turn her hand to any thing, and did not mind hard knocks.

"We ain't playing now, and our side beat without you."

"I can beat you in running, any way," returned Nan, falling back on her strong point.

"Can she?" asked Nat of Jack.

"She runs very well for a girl," answered Jack, who looked down upon Nan with condescending approval.

"Will you try?" said Nan, longing to display her powers.

"It's too hot," and Tommy languished against the wall as if quite exhausted.

"What's the matter with Stuffy?" asked Nan, whose quick eyes were roving from face to face.

"Ball hurt his hand; he howls at every thing," answered Jack scornfully.

"I don't, I never cry, no matter how I'm hurt; it's babyish," said Nan, loftily.

"Pooh! I could make you cry in two minutes," returned Stuffy, rousing up.

"See if you can."

"Go and pick that bunch of nettles, then," and Stuffy pointed to a sturdy specimen of that prickly plant growing by the wall.

Nan instantly "grasped the nettle," pulled it up, and held it with a defiant gesture, in spite of the almost unbearable sting.

"Good for you," cried the boys, quick to acknowledge courage even in one of the weaker sex.

More nettled than she was, Stuffy determined to get a cry out of her somehow, and he said tauntingly, "You are used to poking your hands into every thing, so that isn't fair. Now go and bump your head real hard against the barn, and see if you don't howl then."

"Don't do it," said Nat, who hated cruelty.

But Nan was off, and running straight at the barn, she gave her head a blow that knocked her flat, and sounded like a battering-ram. Dizzy, but undaunted, she staggered up, saying stoutly, though her face was drawn with pain,

"That hurt, but I don't cry."

"Do it again," said Stuffy angrily; and Nan would have done it, but Nat held her; and Tommy, forgetting the heat, flew at Stuffy like a little game-cock, roaring out,

"Stop it, or I'll throw you over the barn!" and so shook and hustled poor Stuffy that for a minute he did not know whether he was on his head or his heels.

"She told me to," was all he could say, when Tommy let him alone.

"Never mind if she did; it is awfully mean to hurt a little girl," said Demi, reproachfully.

"Ho! I don't mind; I ain't a little girl, I'm older than you and Daisy; so now," cried Nan, ungratefully.

"Don't preach, Deacon, you bully Posy every day of your life," called out the Commodore, who just then hove in sight.
"I don't hurt her; do I, Daisy?" and Demi turned to his sister, who was "pooring" Nan's tingling hands, and recommending water for the purple lump rapidly developing itself on her forehead.

"You are the best boy in the world," promptly answered Daisy; adding, as truth compelled her to do, "You hurt me sometimes, but you don't mean to."

"Put away the bats and things, and mind what you are about, my hearties. No fighting allowed aboard this ship," said Emil, who rather lorded it over the others.

"How do you do, Madge Wildfire?" said Mr. Bhaer, as Nan came in with the rest to supper. "Give the right hand, little daughter, and mind thy manners," he added, as Nan offered him her left.

"The other hurts me."

"The poor little hand! what has it been doing to get those blisters?" he asked, drawing it from behind her back, where she had put it with a look which made him think she had been in mischief.

Before Nan could think of any excuse, Daisy burst out with the whole story, during which Stuffy tried to hide his face in a bowl of bread and milk. When the tale was finished, Mr. Bhaer looked down the long table towards his wife, and said with a laugh in his eyes,

"This rather belongs to your side of the house, so I won't meddle with it, my dear."

Mrs. Jo knew what he meant, but she liked her little black sheep all the better for her pluck, though she only said in her soberest way,

"Do you know why I asked Nan to come here?"

"To plague me," muttered Stuffy, with his mouth full.

"To help make little gentlemen of you, and I think you have shown that some of you need it."

Here Stuffy retired into his bowl again, and did not emerge till Demi made them all laugh by saying, in his slow wondering way,

"How can she, when she's such a tomboy?"
"That's just it, she needs help as much as you, and I expect you set her an example of good manners."

"Is she going to be a little gentleman too?" asked Rob.

"She'd like it; wouldn't you, Nan?" added Tommy.

"No, I shouldn't; I hate boys!" said Nan fiercely, for her hand still smarted, and she began to think that she might have shown her courage in some wiser way.

"I am sorry you hate my boys, because they can be well-mannered, and most agreeable when they choose. Kindness in looks and words and ways is true politeness, and any one can have it if they only try to treat other people as they like to be treated themselves."

Mrs. Bhaer had addressed herself to Nan, but the boys nudged one another, and appeared to take the hint, for that time at least, and passed the butter; said "please," and "thank you," "yes, sir," and "no, ma'am," with unusual elegance and respect. Nan said nothing, but kept herself quiet and refrained from tickling Demi, though strongly tempted to do so, because of the dignified airs he put on. She also appeared to have forgotten her hatred of boys, and played "I spy" with them till dark. Stuffy was observed to offer her frequent sucks on his candy-ball during the game, which evidently sweetened her temper, for the last thing she said on going to bed was,

"When my battledore and shuttle-cock comes, I'll let you all play with 'em."

Her first remark in the morning was "Has my box come?" and when told that it would arrive sometime during the day, she fretted and fumed, and whipped her doll, till Daisy was shocked. She managed to exist, however, till five o'clock, when she disappeared, and was not missed till supper-time, because those at home thought she had gone to the hill with Tommy and Demi.

"I saw her going down the avenue alone as hard as she could pelt," said Mary Ann, coming in with the hasty-pudding, and finding every one asking, "Where is Nan?"

"She has run home, little gypsy!" cried Mrs. Bhaer, looking anxious.

"Perhaps she has gone to the station to look after her luggage," suggested Franz.

"That is impossible, she does not know the way, and if she found it, she could never carry the box a mile," said Mrs. Bhaer, beginning to think that her new idea might be rather a hard one to carry out.

"It would be like her," and Mr. Bhaer caught up his hat to go and find the child, when a shout from Jack, who was at the window, made everyone hurry to the door.

There was Miss Nan, to be sure, tugging along a very large band-box tied up in linen bag. Very hot and dusty and tired did she look, but marched stoutly along, and came puffing up to the steps, where she dropped her load with a sigh of relief, and sat down upon it, observed as she crossed her tired arms,

"I couldn't wait any longer, so I went and got it."

"But you did not know the way," said Tommy, while the rest stood round enjoying the joke.

"Oh, I found it, I never get lost."

"It's a mile, how could you go so far?"

"Well, it was pretty far, but I rested a good deal."

"Wasn't that thing very heavy?"

"It's so round, I couldn't get hold of it good, and I thought my arms would break right off."

"I don't see how the station-master let you have it," said Tommy.

"I didn't say anything to him. He was in the little ticket place, and didn't see me, so I just took it off the platform."

"Run down and tell him it is all right, Franz, or old Dodd will think it is stolen," said Mr. Bhaer, joining in the shout of laughter at Nan's coolness.

"I told you we would send for it if it did not come. Another time you must wait, for you will get into trouble if you run away. Promise me this, or I shall not dare to trust you out of my sight," said Mrs. Bhaer, wiping the dust off Nan's little hot face.

"Well, I won't, only papa tells me not to put off doing things, so I don't."

"That is rather a poser; I think you had better give her some supper now, and a private lecture by and by," said Mr. Bhaer, too much amused to be angry at the young lady's exploit.

The boys thought it "great fun," and Nan entertained them all supper-time with an account of her adventures; for a big dog had barked at her, a man had laughed at her, a woman had given her a doughnut, and her hat had fallen into the brook when she stopped to drink, exhausted with her exertion.

"I fancy you will have your hands full now, my dear; Tommy and Nan are quite enough for one woman," said Mr. Bhaer, half an hour later.

"I know it will take some time to tame the child, but she is such a generous, warm-hearted little thing, I should love her even if she were twice as naughty," answered Mrs. Jo, pointing to the merry group, in the middle of which stood Nan, giving away her things right and left, as lavishly as if the big band-box had no bottom.

It was those good traits that soon made little "Giddygaddy," as they called her, a favorite with every one. Daisy never complained of being dull again, for Nan invented the most delightful plays, and her pranks rivalled Tommy's, to the amusement of the whole school. She buried her big doll and forgot it for a week, and found it well mildewed when she dragged it up. Daisy was in despair, but Nan took it to the painter who as at work about the house, got him to paint it brick red, with staring black eyes, then she dressed it up with feathers, and scarlet flannel, and one of Ned's leaden hatchets; and in the character of an Indian chief, the late Poppydilla tomahawked all the other dolls, and caused the nursery to run red with imaginary gore. She gave away her new shoes to a beggar child, hoping to be allowed to go barefoot, but found it impossible to combine charity and comfort, and was ordered to ask leave before disposing of her clothes. She delighted the boys by making a fire-ship out of a shingle with two large sails wet with turpentine, which she lighted, and then sent the little vessel floating down the brook at dusk. She harnessed the old turkey-cock to a straw wagon, and made him trot round the house at a tremendous pace. She gave her coral necklace for four unhappy kittens, which had been tormented by some heartless lads, and tended them for days as gently as a mother, dressing their wounds with cold cream, feeding them with a doll's spoon, and mourning over them when they died, till she was consoled by one of Demi's best turtles. She made Silas tattoo an anchor on her arm like his, and begged hard to have a blue star on each cheek, but he dared not do it, though she coaxed and scolded till the soft-hearted fellow longed to give in. She rode every animal on the place, from the big horse Andy to the cross pig, from whom she was rescued with difficulty. Whatever the boys dared her to do she instantly attempted, no matter how dangerous it might be, and they were never tired of testing her courage.

Mr. Bhaer suggested that they should see who would study best, and Nan found as much pleasure in using her quick wits and fine memory as her active feet and merry tongue, while the lads had to do their best to keep their places, for Nan showed them that girls could do most things as well as boys, and some things better. There were no rewards in school, but Mr. Bhaer's "Well done!" and Mrs. Bhaer's good report on the conscience book, taught them to love duty for its own sake, and try to do it faithfully, sure sooner or later the recompense would come. Little Nan was quick to feel the new atmosphere, to enjoy it, to show that it was what she needed; for this little garden was full of sweet flowers, half hidden by the weeds; and when kind hands gently began to cultivate it, all sorts of green shoots sprung up, promising to blossom beautifully in the warmth of love and care, the best climate for young hearts and souls all the world over.

Lesson 108

1. Read the title of Chapter 8. What do you predict might happen in this chapter?
2. Read chapter 8.
3. Tell someone what happened in the chapter.
4. Read aloud the verse to an audience. What does it mean?
5. What surprised you in this chapter?

Chapter VIII. Pranks and Plays

As there is no particular plan to this story, except to describe a few scenes in the life at Plumfield for the amusement of certain little persons, we will gently ramble along in this chapter and tell some of the pastimes of Mrs. Jo's boys. I beg leave to assure my honored readers that most of the incidents are taken from real life, and that the oddest are the truest; for no person, no matter how vivid an imagination he may have, can invent anything half so droll as the freaks and fancies that originate in the lively brains of little people.

Daisy and Demi were full of these whims, and lived in a world of their own, peopled with lovely or grotesque creatures, to whom they gave the queerest names, and with whom they played the queerest games. One of these nursery inventions was an invisible sprite called "The Naughty Kitty-mouse," whom the children had believed in, feared, and served for a long time. They seldom spoke of it to any one else, kept their rites as private as possible; and, as they never tried to describe it even to themselves, this being had a vague mysterious charm very agreeable to Demi, who delighted in elves and goblins. A most whimsical and tyrannical imp was the Naughty Kitty-mouse, and Daisy found a fearful pleasure in its service, blindly obeying its most absurd demands, which were usually proclaimed from the lips of Demi, whose powers of invention were great. Rob and Teddy sometimes joined in these ceremonies, and considered them excellent fun, although they did not understand half that went on.

One day after school Demi whispered to his sister, with an ominous wag of the head,

"The Kitty-mouse wants us this afternoon."

"What for?" asked Daisy, anxiously.

"A sackerryfice," answered Demi, solemnly. "There must be a fire behind the big rock at two o'clock, and we must all bring the things we like best, and burn them!" he added, with an awful emphasis on the last words.

"Oh, dear! I love the new paper dollies Aunt Amy painted for me best of any thing; must I burn them up?" cried Daisy, who never thought of denying the unseen tyrant any thing it demanded.

"Every one. I shall burn my boat, my best scrapbook, and all my soldiers," said Demi firmly.

"Well, I will; but it's too bad of Kitty-mouse to want our very nicest things," sighed Daisy.

"A sackerryfice means to give up what you are fond of, so we must," explained Demi, to whom the new idea had been suggested by hearing Uncle Fritz describe the customs of the Greeks to the big boys who were reading about them in school.

"Is Rob coming too," asked Daisy.

"Yes, and he is going to bring his toy village; it is all made of wood, you know, and will burn nicely. We'll have a grand bonfire, and see them blaze up, won't we?"

This brilliant prospect consoled Daisy, and she ate her dinner with a row of paper dolls before her, as a sort of farewell banquet.

At the appointed hour the sacrificial train set forth, each child bearing the treasures demanded by the insatiable Kitty-mouse. Teddy insisted on going also, and seeing that all the others had toys, he tucked a squeaking lamb under one arm, and old Annabella under the other, little dreaming what anguish the latter idol was to give him.

"Where are you going, my chickens?" asked Mrs. Jo, as the flock passed her door.

"To play by the big rock; can't we?"

"Yes, only don't do near the pond, and take good care of baby."

"I always do," said Daisy, leading forth her charge with a capable air.

"Now, you must all sit round, and not move till I tell you. This flat stone is an altar, and I am going to make a fire on it."

Demi then proceeded to kindle up a small blaze, as he had seen the boys do at picnics. When the flame burned well, he ordered the company to march round it three times and then stand in a circle.

"I shall begin, and as fast as my things are burnt, you must bring yours."

With that he solemnly laid on a little paper book full of pictures, pasted in by himself; this was followed by a dilapidated boat, and then one by one the unhappy leaden soldiers marched to death. Not one faltered or hung back, from the splendid red and yellow captain to the small drummer who had lost his legs; all vanished in the flames and mingled in one common pool of melted lead.

"Now, Daisy!" called the high priest of Kitty-mouse, when his rich offerings had been consumed, to the great satisfaction of the children.

"My dear dollies, how can I let them go?" moaned Daisy, hugging the entire dozen with a face full of maternal woe.

"You must," commanded Demi; and with a farewell kiss to each, Daisy laid her blooming dolls upon the coals.

"Let me keep one, the dear blue thing, she is so sweet," besought the poor little mamma, clutching her last in despair.

"More! more!" growled an awful voice, and Demi cried, "that's the Kitty-mouse! she must have every one, quick, or she will scratch us."

In went the precious blue belle, flounces, rosy hat, and all, and nothing but a few black flakes remained of that bright band.

"Stand the houses and trees round, and let them catch themselves; it will be like a real fire then," said Demi, who liked variety even in his "sackerryfices."

Charmed by this suggestion, the children arranged the doomed village, laid a line of coals along the main street, and then sat down to watch the conflagration. It was somewhat slow to kindle owing to the paint, but at last one ambitious little cottage blazed up, fired a tree of the palm species, which fell on to the roof of a large family mansion, and in a few minutes the whole town was burning merrily. The wooden population stood and stared at the destruction like blockheads, as they were, till they also caught and blazed away without a cry. It took some time to reduce the town to ashes, and the lookers-on enjoyed the spectacle immensely, cheering as each house fell, dancing like wild Indians when the steeple flamed aloft, and actually casting one wretched little churn-shaped lady, who had escaped to the suburbs, into the very heart of the fire.

The superb success of this last offering excited Teddy to such a degree, that he first threw his lamb into the conflagration, and before it had time even to roast, he planted poor Annabella on the funeral pyre. Of course she did not like it, and expressed her anguish and resentment in a way that terrified her infant destroyer. Being covered with kid, she did not blaze, but did what was worse, she squirmed. First one leg curled up, then the other, in a very awful and lifelike manner; next she flung her arms over her head as if in great agony; her head itself turned on her shoulders, her glass eyes fell out, and with one final writhe of her whole body, she sank down a blackened mass on the ruins of the town. This unexpected demonstration startled every one and frightened Teddy half out of his little wits. He looked, then screamed and fled toward the house, roaring "Marmar" at the top of his voice.

Mrs. Bhaer heard the outcry and ran to the rescue, but Teddy could only cling to her and pour out in his broken way something about "poor Bella hurted," "a dreat fire," and "all the dollies dorn." Fearing some dire mishap, his mother caught him up and hurried to the scene of action, where she found the blind worshippers of Kitty-mouse mourning over the charred remains of the lost darling.

"What have you been at? Tell me all about it," said Mrs. Jo, composing herself to listen patiently, for the culprits looked so penitent, she forgave them beforehand.

With some reluctance Demi explained their play, and Aunt Jo laughed till the tears ran down her cheeks, the children were so solemn, and the play was so absurd.

"I thought you were too sensible to play such a silly game as this. If I had any Kitty-mouse I'd have a good one who liked you to play in safe pleasant ways, and not destroy and frighten. Just see what a ruin you have made; all Daisy's pretty dolls, Demi's soldiers, and Rob's new village beside poor Teddy's pet lamb, and dear old Annabella. I shall have to write up in the nursery the verse that used to come in the boxes of toys,

> The children of Holland take pleasure in making,
> What the children of Boston take pleasure in breaking.

"Only I shall put Plumfield instead of Boston."

"We never will again, truly, truly!" cried the repentant little sinners, much abashed at this reproof.

"Demi told us to," said Rob.

"Well, I heard Uncle tell about the Greece people, who had altars and things, and so I wanted to be like them, only I hadn't any live creatures to sackerryfice, so we burnt up our toys."

"Dear me, that is something like the bean story," said Aunt Jo, laughing again.

"Tell about it," suggested Daisy, to change the subject.

"Once there was a poor woman who had three or four little children, and she used to lock them up in her room when she went out to work, to keep them safe. On day when she was going away she said, 'Now, my dears, don't let baby fall out of window, don't play with the matches, and don't put beans up your noses.' Now the children had never dreamed of doing that last thing, but she put it into their heads, and the minute she was gone, they ran and stuffed their naughty little noses full of beans, just to see how it felt, and she found them all crying when she came home."

"Did it hurt?" asked Rob, with such intense interest that his mother hastily added a warning sequel, lest a new edition of the bean story should appear in her own family.

"Very much, as I know, for when my mother told me this story, I was so silly that I went and tried it myself. I had no beans, so I took some little pebbles, and poked several into my nose. I did not like it at all, and wanted to take them out again very soon, but one would not come, and I was so ashamed to tell what a goose I been that I went for hours with the stone hurting me very much. At last the pain got so bad I had to tell, and when my mother could not get it out the doctor came. Then I was put in a chair and held tight, Rob, while he used his ugly little pincers till the stone hopped out. Dear me! how my wretched little nose did ache, and how people laughed at me!" and Mrs. Jo shook her head in a dismal way, as if the memory of her sufferings was too much for her.

Rob looked deeply impressed and I am glad to say took the warning to heart. Demi proposed that they should bury poor Annabella, and in the interest of the funeral Teddy forgot his fright. Daisy was soon consoled by another batch of dolls from Aunt Amy, and the Naughty Kitty-mouse seemed to be appeased by the last offerings, for she tormented them no more.

"Brops" was the name of a new and absorbing play, invented by Bangs. As this interesting animal is not to be found in any Zoological Garden, unless Du Chaillu has recently brought one from the wilds of Africa, I will mention a few of its peculiar habits and traits, for the benefit of inquiring minds. The Brop is a winged quadruped, with a human face of a youthful and merry aspect. When it walks the earth it grunts, when it soars it gives a shrill hoot, occasionally it goes erect, and talks good English. Its body is usually covered with a substance much resembling a shawl, sometimes red, sometimes blue, often plaid, and, strange to say, they frequently change skins with one another. On their heads they have a horn very like a stiff brown paper lamp-lighter. Wings of the same substance flap upon their shoulders when they fly; this is never very far from the ground, as they usually fall with violence if they attempt any lofty flights. They browse over the earth, but can sit up and eat like the squirrel. Their favorite nourishment is the seed-cake; apples also are freely taken, and sometimes raw carrots are nibbled when food is scarce. They live in dens, where they have a sort of nest, much like a clothes-basket, in which the little Brops play till their wings are grown. These singular animals quarrel at times, and it is on these occasions that they burst into human speech, call each other names, cry, scold, and sometimes tear off horns and skin, declaring fiercely that they "won't play." The few privileged persons who have studied them are inclined to think them a remarkable mixture of the monkey, the sphinx, the roc, and the queer creatures seen by the famous Peter Wilkins.

This game was a great favorite, and the younger children beguiled many a rainy afternoon flapping or creeping about the nursery, acting like little bedlamites and being as merry as little grigs. To be sure, it was rather hard upon clothes, particularly trouser-knees, and jacket-elbows; but Mrs. Bhaer only said, as she patched and darned,

"We do things just as foolish, and not half so harmless. If I could get as much happiness out of it as the little dears do, I'd be a Brop myself."

Nat's favorite amusements were working in his garden, and sitting in the willow-tree with his violin, for that green nest was a fairy world to him, and there he loved to perch, making music like a happy bird. The lads called him "Old Chirper," because he was always humming, whistling, or fiddling, and they often stopped a minute in their work or play to listen to the soft tones of the violin, which seemed to lead a little orchestra of summer sounds. The birds appeared to regard him as one of themselves, and fearlessly sat on the fence or lit among the boughs to watch him with their quick bright eyes. The robins in the apple-tree near by evidently considered him a friend, for the father bird hunted insects close beside him, and the little mother brooded as confidingly over her blue eggs as if the boy was only a new sort of blackbird who cheered her patient watch with his song. The brown brook babbled and sparkled below him, the bees haunted the clover fields on either side, friendly faces peeped at him as they passed, the old house stretched its wide wings hospitably toward him, and with a blessed sense of rest and love and happiness, Nat dreamed for hours in this nook, unconscious what healthful miracles were being wrought upon him.

One listener he had who never tired, and to whom he was more than a mere schoolmate. Poor Billy's chief delight was to lie beside the brook, watching leaves and bits of foam dance by, listening dreamily to the music in the willow-tree. He seemed to think Nat a sort of angel who sat aloft and sang, for a few baby memories still lingered in his mind and seemed to grow brighter at these times. Seeing the interest he took in Nat, Mr. Bhaer begged him to help them lift the cloud from the feeble brain by this gentle spell. Glad to do any thing to show his gratitude, Nat always smiled on Billy when he followed him about, and let him listen undisturbed to the music which seemed to speak a language he could understand. "Help one another," was a favorite Plumfield motto, and Nat learned how much sweetness is added to life by trying to live up to it.

Jack Ford's peculiar pastime was buying and selling; and he bid fair to follow in the footsteps of his uncle, a country merchant, who sold a little of every thing and made money fast. Jack had seen the sugar sanded, the molasses watered, the butter mixed with lard, and things of that kind, and labored under the delusion that it was all a proper part of the business. His stock in trade was of a different sort, but he made as much as he could out of every worm he sold, and always got the best of the bargain when he traded with the boys for string, knives, fish-hooks, or whatever the article might be. The boys who all had nicknames, called him "Skinflint," but Jack did not care as long as the old tobacco-pouch in which he kept his money grew heavier and heavier.

He established a sort of auction-room, and now and then sold off all the odds and ends he had collected, or helped the lads exchange things with one another. He got bats, balls, hockey-sticks, etc., cheap, from one set of mates, furbished them up, and let them for a few cents a time to another set, often extending his business beyond the gates of Plumfield in spite of the rules. Mr. Bhaer put a stop to some of his speculations, and tried to give him a better idea of business talent than mere sharpness in overreaching his neighbors. Now and then Jack made a bad bargain, and felt worse about it than about any failure in lessons or conduct, and took his revenge on the next innocent customer who came along. His account-book was a curiosity; and his quickness at figures quite remarkable. Mr. Bhaer praised him for this, and tried to make his sense of honesty and honor as quick; and, by and by, when Jack found that he could not get on without these virtues, he owned that his teacher was right.

Cricket and football the boys had of course; but, after the stirring accounts of these games in the immortal "Tom Brown at Rugby," no feeble female pen may venture to do more than respectfully allude to them.

Emil spent his holidays on the river or the pond, and drilled the elder lads for a race with certain town boys, who now and then invaded their territory. The race duly came off, but as it ended in a general shipwreck, it was not mentioned in public; and the Commodore had serious thoughts of retiring to a desert island, so disgusted was he with his kind for a time. No desert island being convenient, he was forced to remain among his friends, and found consolation in building a boat-house.

The little girls indulged in the usual plays of their age, improving upon them somewhat as their lively fancies suggested. The chief and most absorbing play was called "Mrs. Shakespeare Smith;" the name was provided by Aunt Jo, but the trials of the poor lady were quite original. Daisy was Mrs. S. S., and Nan by turns her daughter or a neighbor, Mrs. Giddygaddy.

No pen can describe the adventures of these ladies, for in one short afternoon their family was the scene of births, marriages, deaths, floods, earthquakes, tea-parties, and balloon ascensions. Millions of miles did these energetic women travel, dressed in hats and habits never seen before by mortal eye, perched on the bed, driving the posts like mettlesome steeds, and bouncing up and down till their heads spun. Fits and fires were the pet afflictions, with a general massacre now and then by way of change. Nan was never tired of inventing fresh combinations, and Daisy followed her leader with blind admiration. Poor Teddy was a frequent victim, and was often rescued from real danger, for the excited ladies were apt to forget that he was not of the same stuff their longsuffering dolls. Once he was shut into the closet for a dungeon, and forgotten by the girls, who ran off to some out-of-door game. Another time he was half drowned in the bath-tub, playing be a "cunning little whale." And, worst of all, he was cut down just in time after being hung up for a robber.

But the institution most patronized by all was the Club. It had no other name, and it needed none, being the only one in the neighborhood. The elder lads got it up, and the younger were occasionally admitted if they behaved well. Tommy and Demi were honorary members, but were always obliged to retire unpleasantly early, owing to circumstances over which they had no control. The proceedings of this club were somewhat peculiar, for it met at all sorts of places and hours, had all manner of queer ceremonies and amusements, and now and then was broken up tempestuously, only to be re-established, however, on a firmer basis.

Rainy evenings the members met in the schoolroom, and passed the time in games: chess, morris, backgammon, fencing matches, recitations, debates, or dramatic performances of a darkly tragical nature. In summer the barn was the rendezvous, and what went on there no uninitiated mortal knows. On sultry evenings the Club adjourned to the brook for aquatic exercises, and the members sat about in airy attire, frog-like and cool. On such occasions the speeches were unusually eloquent, quite flowing, as one might say; and if any orator's remarks displeased the audience, cold water was thrown upon him till his ardor was effectually quenched. Franz was president, and maintained order admirably, considering the unruly nature of the members. Mr. Bhaer never interfered with their affairs, and was rewarded for this wise forbearance by being invited now and then to behold the mysteries unveiled, which he appeared to enjoy much.

When Nan came she wished to join the Club, and caused great excitement and division among the gentlemen by presenting endless petitions, both written and spoken, disturbing their solemnities by insulting them through the key-hole, performing vigorous solos on the door, and writing up derisive remarks on walls and fences, for she belonged to the "Irrepressibles." Finding these appeals in vain, the girls, by the advice of Mrs. Jo, got up an institution of their own, which they called the Cosy Club. To this they magnanimously invited the gentlemen whose youth excluded them from the other one, and entertained these favored beings so well with little suppers, new games devised by Nan, and other pleasing festivities, that, one by one, the elder boys confessed a desire to partake of these more elegant enjoyments, and, after much consultation, finally decided to propose an interchange of civilities.

The members of the Cosy Club were invited to adorn the rival establishment on certain evenings, and to the surprise of the gentlemen their presence was not found to be a restraint upon the conversation or amusement of the regular frequenters; which could not be said of all Clubs, I fancy. The ladies responded handsomely and hospitably to these overtures of peace, and both institutions flourished long and happily.

Lesson 109

1. Read the title to chapter 9. What are you thinking?
2. Read chapter 9.

3. Read aloud the verse to an audience. What does it mean?

4. What are you thinking now?

5. Do you think the "punishment" for the boys, excluding them from the girls' company and even Mrs. Jo's, was a fair one? Why or why not?

Chapter IX. Daisy's Ball

"Mrs. Shakespeare Smith would like to have Mr. John Brooke, Mr. Thomas Bangs, and Mr. Nathaniel Blake to come to her ball at three o'clock today.

"P.S. Nat must bring his fiddle, so we can dance, and all the boys must be good, or they cannot have any of the nice things we have cooked."

This elegant invitation would, I fear, have been declined, but for the hint given in the last line of the postscript.

"They have been cooking lots of goodies, I smelt 'em. Let's go," said Tommy.

"We needn't stay after the feast, you know," added Demi.

"I never went to a ball. What do you have to do?" asked Nat.

"Oh, we just play be men, and sit round stiff and stupid like grown-up folks, and dance to please the girls. Then we eat up everything, and come away as soon as we can."

"I think I could do that," said Nat, after considering Tommy's description for a minute.

"I'll write and say we'll come;" and Demi despatched the following gentlemanly reply,

"We will all come. Please have lots to eat. J. B. Esquire."

Great was the anxiety of the ladies about their first ball, because if every thing went well they intended to give a dinner-party to the chosen few.

"Aunt Jo likes to have the boys play with us, if they are not rough; so we must make them like our balls, then they will do them good," said Daisy, with her maternal air, as she set the table and surveyed the store of refreshments with an anxious eye.

"Demi and Nat will be good, but Tommy will do something bad, I know he will," replied Nan, shaking her head over the little cake-basket which she was arranging.

"Then I shall send him right home," said Daisy, with decision.

"People don't do so at parties, it isn't proper."

"I shall never ask him any more."

"That would do. He'd be sorry not to come to the dinner-ball, wouldn't he?"

"I guess he would! we'll have the splendidest things ever seen, won't we? Real soup with a ladle and a tureem [she meant tureen] and a little bird for turkey, and gravy, and all kinds of nice vegytubbles." Daisy never could say vegetables properly, and had given up trying.

"It is 'most three, and we ought to dress," said Nan, who had arranged a fine costume for the occasion, and was anxious to wear it.

"I am the mother, so I shan't dress up much," said Daisy, putting on a night-cap ornamented with a red bow, one of her aunt's long skirts, and a shawl; a pair of spectacles and large pocket handkerchief completed her toilette, making a plump, rosy little matron of her.

Nan had a wreath of artificial flowers, a pair of old pink slippers, a yellow scarf, a green muslin skirt, and a fan made of feathers from the duster; also, as a last touch of elegance, a smelling-bottle without any smell in it.

"I am the daughter, so I rig up a good deal, and I must sing and dance, and talk more than you do. The mothers only get the tea and be proper, you know."

A sudden very loud knock caused Miss Smith to fly into a chair, and fan herself violently, while her mamma sat bolt upright on the sofa, and tried to look quite calm and "proper." Little Bess, who was on a visit, acted the part of maid, and opened the door, saying with a smile, "Wart in, gemplemun; it's all weady."

In honor of the occasion, the boys wore high paper collars, tall black hats, and gloves of every color and material, for they were an afterthought, and not a boy among them had a perfect pair.

"Good day, mum," said Demi, in a deep voice, which was so hard to keep up that his remarks had to be extremely brief.

Every one shook hands and then sat down, looking so funny, yet so sober, that the gentlemen forgot their manners, and rolled in their chairs with laughter.

"Oh, don't!" cried Mrs. Smith, much distressed.

"You can't ever come again if you act so," added Miss Smith, rapping Mr. Bangs with her bottle because he laughed loudest.

"I can't help it, you look so like fury," gasped Mr. Bangs, with most uncourteous candor.

"So do you, but I shouldn't be so rude as to say so. He shan't come to the dinner-ball, shall he, Daisy?" cried Nan, indignantly.

"I think we had better dance now. Did you bring your fiddle, sir?" asked Mrs. Smith, trying to preserve her polite composure.

"It is outside the door," and Nat went to get it.

"Better have tea first," proposed the unabashed Tommy, winking openly at Demi to remind him that the sooner the refreshments were secured, the sooner they could escape.

"No, we never have supper first; and if you don't dance well you won't have any supper at all, not one bit, sir," said Mrs. Smith, so sternly that her wild guests saw she was not to be trifled with, and grew overwhelmingly civil all at once.

"I will take Mr. Bangs and teach him the polka, for he does not know it fit to be seen," added the hostess, with a reproachful look that sobered Tommy at once.

Nat struck up, and the ball opened with two couples, who went conscientiously through a somewhat varied dance. The ladies did well, because they liked it, but the gentlemen exerted themselves from more selfish motives, for each felt that he must earn his supper, and labored manfully toward that end. When every one was out of breath they were allowed to rest; and, indeed, poor Mrs. Smith needed it, for her long dress had tripped her up many times. The little maid passed round molasses and water in such small cups that one guest actually emptied nine. I refrain from mentioning his name, because this mild beverage affected him so much that he put cup and all into his mouth at the ninth round, and choked himself publicly.

"You must ask Nan to play and sing now," said Daisy to her brother, who sat looking very much like an owl, as he gravely regarded the festive scene between his high collars.

"Give us a song, mum," said the obedient guest, secretly wondering where the piano was.

Miss Smith sailed up to an old secretary which stood in the room, threw back the lid of the writing-desk, and sitting down before it, accompanied herself with a vigor which made the old desk rattle as she sang that new and lovely song, beginning-

> "Gaily the troubadour
> Touched his guitar,
> As he was hastening
> Home from the war."

The gentlemen applauded so enthusiastically that she gave them "Bounding Billows," "Little Bo-Peep," and other gems of song, till they were obliged to hint that they had had enough. Grateful for the praises bestowed upon her daughter, Mrs. Smith graciously announced,

"Now we will have tea. Sit down carefully, and don't grab."

It was beautiful to see the air of pride with which the good lady did the honors of her table, and the calmness with which she bore the little mishaps that occurred. The best pie flew wildly on the floor when she tried to cut it with a very dull knife; the bread and butter vanished with a rapidity calculated to dismay a housekeeper's soul; and, worst of all, the custards were so soft that they had to be drunk up, instead of being eaten elegantly with the new tin spoons.

I grieve to state that Miss Smith squabbled with the maid for the best jumble, which caused Bess to toss the whole dish into the air, and burst out crying amid a rain of falling cakes. She was comforted by a seat at the table, and the sugar-bowl to empty; but during this flurry a large plate of patties was mysteriously lost, and could not be found. They were the chief ornament of the feast, and Mrs. Smith was indignant at the loss, for she had made them herself, and they were beautiful to behold. I put it to any lady if it was not hard to have one dozen delicious patties (made of flour, salt, and water, with a large raisin in the middle of each, and much sugar over the whole) swept away at one fell swoop?

"You hid them, Tommy; I know you did!" cried the outraged hostess, threatening her suspected guest with the milk-pot.

"I didn't!"

"You did!"

"It isn't proper to contradict," said Nan, who was hastily eating up the jelly during the fray.

"Give them back, Demi," said Tommy.

"That's a fib, you've got them in your own pocket," bawled Demi, roused by the false accusation.

"Let's take 'em away from him. It's too bad to make Daisy cry," suggested Nat, who found his first ball more exciting than he expected.

Daisy was already weeping, Bess like a devoted servant mingled her tears with those of her mistress, and Nan denounced the entire race of boys as "plaguey things." Meanwhile the battle raged among the gentlemen, for, when the two defenders of innocence fell upon the foe, that hardened youth intrenched himself behind a table and pelted them with the stolen tarts, which were very effective missiles, being nearly as hard as bullets. While his ammunition held out the besieged prospered, but the moment the last patty flew over the parapet, the villain was seized, dragged howling from the room, and cast upon the hall floor in an ignominious heap. The conquerors then returned flushed with victory, and while Demi consoled poor Mrs. Smith, Nat and Nan collected the scattered tarts, replaced each raisin in its proper bed, and rearranged the dish so that it really looked almost as well as ever. But their glory had departed, for the sugar was gone, and no one cared to eat them after the insult offered to them.

"I guess we had better go," said Demi, suddenly, as Aunt Jo's voice was heard on the stairs.

"P'r'aps we had," and Nat hastily dropped a stray jumble that he had just picked up.

But Mrs. Jo was among them before the retreat was accomplished, and into her sympathetic ear the young ladies poured the story of their woes.

"No more balls for these boys till they have atoned for this bad behavior by doing something kind to you," said Mrs. Jo, shaking her head at the three culprits.

"We were only in fun," began Demi.

"I don't like fun that makes other people unhappy. I am disappointed in you, Demi, for I hoped you would never learn to tease Daisy. Such a kind little sister as she is to you."

"Boys always tease their sisters; Tom says so," muttered Demi.

"I don't intend that my boys shall, and I must send Daisy home if you cannot play happily together," said Aunt Jo, soberly.

At this awful threat, Demi sidled up to his sister, and Daisy hastily dried her tears, for to be separated was the worst misfortune that could happen to the twins.

"Nat was bad, too, and Tommy was baddest of all," observed Nan, fearing that two of the sinners would not get their fair share of punishment.

"I am sorry," said Nat, much ashamed.

"I ain't!" bawled Tommy through the keyhole, where he was listening with all his might.

Mrs. Jo wanted very much to laugh, but kept her countenance, and said impressively, as she pointed to the door,

"You can go, boys, but remember, you are not to speak to or play with the little girls till I give you leave. You don't deserve the pleasure, so I forbid it."

The ill-mannered young gentlemen hastily retired, to be received outside with derision and scorn by the unrepentant Bangs, who would not associate with them for at least fifteen minutes. Daisy was soon consoled for the failure of her ball, but lamented the edict that parted her from her brother, and mourned over his short-comings in her tender little heart. Nan rather enjoyed the trouble, and went about turning up her pug nose at the three, especially Tommy, who pretended not to care, and loudly proclaimed his satisfaction at being rid of those "stupid girls." But in his secret soul he soon repented of the rash act that caused this banishment from the society he loved, and every hour of separation taught him the value of the "stupid girls."

The others gave in very soon, and longed to be friends, for now there was no Daisy to pet and cook for them; no Nan to amuse and doctor them; and, worst of all, no Mrs. Jo to make home life pleasant and life easy for them. To their great affliction, Mrs. Jo seemed to consider herself one of the offended girls, for she hardly spoke to the outcasts, looked as if she did not see them when she passed, and was always too busy now to attend to their requests. This sudden and entire exile from favor cast a gloom over their souls, for when Mother Bhaer deserted them, their sun had set at noon-day, as it were, and they had no refuge left.

This unnatural state of things actually lasted for three days, then they could bear it no longer, and fearing that the eclipse might become total, went to Mr. Bhaer for help and counsel.

It is my private opinion that he had received instructions how to behave if the case should be laid before him. But no one suspected it, and he gave the afflicted boys some advice, which they gratefully accepted and carried out in the following manner:

Secluding themselves in the garret, they devoted several play-hours to the manufacture of some mysterious machine, which took so much paste that Asia grumbled, and the little girls wondered mightily. Nan nearly got her inquisitive nose pinched in the door, trying to see what was going on, and Daisy sat about, openly lamenting that they could not all play nicely together, and not have any dreadful secrets. Wednesday afternoon was fine, and after a good deal of consultation about wind and weather, Nat and Tommy went off, bearing an immense flat parcel hidden under many newspapers. Nan nearly died with suppressed curiosity, Daisy nearly cried with vexation, and both quite trembled with interest when Demi marched into Mrs. Bhaer's room, hat in hand, and said, in the politest tone possible to a mortal boy of his years,

"Please, Aunt Jo, would you and the girls come out to a surprise party we have made for you? Do it's a very nice one."

"Thank you, we will come with pleasure; only, I must take Teddy with me," replied Mrs. Bhaer, with a smile that cheered Demi like sunshine after rain.

"We'd like to have him. The little wagon is all ready for the girls; you won't mind walking just up to Pennyroyal Hill, will you Aunty?"

"I should like it exceedingly; but are you quite sure I shall not be in the way?"

"Oh, no, indeed! we want you very much; and the party will be spoilt if you don't come," cried Demi, with great earnestness.

"Thank you kindly, sir;" and Aunt Jo made him a grand curtsey, for she liked frolics as well as any of them.

"Now, young ladies, we must not keep them waiting; on with the hats, and let us be off at once. I'm all impatience to know what the surprise is."

As Mrs. Bhaer spoke every one bustled about, and in five minutes the three little girls and Teddy were packed into the "clothes-basket," as they called the wicker wagon which Toby drew. Demi walked at the head of the procession, and Mrs. Jo brought up the rear, escorted by Kit. It was a most imposing party, I assure you, for Toby had a red feather-duster in his head, two remarkable flags waved over the carriage, Kit had a blue bow on his neck, which nearly drove him wild, Demi wore a nosegay of dandelions in his buttonhole, and Mrs. Jo carried the queer Japanese umbrella in honor of the occasion.

The girls had little flutters of excitement all the way; and Teddy was so charmed with the drive that he kept dropping his hat overboard, and when it was taken from him he prepared to tumble out himself, evidently feeling that it behooved him to do something for the amusement of the party.

When they came to the hill "nothing was to be seen but the grass blowing in the wind," as the fairy books say, and the children looked disappointed. But Demi said, in his most impressive manner,

"Now, you all get out and stand still, and the surprise party with come in;" with which remark he retired behind a rock, over which heads had been bobbing at intervals for the last half-hour.

A short pause of intense suspense, and then Nat, Demi, and Tommy marched forth, each bearing a new kite, which they presented to the three young ladies. Shrieks of delight arose, but were silenced by the boys, who said, with faces brimful of merriment, "That isn't all the surprise;" and, running behind the rock, again emerged bearing a fourth kite of superb size, on which was printed, in bright yellow letters, "For Mother Bhaer."

"We thought you'd like one, too, because you were angry with us, and took the girls' part," cried all three, shaking with laughter, for this part of the affair evidently was a surprise to Mrs. Jo.

She clapped her hands, and joined in the laugh, looking thoroughly tickled at the joke.

"Now, boys, that is regularly splendid! Who did think of it?" she asked, receiving the monster kite with as much pleasure as the little girls did theirs.

"Uncle Fritz proposed it when we planned to make the others; he said you'd like it, so we made a bouncer," answered Demi, beaming with satisfaction at the success of the plot.

"Uncle Fritz knows what I like. Yes, these are magnificent kites, and we were wishing we had some the other day when you were flying yours, weren't we, girls?"

"That's why we made them for you," cried Tommy, standing on his head as the most appropriate way of expressing his emotions.

"Let us fly them," said energetic Nan.

"I don't know how," began Daisy.

"We'll show you, we want to!" cried all the boys in a burst of devotion, as Demi took Daisy's, Tommy Nan's, and Nat, with difficulty, persuaded Bess to let go her little blue one.

"Aunty, if you will wait a minute, we'll pitch yours for you," said Demi, feeling that Mrs. Bhaer's favor must not be lost again by any neglect of theirs.

"Bless your buttons, dear, I know all about it; and here is a boy who will toss up for me," added Mrs. Jo, as the professor peeped over the rock with a face full of fun.

He came out at once, tossed up the big kite, and Mrs. Jo ran off with it in fine style, while the children stood and enjoyed the spectacle. One by one all the kites went up, and floated far overhead like gay birds, balancing themselves on the fresh breeze that blew steadily over the hill. Such a merry time as they had! running and shouting, sending up the kites or pulling them down, watching their antics in the air, and feeling them tug at the string like live creatures trying to escape. Nan was quite wild with the fun, Daisy thought the new play nearly as interesting as dolls, and little Bess was so fond of her "boo tite," that she would only let it go on very short flights, preferring to hold it in her lap and look at the remarkable pictures painted on it by Tommy's dashing brush. Mrs. Jo enjoyed hers immensely, and it acted as if it knew who owned it, for it came tumbling down head first when least expected, caught on trees, nearly pitched into the river, and finally darted away to such a height that it looked a mere speck among the clouds.

By and by every one got tired, and fastening the kite-strings to trees and fences, all sat down to rest, except Mr. Bhaer, who went off to look at the cows, with Teddy on his shoulder.

"Did you ever have such a good time as this before?" asked Nat, as they lay about on the grass, nibbling pennyroyal like a flock of sheep.

"Not since I last flew a kite, years ago, when I was a girl," answered Mrs. Jo.

"I'd like to have known you when you were a girl, you must have been so jolly," said Nat.
"I was a naughty little girl, I am sorry to say."

"I like naughty little girls," observed Tommy, looking at Nan, who made a frightful grimace at him in return for the compliment.

"Why don't I remember you then, Aunty? Was I too young?" asked Demi.

"Rather, dear."

"I suppose my memory hadn't come then. Grandpa says that different parts of the mind unfold as we grow up, and the memory part of my mind hadn't unfolded when you were little, so I can't remember how you looked," explained Demi.

"Now, little Socrates, you had better keep that question for grandpa, it is beyond me," said Aunt Jo, putting on the extinguisher.

"Well, I will, he knows about those things, and you don't," returned Demi, feeling that on the whole kites were better adapted to the comprehension of the present company.

"Tell about the last time you flew a kite," said Nat, for Mrs. Jo had laughed as she spoke of it, and he thought it might be interesting.

"Oh, it was only rather funny, for I was a great girl of fifteen, and was ashamed to be seen at such a play. So Uncle Teddy and I privately made our kites, and stole away to fly them. We had a capital time, and were resting as we are now, when suddenly we heard voices, and saw a party of young ladies and gentlemen coming back from a picnic. Teddy did not mind, though he was rather a large boy to be playing with a kite, but I was in a great flurry, for I knew I should be sadly laughed at, and never hear the last of it, because my wild ways amused the neighbors as much as Nan's do us.

"'What shall I do?' I whispered to Teddy, as the voices drew nearer and nearer.

"'I'll show you,' he said, and whipping out his knife he cut the strings. Away flew the kites, and when the people came up we were picking flowers as properly as you please. They never suspected us, and we had a grand laugh over our narrow escape."

"Were the kites lost, Aunty?" asked Daisy.

"Quite lost, but I did not care, for I made up my mind that it would be best to wait till I was an old lady before I played with kites again; and you see I have waited," said Mrs. Jo, beginning to pull in the big kite, for it was getting late.

"Must we go now?"

"I must, or you won't have any supper; and that sort of surprise party would not suit you, I think, my chickens."

"Hasn't our party been a nice one?" asked Tommy, complacently.

"Splendid!" answered every one.

"Do you know why? It is because your guests have behaved themselves, and tried to make everything go well. You understand what I mean, don't you?"

"Yes'm," was all the boys said, but they stole a shamefaced look at one another, as they meekly shouldered their kites and walked home, thinking of another party where the guests had not behaved themselves, and things had gone badly on account of it.

Lesson 110

1. What is the title of Chapter 10? What are you thinking?
2. Read the first half of chapter 10.
3. Why is Dan is called a Spartan? If you have studied ancient history, you will know who the Spartans were. They lived in the ancient Greek city of Sparta and spent their whole lives training for battle.
4. In the beginning of the chapter the weather is balmy. Find out what that means if you don't know.
5. How are you feeling about Dan now? Why?
6. What do you think will happen in the rest of the chapter?

Chapter X. Home Again

July had come, and haying begun; the little gardens were doing finely and the long summer days were full of pleasant hours. The house stood open from morning till night, and the lads lived out of doors, except at school time. The lessons were short, and there were many holidays, for the Bhaers believed in cultivating healthy bodies by much exercise, and our short summers are best used in out-of-door work. Such a rosy, sunburnt, hearty set as the boys became; such appetites as they had; such sturdy arms and legs, as outgrew jackets and trousers; such laughing and racing all over the place; such antics in house and barn; such adventures in the tramps over hill and dale; and such satisfaction in the hearts of the worthy Bhaers, as they saw their flock prospering in mind and body, I cannot begin to describe. Only one thing was needed to make them quite happy, and it came when they least expected it.

One balmy night when the little lads were in bed, the elder ones bathing down at the brook, and Mrs. Bhaer undressing Teddy in her parlor, he suddenly cried out, "Oh, my Danny!" and pointed to the window, where the moon shone brightly.

"No, lovey, he is not there, it was the pretty moon," said his mother.

"No, no, Danny at a window; Teddy saw him," persisted baby, much excited.

"It might have been," and Mrs. Bhaer hurried to the window, hoping it would prove true. But the face was gone, and nowhere appeared any signs of a mortal boy; she called his name, ran to the front door with Teddy in his little shirt, and made him call too, thinking the baby voice might have more effect than her own. No one answered, nothing appeared , and they went back much disappointed. Teddy would not be satisfied with the moon, and after he was in his crib kept popping up his head to ask if Danny was not "tummin' soon."

By and by he fell asleep, the lads trooped up to bed, the house grew still, and nothing but the chirp of the crickets broke the soft silence of the summer night. Mrs. Bhaer sat sewing, for the big basket was always piled with socks, full of portentous holes, and thinking of the lost boy. She had decided that baby had been mistaken, and did not even disturb Mr. Bhaer by telling him of the child's fancy, for the poor man got little time to himself till the boys were abed, and he was busy writing letters. It was past ten when she rose to shut up the house. As she paused a minute to enjoy the lovely scene from the steps, something white caught her eye on one of the hay-cocks scattered over the lawn. The children had been playing there all the afternoon, and, fancying that Nan had left her hat as usual, Mrs. Bhaer went out to get it. But as she approached, she saw that it was neither hat nor handkerchief, but a shirt sleeve with a brown hand sticking out of it. She hurried round the hay-cock, and there lay Dan, fast asleep.

Ragged, dirty, thin, and worn-out he looked; one foot was bare, the other tied up in the old gingham jacket which he had taken from his own back to use as a clumsy bandage for some hurt. He seemed to have hidden himself behind the hay-cock, but in his sleep had thrown out the arm that had betrayed him. He sighed and muttered as if his dreams disturbed him, and once when he moved, he groaned as if in pain, but still slept on quite spent with weariness.

"He must not lie here," said Mrs. Bhaer, and stooping over him she gently called his name. He opened his eyes and looked at her, as if she was a part of his dream, for he smiled and said drowsily, "Mother Bhaer, I've come home."

The look, the words, touched her very much, and she put her hand under his head to lift him up, saying in her cordial way,

"I thought you would, and I'm so glad to see you, Dan." He seemed to wake thoroughly then, and started up looking about him as if he suddenly remembered where he was, and doubted even that kind welcome. His face changed, and he said in his old rough way,

"I was going off in the morning. I only stopped to peek in, as I went by."

"But why not come in, Dan? Didn't you hear us call you? Teddy saw, and cried for you."

"Didn't suppose you'd let me in," he said, fumbling with a little bundle which he had taken up as if going immediately.

"Try and see," was all Mrs. Bhaer answered, holding out her hand and pointing to the door, where the light shone hospitably.

With a long breath, as if a load was off his mind, Dan took up a stout stick, and began to limp towards the house, but stopped suddenly, to say inquiringly,

"Mr. Bhaer won't like it. I ran away from Page."

"He knows it, and was sorry, but it will make no difference. Are you lame?" asked Mrs. Jo, as he limped on again.

"Getting over a wall a stone fell on my foot and smashed it. I don't mind," and he did his best to hide the pain each step cost him.

Mrs. Bhaer helped him into her own room, and, once there, he dropped into a chair, and laid his head back, white and faint with weariness and suffering.

"My poor Dan! drink this, and then eat a little; you are at home now, and Mother Bhaer will take good care of you."

He only looked up at her with eyes full of gratitude, as he drank the wine she held to his lips, and then began slowly to eat the food she brought him. Each mouthful seemed to put heart into him, and presently he began to talk as if anxious to have her know all about him.

"Where have you been, Dan?" she asked, beginning to get out some bandages.

"I ran off more'n a month ago. Page was good enough, but too strict. I didn't like it, so I cut away down the river with a man who was going in his boat. That's why they couldn't tell where I'd gone. When I left the man, I worked for a couple of weeks with a farmer, but I thrashed his boy, and then the old man thrashed me, and I ran off again and walked here."

"All the way?"

"Yes, the man didn't pay me, and I wouldn't ask for it. Took it out in beating the boy," and Dan laughed, yet looked ashamed, as he glanced at his ragged clothes and dirty hands.

"How did you live? It was a long, long tramp for a boy like you."

"Oh, I got on well enough, till I hurt my foot. Folks gave me things to eat, and I slept in barns and tramped by day. I got lost trying to make a short cut, or I'd have been here sooner."

"But if you did not mean to come in and stay with us, what were you going to do?"

"I thought I'd like to see Teddy again, and you; and then I was going back to my old work in the city, only I was so tired I went to sleep on the hay. I'd have been gone in the morning, if you hadn't found me."

"Are you sorry I did?" and Mrs. Jo looked at him with a half merry, half reproachful look, as she knelt down to look at his wounded foot.

The color came up into Dan's face, and he kept his eyes fixed on his plate, as he said very low, "No, ma'am, I'm glad, I wanted to stay, but I was afraid you-"

He did not finish, for Mrs. Bhaer interrupted him by an exclamation of pity, as she saw his foot, for it was seriously hurt.

"When did you do it?"

"Three days ago."

"And you have walked on it in this state?"

"I had a stick, and I washed it at every brook I came to, and one woman gave me a rag to put on it."

"Mr. Bhaer must see and dress it at once," and Mrs. Jo hastened into the next room, leaving the door ajar behind her, so that Dan heard all that passed.

"Fritz, the boy has come back."

"Who? Dan?"

"Yes, Teddy saw him at the window, and he called to him, but he went away and hid behind the hay-cocks on the lawn. I found him there just now fast asleep, and half dead with weariness and pain. He ran away from Page a month ago, and has been making his way to us ever since. He pretends that he did not mean to let us see him, but go on to the city, and his old work, after a look at us. It is evident, however, that the hope of being taken in has led him here through every thing, and there he is waiting to know if you will forgive and take him back."

"Did he say so?"

"His eyes did, and when I waked him, he said, like a lost child, 'Mother Bhaer, I've come home.' I hadn't the heart to scold him, and just took him in like a poor little black sheep come back to the fold. I may keep him, Fritz?"

"Of course you may! This proves to me that we have a hold on the boy's heart, and I would no more send him away now than I would my own Rob."

Dan heard a soft little sound, as if Mrs. Jo thanked her husband without words, and, in the instant's silence that followed, two great tears that had slowly gathered in the boy's eyes brimmed over and rolled down his dusty cheeks. No one saw them, for he brushed them hastily away; but in that little pause I think Dan's old distrust for these good people vanished for ever, the soft spot in his heart was touched, and he felt an impetuous desire to prove himself worthy of the love and pity that was so patient and forgiving. He said nothing, he only wished the wish with all his might, resolved to try in his blind boyish way, and sealed his resolution with the tears which neither pain, fatigue, nor loneliness could wring from him.

"Come and see his foot. I am afraid it is badly hurt, for he has kept on three days through heat and dust, with nothing but water and an old jacket to bind it up with. I tell you, Fritz, that boy is a brave lad, and will make a fine man yet."

"I hope so, for your sake, enthusiastic woman, your faith deserves success. Now, I will go and see your little Spartan. Where is he?"

"In my room; but, dear, you'll be very kind to him, no matter how gruff he seems. I am sure that is the way to conquer him. He won't bear sternness nor much restraint, but a soft word and infinite patience will lead him as it used to lead me."

"As if you ever like this little rascal!" cried Mr. Bhaer, laughing, yet half angry at the idea.

"I was in spirit, though I showed it in a different way. I seem to know by instinct how he feels, to understand what will win and touch him, and to sympathize with his temptations and faults. I am glad I do, for it will help me to help him; and if I can make a good man of this wild boy, it will be the best work of my life."

"God bless the work, and help the worker!"

Mr. Bhaer spoke now as earnestly as she had done, and both came in together to find Dan's head down upon his arm, as if he was quite overcome by sleep. But he looked up quickly, and tried to rise as Mr. Bhaer said pleasantly,

"So you like Plumfield better than Page's farm. Well, let us see if we can get on more comfortably this time than we did before."

"Thanky, sir," said Dan, trying not to be gruff, and finding it easier than he expected.

"Now, the foot! Ach! this is not well. We must have Dr. Firth to-morrow. Warm water, Jo, and old linen."

Mr. Bhaer bathed and bound up the wounded foot, while Mrs. Jo prepared the only empty bed in the house. It was in the little guest-chamber leading from the parlor, and often used when the lads were poorly, for it saved Mrs. Jo from running up and down, and the invalids could see what was going on. When it was ready, Mr. Bhaer took the boy in his arms, and carried him in, helped him undress, laid him on the little white bed, and left him with another hand-shake, and a fatherly "Good-night, my son."

Dan dropped asleep at once, and slept heavily for several hours; then his foot began to throb and ache, and he awoke to toss about uneasily, trying not to groan lest any one should hear him, for he was a brave lad, and did bear pain like "a little Spartan," as Mr. Bhaer called him.

Mrs. Jo had a way of flitting about the house at night, to shut the windows if the wind grew chilly, to draw mosquito curtains over Teddy, or look after Tommy, who occasionally walked in his sleep. The least noise waked her, and as she often heard imaginary robbers, cats, and conflagrations, the doors stood open all about, so her quick ear caught the sound of Dan's little moans, and she was up in a minute. He was just giving his hot pillow a despairing thump when a light came glimmering through the hall, and Mrs. Jo crept in, looking like a droll ghost, with her hair in a great knob on the top of her head, and a long gray dressing-gown trailing behind her.

"Are you in pain, Dan?"

"It's pretty bad; but I didn't mean to wake you."

"I'm a sort of owl, always flying about at night. Yes, your foot is like fire; the bandages must be wet again," and away flapped the maternal owl for more cooling stuff, and a great mug of ice water.

"Oh, that's so nice!" sighed Dan, the wet bandages went on again, and a long draught of water cooled his thirsty throat.

"There, now, sleep your best, and don't be frightened if you see me again, for I'll slip down by and by, and give you another sprinkle."

As she spoke, Mrs. Jo stooped to turn the pillow and smooth the bed-clothes, when, to her great surprise, Dan put his arm around her neck, drew her face down to his, and kissed her, with a broken "Thank you, ma'am," which said more than the most eloquent speech could have done; for the hasty kiss, the muttered words, meant, "I'm sorry, I will try." She understood it, accepted the unspoken confession, and did not spoil it by any token of surprise. She only remembered that he had no mother, kissed the brown cheek half hidden on the pillow, as if ashamed of the little touch of tenderness, and left him, saying, what he long remembered, "You are my boy now, and if you choose you can make me proud and glad to say so."

Once again, just at dawn, she stole down to find him so fast asleep that he did not wake, and showed no sign of consciousness as she wet his foot, except that the lines of pain smoothed themselves away, and left his face quite peaceful.

The day was Sunday, and the house so still that he never waked till near noon, and, looking round him, saw an eager little face peering in at the door. He held out his arms, and Teddy tore across the room to cast himself bodily upon the bed, shouting, "My Danny's tum!" as he hugged and wriggled with delight. Mrs. Bhaer appeared next, bringing breakfast, and never seeming to see how shamefaced Dan looked at the memory of the little scene last night. Teddy insisted on giving him his "betfus," and fed him like a baby, which, as he was not very hungry, Dan enjoyed very much.

Then came the doctor, and the poor Spartan had a bad time of it, for some of the little bones in his foot were injured, and putting them to rights was such a painful job, that Dan's lips were white, and great drops stood on his forehead, though he never cried out, and only held Mrs. Jo's hand so tight that it was red long afterwards.

"You must keep this boy quiet, for a week at least, and not let him put his foot to the ground. By that time, I shall know whether he may hop a little with a crutch, or stick to his bed for a while longer," said Dr. Firth, putting up the shining instruments that Dan did not like to see.

"It will get well sometime, won't it?" he asked, looking alarmed at the word "crutches."

"I hope so;" and with that the doctor departed, leaving Dan much depressed; for the loss of a foot is a dreadful calamity to an active boy.

"Don't be troubled, I am a famous nurse, and we will have you tramping about as well as ever in a month," said Mrs. Jo, taking a hopeful view of the case.

But the fear of being lame haunted Dan, and even Teddy's caresses did not cheer him; so Mrs. Jo proposed that one or two of the boys should come in and pay him a little visit, and asked whom he would like to see.

"Nat and Demi; I'd like my hat too, there's something in it I guess they'd like to see. I suppose you threw away my bundle of plunder?" said Dan, looking rather anxious as he put the question.

"No, I kept it, for I thought they must be treasures of some kind, you took such care of them;" and Mrs. Jo brought him his old straw hat stuck full of butterflies and beetles, and a handkerchief containing a collection of odd things picked up on his way: birds' eggs, carefully done up in moss, curious shells and stones, bits of fungus, and several little crabs, in a state of great indignation at their imprisonment.

"Could I have something to put these fellers in? Mr. Hyde and I found 'em, and they are first-rate ones, so I'd like to keep and watch 'em; can I?" asked Dan, forgetting his foot, and laughing to see the crabs go sidling and backing over the bed.

"Of course you can; Polly's old cage will be just the thing. Don't let them nip Teddy's toes while I get it;" and away went Mrs. Jo, leaving Dan overjoyed to find that his treasures were not considered rubbish, and thrown away.

Nat, Demi, and the cage arrived together, and the crabs were settled in their new house, to the great delight of the boys, who, in the excitement of the performance, forgot any awkwardness they might otherwise have felt in greeting the runaway. To these admiring listeners Dan related his adventures much more fully than he had done to the Bhaers. Then he displayed his "plunder," and described each article so well, that Mrs. Jo, who had retired to the next room to leave them free, was surprised and interested, as well as amused, at their boyish chatter.

Lesson 111

1. Finish chapter 10.
2. Summarize the chapter for someone.

Vocabulary

1. Practice your vocabulary by going to Lesson 15 and Lesson 31 to review.

Chapter X. continued

"How much the lad knows of these things! how absorbed he is in them! and what a mercy it is just now, for he cares so little for books, it would be hard to amuse him while he is laid up; but the boys can supply him with beetles and stones to any extent, and I am glad to find out this taste of his; it is a good one, and may perhaps prove the making of him. If he should turn out a great naturalist, and Nat a musician, I should have cause to be proud of this year's work;" and Mrs. Jo sat smiling over her book as she built castles in the air, just as she used to do when a girl, only then they were for herself, and now they were for other people, which is the reason perhaps that some of them came to pass in reality for charity is an excellent foundation to build anything upon.

Nat was most interested in the adventures, but Demi enjoyed the beetles and butterflies immensely, drinking in the history of their changeful little lives as if it were a new and lovely sort of fairy tale for, even in his plain way, Dan told it well, and found great satisfaction in the thought that here at least the small philosopher could learn of him. So interested were they in the account of catching a musk rat, whose skin was among the treasures, that Mr. Bhaer had to come himself to tell Nat and Demi it was time for the walk. Dan looked so wistfully after them as they ran off that Father Bhaer proposed carrying him to the sofa in the parlor for a little change of air and scene.

When he was established, and the house quiet, Mrs. Jo, who sat near by showing Teddy pictures, said, in an interested tone, as she nodded towards the treasures still in Dan's hands,

"Where did you learn so much about these things?"

"I always liked 'em, but didn't know much till Mr. Hyde told me."

"Oh, he was a man who lived round in the woods studying these things I don't know what you call him and wrote about frogs, and fishes, and so on. He stayed at Page's, and used to want me to go and help him, and it was great fun, 'cause he told me ever so much, and was uncommon jolly and wise. Hope I'll see him again sometime."

"I hope you will," said Mrs. Jo, for Dan's face had brightened up, and he was so interested in the matter that he forgot his usual taciturnity.

"Why, he could make birds come to him, and rabbits and squirrels didn't mind him any more than if he was a tree. Did you ever tickle a lizard with a straw?" asked Dan, eagerly.

"No, but I should like to try it."

"Well, I've done it, and it's so funny to see 'em turn over and stretch out, they like it so much. Mr. Hyde used to do it; and he'd make snakes listen to him while he whistled, and he knew just when certain flowers would blow, and bees wouldn't sting him, and he'd tell the wonderfullest things about fish and flies, and the Indians and the rocks."

"I think you were so fond of going with Mr. Hyde, you rather neglected Mr. Page," said Mrs. Jo, slyly.

"Yes, I did; I hated to have to weed and hoe when I might be tramping round with Mr. Hyde. Page thought such things silly, and called Mr. Hyde crazy because he'd lay hours watching a trout or a bird."

"Suppose you say lie instead of lay, it is better grammar," said Mrs. Jo, very gently; and then added, "Yes, Page is a thorough farmer, and would not understand that a naturalist's work was just as interesting, and perhaps just as important as his own. Now, Dan, if you really love these things, as I think you do, and I am glad to see it, you shall have time to study them and books to help you; but I want you to do something besides, and to do it faithfully, else you will be sorry by and by, and find that you have got to begin again."

"Yes, ma'am," said Dan, meekly, and looked a little scared by the serious tone of the last remarks, for he hated books, yet had evidently made up his mind to study anything she proposed.

"Do you see that cabinet with twelve drawers in it?" was the next very unexpected question.

Dan did see two tall old-fashioned ones standing on either side of the piano; he knew them well, and had often seen nice bits of string, nails, brown paper, and such useful matters come out of the various drawers. He nodded and smiled. Mrs. Jo went on,

"Well, don't you think those drawers would be good places to put your eggs, and stones, and shells, and lichens?"

"Oh, splendid, but you wouldn't like my things 'clutterin' round,' as Mr. Page used to say, would you?" cried Dan, sitting up to survey the old piece of furniture with sparkling eyes.

"I like litter of that sort; and if I didn't, I should give you the drawers, because I have a regard for children's little treasures, and I think they should be treated respectfully. Now, I am going to make a bargain with you, Dan, and I hope you will keep it honorably. Here are twelve good-sized drawers, one for each month of the year, and they shall be yours as fast as you earn them, by doing the little duties that belong to you. I believe in rewards of a certain kind, especially for young folks; they help us along, and though we may begin by being good for the sake of the reward, if it is rightly used, we shall soon learn to love goodness for itself."

"Do you have 'em?" asked Dan, looking as if this was new talk for him.

"Yes, indeed! I haven't learnt to get on without them yet. My rewards are not drawers, or presents, or holidays, but they are things which I like as much as you do the others. The good behavior and success of my boys is one of the rewards I love best, and I work for it as I want you to work for your cabinet. Do what you dislike, and do it well, and you get two rewards, one, the prize you see and hold; the other, the satisfaction of a duty cheerfully performed. Do you understand that?"

"Yes, ma'am."

"We all need these little helps; so you shall try to do your lessons and your work, play kindly with all the boys, and use your holidays well; and if you bring me a good report, or if I see and know it without words for I'm quick to spy out the good little efforts of my boys you shall have a compartment in the drawer for your treasures. See, some are already divided into four parts, and I will have the others made in the same way, a place for each week; and when the drawer is filled with curious and pretty things, I shall be as proud of it as you are; prouder, I think for in the pebbles, mosses, and gay butterflies, I shall see good resolutions carried out, conquered faults, and a promise well kept. Shall we do this, Dan?"

The boys answered with one of the looks which said much, for it showed that he felt and understood her wish and words, although he did not know how to express his interest and gratitude for such care and kindness. She understood the look, and seeing by the color that flushed up to his forehead that he was touched, as she wished him to be, she said no more about that side of the new plan, but pulled out the upper drawer, dusted it, and set it on two chairs before the sofa, saying briskly,

"Now, let us begin at once by putting those nice beetles in a safe place. These compartments will hold a good deal, you see. I'd pin the butterflies and bugs round the sides; they will be quite safe there, and leave room for the heavy things below. I'll give you some cotton wool, and clean paper and pins, and you can get ready for the week's work."

"But I can't go out to find any new things," said Dan, looking piteously at his foot.

"That's true; never mind, we'll let these treasures do for this week, and I dare say the boys will bring you loads of things if you ask them."

"They don't know the right sort; besides, if I lay, no, lie here all the time, I can't work and study, and earn my drawers."

"There are plenty of lessons you can learn lying there, and several little jobs of work you can do for me."

"Can I?" and Dan looked both surprised and pleased.

"You can learn to be patient and cheerful in spite of pain and no play. You can amuse Teddy for me, wind cotton, read to me when I sew, and do many things without hurting your foot, which will make the days pass quickly, and not be wasted ones."

Here Demi ran in with a great butterfly in one hand, and a very ugly little toad in the other.

"See, Dan, I found them, and ran back to give them to you; aren't they beautiful ones?" panted Demi, all out of breath.

Dan laughed at the toad, and said he had no place to put him, but the butterfly was a beauty, and if Mrs. Jo would give him a big pin, he would stick it right up in the drawer.

"I don't like to see the poor thing struggle on a pin; if it must be killed, let us put it out of pain at once with a drop of camphor," said Mrs. Jo, getting out the bottle.

"I know how to do it Mr. Hyde always killed 'em that way but I didn't have any camphor, so I use a pin," and Dan gently poured a drop on the insect's head, when the pale green wings fluttered an instant, and then grew still.

This dainty little execution was hardly over when Teddy shouted from the bedroom, "Oh, the little trabs are out, and the big one's eaten 'em all up." Demi and his aunt ran to the rescue, and found Teddy dancing excitedly in a chair, while two little crabs were scuttling about the floor, having got through the wires of the cage. A third was clinging to the top of the cage, evidently in terror of his life, for below appeared a sad yet funny sight. The big crab had wedged himself into the little recess where Polly's cup used to stand, and there he sat eating one of his relations in the coolest way. All the claws of the poor victim were pulled off, and he was turned upside down, his upper shell held in one claw close under the mouth of the big crab like a dish, while he leisurely ate out of it with the other claw, pausing now and then to turn his queer bulging eyes from side to side, and to put out a slender tongue and lick them in a way that made the children scream with laughter. Mrs. Jo carried the cage in for Dan to see the sight, while Demi caught and confined the wanderers under an inverted wash-bowl.

"I'll have to let these fellers go, for I can't keep 'em in the house," said Dan, with evident regret.

"I'll take care of them for you, if you will tell me how, and they can live in my turtle-tank just as well as not," said Demi, who found them more interesting even that his beloved slow turtles. So Dan gave him directions about the wants and habits of the crabs, and Demi bore them away to introduce them to their new home and neighbors. "What a good boy he is!" said Dan, carefully settling the first butterfly, and remembering that Demi had given up his walk to bring it to him.

"He ought to be, for a great deal has been done to make him so."

"He's had folks to tell him things, and to help him; I haven't," said Dan, with a sigh, thinking of his neglected childhood, a thing he seldom did, and feeling as if he had not had fair play somehow.

"I know it, dear, and for that reason I don't expect as much from you as from Demi, though he is younger; you shall have all the help that we can give you now, and I hope to teach you how to help yourself in the best way. Have you forgotten what Father Bhaer told you when you were here before, about wanting to be good, and asking God to help you?"

"No, ma'am," very low.

"Do you try that way still?"

"No, ma'am," lower still.

"Will you do it every night to please me?"

"Yes, ma'am," very soberly.

"I shall depend on it, and I think I shall know if you are faithful to your promise, for these things always show to people who believe in them, though not a word is said. Now here is a pleasant story about a boy who hurt his foot worse than you did yours; read it, and see how bravely he bore his troubles."

She put that charming little book, "The Crofton Boys," into his hands, and left him for an hour, passing in and out from time to time that he might not feel lonely. Dan did not love to read, but soon got so interested that he was surprised when the boys came home. Daisy brought him a nosegay of wild flowers, and Nan insisted on helping bring him his supper, as he lay on the sofa with the door open into the dining-room, so that he could see the lads at table, and they could nod socially to him over their bread and butter.

Mr. Bhaer carried him away to his bed early, and Teddy came in his night-gown to say good-night, for he went to his little nest with the birds.

"I want to say my prayers to Danny; may I?" he asked; and when his mother said, "Yes," the little fellow knelt down by Dan's bed, and folding his chubby hands, said softly,

"Pease Dod bess everybody, and hep me to be dood."

Then he went away smiling with sleepy sweetness over his mother's shoulder.

But after the evening talk was done, the evening song sung, and the house grew still with beautiful Sunday silence, Dan lay in his pleasant room wide awake, thinking new thoughts, feeling new hopes and desires stirring in his boyish heart, for two good angels had entered in: love and gratitude began the work which time and effort were to finish; and with an earnest wish to keep his first promise, Dan folded his hands together in the Darkness, and softly whispered Teddy's little prayer,

"Please God bless every one, and help me to be good."

Lesson 112

1. What is the title of Chapter 11?
2. What do you already know about Uncle Teddy? What more would you like to find out?
3. Read the beginning of chapter 11.

Chapter XI. Uncle Teddy

For a week Dan only moved from bed to sofa; a long week and a hard one, for the hurt foot was very painful at times, the quiet days were very wearisome to the active lad, longing to be out enjoying the summer weather, and especially difficult was it to be patient. But Dan did his best, and every one helped him in their various ways; so the time passed, and he was rewarded at last by hearing the doctor say, on Saturday morning, "This foot is doing better than I expected. Give the lad the crutch this afternoon, and let him stump about the house a little."

"Hooray!" shouted Nat, and raced away to tell the other boys the good news.

Everybody was very glad, and after dinner the whole flock assembled to behold Dan crutch himself up and down the hall a few times before he settled in the porch to hold a sort of levee. He was much pleased at the interest and good-will shown him, and brightened up more and more every minute; for the boys came to pay their respects, the little girls fussed about him with stools and cushions, and Teddy watched over him as if he was a frail creature unable to do anything for himself. They were still sitting and standing about the steps, when a carriage stopped at the gate, a hat was waved from it, and with a shout of "Uncle Teddy! Uncle Teddy!" Rob scampered down the avenue as fast as his short legs would carry him. All the boys but Dan ran after him to see who should be first to open the gate, and in a moment the carriage drove up with boys swarming all over it, while Uncle Teddy sat laughing in the midst, with his little daughter on his knee.

"Stop the triumphal car and let Jupiter descend," he said, and jumping out ran up the steps to meet Mrs. Bhaer, who stood smiling and clapping her hands like a girl.

"How goes it, Teddy?"

"All right, Jo."

Then they shook hands, and Mr. Laurie put Bess into her aunt's arms, saying, as the child hugged her tight, "Goldilocks wanted to see you so much that I ran away with her, for I was quite pining for a sight of you myself. We want to play with your boys for an hour or so, and to see how 'the old woman who lived in a shoe, and had so many children she did not know what to do,' is getting on."

"I'm so glad! Play away, and don't get into mischief," answered Mrs. Jo, as the lads crowded round the pretty child, admiring her long golden hair, dainty dress, and lofty ways, for the little "Princess," as they called her, allowed no one to kiss her, but sat smiling down upon them, and graciously patting their heads with her little, white hands. They all adored her, especially Rob, who considered her a sort of doll, and dared not touch her lest she should break, but worshipped her at a respectful distance, made happy by an occasional mark of favor from her little highness. As she immediately demanded to see Daisy's kitchen, she was borne off by Mrs. Jo, with a train of small boys following. The others, all but Nat and Demi, ran away to the menagerie and gardens to have all in order; for Mr. Laurie always took a general survey, and looked disappointed if things were not flourishing.

Standing on the steps, he turned to Dan, saying like an old acquaintance, though he had only seen him once or twice before,

"How is the foot?"

"Better, sir."

"Rather tired of the house, aren't you?"

"Guess I am!" and Dan's eyes roved away to the green hills and woods where he longed to be.

"Suppose we take a little turn before the others come back? That big, easy carriage will be quite safe and comfortable, and a breath of fresh air will do you good. Get a cushion and a shawl, Demi, and let's carry Dan off."

The boys thought it a capital joke, and Dan looked delighted, but asked, with an unexpected burst of virtue,

"Will Mrs. Bhaer like it?"

"Oh, yes; we settled all that a minute ago."

"You didn't say any thing about it, so I don't see how you could," said Demi, inquisitively.

"We have a way of sending messages to one another, without any words. It is a great improvement on the telegraph."

"I know it's eyes; I saw you lift your eyebrows, and nod toward the carriage, and Mrs. Bhaer laughed and nodded back again," cried Nat, who was quite at his ease with kind Mr. Laurie by this time.

"Right. Now them, come on," and in a minute Dan found himself settled in the carriage, his foot on a cushion on the seat opposite, nicely covered with a shawl, which fell down from the upper regions in a most mysterious manner, just when they wanted it. Demi climbed up to the box beside Peter, the black coachman. Nat sat next Dan in the place of honor, while Uncle Teddy would sit opposite, to take care of the foot, he said, but really that he might study the faces before him both so happy, yet so different, for Dan's was square, and brown, and strong, while Nat's was long, and fair, and rather weak, but very amiable with its mild eyes and good forehead.

"By the way, I've got a book somewhere here that you may like to see," said the oldest boy of the party, diving under the seat and producing a book which make Dan exclaim,

"Oh! by George, isn't that a stunner?" as he turned the leaves, and saw fine plates of butterflies, and birds, and every sort of interesting insect, colored like life. He was so charmed that he forgot his thanks, but Mr. Laurie did not mind, and was quite satisfied to see the boy's eager delight, and to hear this exclamations over certain old friends as he came to them. Nat leaned on his shoulder to look, and Demi turned his back to the horses, and let his feet dangle inside the carriage, so that he might join in the conversation.

When they got among the beetles, Mr. Laurie took a curious little object out of his vest-pocket, and laying it in the palm of his hand, said,

"There's a beetle that is thousands of years old;" and then, while the lads examined the queer stone-bug, that looked so old and gray, he told them how it came out of the wrappings of a mummy, after lying for ages in a famous tomb. Finding them interested, he went on to tell about the Egyptians, and the strange and splendid ruins they have left behind them the Nile, and how he sailed up the mighty river, with the handsome dark men to work his boat; how he shot alligators, saw wonderful beasts and birds; and afterwards crossed the desert on a camel, who pitched him about like a ship in a storm.

"Uncle Teddy tells stories 'most as well as Grandpa," said Demi, approvingly, when the tale was done, and the boys' eyes asked for more.

"Thank you," said Mr. Laurie, quite soberly, for he considered Demi's praise worth having, for children are good critics in such cases, and to suit them is an accomplishment that any one may be proud of.

"Here's another trifle or two that I tucked into my pocket as I was turning over my traps to see if I had any thing that would amuse Dan," and Uncle Teddy produced a fine arrow-head and a string of wampum.

"Oh! tell about the Indians," cried Demi, who was fond of playing wigwam.

"Dan knows lots about them," added Nat.

"More than I do, I dare say. Tell us something," and Mr. Laurie looked as interested as the other two.

"Mr. Hyde told me; he's been among 'em, and can talk their talk, and likes 'em," began Dan, flattered by their attention, but rather embarrassed by having a grown-up listener.

"What is wampum for?" asked curious Demi, from his perch.

The others asked questions likewise, and, before he knew it, Dan was reeling off all Mr. Hyde had told him, as they sailed down the river a few weeks before. Mr. Laurie listened well, but found the boy more interesting than the Indians, for Mrs. Jo had told him about Dan, and he rather took a fancy to the wild lad, who ran away as he himself had often longed to do, and who was slowly getting tamed by pain and patience.

"I've been thinking that it would be a good plan for you fellows to have a museum of your own; a place in which to collect all the curious and interesting things that you find, and make, and have given you. Mrs. Jo is too kind to complain, but it is rather hard for her to have the house littered up with all sorts of rattletraps, half-a-pint of dor-bugs in one of her best vases, for instance, a couple of dead bats nailed up in the back entry, wasps nests tumbling down on people's heads, and stones lying round everywhere, enough to pave the avenue. There are not many women who would stand that sort of thing, are there, now?"

As Mr. Laurie spoke with a merry look in his eyes, the boys laughed and nudged one another, for it was evident that some one told tales out of school, else how could he know of the existence of these inconvenient treasures.

"Where can we put them, then?" said Demi, crossing his legs and leaning down to argue the question.

"In the old carriage-house."

"But it leaks, and there isn't any window, nor any place to put things, and it's all dust and cobwebs," began Nat.

"Wait till Gibbs and I have touched it up a bit, and then see how you like it. He is to come over on Monday to get it ready; then next Saturday I shall come out, and we will fix it up, and make the beginning, at least, of a fine little museum. Every one can bring his things, and have a place for them; and Dan is to be the head man, because he knows most about such matters, and it will be quiet, pleasant work for him now that he can't knock about much."

"Won't that be jolly?" cried Nat, while Dan smiled all over his face and had not a word to say, but hugged his book, and looked at Mr. Laurie as if he thought him one of the greatest public benefactors that ever blessed the world.

"Shall I go round again, sir?" asked Peter, as they came to the gate, after two slow turns about the half-mile triangle.

"No, we must be prudent, else we can't come again. I must go over the premises, take a look at the carriage-house, and have a little talk with Mrs. Jo before I go;" and, having deposited Dan on his sofa to rest and enjoy his book, Uncle Teddy went off to have a frolic with the lads who were raging about the place in search of him. Leaving the little girls to mess up-stairs, Mrs. Bhaer sat down by Dan, and listened to his eager account of the drive till the flock returned, dusty, warm, and much excited about the new museum, which every one considered the most brilliant idea of the age.

"I always wanted to endow some sort of an institution, and I am going to begin with this," said Mr. Laurie, sitting down on a stool at Mrs. Jo's feet.

"You have endowed one already. What do you call this?" and Mrs. Jo pointed to the happy-faced lads, who had camped upon the floor about him.

"I call it a very promising Bhaer-garden, and I'm proud to be a member of it. Did you know I was the head boy in this school?" he asked, turning to Dan, and changing the subject skilfully, for he hated to be thanked for the generous things he did.

"I thought Franz was!" answered Dan, wondering what the man meant.

"Oh, dear no! I'm the first boy Mrs. Jo ever had to take care of, and I was such a bad one that she isn't done with me yet, though she has been working at me for years and years."

"How old she must be!" said Nat, innocently.

"She began early, you see. Poor thing! she was only fifteen when she took me, and I led her such a life, it's a wonder she isn't wrinkled and gray, and quite worn out," and Mr. Laurie looked up at her laughing.

"Don't Teddy; I won't have you abuse yourself so;" and Mrs. Jo stroked the curly black head at her knee as affectionately as ever, for, in spite of every thing Teddy was her boy still.

"If it hadn't been for you, there never would have been a Plumfield. It was my success with you, sir, that gave me courage to try my pet plan. So the boys may thank you for it, and name the new institution 'The Laurence Museum,' in honor of its founder, won't we, boys?" she added, looking very like the lively Jo of old times.

"We will! we will!" shouted the boys, throwing up their hats, for though they had taken them off on entering the house, according to rule, they had been in too much of a hurry to hang them up.

"I'm as hungry as a bear, can't I have a cookie?" asked Mr. Laurie, when the shout subsided and he had expressed his thanks by a splendid bow.

"Trot out and ask Asia for the gingerbread-box, Demi. It isn't in order to eat between meals, but, on this joyful occasion, we won't mind, and have a cookie all round," said Mrs. Jo; and when the box came she dealt them out with a liberal hand, every one munching away in a social circle.

Lesson 113

1. Finish chapter 11.
2. Write a summary of the chapter.
3. What questions do you still have about Uncle Teddy? How is he related to Mother Jo? If you could ask him something, what would you ask him?

Chapter XI. continued

Suddenly, in the midst of a bite, Mr. Laurie cried out, "Bless my heart, I forgot grandma's bundle!" and running out to the carriage, returned with an interesting white parcel, which, being opened, disclosed a choice collection of beasts, birds, and pretty things cut out of crisp sugary cake, and baked a lovely brown.

"There's one for each, and a letter to tell which is whose. Grandma and Hannah made them, and I tremble to think what would have happened to me if I had forgotten to leave them."

Then, amid much laughing and fun, the cakes were distributed. A fish for Dan, a fiddle for Nat, a book for Demi, a money for Tommy, a flower for Daisy, a hoop for Nan, who had driven twice round the triangle without stopping, a star for Emil, who put on airs because he studied astronomy, and, best of all, an omnibus for Franz, whose great delight was to drive the family bus. Stuffy got a fat pig, and the little folks had birds, and cats, and rabbits, with black currant eyes.

"Now I must go. Where is my Goldilocks? Mamma will come flying out to get her if I'm not back early," said Uncle Teddy, when the last crumb had vanished, which it speedily did, you may be sure.

The young ladies had gone into the garden, and while they waited till Franz looked them up, Jo and Laurie stood at the door talking together.

"How does little Giddy-gaddy come on?" he asked, for Nan's pranks amused him very much, and he was never tired of teasing Jo about her.

"Nicely; she is getting quite mannerly, and begins to see the error of her wild ways."

"Don't the boys encourage her in them?"

"Yes; but I keep talking, and lately she has improved much. You saw how prettily she shook hands with you, and how gentle she was with Bess. Daisy's example has its effect upon her, and I'm quite sure that a few months will work wonders."

Here Mrs. Jo's remarks were cut short by the appearance of Nan tearing round the corner at a break-neck pace, driving a mettlesome team of four boys, and followed by Daisy trundling Bess in a wheelbarrow. Hat off, hair flying, whip cracking, and barrow bumping, up they came in a cloud of dust, looking as wild a set of little hoydens as one would wish to see.

"So, these are the model children, are they? It's lucky I didn't bring Mrs. Curtis out to see your school for the cultivation of morals and manners; she would never have recovered from the shock of this spectacle," said Mr. Laurie, laughing at Mrs. Jo's premature rejoicing over Nan's improvement.

"Laugh away; I'll succeed yet. As you used to say at College, quoting some professor, 'Though the experiment has failed, the principle remains the same,' " said Mrs. Bhaer, joining in the merriment.

"I'm afraid Nan's example is taking effect upon Daisy, instead of the other way. Look at my little princess! she has utterly forgotten her dignity, and is screaming like the rest. Young ladies, what does this mean?" and Mr. Laurie rescued his small daughter from impending destruction, for the four horses were champing their bits and curvetting madly all about her, as she sat brandishing a great whip in both hands.

"We're having a race, and I beat," shouted Nan.

"I could have run faster, only I was afraid of spilling Bess," screamed Daisy.

"Hi! go long!" cried the princess, giving such a flourish with her whip that the horses ran away, and were seen no more.

"My precious child! come away from this ill-mannered crew before you are quite spoilt. Good-by, Jo! Next time I come, I shall expect to find the boys making patchwork."

"It wouldn't hurt them a bit. I don't give in, mind you; for my experiments always fail a few times before they succeed. Love to Amy and my blessed Marmee," called Mrs. Jo, as the carriage drove away; and the last Mr. Laurie saw of her, she was consoling Daisy for her failure by a ride in the wheelbarrow, and looking as if she liked it.

Great was the excitement all the week about the repairs in the carriage-house, which went briskly on in spite of the incessant questions, advice, and meddling of the boys. Old Gibbs was nearly driven wild with it all, but managed to do his work nevertheless; and by Friday night the place was all in order roof mended, shelves up, walls whitewashed, a great window cut at the back, which let in a flood of sunshine, and gave them a fine view of the brook, the meadows, and the distant hills; and over the great door, painted in red letters, was "The Laurence Museum."

All Saturday morning the boys were planning how it should be furnished with their spoils, and when Mr. Laurie arrived, bringing an aquarium which Mrs. Amy said she was tired of, their rapture was great.

The afternoon was spent in arranging things, and when the running and lugging and hammering was over, the ladies were invited to behold the institution.

It certainly was a pleasant place, airy, clean, and bright. A hop-vine shook its green bells round the open window, the pretty aquarium stood in the middle of the room, with some delicate water plants rising above the water, and gold-fish showing their brightness as they floated to and fro below. On either side of the window were rows of shelves ready to receive the curiosities yet to be found. Dan's tall cabinet stood before the great door which was fastened up, while the small door was to be used. On the cabinet stood a queer Indian idol, very ugly, but very interesting; old Mr. Laurence sent it, as well as a fine Chinese junk in full sail, which had a conspicuous place on the long table in the middle of the room. Above, swinging in a loop, and looking as if she was alive, hung Polly, who died at an advanced age, had been carefully stuffed, and was no presented by Mrs. Jo. The walls were decorated with all sorts of things. A snake's skin, a big wasp's nest, a birch-bark canoe, a string of birds' eggs, wreaths of gray moss from the South, and a bunch of cotton-pods. The dead bats had a place, also a large turtle-shell, and an ostrich-egg proudly presented by Demi, who volunteered to explain these rare curiosities to guests whenever they liked. There were so many stones that it was impossible to accept them all, so only a few of the best were arranged among the shells on the shelves, the rest were piled up in corners, to be examined by Dan at his leisure.

Every one was eager to give something, even Silas, who sent home for a stuffed wild-cat killed in his youth. It was rather moth-eaten and shabby, but on a high bracket and best side foremost the effect was fine, for the yellow glass eyes glared, and the mouth snarled so naturally, that Teddy shook in his little shoes at sight of it, when he came bringing his most cherished treasure, one cocoon, to lay upon the shrine of science.

"Isn't it beautiful? I'd no idea we had so many curious things. I gave that; don't it look well? We might make a lot by charging something for letting folks see it."

Jack added that last suggestion to the general chatter that went on as the family viewed the room.

"This is a free museum and if there is any speculating on it I'll paint out the name over the door," said Mr. Laurie, turning so quickly that Jack wished he had held his tongue.

"Hear! hear!" cried Mr. Bhaer.

"Speech! speech!" added Mrs. Jo.

"Can't, I'm too bashful. You give them a lecture yourself you are used to it," Mr. Laurie answered, retreating towards the window, meaning to escape. But she held him fast, and said, laughing as she looked at the dozen pairs of dirty hands about her,

"If I did lecture, it would on the chemical and cleansing properties of soap. Come now, as the founder of the institution, you really ought to give us a few moral remarks, and we will applaud tremendously."

Seeing that there was no way of escaping, Mr. Laurie looked up at Polly hanging overhead, seemed to find inspiration in the brilliant old bird, and sitting down upon the table, said, in his pleasant way,

"There is one thing I'd like to suggest, boys, and that is, I want you to get some good as well as much pleasure out of this. Just putting curious or pretty things here won't do it; so suppose you read up about them, so that when anybody asks questions you can answer them, and understand the matter. I used to like these things myself, and should enjoy hearing about them now, for I've forgotten all I once knew. It wasn't much, was it, Jo? Here's Dan now, full of stories about birds, and bugs, and so on; let him take care of the museum, and once a week the rest of you take turns to read a composition, or tell about some animal, mineral, or vegetable. We should all like that, and I think it would put considerable useful knowledge into our heads. What do you say, Professor?"

"I like it much, and will give the lads all the help I can. But they will need books to read up these new subjects, and we have not many, I fear," began Mr. Bhaer, looking much pleased, planning many fine lectures on geology, which he liked. "We should have a library for the special purpose."

"Is that a useful sort of book, Dan?" asked Mr. Laurie, pointing to the volume that lay open by the cabinet.

"Oh, yes! it tells all I want to know about insects. I had it here to see how to fix the butterflies right. I covered it, so it is not hurt;" and Dan caught it up, fearing the lender might think him careless.

"Give it here a minute;" and, pulling out his pencil, Mr. Laurie wrote Dan's name in it, saying, as he set the book up on one of the corner shelves, where nothing stood but a stuffed bird without a tail, "There, that is the beginning of the museum library. I'll hunt up some more books, and Demi shall keep them in order. Where are those jolly little books we used to read, Jo? 'Insect Architecture' or some such name, all about ants having battles, and bees having queens, and crickets eating holes in our clothes and stealing milk, and larks of that sort."

"In the garret at home. I'll have them sent out, and we will plunge into Natural History with a will," said Mrs. Jo, ready for any thing.

"Won't it be hard to write about such things?" asked Nat, who hated compositions.

"At first, perhaps; but you will soon like it. If you think that hard, how would you like to have this subject given to you, as it was to a girl of thirteen: A conversation between Themistocles, Aristides, and Pericles on the proposed appropriation of funds of the confederacy of Delos for the ornamentation of Athens?" said Mrs. Jo.

The boys groaned at the mere sound of the long names, and the gentlemen laughed at the absurdity of the lesson.

"Did she write it?" asked Demi, in an awe-stricken tone.

"Yes, but you can imagine what a piece of work she make of it, though she was rather a bright child."

"I'd like to have seen it," said Mr. Bhaer.

"Perhaps I can find it for you; I went to school with her," and Mrs. Jo looked so wicked that every one knew who the little girl was.

Hearing of this fearful subject for a composition quite reconciled the boys to the thought of writing about familiar things. Wednesday afternoon was appointed for the lectures, as they preferred to call them, for some chose to talk instead of write. Mr. Bhaer promised a portfolio in which the written productions should be kept, and Mrs. Bhaer said she would attend the course with great pleasure.

Then the dirty-handed society went off the wash, followed by the Professor, trying to calm the anxiety of Rob, who had been told by Tommy that all water was full of invisible pollywogs.

"I like your plan very much, only don't be too generous, Teddy," said Mrs. Bhaer, when they were left alone. "You know most of the boys have got to paddle their own canoes when they leave us, and too much sitting in the lap of luxury will unfit them for it."

"I'll be moderate, but do let me amuse myself. I get desperately tired of business sometimes, and nothing freshens me up like a good frolic with your boys. I like that Dan very much, Jo. He isn't demonstrative; but he has the eye of a hawk, and when you have tamed him a little he will do you credit."

"I'm so glad you think so. Thank you very much for your kindness to him, especially for this museum affair; it will keep him happy while he is lame, give me a chance to soften and smooth this poor, rough lad, and make him love us. What did inspire you with such a beautiful, helpful idea, Teddy?" asked Mrs. Bhaer, glancing back at the pleasant room, as she turned to leave it.

Laurie took both her hands in his, and answered, with a look that made her eyes fill with happy tears,

"Dear Jo! I have known what it is to be a motherless boy, and I never can forget how much you and yours have done for me all these years."

Lesson 114

1. Read the title of chapter 12. What are you picturing?
2. Read the beginning of chapter 12.

Speech

1. Read the poem from the chapter out loud in front of an audience.

Chapter XII. Huckleberries

There was a great clashing of tin pails, much running to and fro, and frequent demands for something to eat, one August afternoon, for the boys were going huckleberrying, and made as much stir about it as if they were setting out to find the North West Passage.

"Now, my lads, get off as quietly as you can, for Rob is safely out of the way, and won't see you," said Mrs. Bhaer, as she tied Daisy's broad-brimmed hat, and settled the great blue pinafore in which she had enveloped Nan.

But the plan did not succeed, for Rob had heard the bustle, decided to go, and prepared himself, without a thought of disappointment. The troop was just getting under way when the little man came marching downstairs with his best hat on, a bright tin pail in his hand, and a face beaming with satisfaction.

"Oh, dear! now we shall have a scene," sighed Mrs. Bhaer, who found her eldest son very hard to manage at times.

"I'm all ready," said Rob, and took his place in the ranks with such perfect unconsciousness of his mistake, that it really was very hard to undeceive him.

"It's too far for you, my love; stay and take care of me, for I shall be all alone," began his mother.

"You've got Teddy. I'm a big boy, so I can go; you said I might when I was bigger, and I am now," persisted Rob, with a cloud beginning to dim the brightness of his happy face.

"We are going up to the great pasture, and it's ever so far; we don't want you tagging on," cried Jack, who did not admire the little boys.

"I won't tag, I'll run and keep up. O Mamma! let me go! I want to fill my new pail, and I'll bring 'em all to you. Please, please, I will be good!" prayed Robby, looking up at his mother, so grieved and disappointed that her heart began to fail her.

"But, my deary, you'll get so tired and hot you won't have a good time. Wait till I go, and then we will stay all day, and pick as many berries as you want."

"You never do go, you are so busy, and I'm tired of waiting. I'd rather go and get the berries for you all myself. I love to pick 'em, and I want to fill my new pail dreffly," sobbed Rob.

The pathetic sight of great tears tinkling into the dear new pail, and threatening to fill it with salt water instead of huckleberries, touched all the ladies present. His mother patted the weeper on his back; Daisy offered to stay home with him; and Nan said, in her decided way,

"Let him come; I'll take care of him."

"If Franz was going I wouldn't mind, for he is very careful; but he is haying with the father, and I'm not sure about the rest of you," began Mrs. Bhaer.

"It's so far," put in Jack.

"I'd carry him if I was going wish I was," said Dan, with a sigh.

"Thank you, dear, but you must take care of your foot. I wish I could go. Stop a minute, I think I can manage it after all;" and Mrs. Bhaer ran out to the steps, waving her apron wildly.

Silas was just driving away in the hay-cart, but turned back, and agreed at once, when Mrs. Jo proposed that he should take the whole party to the pasture, and go for them at five o'clock.

"It will delay your work a little, but never mind; we will pay you in huckleberry pies," said Mrs. Jo, knowing Silas's weak point.

His rough, brown face brightened up, and he said, with a cheery "Haw! haw!" - "Wal now, Mis' Bhaer, if you go to bribin' of me, I shall give in right away."

"Now, boys, I have arranged it so that you can all go," said Mrs. Bhaer, running back again, much relieved, for she loved to make them happy, and always felt miserable when she had disturbed the serenity of her little sons; for she believed that the small hopes and plans and pleasures of children should be tenderly respected by grown-up people, and never rudely thwarted or ridiculed.

"Can I go?" said Dan, delighted.

"I thought especially of you. Be careful, and never mind the berries, but sit about and enjoy the lovely things which you know how to find all about you," answered Mrs. Bhaer, who remembered his kind offer to her boy.

"Me too! me too!" sung Rob, dancing with joy, and clapping his precious pail and cover like castanets.

"Yes, and Daisy and Nan must take good care of you. Be at the bars at five o'clock, and Silas will come for you all."

Robby cast himself upon his mother in a burst of gratitude, promising to bring her every berry he picked, and not eat one. Then they were all packed into the hay-cart, and went rattling away, the brightest face among the dozen being that of Rob, as he sat between his two temporary little mothers, beaming upon the whole world, and waving his best hat; for his indulgent mamma had not the heart to bereave him of it, since this was a gala-day to him.

Such a happy afternoon as they had, in spite of the mishaps which usually occur on such expeditions! Of course Tommy came to grief, tumbled upon a hornet's nest and got stung; but being used to woe, he bore the smart manfully, till Dan suggested the application of damp earth, which much assuaged the pain. Daisy saw a snake, and flying from it lost half her berries; but Demi helped her to fill up again, and discussed reptiles most learnedly the while. Ned fell out of a tree, and split his jacket down the back, but suffered no other fracture. Emil and Jack established rival claims to a certain thick patch, and while they were squabbling about it, Stuffy quickly and quietly stripped the bushes and fled to the protection of Dan, who was enjoying himself immensely. The crutch was no longer necessary, and he was delighted to see how strong his foot felt as he roamed about the great pasture, full of interesting rocks and stumps, with familiar little creatures in the grass, and well-known insects dancing in the air.

But of all the adventures that happened on this afternoon that which befell Nan and Rob was the most exciting, and it long remained one of the favorite histories of the household. Having explored the country pretty generally, torn three rents in her frock, and scratched her face in a barberry-bush, Nan began to pick the berries that shone like big, black beads on the low, green bushes. Her nimble fingers flew, but still her basket did not fill up as rapidly as she desired, so she kept wandering here and there to search for better places, instead of picking contentedly and steadily as Daisy did. Rob followed Nan, for her energy suited him better than his cousin's patience, and he too was anxious to have the biggest and best berries for Marmar.

"I keep putting 'em in, but it don't fill up, and I'm so tired," said Rob, pausing a moment to rest his short legs, and beginning to think huckleberrying was not all his fancy painted it; for the sun blazed, Nan skipped hither and thither like a grasshopper, and the berries fell out of his pail almost as fast as he put them in, because, in his struggles with the bushes, it was often upside-down.

"Last time we came they were ever so much thicker over that wall great bouncers; and there is a cave there where the boys made a fire. Let's go and fill our things quick, and then hide in the cave and let the others find us," proposed Nan, thirsting for adventures.

Rob consented, and away they went, scrambling over the wall and running down the sloping fields on the other side, till they were hidden among the rocks and underbrush. The berries were thick, and at last the pails were actually full. It was shady and cool down there, and a little spring gave the thirsty children a refreshing drink out of its mossy cup.

"Now we will go and rest in the cave, and eat our lunch," said Nan, well satisfied with her success so far.

"Do you know the way?" asked Rob.

"'Course I do; I've been once, and I always remember. Didn't I go and get my box all right?"

That convinced Rob, and he followed blindly as Nan led him over stock and stone, and brought him, after much meandering, to a small recess in the rock, where the blackened stones showed that fires had been made.

"Now, isn't it nice?" asked Nan, as she took out a bit of bread-and-butter, rather damaged by being mixed up with nails, fishhooks, stones and other foreign substances, in the young lady's pocket.

"Yes; do you think they will find us soon?" asked Rob, who found the shadowy glen rather dull, and began to long for more society.

"No, I don't; because if I hear them, I shall hide, and have fun making them find me."

"P'raps they won't come."

"Don't care; I can get home myself."

"Is it a great way?" asked Rob, looking at his little stubby boots, scratched and wet with his long wandering.

"It's six miles, I guess." Nan's ideas of distance were vague, and her faith in her own powers great.

"I think we better go now," suggested Rob, presently.

"I shan't till I have picked over my berries;" and Nan began what seemed to Rob an endless task.

"Oh, dear! you said you'd take good care of me," he sighed, as the sun seemed to drop behind the hill all of a sudden.

"Well I am taking good care of you as hard as I can. Don't be cross, child; I'll go in a minute," said Nan, who considered five-year-old Robby a mere infant compared to herself.

So little Rob sat looking anxiously about him, and waiting patiently, for, spite of some misgivings, he felt great confidence in Nan.

"I guess it's going to be night pretty soon," he observed, as if to himself, as a mosquito bit him, and the frogs in a neighboring marsh began to pipe up for the evening concert.

"My goodness me! so it is. Come right away this minute, or they will be gone," cried Nan, looking up from her work, and suddenly perceiving that the sun was down.

"I heard a horn about an hour ago; may be they were blowing for us," said Rob, trudging after his guide as she scrambled up the steep hill.

"Where was it?" asked Nan, stopping short.

"Over that way;" he pointed with a dirty little finger in an entirely wrong direction.

"Let's go that way and meet them;" and Nan wheeled about, and began to trot through the bushes, feeling a trifle anxious, for there were so many cow-paths all about she could not remember which way they came.

On they went over stock and stone again, pausing now and then to listen for the horn, which did not blow any more, for it was only the moo of a cow on her way home.

"I don't remember seeing that pile of stones do you?" asked Nan, as she sat on a wall to rest a moment and take an observation.

"I don't remember any thing, but I want to go home," and Rob's voice had a little tremble in it that made Nan put her arms round him and lift him gently down, saying, in her most capable way,

"I'm going just as fast as I can, dear. Don't cry, and when we come to the road, I'll carry you."

"Where is the road?" and Robby wiped his eyes to look for it.

"Over by that big tree. Don't you know that's the one Ned tumbled out of?"

"So it is. May be they waited for us; I'd like to ride home wouldn't you?" and Robby brightened up as he plodded along toward the end of the great pasture.

"No, I'd rather walk," answered Nan, feeling quite sure that she would be obliged to do so, and preparing her mind for it.

Another long trudge through the fast-deepening twilight and another disappointment, for when they reached the tree, they found to their dismay that it was not the one Ned climbed, and no road anywhere appeared.

"Are we lost?" quavered Rob, clasping his pail in despair.

"Not much. I don't just see which way to go, and I guess we'd better call."

So they both shouted till they were hoarse, yet nothing answered but the frogs in full chorus.

"There is another tall tree over there, perhaps that's the one," said Nan, whose heart sunk within her, though she still spoke bravely.

"I don't think I can go any more; my boots are so heavy I can't pull 'em;" and Robby sat down on a stone quite worn out.

"Then we must stay here all night. I don't care much, if snakes don't come."

"I'm frightened of snakes. I can't stay all night. Oh, dear! I don't like to be lost," and Rob puckered up his face to cry, when suddenly a thought occurred to him, and he said, in a tone of perfect confidence,

"Marmar will come and find me she always does; I ain't afraid now."

"She won't know where we are."

"She didn't know I was shut up in the ice-house, but she found me. I know she'll come," returned Robby, so trustfully, that Nan felt relieved, and sat down by him, saying, with a remorseful sigh,

"I wish we hadn't run away."

"You made me; but I don't mind much Marmar will love me just the same," answered Rob, clinging to his sheet-anchor when all other hope was gone.

"I'm so hungry. Let's eat our berries," proposed Nan, after a pause, during which Rob began to nod.

"So am I, but I can't eat mine, 'cause I told Marmar I'd keep them all for her."

"You'll have to eat them if no one comes for us," said Nan, who felt like contradicting every thing just then. "If we stay here a great many days, we shall eat up all the berries in the field, and then we shall starve," she added grimly.

"I shall eat sassafras. I know a big tree of it, and Dan told me how squirrels dig up the roots and eat them, and I love to dig," returned Rob, undaunted by the prospect of starvation.

"Yes; and we can catch frogs, and cook them. My father ate some once, and he said they were nice," put in Nan, beginning to find a spice of romance even in being lost in a huckleberry pasture.

"How could we cook frogs? we haven't got any fire."

"I don't know; next time I'll have matches in my pocket," said Nan, rather depressed by this obstacle to the experiment in frog-cookery.

"Couldn't we light a fire with a fire-fly?" asked Rob, hopefully, as he watched them flitting to and fro like winged sparks.

"Let's try;" and several minutes were pleasantly spent in catching the flies, and trying to make them kindle a green twig or two. "It's a lie to call them fireflies when there isn't a fire in them," Nan said, throwing one unhappy insect away with scorn, though it shone its best, and obligingly walked up and down the twigs to please the innocent little experimenters.

"Marmar's a good while coming," said Rob, after another pause, during which they watched the stars overhead, smelt the sweet fern crushed under foot, and listened to the crickets' serenade.

"I don't see why God made any night; day is so much pleasanter," said Nan, thoughtfully.

"It's to sleep in," answered Rob, with a yawn.

"Then do go to sleep," said Nan, pettishly.

"I want my own bed. Oh, I wish I could see Teddy!" cried Rob, painfully reminded of home by the soft chirp of birds safe in their little nests.

"I don't believe your mother will ever find us," said Nan, who was becoming desperate, for she hated patient waiting of any sort. "It's so dark she won't see us."

"It was all black in the ice-house, and I was so scared I didn't call her, but she saw me; and she will see me now, no matter how dark it is," returned confiding Rob, standing up to peer into the gloom for the help which never failed him.

"I see her! I see her!" he cried, and ran as fast as his tired legs would take him toward a dark figure slowly approaching. Suddenly he stopped, then turned about, and came stumbling back, screaming in a great panic,

"No, it's a bear, a big black one!" and hid his face in Nan's skirts.

For a moment Nan quailed; ever her courage gave out at the thought of a real bear, and she was about to turn and flee in great disorder, when a mild "Moo!" changed her fear to merriment, as she said, laughing,

"It's a cow, Robby! the nice, black cow we saw this afternoon."

The cow seemed to feel that it was not just the thing to meet two little people in her pasture after dark, and the amiable beast paused to inquire into the case. She let them stroke her, and stood regarding them with her soft eyes so mildly, that Nan, who feared no animal but a bear, was fired with a desire to milk her.

"Silas taught me how; and berries and milk would be so nice," she said, emptying the contents of her pail into her hat, and boldly beginning her new task, while Rob stood by and repeated, at her command, the poem from Mother Goose:

> Cushy cow, bonny, let down your milk,
> Let down your milk to me,
> And I will give you a gown of silk,
> A gown of silk and a silver tee.

But the immortal rhyme had little effect, for the benevolent cow had already been milked, and had only half a gill to give the thirsty children.

"Shoo! get away! you are an old cross patch," cried Nan, ungratefully, as she gave up the attempt in despair; and poor Molly walked on with a gentle gurgle of surprise and reproof.

"Each can have a sip, and then we must take a walk. We shall go to sleep if we don't; and lost people mustn't sleep. Don't you know how Hannah Lee in the pretty story slept under the snow and died?"

"But there isn't any snow now, and it's nice and warm," said Rob, who was not blessed with as lively a fancy as Nan.

"No matter, we will poke about a little, and call some more; and then, if nobody comes, we will hide under the bushes, like Hop-'o-my-thumb and his brothers."

It was a very short walk, however, for Rob was so sleepy he could not get on, and tumbled down so often that Nan entirely lost patience, being half distracted by the responsibility she had taken upon herself.

"If you tumble down again, I'll shake you," she said, lifting the poor little man up very kindly as she spoke, for Nan's bark was much worse than her bite.

"Please don't. It's my boots they keep slipping so;" and Rob manfully checked the sob just ready to break out, adding, with a plaintive patience that touched Nan's heart, "If the skeeters didn't bite me so, I could go to sleep till Marmar comes."

"Put your head on my lap, and I'll cover you up with my apron; I'm not afraid of the night," said Nan, sitting down and trying to persuade herself that she did not mind the shadow nor the mysterious rustlings all about her.

"Wake me up when she comes," said Rob, and was fast asleep in five minutes with his head in Nan's lap under the pinafore.

The little girl sat for some fifteen minutes, staring about her with anxious eyes, and feeling as if each second was an hour. Then a pale light began to glimmer over the hill-top and she said to herself, "I guess the night is over and morning is coming. I'd like to see the sun rise, so I'll watch, and when it comes up we can find our way right home."

But before the moon's round face peeped above the hill to destroy her hope, Nan had fallen asleep, leaning back in a little bower of tall ferns, and was deep in a mid-summer night's dream of fire-flies and blue aprons, mountains of huckleberries, and Robby wiping away the tears of a black cow, who sobbed, "I want to go home! I want to go home!"

While the children were sleeping, peacefully lulled by the drowsy hum of many neighborly mosquitoes, the family at home were in a great state of agitation. The hay-cart came at five, and all but Jack, Emil, Nan, and Rob were at the bars ready for it. Franz drove instead of Silas, and when the boys told him that the others were going home through the wood, he said, looking ill-pleased, "They ought to have left Rob to ride, he will be tired out by the long walk."

"It's shorter that way, and they will carry him," said Stuffy, who was in a hurry for his supper.

"You are sure Nan and Rob went with them?"

"Of course they did; I saw them getting over the wall, and sung out that it was most five, and Jack called back that they were going the other way," explained Tommy.

"Very well, pile in then," and away rattled the hay-cart with the tired children and the full pails.

Mrs. Jo looked sober when she heard of the division of the party, and sent Franz back with Toby to find and bring the little ones home. Supper was over, and the family sitting about in the cool hall as usual, when Franz came trotting back, hot, dusty, and anxious.

"Have they come?" he called out when half-way up the avenue.

"No!" and Mrs. Jo flew out of her chair looking so alarmed that every one jumped up and gathered round Franz.

"I can't find them anywhere," he began; but the words were hardly spoken when a loud "Hullo!" startled them all, and the next minute Jack and Emil came round the house.

"Where are Nan and Rob?" cried Mrs. Jo, clutching Emil in a way that caused him to think his aunt had suddenly lost her wits.
"I don't know. They came home with the others, didn't they?" he answered, quickly.

"No; George and Tommy said they went with you."

"Well, they didn't. Haven't seen them. We took a swim in the pond, and came by the wood," said Jack, looking alarmed, as well he might.

146

"Call Mr. Bhaer, get the lanterns, and tell Silas I want him."

That was all Mrs. Jo said, but they knew what she meant, and flew to obey her orders. In ten minutes, Mr. Bhaer and Silas were off to the wood, and Franz tearing down the road on old Andy to search the great pasture. Mrs. Jo caught up some food from the table, a little bottle of brandy from the medicine-closet, took a lantern, and bidding Jack and Emil come with her, and the rest not stir, she trotted away on Toby, never stopping for hat or shawl. She heard some one running after her, but said not a word till, as she paused to call and listen, the light of her lantern shone on Dan's face.

Lesson 115

1. Do you think the family will have a hard time finding Nan and Rob? Why or why not?
2. Finish chapter 12.
3. What are you thinking about Nan's punishment?
4. Describe to someone the setting of this chapter. Think of what details the author includes.
5. Do you have a memory about a time when you were lost or thought you were lost or thought you had lost someone for whom you were responsible? How did you feel?

Chapter XII. continued

"You here! I told Jack to come," she said, half-inclined to send him back, much as she needed help.

"I wouldn't let him; he and Emil hadn't had any supper, and I wanted to come more than they did," he said, taking the lantern from her and smiling up in her face with the steady look in his eyes that made her feel as if, boy though he was, she had some one to depend on.

Off she jumped, and ordered him on to Toby, in spite of his pleading to walk; then they went on again along the dusty, solitary road, stopping every now and then to call and hearken breathlessly for little voices to reply.

When they came to the great pasture, other lights were already flitting to and fro like will-o'-the-wisps, and Mr. Bhaer's voice was heard shouting, "Nan! Rob! Rob! Nan!" in every part of the field. Silas whistled and roared, Dan plunged here and there on Toby, who seemed to understand the case, and went over the roughest places with unusual docility. Often Mrs. Jo hushed them all, saying, with a sob in her throat, "The noise may frighten them, let me call; Robby will know my voice;" and then she would cry out the beloved little name in every tone of tenderness, till the very echoes whispered it softly, and the winds seemed to waft it willingly; but still no answer came.

The sky was overcast now, and only brief glimpses of the moon were seen, heat-lightning darted out of the dark clouds now and then, and a faint far-off rumble as of thunder told that a summer-storm was brewing.

"O my Robby! my Robby!" mourned poor Mrs. Jo, wandering up and down like a pale ghost, while Dan kept beside her like a faithful fire-fly. "What shall I say to Nan's father if she comes to harm? Why did I ever trust my darling so far away? Fritz, do you hear any thing?" and when a mournful, "No" came back, she wrung her hands so despairingly that Dan sprung down from Toby's back, tied the bridle to the bars, and said, in his decided way,

"They may have gone down the spring I'm going to look."

He was over the wall and away so fast that she could hardly follow him; but when she reached the spot, he lowered the lantern and showed her with joy the marks of little feet in the soft ground about the spring. She fell down on her knees to examine the tracks, and then sprung up, saying eagerly,

"Yes; that is the mark of my Robby's little boots! Come this way, they must have gone on."

Such a weary search! But now some inexplicable instinct seemed to lead the anxious mother, for presently Dan uttered a cry, and caught up a little shining object lying in the path. It was the cover of the new tin pail, dropped in the first alarm of being lost. Mrs. Jo hugged and kissed it as if it were a living thing; and when Dan was about to utter a glad shout to bring the others to the spot, she stopped him, saying, as she hurried on, "No, let me find them; I let Rob go, and I want to give him back to his father all myself."

A little farther on Nan's hat appeared, and after passing the place more than once, they came at last upon the babes in the wood, both sound asleep. Dan never forgot the little picture on which the light of his lantern shone that night. He thought Mrs. Jo would cry out, but she only whispered, "Hush!" as she softly lifted away the apron, and saw the little ruddy face below. The berry-stained lips were half-open as the breath came and went, the yellow hair lay damp on the hot forehead, and both the chubby hands held fast the little pail still full.

The sight of the childish harvest, treasured through all the troubles of that night for her, seemed to touch Mrs. Jo to the heart, for suddenly she gathered up her boy, and began to cry over him, so tenderly, yet so heartily, that he woke up, and at first seemed bewildered. Then he remembered, and hugged her close, saying with a laugh of triumph,

"I knew you'd come! O Marmar! I did want you so!" For a moment they kissed and clung to one another, quite forgetting all the world; for no matter how lost and soiled and worn-out wandering sons may be, mothers can forgive and forget every thing as they fold them in their fostering arms. Happy the son whose faith in his mother remains unchanged, and who, through all his wanderings, has kept some filial token to repay her brave and tender love.

Dan meantime picked Nan out of her bush, and, with a gentleness none but Teddy ever saw in him before, he soothed her first alarm at the sudden waking, and wiped away her tears; for Nan also began to cry for joy, it was so good to see a kind face and feel a strong arm round her after what seemed to her ages of loneliness and fear.

"My poor little girl, don't cry! You are all safe now, and no one shall say a word of blame to-night," said Mrs. Jo, taking Nan into her capacious embrace, and cuddling both children as a hen might gather her lost chickens under her motherly wings.

"It was my fault; but I am sorry. I tried to take care of him, and I covered him up and let him sleep, and didn't touch his berries, though I was so hungry; and I never will do it again truly, never, never," sobbed Nan, quite lost in a sea of penitence and thankfulness.

"Call them now, and let us get home," said Mrs. Jo; and Dan, getting upon the wall, sent a joyful word "Found!" ringing over the field.

How the wandering lights came dancing from all sides, and gathered round the little group among the sweet fern bushes! Such a hugging, and kissing, and talking, and crying, as went on must have amazed the glowworms, and evidently delighted the mosquitoes, for they hummed frantically, while the little moths came in flocks to the party, and the frogs croaked as if they could not express their satisfaction loudly enough.

Then they set out for home, a queer party, for Franz rode on to tell the news; Dan and Toby led the way; then came Nan in the strong arms of Silas, who considered her "the smartest little baggage he ever saw," and teased her all the way home about her pranks. Mrs. Bhaer would let no one carry Rob but himself, and the little fellow, refreshed by sleep, sat up, and chattered gayly, feeling himself a hero, while his mother went beside him holding on to any pat of his precious little body that came handy, and never tired of hearing him say, "I knew Marmar would come," or seeing him lean down to kiss her, and put a plump berry into her mouth, "'Cause he picked 'em all for her."

The moon shone out just as they reached the avenue, and all the boys came shouting to meet them, so the lost lambs were borne in triumph and safety, and landed in the dining-room, where the unromantic little things demanded supper instead of preferring kisses and caresses. They were set down to bread and milk, while the entire household stood round to gaze upon them. Nan soon recovered her spirits, and recounted her perils with a relish now that they were all over. Rob seemed absorbed in his food, but put down his spoon all of a sudden, and set up a doleful roar.

"My precious, why do you cry?" asked his mother, who still hung over him.

"I'm crying 'cause I was lost," bawled Rob, trying to squeeze out a tear, and failing entirely.

"But you are found now. Nan says you didn't cry out in the field, and I was glad you were such a brave boy."

"I was so busy being frightened I didn't have any time then. But I want to cry now, 'cause I don't like to be lost," explained Rob, struggling with sleep, emotion, and a mouthful of bread and milk.

The boys set up such a laugh at this funny way of making up for lost time, that Rob stopped to look at them, and the merriment was so infectious, that after a surprised stare he burst out into a merry, "Ha, ha!" and beat his spoon upon the table as if he enjoyed the joke immensely.

"It is ten o'clock; into bed, every man of you," said Mr. Bhaer, looking at his watch.

"And, thank Heaven! there will be no empty ones to-night," added Mrs. Bhaer, watching, with full eyes, Robby going up in his father's arms, and Nan escorted by Daisy and Demi, who considered her the most interesting heroine of their collection.

"Poor Aunt Jo is so tired she ought to be carried up herself," said gentle Franz, putting his arm round her as she paused at the stair-foot, looking quite exhausted by her fright and long walk.

"Let's make an arm-chair," proposed Tommy.

"No, thank you, my lads; but somebody may lend me a shoulder to lean on," answered Mrs. Jo.
"Me! me!" and half-a-dozen jostled one another, all eager to be chosen, for there was something in the pale motherly face that touched the warm hearts under the round jackets.

Seeing that they considered it an honor, Mrs. Jo gave it to the one who had earned it, and nobody grumbled when she put her arm on Dan's broad shoulder, saying, with a look that made him color up with pride and pleasure,

"He found the children; so I think he must help me up."

Dan felt richly rewarded for his evening's work, not only that he was chosen from all the rest to go proudly up bearing the lamp, but because Mrs. Jo said heartily, "Good-night, my boy! God bless you!" as he left her at her door.

"I wish I was your boy," said Dan, who felt as if danger and trouble had somehow brought him nearer than ever to her.

"You shall be my oldest son," and she sealed her promise with a kiss that made Dan hers entirely.

Little Rob was all right next day, but Nan had a headache, and lay on Mother Bhaer's sofa with cold-cream upon her scratched face. Her remorse was quite gone, and she evidently thought being lost rather a fine amusement. Mrs. Jo was not pleased with this state of things, and had no desire to have her children led from the paths of virtue, or her pupils lying round loose in huckleberry fields. So she talked soberly to Nan, and tried to impress upon her mind the difference between liberty and license, telling several tales to enforce her lecture. She had not decided how to punish Nan, but one of these stories suggested a way, and as Mrs. Jo liked odd penalties, she tried it.

"All children run away," pleaded Nan, as if it was as natural and necessary a thing as measles or hooping cough.

"Not all, and some who do run away don't get found again," answered Mrs. Jo.

"Didn't you do it yourself?" asked Nan, whose keen little eyes saw some traces of a kindred spirit in the serious lady who was sewing so morally before her.

Mrs. Jo laughed, and owned that she did.

"Tell about it," demanded Nan, feeling that she was getting the upper hand in the discussion.
Mrs. Jo saw that, and sobered down at once, saying, with a remorseful shake of the head,

"I did it a good many times, and led my poor mother rather a hard life with my pranks, till she cured me."

"How?" and Nan sat up with a face full of interest.

"I had a new pair of shoes once, and wanted to show them; so, though I was told not to leave the garden, I ran away and was wandering about all day. It was in the city, and why I wasn't killed I don't know. Such a time as I had. I frolicked in the park with dogs, sailed boats in the Back Bay with strange boys, dined with a little Irish beggar-girl on salt fish and potatoes, and was found at last fast asleep on a door-step with my arms round a great dog. It was late in the evening, and I was a dirty as a little pig, and the new shoes were worn out I had travelled so far."

"How nice!" cried Nan, looking all ready to go and do it herself.

"It was not nice next day;" and Mrs. Jo tried to keep her eyes from betraying how much she enjoyed the memory of her early capers.

"Did your mother whip you?" asked Nan, curiously.

"She never whipped me but once, and then she begged my pardon, or I don't think I ever should have forgiven her, it hurt my feelings so much."

"Why did she beg your pardon? my father don't."

"Because, when she had done it, I turned round and said, 'Well, you are mad yourself, and ought to be whipped as much as me.' She looked at me a minute, then her anger all died out, and she said, as if ashamed, 'You are right, Jo, I am angry; and why should I punish you for being in a passion when I set you such a bad example? Forgive me, dear, and let us try to help one another in a better way.' I never forgot it, and it did me more good than a dozen rods."

Nan sat thoughtfully turning the little cold-cream jar for a minute, and Mrs. Jo said nothing, but let that idea get well into the busy little mind that was so quick to see and feel what went on about her.

"I like that," said Nan, presently, and her face looked less elfish, with its sharp eyes, inquisitive nose, and mischievous mouth. "What did your mother do to you when you ran away that time?"

"She tied me to the bed-post with a long string, so that I could not go out of the room, and there I stayed all day with the little worn-out shoes hanging up before me to remind me of my fault."

"I should think that would cure anybody," cried Nan, who loved her liberty above all things.

"It did cure me, and I think it will you, so I am going to try it," said Mrs. Jo, suddenly taking a ball of strong twine out of a drawer in her work-table.

Nan looked as if she was decidedly getting the worst of the argument now, and sat feeling much crestfallen while Mrs. Jo tied one end round her waist and the other to the arm of the sofa, saying, as she finished,

"I don't like to tie you up like a naughty little dog, but if you don't remember any better than a dog, I must treat you like one."

"I'd just as lief be tied up as not I like to play dog;" and Nan put on a don't-care face, and began to growl and grovel on the floor.

Mrs. Jo took no notice, but leaving a book or two and a handkerchief to hem, she went away, and left Miss Nan to her own devices. This was not agreeable, and after sitting a moment she tried to untie the cord. But it was fastened in the belt of her apron behind, so she began on the knot at the other end. It soon came loose, and, gathering it up, Nan was about to get out of the window, when she heard Mrs. Jo say to somebody as she passed through the hall,

"No, I don't think she will run away now; she is an honorable little girl, and knows that I do it to help her."

In a minute, Nan whisked back, tied herself up, and began to sew violently. Rob came in a moment after, and was so charmed with the new punishment, that he got a jump-rope and tethered himself to the other arm of the sofa in the most social manner.

"I got lost too, so I ought to be tied up as much as Nan," he explained to his mother when she saw the new captive.

"I'm not sure that you don't deserve a little punishment, for you knew it was wrong to go far away from the rest."

"Nan took me," began Rob, willing to enjoy the novel penalty, but not willing to take the blame.

"You needn't have gone. You have got a conscience, though you are a little boy, and you must learn to mind it."

"Well, my conscience didn't prick me a bit when she said 'Let's get over the wall,' " answered Rob, quoting one of Demi's expressions.

"Did you stop to see if it did?"

"No."

"Then you cannot tell."

"I guess it's such a little conscience that it don't prick hard enough for me to feel it," added Rob, after thinking the matter over for a minute.

"We must sharpen it up. It's bad to have a dull conscience; so you may stay here till dinner-time, and talk about it with Nan. I trust you both not to untie yourselves till I say the word."

"No, we won't," said both, feeling a certain sense of virtue in helping to punish themselves.

For an hour they were very good, then they grew tired of one room, and longed to get out. Never had the hall seemed so inviting; even the little bedroom acquired a sudden interest, and they would gladly have gone in and played tent with the curtains of the best bed. The open windows drove them wild because they could not reach them; and the outer world seemed so beautiful, they wondered how they ever found the heart to say it was dull. Nan pined for a race round the lawn, and Rob remembered with dismay that he had not fed his dog that morning, and wondered what poor Pollux would do. They watched the clock, and Nan did some nice calculations in minutes and seconds, while Rob learned to tell all the hours between eight and one so well that he never forgot them. It was maddening to smell the dinner, to know that there was to be succotash and huckleberry pudding, and to feel that they would not be on the spot to secure good helps of both. When Mary Ann began to set the table, they nearly cut themselves in two trying to see what meat there was to be; and Nan offered to help her make the beds, if she would only see that she had "lots of sauce on her pudding."

When the boys came bursting out of school, they found the children tugging at their halters like a pair of restive little colts, and were much edified, as well as amused, by the sequel to the exciting adventures of the night.

"Untie me now, Marmar; my conscience will prick like a pin next time, I know it will," said Rob, as the bell rang, and Teddy came to look at him with sorrowful surprise.

"We shall see," answered his mother, setting him free. He took a good run down the hall, back through the dining-room, and brought up beside Nan, quite beaming with virtuous satisfaction.

"I'll bring her dinner to her, may I?" he asked, pitying his fellow-captive.

"That's my kind little son! Yes, pull out the table, and get a chair;" and Mrs. Jo hurried away to quell the ardor of the others, who were always in a raging state of hunger at noon.

Nan ate alone, and spent a long afternoon attached to the sofa. Mrs. Bhaer lengthened her bonds so that she could look out of the window; and there she stood watching the boys play, and all the little summer creatures enjoying their liberty. Daisy had a picnic for the dolls on the lawn, so that Nan might see the fun if she could not join in it. Tommy turned his best somersaults to console her; Demi sat on the steps reading aloud to himself, which amused Nan a good deal; and Dan brought a little tree-toad to show her as the most delicate attention in his power.

But nothing atoned for the loss of freedom; and a few hours of confinement taught Nan how precious it was. A good many thoughts went through the little head that lay on the window-sill during the last quiet hour when all the children went to the brook to see Emil's new ship launched. She was to have christened it, and had depended on smashing a tiny bottle of currant-wine over the prow as it was named Josephine in honor of Mrs. Bhaer. Now she had lost her chance, and Daisy wouldn't do it half so well. Tears rose to her eyes as she remembered that it was all her own fault; and she said aloud, addressing a fat bee who was rolling about in the yellow heart of a rose just under the window,

"If you have run away, you'd better go right home, and tell your mother you are sorry, and never do so any more."

"I am glad to hear you give him such good advice, and I think he has taken it," said Mrs. Jo, smiling, as the bee spread his dusty wings and flew away.

Nan brushed off a bright drop or two that shone on the window-sill, and nestled against her friend as she took her on her knee, adding kindly for she had seen the little drops, and knew what they meant, "Do you think my mother's cure for running away a good one?"

"Yes, ma'am," answered Nan, quite subdued by her quiet day.

"I hope I shall not have to try it again."

"I guess not;" and Nan looked up with such an earnest little face that Mrs. Jo felt satisfied, and said no more, for she liked to have her penalties do their own work, and did not spoil the effect by too much moralizing.

Here Rob appeared, bearing with infinite care what Asia called a "sarcer pie," meaning one baked in a saucer.

"It's made out of some of my berries, and I'm going to give you half at supper-time," he announced with a flourish.

"What makes you, when I'm so naughty?" asked Nan, meekly.

"Because we got lost together. You ain't going to be naughty again, are you?"

"Never," said Nan, with great decision.

"Oh, goody! now let's go and get Mary Ann to cut this for us all ready to eat; it's 'most tea time;" and Rob beckoned with the delicious little pie.

Nan started to follow, then stopped, and said,

"I forgot, I can't go."

"Try and see," said Mrs. Bhaer, who had quietly untied the cord sash while she had been talking.

Nan saw that she was free, and with one tempestuous kiss to Mrs. Jo, she was off like a humming-bird, followed by Robby, dribbling huckleberry juice as he ran.

Lesson 116

1. What do you picture when you read the title of Chapter 13? What do you think this chapter might be about?
2. Read chapter 13. What are you thinking after you have finished your reading?
3. The point of view of a story is who is telling the story. It could be the main character within the story, the "I" character. The story could also be told in the third person (by some all-

knowing narrator telling the story). With this point of view there is no "I" character telling what's going on around him and what he is thinking. The all-knowing story teller can tell us what every character is doing and thinking.

4. Here's an example of each. Which is which? One is told in the first person, with an "I" character. One is told in the third person, no "I" character. (Answers)

    -   He ran home as fast as possible to find out what was going to happen.

    -   Running home as fast as I could, I couldn't help being anxious to find out what was going to happen.

Chapter XIII. Goldilocks

After the last excitement peace descended upon Plumfield and reigned unbroken for several weeks, for the elder boys felt that the loss of Nan and Rob lay at their door, and all became so paternal in their care that they were rather wearying; while the little ones listened to Nan's recital of her perils so many times, that they regarded being lost as the greatest ill humanity was heir to, and hardly dared to put their little noses outside the great gate lest night should suddenly descend upon them, and ghostly black cows come looming through the dusk.

"It is too good to last," said Mrs. Jo; for years of boy-culture had taught her that such lulls were usually followed by outbreaks of some sort, and when less wise women would have thought that the boys had become confirmed saints, she prepared herself for a sudden eruption of the domestic volcano.

One cause of this welcome calm was a visit from little Bess, whose parents lent her for a week while they were away with Grandpa Laurence, who was poorly. The boys regarded Goldilocks as a mixture of child, angel, and fairy, for she was a lovely little creature, and the golden hair which she inherited from her blonde mamma enveloped her like a shining veil, behind which she smiled upon her worshippers when gracious, and hid herself when offended. Her father would not have it cut and it hung below her waist, so soft and fine and bright, that Demi insisted that it was silk spun from a cocoon. Every one praised the little Princess, but it did not seem to do her harm, only to teach her that her presence brought sunshine, her smiles made answering smiles on other faces, and her baby griefs filled every heart with tenderest sympathy.

Unconsciously, she did her young subjects more good than many a real sovereign, for her rule was very gentle and her power was felt rather than seen. Her natural refinement made her dainty in all things, and had a good effect upon the careless lads about her. She would let no one touch her roughly or with unclean hands, and more soap was used during her visits than at any other time, because the boys considered it the highest honor to be allowed to carry her highness, and the deepest disgrace to be repulsed with the disdainful command, "Do away, dirty boy!"

Loud voices displeased her and quarrelling frightened her; so gentler tones came into the boyish voices as they addressed her, and squabbles were promptly suppressed in her presence by lookers-on if the principles could not restrain themselves. She liked to be waited on, and the biggest boys did her little errands without a murmur, while the small lads were her devoted slaves in all things. They begged to be allowed to draw her carriage, bear her berry-basket, or pass her plate at table. No service was too humble, and Tommy and Ned came to blows before they could decide which should have the honor of blacking her little boots.

Nan was especially benefited by a week in the society of a well-bred lady, though such a very small one; for Bess would look at her with a mixture of wonder and alarm in her great blue eyes when the hoyden screamed and romped; and she shrunk from her as if she thought her a sort of wild animal. Warm-hearted Nan felt this very much. She said at first, "Pooh! I don't care!" But she did care, and was so hurt when Bess said, "I love my tuzzin best, tause she is twiet," that she shook poor Daisy till her teeth chattered in her head, and then fled to the barn to cry dismally. In that general refuge for perturbed spirits she found comfort and good counsel from some source or other. Perhaps the swallows from their mud-built nests overhead twittered her a little lecture on the beauty of gentleness. However that might have been, she came out quite subdued, and carefully searched the orchard for a certain kind of early apple that Bess liked because it was sweet and small and rosy. Armed with this peace-offering, she approached the little Princess, and humbly presented it. To her great joy it was graciously accepted, and when Daisy gave Nan a forgiving kiss, Bess did likewise, as if she felt that she had been too severe, and desired to apologize. After this they played pleasantly together, and Nan enjoyed the royal favor for days. To be sure she felt a little like a wild bird in a pretty cage at first, and occasionally had to slip out to stretch her wings in a long flight, or to sing at the top of her voice, where neither would disturb the plump turtle-dove Daisy, nor the dainty golden canary Bess. But it did her good; for, seeing how every one loved the little Princess for her small graces and virtues, she began to imitate her, because Nan wanted much love, and tried hard to win it.

Not a boy in the house but felt the pretty child's influence, and was improved by it without exactly knowing how or why, for babies can work miracles in the hearts that love them. Poor Billy found infinite satisfaction in staring at her, and though she did not like it she permitted without a frown, after she had been made to understand that he was not quite like the others, and on that account must be more kindly treated. Dick and Dolly overwhelmed her with willow whistles, the only thing they knew how to make, and she accepted but never used them. Rob served her like he was in love with her, and Teddy followed her like a pet dog. Jack she did not like, because he was afflicted with warts and had a harsh voice. Stuffy displeased her because he did not eat tidily, and George tried hard not to gobble, that he might not disgust the dainty little lady opposite. Ned was banished from court in utter disgrace when he was discovered tormenting some unhappy field-mice. Goldilocks could never forget the sad spectacle, and retired behind her veil when he approached, waving him away with an imperious little hand, and crying, in a tone of mingled grief and anger,

"No, I tarn't love him; he tut the poor mouses' little tails off, and they queeked!"

Daisy promptly abdicated when Bess came, and took the humble post of chief cook, while Nan was first maid of honor; Emil was chancellor of the exchequer, and spent the public monies lavishly in getting up spectacles that cost whole ninepences. Franz was prime minister, and directed her affairs of state, planned royal progresses through the kingdom, and kept foreign powers in order. Demi was her philosopher, and fared much better than such gentlemen usually do among crowned heads. Dan was her standing army, and defended her territories gallantly; Tommy was court fool, and Nat a tuneful Rizzio to this innocent little Mary.

Uncle Fritz and Aunt Jo enjoyed this peaceful episode, and looked on at the pretty play in which the young folk unconsciously imitated their elders, without adding the tragedy that is so apt to spoil the dramas acted on the larger stage.

"They teach us quite as much as we teach them," said Mr. Bhaer.

"Bless the dears! they never guess how many hints they give us as to the best way of managing them," answered Mrs. Jo.

"I think you were right about the good effect of having girls among the boys. Nan has stirred up Daisy, and Bess is teaching the little bears how to behave better than we can. If this reformation goes on as it has begun, I shall soon feel like Dr. Blimber with his model young gentlemen," said Professor, laughing, as he saw Tommy not only remove his own hat, but knock off Ned's also, as they entered the hall where the Princess was taking a ride on the rocking-horse, attended by Rob and Teddy astride of chairs, and playing gallant knights to the best of their ability.

"You will never be a Blimber, Fritz, you couldn't do it if you tried; and our boys will never submit to the forcing process of that famous hot-bed. No fear that they will be too elegant: American boys like liberty too well. But good manners they cannot fail to have, if we give them the kindly spirit that shines through the simplest demeanor, making it courteous and cordial, like yours, my dear old boy."

"Tut! tut! we will not compliment; for if I begin you will run away, and I have a wish to enjoy this happy half hour to the end;" yet Mr. Bhaer looked pleased with the compliment, for it was true, and Mrs. Jo felt that she had received the best her husband could give her, by saying that he found his truest rest and happiness in her society.

"To return to the children: I have just had another proof of Goldilocks' good influence," said Mrs. Jo, drawing her chair nearer the sofa, where the Professor lay resting after a long day's work in his various gardens. "Nan hates sewing, but for love of Bess has been toiling half the afternoon over a remarkable bag in which to present a dozen of our love-apples to her idol when she goes. I praised her for it, and she said, in her quick way, 'I like to sew for other people; it is stupid sewing for myself.' I took the hint, and shall give her some little shirts and aprons for Mrs. Carney's children. She is so generous, she will sew her fingers sore for them, and I shall not have to make a task of it."

"But needlework is not a fashionable accomplishment, my dear."

"Sorry for it. My girls shall learn all I can teach them about it, even if they give up the Latin, Algebra, and half-a-dozen ologies it is considered necessary for girls to muddle their poor brains over now-a-days. Amy means to make Bess an accomplished woman, but the dear's mite of a forefinger has little pricks on it already, and her mother has several specimens of needlework which she values more than the clay bird without a bill, that filled Laurie with such pride when Bess made it."

"I also have proof of the Princess's power," said Mrs. Bhaer, after he had watched Mrs. Jo sew on a button with an air of scorn for the whole system of fashionable education. "Jack is so unwilling to be classed with Stuffy and Ned, as distasteful to Bess, that he came to me a little while ago, and asked me to touch his warts with caustic. I have often proposed it, and he never would consent; but now he bore the smart manfully, and consoles his present discomfort by hopes of future favor, when he can show her fastidious ladyship a smooth hand."

Mrs. Bhaer laughed at the story, and just then Stuffy came in to ask if he might give Goldilocks some of the bonbons his mother had sent him.

"She is not allowed to eat sweeties; but if you like to give her the pretty box with the pink sugar-rose in it, she would like it very much," said Mrs. Jo, unwilling to spoil this unusual piece of self-denial, for the "fat boy" seldom offered to share his sugar-plums.

"Won't she eat it? I shouldn't like to make her sick," said Stuffy, eyeing the delicate sweetmeat lovingly, yet putting it into the box.

"Oh, no, she won't touch it, if I tell her it is to look at, not to eat. She will keep it for weeks, and never think of tasting it. Can you do as much?"

"I should hope so! I'm ever so much older than she is," cried Stuffy, indignantly.

"Well, suppose we try. Here, put your bonbons in this bag, and see how long you can keep them. Let me count two hearts, four red fishes, three barley-sugar horses, nine almonds, and a dozen chocolate drops. Do you agree to that?" asked sly Mrs. Jo, popping the sweeties into her little spool-bag.

"Yes," said Stuffy, with a sigh; and pocketing the forbidden fruit, he went away to give Bess the present, that won a smile from her, and permission to escort her round the garden.

"Poor Stuffy's heart has really got the better of his stomach at last, and his efforts will be much encouraged by the rewards Bess gives him," said Mrs. Jo.

"Happy is the man who can put temptation in his pocket and learn self-denial from so sweet a little teacher!" added Mr. Bhaer, as the children passed the window, Stuffy's fat face full of placid satisfaction, and Goldilocks surveying her sugar-rose with polite interest, though she would have preferred a real flower with a "pitty smell."

When her father came to take her home, a universal wail arose, and the parting gifts showered upon her increased her luggage to such an extent that Mr. Laurie proposed having out the big wagon to take it into town. Every one had given her something; and it was found difficult to pack white mice, cake, a parcel of shells, apples, a rabbit kicking violently in a bag, a large cabbage for his refreshment, a bottle of minnows, and a mammoth bouquet. The farewell scene was moving, for the Princess sat upon the hall-table, surrounded by her subjects. She kissed her cousins, and held out her hand to the other boys, who shook it gently with various soft speeches, for they were taught not to be ashamed of showing their emotions.

"Come again soon, little dear," whispered Dan, fastening his best green-and-gold beetle in her hat.

"Don't forget me, Princess, whatever you do," said the engaging Tommy, taking a last stroke of the pretty hair.

"I am coming to your house next week, and then I shall see you, Bess," added Nat, as if he found consolation in the thought.

"Do shake hands now," cried Jack, offering a smooth paw.

"Here are two nice new ones to remember us by," said Dick and Dolly, presenting fresh whistles, quite unconscious that seven old ones had been privately deposited in the kitchen-stove.

"My little precious! I shall work you a book-mark right away, and you must keep it always," said Nan, with a warm embrace.

But of all the farewells, poor Billy's was the most pathetic, for the thought that she was really going became so unbearable that he cast himself down before her, hugging her little blue boots and blubbering despairingly, "Don't go away! oh, don't!" Goldilocks was so touched by this burst of feeling, that she leaned over and lifting the poor lad's head, said, in her soft, little voice,

"Don't cry, poor Billy! I will tiss you and tum adain soon."

This promise consoled Billy, and he fell back beaming with pride at the unusual honor conferred upon him.

"Me too! me too!" clamored Dick and Dolly, feeling that their devotion deserved some return. The others looked as if they would like to join in the cry; and something in the kind, merry faces about her moved the Princess to stretch out her arms and say, with reckless condescension,

"I will tiss evvybody!"

Like a swarm of bees about a very sweet flower, the affectionate lads surrounded their pretty playmate, and kissed her till she looked like a little rose, not roughly, but so enthusiastically that nothing but the crown of her hat was visible for a moment. Then her father rescued her, and she drove away still smiling and waving her hands, while the boys sat on the fence screaming like a flock of guinea-fowls, "Come back! come back!" till she was out of sight.

They all missed her, and each dimly felt that he was better for having known a creature so lovely, delicate, and sweet; for little Bess appealed to the chivalrous instinct in them as something to love, admire, and protect with a tender sort of reverence. Many a man remembers some pretty child who has made a place in his heart and kept her memory alive by the simple magic of her innocence; these little men were just learning to feel this power, and to love it for its gentle influence, not ashamed to let the small hand lead them, nor to own their loyalty to womankind, even in the bud.

Lesson 117

1. Read the title of Chapter 14. Damon and Pythias were two Greeks famous for their loyal friendship, a little like David and Jonathan in the Bible. What do you think might happen in this chapter?

2. Read the first part of chapter 14.

3. What is your answer to the mysterious disappearance of Tommy's money?

4. What point of view is *Little Men* told from? (Answers)

Chapter XIV. Damon and Pythias

Mrs. Bhaer was right; peace was only a temporary lull, a storm was brewing, and two days after Bess left, a moral earthquake shook Plumfield to its centre.

Tommy's hens were at the bottom of the trouble, for if they had not persisted in laying so many eggs, he could not have sold them and made such sums. Money is the root of all evil, and yet it is such a useful root that we cannot get on without it any more than we can without potatoes. Tommy certainly could not, for he spent his income so recklessly, that Mr. Bhaer was obliged to insist on a savings-bank, and presented him with a private one an imposing tin edifice, with the name over the door, and a tall chimney, down which the pennies were to go, there to rattle temptingly till leave was given to open a sort of trap-door in the floor.

The house increased in weight so rapidly, that Tommy soon became satisfied with his investment, and planned to buy unheard-of treasures with his capital. He kept account of the sums deposited, and was promised that he might break the bank as soon as he had five dollars, on condition that he spent the money wisely. Only one dollar was needed, and the day Mrs. Jo paid him for four dozen eggs, he was so delighted, that he raced off to the barn to display the bright quarters to Nat, who was also laying by money for the long-desired violin.

"I wish I had 'em to put with my three dollars, then I'd soon get enough to buy my fiddle," he said, looking wistfully at the money.

"P'raps I'll lend you some. I haven't decided yet what I'll do with mine," said Tommy, tossing up his quarters and catching them as they fell.

"Hi! boys! come down to the brook and see what a jolly great snake Dan's got!" called a voice from behind the barn.

"Come on," said Tommy; and, laying his money inside the old winnowing machine, away he ran, followed by Nat.

The snake was very interesting, and then a long chase after a lame crow, and its capture, so absorbed Tommy's mind and time, that he never thought of his money till he was safely in bed that night.

"Never mind, no one but Nat knows where it is," said the easy-going lad, and fell asleep untroubled by any anxiety about his property.

Next morning, just as the boys assembled for school, Tommy rushed into the room breathlessly, demanding,

"I say, who has got my dollar?"

"What are you talking about?" asked Franz.

Tommy explained, and Nat corroborated his statement.

Every one else declared they knew nothing about it, and began to look suspiciously at Nat, who got more and more alarmed and confused with each denial.

"Somebody must have taken it," said Franz, as Tommy shook his fist at the whole party, and wrathfully declared that-

"By thunder turtles! if I get hold of the thief, I'll give him what he won't forget in a hurry."

"Keep cool, Tom; we shall find him out; thieves always come to grief," said Dan, as one who knew something of the matter.

"May be some tramp slept in the barn and took it," suggested Ned.

"No, Silas don't allow that; besides, a tramp wouldn't go looking in that old machine for money," said Emil, with scorn.

"Wasn't it Silas himself?" said Jack.

"Well, I like that! Old Si is as honest as daylight. You wouldn't catch him touching a penny of ours," said Tommy, handsomely defending his chief admirer from suspicion.

"Whoever it was had better tell, and not wait to be found out," said Demi, looking as if an awful misfortune had befallen the family.

"I know you think it's me," broke out Nat, red and excited.

"You are the only one who knew where it was," said Franz.

"I can't help it I didn't take it. I tell you I didn't I didn't!" cried Nat, in a desperate sort of way.

"Gently, gently, my son! What is all this noise about?" and Mr. Bhaer walked in among them.

Tommy repeated the story of his loss, and, as he listened, Mr. Bhaer's face grew graver and graver; for, with all their faults and follies, the lads till now had been honest.

"Take your seats," he said; and, when all were in their places, he added slowly, as his eye went from face to face with a grieved look, that was harder to bear than a storm of words,

"Now, boys, I shall ask each one of you a single question, and I want an honest answer. I am not going to try to frighten, bribe, or surprise the truth out of you, for every one of you have got a conscience, and know what it is for. Now is the time to undo the wrong done to Tommy, and set yourselves right before us all. I can forgive the yielding to sudden temptation much easier than I can deceit. Don't add a lie to the theft, but confess frankly, and we will all try to help you make us forget and forgive."

He paused a moment, and one might have heard a pin drop, the room was so still; then slowly and impressively he put the question to each one, receiving the same answer in varying tones from all. Every face was flushed and excited, so that Mr. Bhaer could not take color as a witness, and some of the little boys were so frightened that they stammered over the two short words as if guilty, though it was evident that they could not be. When he came to Nat, his voice softened, for the poor lad looked so wretched, Mr. Bhaer felt for him. He believed him to be the culprit, and hoped to save the boy from another lie, by winning him to tell the truth without fear.

"Now, my son, give me an honest answer. Did you take the money?"

"No, sir!" and Nat looked up at him imploringly.

As the words fell from his trembling lips, somebody hissed.

"Stop that!" cried Mr. Bhaer, with a sharp rap on his desk, as he looked sternly toward the corner whence the sound came.

Ned, Jack, and Emil sat there, and the first two looked ashamed of themselves, but Emil called out,

"It wasn't me, uncle! I'd be ashamed to hit a fellow when he is down."

"Good for you!" cried Tommy, who was in a sad state of affliction at the trouble his unlucky dollar had made.

"Silence!" commanded Mr. Bhaer; and when it came, he said soberly,

"I am very sorry, Nat, but evidences are against you, and your old fault makes us more ready to doubt you than we should be if we could trust you as we do some of the boys, who never fib. But mind, my child, I do not charge you with this theft; I shall not punish you for it till I am perfectly sure, nor ask any thing more about it. I shall leave it for you to settle with your own conscience. If you are guilty, come to me at any hour of the day or night and confess it, and I will forgive and help you to amend. If you are innocent, the truth will appear sooner or later, and the instant it does, I will be the first to beg your pardon for doubting you, and will so gladly do my best to clear your character before us all."

"I didn't! I didn't!" sobbed Nat, with his head down upon his arms, for he could not bear the look of distrust and dislike which he read in the many eyes fixed on him.

"I hope not." Mr. Bhaer paused a minute, as if to give the culprit, whoever he might be, one more chance. Nobody spoke, however, and only sniffs of sympathy from some of the little fellows broke the silence. Mr. Bhaer shook his head, and added, regretfully,

"There is nothing more to be done, then, and I have but one thing to say: I shall not speak of this again, and I wish you all to follow my example. I cannot expect you to feel as kindly toward any one whom you suspect as before this happened, but I do expect and desire that you will not torment the suspected person in any way, he will have a hard enough time without that. Now go to your lessons."

"Father Bhaer let Nat off too easy," muttered Ned to Emil, as they got out their books.

"Hold your tongue," growled Emil, who felt that this event was a blot upon the family honor.

Many of the boys agreed with Ned, but Mr. Bhaer was right, nevertheless; and Nat would have been wiser to confess on the spot and have the trouble over, for even the hardest whipping he ever received from his father was far easier to bear than the cold looks, the avoidance, and general suspicion that met him on all sides. If ever a boy was sent to Coventry and kept there, it was poor Nat; and he suffered a week of slow torture, though not a hand was raised against him, and hardly a word said.

That was the worst of it; if they would only have talked it out, or even have thrashed him all round, he could have stood it better than the silent distrust that made very face so terrible to meet. Even Mrs. Bhaer's showed traces of it, though her manner was nearly as kind as ever; but the sorrowful anxious look in Father Bhaer's eyes cut Nat to the heart, for he loved his teacher dearly, and knew that he had disappointed all his hopes by this double sin.

Only one person in the house entirely believed in him, and stood up for him stoutly against all the rest. This was Daisy. She could not explain why she trusted him against all appearances, she only felt that she could not doubt him, and her warm sympathy made her strong to take his part. She would not hear a word against him from any one, and actually slapped her beloved Demi when he tried to convince her that it must have been Nat, because no one else knew where the money was.

"Maybe the hens ate it; they are greedy old things," she said; and when Demi laughed, she lost her temper, slapped the amazed boy, and then burst out crying and ran away, still declaring, "He didn't! he didn't! he didn't!"

Neither aunt nor uncle tried to shake the child's faith in her friend, but only hoped her innocent instinct might prove sure, and loved her all the better for it. Nat often said, after it was over, that he couldn't have stood it, if it had not been for Daisy. When the others shunned him, she clung to him closer than ever, and turned her back on the rest. She did not sit on the stairs now when he solaced himself with the old fiddle, but went in and sat beside him, listening with a face so full of confidence and affection, that Nat forgot disgrace for a time, and was happy. She asked him to help her with her lessons, she cooked him marvelous messes in her kitchen, which he ate manfully, no matter what they were, for gratitude gave a sweet flavor to the most distasteful. She proposed impossible games of cricket and ball, when she found that he shrank from joining the other boys. She put little nosegays from her garden on his desk, and tried in every way to show that she was not a fair-weather friend, but faithful through evil as well as good repute. Nan soon followed her example, in kindness at least; curbed her sharp tongue, and kept her scornful little nose from any demonstration of doubt or dislike, which was good of Madame Giddy-gaddy, for she firmly believed that Nat took the money.

Most of the boys let him severely alone, but Dan, though he said he despised him for being a coward, watched over him with a grim sort of protection, and promptly cuffed any lad who dared to molest his mate or make him afraid. His idea of friendship was as high as Daisy's, and, in his own rough way, he lived up to it as loyally.

Sitting by the brook one afternoon, absorbed in the study of the domestic habits of water-spiders, he overheard a bit of conversation on the other side of the wall. Ned, who was intensely inquisitive, had been on tenterhooks to know certainly who was the culprit; for of late one or two of the boys had begun to think that they were wrong, Nat was so steadfast in his denials, and so meek in his endurance of their neglect. This doubt had teased Ned past bearing, and he had several times privately beset Nat with questions, regardless of Mr. Bhaer's express command. Finding Nat reading alone on the shady side of the wall, Ned could not resist stopping for a nibble at the forbidden subject. He had worried Nat for some ten minutes before Dan arrived, and the first words the spider-student heard were these, in Nat's patient, pleading voice,

"Don't, Ned! oh, don't! I can't tell you because I don't know, and it's mean of you to keep nagging at me on the sly, when Father Bhaer told you not to plague me. You wouldn't dare to if Dan was round."

"I ain't afraid of Dan; he's nothing but an old bully. Don't believe but what he took Tom's money, and you know it, and won't tell. Come, now!"

"He didn't, but, if he did, I would stand up for him, he has always been so good to me," said Nat, so earnestly that Dan forgot his spiders, and rose quickly to thank him, but Ned's next words arrested him.

"I know Dan did it, and gave the money to you. Shouldn't wonder if he got his living picking pockets before he came here, for nobody knows any thing about him but you," said Ned, not believing his own words, but hoping to get the truth out of Nat by making him angry.

He succeeded in a part of his ungenerous wish, for Nat cried out, fiercely,

"If you say that again I'll go and tell Mr. Bhaer all about it. I don't want to tell tales, but, by George! I will, if you don't let Dan alone."

"Then you'll be a sneak, as well as a liar and a thief," began Ned, with a jeer, for Nat had borne insult to himself so meekly, the other did not believe he would dare to face the master just to stand up for Dan.

What he might have added I cannot tell, for the words were hardly out of his mouth when a long arm from behind took him by the collar, and, jerking him over the wall in a most promiscuous way, landed him with a splash in the middle of the brook.

"Say that again and I'll duck you till you can't see!" cried Dan, looking like a modern Colossus of Rhodes as he stood, with a foot on either side of the narrow stream, glaring down at the discomfited youth in the water.

"I was only in fun," said Ned.

"You are a sneak yourself to badger Nat round the corner. Let me catch you at it again, and I'll souse you in the river next time. Get up, and clear out!" thundered Dan, in a rage.

Ned fled, dripping, and his impromptu sitz-bath evidently did him good, for he was very respectful to both the boys after that, and seemed to have left his curiosity in the brook. As he vanished Dan jumped over the wall, and found Nat lying, as if quite worn out and bowed down with his troubles.

"He won't pester you again, I guess. If he does, just tell me, and I'll see to him," said Dan, trying to cool down.

"I don't mind what he says about me so much, I've got used to it," answered Nat sadly; "but I hate to have him pitch into you."

"How do you know he isn't right?" asked Dan, turning his face away.

"What, about the money?" cried Nat, looking up with a startled air.

"Yes."

"But I don't believe it! You don't care for money; all you want is your old bugs and things," and Nat laughed, incredulously.

"I want a butterfly net as much as you want a fiddle; why shouldn't I steal the money for it as much as you?" said Dan, still turning away, and busily punching holes in the turf with his stick.

"I don't think you would. You like to fight and knock folks round sometimes, but you don't lie, and I don't believe you'd steal," and Nat shook his head decidedly.

"I've done both. I used to fib like fury; it's too much trouble now; and I stole things to eat out of gardens when I ran away from Page, so you see I am a bad lot," said Dan, speaking in the rough, reckless way which he had been learning to drop lately.

"O Dan! don't say it's you! I'd rather have it any of the other boys," cried Nat, in such a distressed tone that Dan looked pleased, and showed that he did, by turning round with a queer expression in his face, though he only answered,

"I won't say any thing about it. But don't you fret, and we'll pull through somehow, see if we don't."

Something in his face and manner gave Nat a new idea; and he said, pressing his hands together, in the eagerness of his appeal,

"I think you know who did it. If you do, beg him to tell, Dan. It's so hard to have 'em all hate me for nothing. I don't think I can bear it much longer. If I had any place to go to, I'd run away, though I love Plumfield dearly; but I'm not brave and big like you, so I must stay and wait till some one shows them that I haven't lied."

As he spoke, Nat looked so broken and despairing, that Dan could not bear it, and, muttered huskily,

"You won't wait long," and he walked rapidly away, and was seen no more for hours.

"What is the matter with Dan?" asked the boys of one another several times during the Sunday that followed a week which seemed as if it would never end. Dan was often moody, but that day he was so sober and silent that no one could get any thing out of him. When they walked he strayed away from the rest, and came home late. He took no part in the evening conversation, but sat in the shadow, so busy with his own thoughts that he scarcely seemed to hear what was going on. When Mrs. Jo showed him an unusually good report in the Conscience Book, he looked at it without a smile, and said, wistfully,

"You think I am getting on, don't you?"

"Excellently, Dan! and I am so pleased, because I always thought you only needed a little help to make you a boy to be proud of."

He looked up at her with a strange expression in his black eyes an expression of mingled pride and love and sorrow which she could not understand then but remembered afterward.

"I'm afraid you'll be disappointed, but I do try," he said, shutting the book with no sign of pleasure in the page that he usually liked so much to read over and talk about.

"Are you sick, dear?" asked Mrs. Jo, with her hand on his shoulder.

"My foot aches a little; I guess I'll go to bed. Good-night, mother," he added, and held the hand against his cheek a minute, then went away looking as if he had said good-bye to something dear.

"Poor Dan! he takes Nat's disgrace to heart sadly. He is a strange boy; I wonder if I ever shall understand him thoroughly?" said Mrs. Jo to herself, as she thought over Dan's late improvement with real satisfaction, yet felt that there was more in the lad than she had at first suspected.

One of things which cut Nat most deeply was an act of Tommy's, for after his loss Tommy had said to him, kindly, but firmly,

"I don't wish to hurt you, Nat, but you see I can't afford to lose my money, so I guess we won't be partners any longer;" and with that Tommy rubbed out the sign, "T. Bangs & Co."

Nat had been very proud of the "Co.," and had hunted eggs industriously, kept his accounts all straight, and had added a good sum to his income from the sale of his share of stock in trade.

"O Tom! must you?" he said, feeling that his good name was gone for ever in the business world if this was done.

"I must," returned Tommy, firmly. "Emil says that when one man 'bezzles (believe that's the word it means to take money and cut away with it) the property of a firm, the other one sues him, or pitches into him somehow, and won't have any thing more to do with him. Now you have 'bezzled my property; I shan't sue you, and I shan't pitch into you, but I must dissolve the partnership, because I can't trust you, and I don't wish to fail."

"I can't make you believe me, and you won't take my money, though I'd be thankful to give all my dollars if you'd only say you don't think I took your money. Do let me hunt for you, I won't ask any wages, but do it for nothing. I know all the places, and I like it," pleaded Nat.

But Tommy shook his head, and his jolly round face looked suspicious and hard as he said, shortly, "Can't do it; wish you didn't know the places. Mind you don't go hunting on the sly, and speculate in my eggs."

Poor Nat was so hurt that he could not get over it. He felt that he had lost not only his partner and patron, but that he was bankrupt in honor, and an outlaw from the business community. No one trusted his word, written or spoken, in spite of his efforts to redeem the past falsehood; the sign was down, the firm broken up, and he a ruined man. The barn, which was the boys' Wall Street, knew him no more. Cockletop and her sisters cackled for him in vain, and really seemed to take his misfortune to heart, for eggs were fewer, and some of the biddies retired in disgust to new nests, which Tommy could not find.

Lesson 118

1. What do you think is going to happen?

2. Finish reading chapter 14.

3. What are you thinking?

4. Read a little more about Damon and Pythias. The story goes that they were best friends. Pythias said something against the king and was sentenced to be executed. He asked to go home to explain to his family and to say goodbye. Damon offered to stay in his place and to be killed in his place if he didn't return, so the king let Pythias go. Pythias did return to keep his friend from being killed as Damon trusted he would. The king was so impressed at their faithful, trusting friendship, that he didn't kill Pythias and kept them on as advisors.

5. Why do you think Louisa Mae Alcott chose this title for Chapter 14? Write an answer in complete sentences. It should start like this, "I think Louisa Mae Alcott chose 'Damon and Pythias' as the title for the chapter because…" Tell why and give an example.

Chapter XIV. continued (Titled: Damon and Pythias)

"They trust me," said Nat, when he heard of it; and though the boys shouted at the idea, Nat found comfort in it, for when one is down in the world, the confidence of even a speckled hen is most consoling.

Tommy took no new partner, however, for distrust had entered in, and poisoned the peace of his once confiding soul. Ned offered to join him, but he declined, saying, with a sense of justice that did him honor,

"It might turn out that Nat didn't take my money, and then we could be partners again. I don't think it will happen, but I will give him a chance, and keep the place open a little longer."

Billy was the only person whom Bangs felt he could trust in his shop, and Billy was trained to hunt eggs, and hand them over unbroken, being quite satisfied with an apple or a sugar-plum for wages. The morning after Dan's gloomy Sunday, Billy said to his employer, as he displayed the results of a long hunt,

"Only two."

"It gets worse and worse; I never saw such provoking old hens," growled Tommy, thinking of the days when he often had six to rejoice over. "Well, put 'em in my hat and give me a new bit of chalk; I must mark 'em up, any way."

Billy mounted a peck-measure, and looked into the top of the machine, where Tommy kept his writing materials.

"There's lots of money in here," said Billy.

"No, there isn't. Catch me leaving my cash round again," returned Tommy.

"I see 'em one, four, eight, two dollars," persisted Billy, who had not yet mastered the figures correctly.

"What a jack you are!" and Tommy hopped up to get the chalk for himself, but nearly tumbled down again, for there actually were four bright quarters in a row, with a bit of paper on them directed to "Tom Bangs," that there might be no mistake.

"Thunder turtles!" cried Tommy, and seizing them he dashed into the house, bawling wildly, "It's all right! Got my money! Where's Nat?"

He was soon found, and his surprise and pleasure were so genuine that few doubted his word when he now denied all knowledge of the money.

"How could I put it back when I didn't take it? Do believe me now, and be good to me again," he said, so imploringly, that Emil slapped him on the back, and declared he would for one.

"So will I, and I'm jolly glad it's not you. But who the dickens is it?" said Tommy, after shaking hands heartily with Nat.

"Never mind, as long as it's found," said Dan with his eyes fixed on Nat's happy face.

"Well, I like that! I'm not going to have my things hooked, and then brought back like the juggling man's tricks," cried Tommy, looking at his money as if he suspected witchcraft.

"We'll find him out somehow, though he was sly enough to print this so his writing wouldn't be known," said Franz, examining the paper.

"Demi prints tip-top," put in Rob, who had not a very clear idea what the fuss was all about.

"You can't make me believe it's him, not if you talk till you are blue," said Tommy, and the others hooted at the mere idea; for the little deacon, as they called him, was above suspicion.

Nat felt the difference in the way they spoke of Demi and himself, and would have given all he had or ever hoped to have to be so trusted; for he had learned how easy it is to lose the confidence of others, how very, very hard to win it back, and truth became to him a precious thing since he had suffered from neglecting it.

Mr. Bhaer was very glad one step had been taken in the right direction, and waited hopefully for yet further revelations. They came sooner than he expected, and in a way that surprised and grieved him very much. As they sat at supper that night, a square parcel was handed to Mrs. Bhaer from Mrs. Bates, a neighbor. A note accompanied the parcel, and, while Mr. Bhaer read it, Demi pulled off the wrapper, exclaiming, as he saw its contents,

"Why, it's the book Uncle Teddy gave Dan!"

"The devil!" broke from Dan, for he had not yet quite cured himself of swearing, though he tried very hard.

Mr. Bhaer looked up quickly at the sound. Dan tried to meet his eyes, but could not; his own fell, and he sat biting his lips, getting redder and redder till he was the picture of shame.

"What is it?" asked Mrs. Bhaer, anxiously.

"I should have preferred to talk about this in private, but Demi has spoilt that plan, so I may as well have it out now," said Mr. Bhaer, looking a little stern, as he always did when any meanness or deceit came up for judgment.

"The note is from Mrs. Bates, and she says that her boy Jimmy told her he bought this book of Dan last Saturday. She saw that it was worth much more than a dollar, and thinking there was some mistake, has sent it to me. Did you sell it, Dan?"

"Yes, sir," was the slow answer.

"Why?"

"Wanted money."

"For what?"

"To pay somebody."

"To whom did you owe it?"

"Tommy."

"Never borrowed a cent of me in his life," cried Tommy, looked scared, for he guessed what was coming now, and felt that on the whole he would have preferred witchcraft, for he admired Dan immensely.

"Perhaps he took it," cried Ned, who owed Dan a grudge for the ducking, and, being a mortal boy, liked to pay it off.

"O Dan!" cried Nat, clasping his hands, regardless of the bread and butter in them.

"It is a hard thing to do, but I must have this settled, for I cannot have you watching each other like detectives, and the whole school disturbed in this way. did you put that dollar in the barn this morning?" asked Mr. Bhaer.

Dan looked him straight in the face, and answered steadily, "Yes, I did."

A murmur went round the table, Tommy dropped his mug with a crash; Daisy cried out, "I knew it wasn't Nat;" Nan began to cry, and Mrs. Jo left the room, looking so disappointed, sorry, and ashamed that Dan could not bear it. He hid his face in his hands a moment, then threw up his head, squared his shoulders as if settling some load upon them, and said, with the dogged look, and half-resolute, half-reckless tone he had used when he first came

"I did it; now you may do what you like to me, but I won't say another word about it."

"Not even that you are sorry?" asked Mr. Bhaer, troubled by the change in him.

"I ain't sorry."

"I'll forgive him without asking," said Tommy, feeling that it was harder somehow to see brave Dan disgraced than timid Nat.

"Don't want to be forgiven," returned Dan, gruffly.

"Perhaps you will when you have thought about it quietly by yourself, I won't tell you now how surprised and disappointed I am, but by and by I will come up and talk to you in your room."

"Won't make any difference," said Dan, trying to speak defiantly, but failing as he looked at Mr. Bhaer's sorrowful face; and, taking his words for a dismissal, Dan left the room as if he found it impossible to stay.

It would have done him good if he had stayed; for the boys talked the matter over with such sincere regret, and pity, and wonder, it might have touched and won him to ask pardon. No one was glad to find that it was he, not even Nat; for, spite of all his faults, and they were many, every one liked Dan now, because under his rough exterior lay some of the manly virtues which we most admire and love. Mrs. Jo had been the chief prop, as well as cultivator, of Dan; and she took it sadly to heart that her last and most interesting boy had turned out so ill. The theft was bad, but the lying about it, and allowing another to suffer so much from an unjust suspicion was worse; and most discouraging of all was the attempt to restore the money in an underhand way, for it showed not only a want of courage, but a power of deceit that boded ill for the future. Still more trying was his steady refusal to talk of the matter, to ask pardon, or express any remorse. Days passed; and he went about his lessons and his work, silent, grim, and unrepentant. As if taking warning by their treatment of Nat, he asked no sympathy of any one, rejected the advances of the boys, and spent his leisure hours roaming about the fields and woods, trying to find playmates in the birds and beasts, and succeeding better than most boys would have done, because he knew and loved them so well.

"If this goes on much longer, I'm afraid he will run away again, for he is too young to stand a life like this," said Mr. Bhaer, quite dejected at the failure of all his efforts.

"A little while ago I should have been quite sure that nothing would tempt him away, but now I am ready of any thing, he is so changed," answered poor Mrs. Jo, who mourned over her boy and could not be comforted, because he shunned her more than any one else, and only looked at her with the half-fierce, half-imploring eyes of a wild animal caught in a trap, when she tried to talk to him alone.

Nat followed him about like a shadow, and Dan did not repulse him as rudely as he did others, but said, in his blunt way, "You are all right; don't worry about me. I can stand it better than you did."

"But I don't like to have you all alone," Nat would say, sorrowfully.

"I like it;" and Dan would tramp away, stifling a sigh sometimes, for he was lonely.

Passing through the birch grove one day, he came up on several of the boys, who were amusing themselves by climbing up the trees and swinging down again, as they slender elastic stems bent till their tops touched the ground. Dan paused a minute to watch the fun, without offering to join in it, and as he stood there Jack took his turn. He had unfortunately chosen too large a tree; for when he swung off, it only bent a little way, and left him hanging at a dangerous height.

"Go back; you can't do it!" called Ned from below.

Jack tried, but the twigs slipped from his hands, and he could not get his legs round the trunk. He kicked, and squirmed, and clutched in vain, then gave it up, and hung breathless, saying helplessly,

"Catch me! help me! I must drop!"

"You'll be killed if you do," cried Ned, frightened out of his wits.

"Hold on!" shouted Dan; and up the tree he went, crashing his way along till he nearly reached Jack, whose face looked up at him, full of fear and hope.

"You'll both come down," said Ned, dancing with excitement on the slope underneath, while Nat held out his arms, in the wild hope of breaking the fall.

"That's what I want; stand from under," answered Dan, coolly; and, as he spoke, his added weight bent the tree many feet nearer the earth.

Jack dropped safely; but the birch, lightened of half its load, flew up again so suddenly, that Dan, in the act of swinging round to drop feet foremost, lost his hold and fell heavily.

"I'm not hurt, all right in a minute," he said, sitting up, a little pale and dizzy, as the boys gathered round him, full of admiration and alarm.

"You're a trump, Dan, and I'm ever so much obliged to you," cried Jack, gratefully.

"It wasn't any thing," muttered Dan, rising slowly.

"I say it was, and I'll shake hands with you, though you are," Ned checked the unlucky word on his tongue, and held out his hand, feeling that it was a handsome thing on his part.

"But I won't shake hands with a sneak;" and Dan turned his back with a look of scorn, that caused Ned to remember the brook, and retire with undignified haste.

"Come home, old chap; I'll give you a lift;" and Nat walked away with him leaving the others to talk over the feat together, to wonder when Dan would "come round," and to wish one and all that Tommy's "confounded money had been in Jericho before it made such a fuss."

When Mr. Bhaer came into school next morning, he looked so happy, that the boys wondered what had happened to him, and really thought he had lost his mind when they saw him go straight to Dan, and, taking him by both hands, say all in one breath, as he shook them heartily,

"I know all about it, and I beg your pardon. It was like you to do it, and I love you for it, though it's never right to tell lies, even for a friend."

"What is it?" cried Nat, for Dan said not a word, only lifted up his head, as if a weight of some sort had fallen off his back.

"Dan did not take Tommy's money;" and Mr. Bhaer quite shouted it, he was so glad.

"Who did?" cried the boys in a chorus.

Mr. Bhaer pointed to one empty seat, and every eye followed his finger, yet no one spoke for a minute, they were so surprised.

"Jack went home early this morning, but he left this behind him;" and in the silence Mr. Bhaer read the note which he had found tied to his door-handle when he rose.

> I took Tommy's dollar. I was peeking in through a crack and saw him put it there. I was afraid to tell before, though I wanted to. I didn't care so much about Nat, but Dan is a trump, and I can't stand it any longer. I never spent the money; it's under the carpet in my room, right behind the washstand. I'm awful sorry. I am going home, and don't think I shall ever come back, so Dan may have my things.
>
> JACK

It was not an elegant confession, being badly written, much blotted, and very short; but it was a precious paper to Dan; and, when Mr. Bhaer paused, the boy went to him, saying, in a rather broken voice, but with clear eyes, and the frank, respectful manner they had tried to teach him,

"I'll say I'm sorry now, and ask you to forgive me, sir."

"It was a kind lie, Dan, and I can't help forgiving it; but you see it did no good," said Mr. Bhaer, with a hand on either shoulder, and a face full of relief and affection.

"It kept the boys from plaguing Nat. That's what I did it for. It made him right down miserable. I didn't care so much," explained Dan, as if glad to speak out after his hard silence.

"How could you do it? You are always so kind to me," faltered Nat, feeling a strong desire to hug his friend and cry. Two girlish performances, which would have scandalized Dan to the last degree.

"It's all right now, old fellow, so don't be a fool," he said, swallowing the lump in his throat, and laughing out as he had not done for weeks. "Does Mrs. Bhaer know?" he asked, eagerly.

"Yes; and she is so happy I don't know what she will do to you," began Mr. Bhaer, but got no farther, for here the boys came crowding about Dan in a tumult of pleasure and curiosity; but before he had answered more than a dozen questions, a voice cried out,

"Three cheers for Dan!" and there was Mrs. Jo in the doorway waving her dish-towel, and looking as if she wanted to dance a jig for joy, as she used to do when a girl.

"Now then," cried Mr. Bhaer, and led off a rousing hurrah, which startled Asia in the kitchen, and made old Mr. Roberts shake his head as he drove by, saying,

"Schools are not what they were when I was young!"

Dan stood it pretty well for a minute, but the sight of Mrs. Jo's delight upset him, and he suddenly bolted across the hall into the parlor, whither she instantly followed, and neither were seen for half an hour.

Mr. Bhaer found it very difficult to calm his excited flock; and, seeing that lessons were an impossibility for a time, he caught their attention by telling them the fine old story of the friends whose fidelity to one another has made their names immortal. The lads listened and remembered, for just then their hearts were touched by the loyalty of a humbler pair of friends. The lie was wrong, but the love that prompted it and the courage that bore in silence the disgrace which belonged to another, made Dan a hero in their eyes. Honesty and honor had a new meaning now; a good name was more precious than gold; for once lost money could not buy it back; and faith in one another made life smooth and happy as nothing else could do.

Tommy proudly restored the name of the firm; Nat was devoted to Dan; and all the boys tried to atone to both for former suspicion and neglect. Mrs. Jo rejoiced over her flock, and Mr. Bhaer was never tired of telling the story of his young Damon and Pythias.

Lesson 119

1. Read the title of Chapter 15. What do you picture?
2. Read the first part of chapter 15.
3. Do you have a memory of a willow tree? Tell or write about it.

Chapter XV. In the Willow

The old tree saw and heard a good many little scenes and confidences that summer, because it became the favorite retreat of all the children, and the willow seemed to enjoy it, for a pleasant welcome always met them, and the quiet hours spent in its arms did them all good. It had a great deal of company one Saturday afternoon, and some little bird reported what went on there.

First came Nan and Daisy with their small tubs and bits of soap, for now and then they were seized with a tidy fit, and washed up all their dolls' clothes in the brook. Asia would not have them "slopping round" in her kitchen, and the bath-room was forbidden since Nan forgot to turn off the water till it overflowed and came gently dripping down through the ceiling. Daisy went systematically to work, washing first the white and then the colored things, rinsing them nicely, and hanging them to dry on a cord fastened from one barberry-bush to another, and pinning them up with a set of tiny clothes-pins Ned had turned for her. But Nan put all her little things to soak in the same tub, and then forgot them while she collected thistledown to stuff a pillow for Semiramis, Queen of Babylon, as one doll was named. This took some time, and when Mrs. Giddy-gaddy came to take out her clothes, deep green stains appeared on every thing, for she had forgotten the green silk lining of a certain cape, and its color had soaked nicely into the pink and blue gowns, the little chemises, and even the best ruffled petticoat.

"Oh me! what a mess!" sighed Nan.

"Lay them on the grass to bleach," said Daisy, with an air of experience.

"So I will, and we can sit up in the nest and watch that they don't blow away."

The Queen of Babylon's wardrobe was spread forth upon the bank, and, turning up their tubs to dry, the little washerwomen climbed into the nest, and fell to talking, as ladies are apt to do in the pauses of domestic labor.

"I'm going to have a feather-bed to go with my new pillow," said Mrs. Giddy-gaddy, as she transferred the thistledown from her pocket to her handkerchief, losing about half in the process.

"I wouldn't; Aunt Jo says feather-beds aren't healthy. I never let my children sleep on any thing but a mattress," returned Mrs. Shakespeare Smith, decidedly.

"I don't care; my children are so strong they often sleep on the floor, and don't mind it," (which was quite true). "I can't afford nine mattresses, and I like to make beds myself."

"Won't Tommy charge for the feathers?"

"May be he will, but I shan't pay him, and he won't care," returned Mrs. G., taking a base advantage of the well-known good nature of T. Bangs.

"I think the pink will fade out of that dress sooner than the green mark will," observed Mrs. S., looking down from her perch, and changing the subject, for she and her gossip differed on many points, and Mrs. Smith was a discreet lady.

"Never mind; I'm tired of dolls, and I guess I shall put them all away and attend to my farm; I like it rather better than playing house," said Mrs. G., unconsciously expressing the desire of many older ladies, who cannot dispose of their families so easily however.

"But you mustn't leave them; they will die without their mother," cried the tender Mrs. Smith.

"Let 'em die then; I'm tired of fussing over babies, and I'm going to play with the boys; they need me to see to 'em," returned the strong-minded lady.

Daisy knew nothing about women's rights; she quietly took all she wanted, and no one denied her claim, because she did not undertake what she could not carry out, but unconsciously used the all-powerful right of her own influence to win from others any privilege for which she had proved her fitness. Nan attempted all sorts of things, undaunted by direful failures, and clamored fiercely to be allowed to do every thing that the boys did. They laughed at her, hustled her out of the way, and protested against her meddling with their affairs. But she would not be quenched and she would be heard, for her will was strong, and she had the spirit of a rampant reformer. Mrs. Bhaer sympathized with her, but tired to curb her frantic desire for entire liberty, showing her that she must wait a little, learn self-control, and be ready to use her freedom before she asked for it. Nan had meek moments when she agreed to this, and the influences at work upon her were gradually taking effect. She no longer declared that she would be engine-driver or a blacksmith, but turned her mind to farming, and found in it a vent for the energy bottled up in her active little body. It did not quite satisfy her, however; for her sage and sweet marjoram were dumb things, and could not thank her for her care. She wanted something human to love, work for, and protect, and was never happier than when the little boys brought their cut fingers, bumped heads, or bruised joints for her to "mend-up." Seeing this, Mrs. Jo proposed that she should learn how to do it nicely, and Nursey had an apt pupil in bandaging, plastering, and fomenting. The boys began to call her "Dr. Giddy-gaddy," and she liked it so well that Mrs. Jo one day said to the Professor

"Fritz, I see what we can do for that child. She wants something to live for even now, and will be one of the sharp, strong, discontented women if she does not have it. Don't let us snub her restless little nature, but do our best to give her the work she likes, and by and by persuade her father to let her study medicine. She will make a capital doctor, for she has courage, strong nerves, a tender heart, and an intense love and pity for the weak and suffering."

Mr. Bhaer smiled at first, but agreed to try, and gave Nan an herb-garden, teaching her the various healing properties of the plants she tended, and letting her try their virtues on the children in the little illnesses they had from time to time. She learned fast, remembered well, and showed a sense and interest most encouraging to her Professor, who did not shut his door in her face because she was a little woman.

She was thinking of this, as she sat in the willow that day, and when Daisy said in her gentle way, "I love to keep house, and mean to have a nice one for Demi when we grow up and live together."

Nan replied with decision, "Well, I haven't got any brother, and I don't want any house to fuss over. I shall have an office, with lots of bottles and drawers and pestle things in it, and I shall drive round in a horse and chaise and cure sick people. That will be such fun."

"Ugh! how can you bear the bad-smelling stuff and the nasty little powders and castor-oil and senna and hive syrup?" cried Daisy, with a shudder.

"I shan't have to take any, so I don't care. Besides, they make people well, and I like to cure folks. Didn't my sage-tea make Mother Bhaer's headache go away, and my hops stop Ned's toothache in five hours? So now!"

"Shall you put leeches on people, and cut off legs and pull out teeth?" asked Daisy, quaking at the thought.

"Yes, I shall do every thing; I don't care if the people are all smashed up, I shall mend them. My grandpa was a doctor, and I saw him sew a great cut in a man's cheek, and I held the sponge, and wasn't frightened a bit, and Grandpa said I was a brave girl."

"How could you? I'm sorry for sick people, and I like to nurse them, but it makes my legs shake so I have to run away. I'm not a brave girl," sighed Daisy.

"Well, you can be my nurse, and cuddle my patients when I have given them the physic and cut off their legs," said Nan, whose practice was evidently to be of the heroic kind.

"Ship ahoy! Where are you, Nan?" called a voice from below.

"Here we are."

"Ay, ay!" said the voice, and Emil appeared holding one hand in the other, with his face puckered up as if in pain.

"Oh, what's the matter?" cried Daisy, anxiously.

"A confounded splinter in my thumb. Can't get it out. Take a pick at it, will you, Nanny?"

"It's in very deep, and I haven't any needle," said Nan, examining a tarry thumb with interest.

"Take a pin," said Emil, in a hurry.

"No, it's too big and hasn't got a sharp point."

Here Daisy, who had dived into her pocket, presented a neat little housewife with four needles in it.

"You are the Posy who always has what we want," said Emil; and Nan resolved to have a needle-book in her own pocket henceforth, for just such cases as this were always occurring in her practice.

Daisy covered her eyes, but Nan probed and picked with a steady hand, while Emil gave directions not down in any medical work or record.

"Starboard now! Steady, boys, steady! Try another tack. Heave ho! there she is!"

"Suck it," ordered the Doctor, surveying the splinter with an experienced eye.

"Too dirty," responded the patient, shaking his bleeding hand.

"Wait; I'll tie it up if you have got a handkerchief."

"Haven't; take one of those rags down there."

"Gracious! no, indeed; they are doll's clothes," cried Daisy, indignantly.

"Take one of mine; I'd like to have you," said Nan; and swinging himself down, Emil caught up the first "rag" he saw. It happened to be the frilled skirt; but Nan tore it up without a murmur; and when the royal petticoat was turned into a neat little bandage, she dismissed her patient with the command

"Keep it wet, and let it alone; then it will heal right up, and not be sore."

"What do you charge?" asked the Commodore, laughing.

"Nothing; I keep a 'spensary; that is a place where poor people are doctored free gratis for nothing," explained Nan, with an air.

"Thank you, Doctor Giddy-gaddy. I'll always call you in when I come to grief;" and Emil departed, but looked back to say - for one good turn deserves another - "Your duds are blowing away, Doctor."

Forgiving the disrespectful word, "duds," the ladies hastily descended, and, gathering up their wash, retired to the house to fire up the little stove, and go to ironing.

A passing breath of air shook the old willow, as if it laughed softly at the childish chatter which went on in the nest, and it had hardly composed itself when another pair of birds alighted for a confidential twitter.

"Now, I'll tell you the secret," began Tommy, who was "swellin' wisibly" with the importance of his news.

"Tell away," answered Nat, wishing he had brought his fiddle, it was so shady and quiet here.

"Well, we fellows were talking over the late interesting case of circumstantial evidence," said Tommy, quoting at random from a speech Franz had made at the club, "and I proposed giving Dan something to make up for our suspecting him, to show our respect, and so on, you know something handsome and useful, that he could keep always and be proud of. What do you think we chose?"

"A butterfly-net; he wants one ever so much," said Nat, looking a little disappointed, for he meant to get it himself.

"No, sir; it's to be a microscope, a real swell one, that we see what-do-you-call-'ems in water with, and stars, and ant-eggs, and all sorts of games, you know. Won't it be a jolly good present?" said Tommy, rather confusing microscopes and telescopes in his remarks.

"Tip-top! I'm so glad! Won't it cost a heap, though?" cried Nat, feeling that his friend was beginning to be appreciated.

"Of course it will; but we are all going to give something. I headed the paper with my five dollars; for if it is done at all, it must be done handsome."

"What! all of it? I never did see such a generous chap as you are;" and Nat beamed upon him with sincere admiration.

"Well, you see, I've been so bothered with my property, that I'm tired of it, and don't mean to save up any more, but give it away as I go along, and then nobody will envy me, or want to steal it, and I shan't be suspecting folks and worrying about my old cash," replied Tommy, on whom the cares and anxieties of a millionaire weighed heavily.

"Will Mr. Bhaer let you do it?"

"He thought it was a first-rate plan, and said that some of the best men he knew preferred to do good with their money instead of laying it up to be squabbled over when they died."

"Your father is rich; does he do that way?"

"I'm not sure; he gives me all I want; I know that much. I'm going to talk to him about it when I go home. Anyhow, I shall set him a good example;" and Tommy was so serious, that Nat did not dare to laugh, but said, respectfully-

"You will be able to do ever so much with your money, won't you?"

"So Mr. Bhaer said, and he promised to advise me about useful ways of spending it. I'm going to begin with Dan; and next time I get a dollar or so, I shall do something for Dick, he's such a good little chap, and only has a cent a week for pocket-money. He can't earn much, you know; so I'm going to kind of see to him;" and good-hearted Tommy quite longed to begin.

"I think that's a beautiful plan, and I'm not going to try to buy a fiddle any more; I'm going to get Dan his net all myself, and if there is any money left, I'll do something to please poor Billy. He's fond of me, and though he isn't poor, he'd like some little thing from me, because I can make out what he wants better than the rest of you." And Nat fell to wondering how much happiness could be got out of his precious three dollars.

"So I would. Now come and ask Mr. Bhaer if you can't go in town with me on Monday afternoon, so you can get the net, while I get the microscope. Franz and Emil are going too, and we'll have a jolly time larking round among the shops."

The lads walked away arm-in-arm, discussing the new plans with droll importance, yet beginning already to feel the sweet satisfaction which comes to those who try, no matter how humbly, to be earthly providences to the poor and helpless, and gild their mite with the gold of charity before it is laid up where thieves cannot break through and steal.

"Come up and rest while we sort the leaves; it's so cool and pleasant here," said Demi, as he and Dan came sauntering home from a long walk in the woods.

"All right!" answered Dan, who was a boy of few words, and up they went.

"What makes birch leaves shake so much more than the others?" asked inquiring Demi, who was always sure of an answer from Dan.

"They are hung differently. Don't you see the stem where it joins the leaf is sort of pinched one way, and where it joins the twig, it is pinched another. This makes it waggle with the least bit of wind, but the elm leaves hang straight, and keep stiller."

"How curious! will this do so?" and Demi held up a sprig of acacia, which he had broken from a little tree on the lawn, because it was so pretty.

"No; that belongs to the sort that shuts up when you touch it. Draw your finger down the middle of the stem, and see if the leaves don't curl up," said Dan, who was examining a bit of mica.

Demi tried it, and presently the little leaves did fold together, till the spray showed a single instead of a double line of leaves.

"I like that; tell me about the others. What do these do?" asked Demi, taking up a new branch.

"Feed silk-worms; they live on mulberry leaves, till they begin to spin themselves up. I was in a silk-factory once, and there were rooms full of shelves all covered with leaves, and worms eating them so fast that it made a rustle. Sometimes they eat so much they die. Tell that to Stuffy," and Dan laughed, as he took up another bit of rock with a lichen on it.

"I know one thing about this mullein leaf: the fairies use them for blankets," said Demi, who had not quite given up his faith in the existence of the little folk in green.

"If I had a microscope, I'd show you something prettier than fairies," said Dan, wondering if he should ever own that coveted treasure. "I knew an old woman who used mullein leaves for a night-cap because she had face-ache. She sewed them together, and wore it all the time."

"How funny! was she your grandmother?"

"Never had any. She was a queer old woman, and lived alone in a little tumble-down house with nineteen cats. Folks called her a witch, but she wasn't, though she looked like an old rag-bag. She was real kind to me when I lived in that place, and used to let me get warm at her fire when the folks at the poorhouse were hard on me."

"Did you live in a poorhouse?"

"A little while. Never mind that I didn't mean to speak of it;" and Dan stopped short in his unusual fit of communicativeness.

"Tell about the cats, please," said Demi, feeling that he had asked an unpleasant question, and sorry for it.

"Nothing to tell; only she had a lot of 'em, and kept 'em in a barrel nights; and I used to go and tip over the barrel sometimes, and let 'em out all over the house, and then she'd scold, and chase 'em and put 'em in again, spitting and yowling like fury."

"Was she good to them?" asked Demi, with a hearty child's laugh, pleasant to hear.

"Guess she was. Poor old soul! she took in all the lost and sick cats in the town; and when anybody wanted one they went to Marm Webber, and she let 'em pick any kind and color they wanted, and only asked ninepence, she was glad to have her pussies get a good home."

Lesson 120

1. Finish reading chapter 15.
2. What are you thinking?
3. Demi said, "It's very singular how hard it is to manage your mind." Do you agree? Why or why not? (You can just tell your answer.)

Chapter XV. continued

"I should like to see Marm Webber. Could I, if I went to that place?"

"She's dead. All my folks are," said Dan, briefly.

"I'm sorry;" and Demi sat silent a minute, wondering what subject would be safe to try next. He felt delicate about speaking of the departed lady, but was very curious about the cats, and could not resist asking softly

"Did she cure the sick ones?"

"Sometimes. One had a broken leg, and she tied it up to a stick, and it got well; and another had fits, and she doctored it with yarbs till it was cured. But some of 'em died, and she buried 'em; and when they couldn't get well, she killed 'em easy."

"How?" asked Demi, feeling that there was a peculiar charm about this old woman, and some sort of joke about the cats, because Dan was smiling to himself.

"A kind lady, who was fond of cats, told her how, and gave her some stuff, and sent all her own pussies to be killed that way. Marm used to put a sponge wet with ether, in the bottom of an old boot, then poke puss in head downwards. The ether put her to sleep in a jiffy, and she was drowned in warm water before she woke up."

"I hope the cats didn't feel it. I shall tell Daisy about that. You have known a great many interesting things, haven't you?" asked Demi, and fell to meditating on the vast experience of a boy who had run away more than once, and taken care of himself in a big city.

"Wish I hadn't sometimes."

"Why? Don't remembering them feel good?"

"No."

"It's very singular how hard it is to manage your mind," said Demi, clasping his hands round his knees, and looking up at the sky as if for information upon his favorite topic.

"Devilish hard no, I don't mean that;" and Dan bit his lips, for the forbidden word slipped out in spite of him, and he wanted to be more careful with Demi than with any of the other boys.

"I'll play I didn't hear it," said Demi; "and you won't do it again, I'm sure."

"Not if I can help it. That's one of the things I don't want to remember. I keep pegging away, but it don't seem to do much good;" and Dan looked discouraged.

"Yes, it does. You don't say half so many bad words as you used to; and Aunt Jo is pleased, because she said it was a hard habit to break up."

"Did she?" and Dan cheered up a bit.

"You must put swearing away in your fault-drawer, and lock it up; that's the way I do with my badness."

"What do you mean?" asked Dan, looking as if he found Demi almost as amusing as a new sort of cockchafer or beetle.

"Well, it's one of my private plays, and I'll tell you, but I think you'll laugh at it," began Demi, glad to hold forth on this congenial subject. "I play that my mind is a round room, and my soul is a little sort of creature with wings that lives in it. The walls are full of shelves and drawers, and in them I keep my thoughts, and my goodness and badness, and all sorts of things. The goods I keep where I can see them, and the bads I lock up tight, but they get out, and I have to keep putting them in and squeezing them down, they are so strong. The thoughts I play with when I am alone or in bed, and I make up and do what I like with them. Every Sunday I put my room in order, and talk with the little spirit that lives there, and tell him what to do. He is very bad sometimes, and won't mind me, and I have to scold him, and take him to Grandpa. He always makes him behave, and be sorry for his faults, because Grandpa likes this play, and gives me nice things to put in the drawers, and tells me how to shut up the naughties. Hadn't you better try that way? It's a very good one;" and Demi looked so earnest and full of faith, that Dan did not laugh at his quaint fancy, but said, soberly,

"I don't think there is a lock strong enough to keep my badness shut up. Any way my room is in such a clutter I don't know how to clear it up."

"You keep your drawers in the cabinet all spandy nice; why can't you do the others?"

"I ain't used to it. Will you show me how?" and Dan looked as if inclined to try Demi's childish way of keeping a soul in order.

"I'd love to, but I don't know how, except to talk as Grandpa does. I can't do it good like him, but I'll try."

"Don't tell any one; only now and then we'll come here and talk things over, and I'll pay you for it by telling all I know about my sort of things. Will that do?" and Dan held out his big, rough hand.

Demi gave his smooth, little hand readily, and the league was made; for in the happy, peaceful world where the younger boy lived, lions and lambs played together, and little children innocently taught their elders.

"Hush!" said Dan, pointing toward the house, as Demi was about to indulge in another discourse on the best way of getting badness down, and keeping it down; and peeping from their perch, they saw Mrs. Jo strolling slowly along, reading as she went, while Teddy trotted behind her, dragging a little cart upside down.

"Wait till they see us," whispered Demi, and both sat still as the pair came nearer, Mrs. Jo so absorbed in her book that she would have walked into the brook if Teddy had not stopped her by saying-

"Marmar, I wanter fis."

Mrs. Jo put down the charming book which she had been trying to read for a week, and looked about her for a fishing-pole, being used to making toys out of nothing. Before she had broken one from the hedge, a slender willow bough fell at her feet; and, looking up, she saw the boys laughing in the nest.

"Up! up!" cried Teddy, stretching his arms and flapping his skirts as if about to fly.

"I'll come down and you come up. I must go to Daisy now;" and Demi departed to rehearse the tale of the nineteen cats, with the exciting boot-and-barrel episodes.

Teddy was speedily whisked up; and then Dan said, laughing, "Come, too; there's plenty of room. I'll lend you a hand."

Mrs. Jo glanced over her shoulder, but no one was in sight; and rather liking the joke of the thing, she laughed back, saying, "Well, if you won't mention it, I think I will;" and with two nimble steps was in the willow.

"I haven't climbed a tree since I was married. I used to be very fond of it when I was a girl," she said, looking well-pleased with her shady perch.

"Now, you read if you want to, and I'll take care of Teddy," proposed Dan, beginning to make a fishing-rod for impatient Baby.

"I don't think I care about it now. What were you and Demi at up here?" asked Mrs. Jo, thinking, from the sober look on Dan's face, that he had something on his mind.

"Oh! we were talking. I'd been telling him about leaves and things, and he was telling me some of his queer plays. Now, then, Major, fish away;" and Dan finished off his work by putting a big blue fly on the bent pin which hung at the end of the cord he had tied to the willow-rod.

Teddy leaned down from the tree, and was soon wrapt up in watching for the fish which he felt sure would come. Dan held him by his little petticoats, lest he should take a "header" into the brook, and Mrs. Jo soon won him to talk by doing so herself.

"I am so glad you told Demi about 'leaves and things;' it is just what he needs; and I wish you would teach him, and take him to walk with you."

"I'd like to, he is so bright; but-"

"But what?"

"I didn't think you'd trust me."

"Why not?"

"Well, Demi is so kind of precious, and so good, and I'm such a bad lot, I thought you'd keep him away from me."

"But you are not a 'bad lot,' as you say; and I do trust you, Dan, entirely, because you honestly try to improve, and do better and better every week."

"Really?" and Dan looked up at her with the cloud of despondency lifting from his face.

"Yes; don't you feel it?"

"I hoped so, but I didn't know."

"I have been waiting and watching quietly, for I thought I'd give you a good trial first; and if you stood it, I would give you the best reward I had. You have stood it well; and now I'm going to trust not only Demi, but my own boy, to you, because you can teach them some things better than any of us."

"Can I?" and Dan looked amazed at the idea.

"Demi has lived among older people so much that he needs just what you have knowledge of common things, strength, and courage. He thinks you are the bravest boy he ever saw, and admires your strong way of doing things. Then you know a great deal about natural objects, and can tell him more wonderful tales of birds, and bees, and leaves, and animals, than his story-books give him; and, being true, these stories will teach and do him good. Don't you see now how much you can help him, and why I like to have him with you?"

"But I swear sometimes, and might tell him something wrong. I wouldn't mean to, but it might slip out, just as 'devil' did a few minutes ago," said Dan, anxious to do his duty, and let her know his shortcomings.

"I know you try not to say or do any thing to harm the little fellow, and here is where I think Demi will help you, because he is so innocent and wise in his small way, and has what I am trying to give you, dear, good principles. It is never too early to try and plant them in a child, and never too late to cultivate them in the most neglected person. You are only boys yet; you can teach one another.

Demi will unconsciously strengthen your moral sense, you will strengthen his common sense, and I shall feel as if I had helped you both."

Words could not express how pleased and touched Dan was by this confidence and praise. No one had ever trusted him before, no one had cared to find out and foster the good in him, and no one had suspected how much there was hidden away in the breast of the neglected boy, going fast to ruin, yet quick to feel and value sympathy and help. No honor that he might earn hereafter would ever be half so precious as the right to teach his few virtues and small store of learning to the child whom he most respected; and no more powerful restraint could have been imposed upon him than the innocent companion confided to his care. He found courage now to tell Mrs. Jo of the plan already made with Demi, and she was glad that the first step had been so naturally taken. Every thing seemed to be working well for Dan, and she rejoiced over him, because it had seemed a hard task, yet, working on with a firm belief in the possibility of reformation in far older and worse subjects than he, there had come this quick and hopeful change to encourage her. He felt that he had friends now and a place in the world, something to live and work for, and, though he said little, all that was best and bravest in a character made old by a hard experience responded to the love and faith bestowed on him, and Dan's salvation was assured.

Their quiet talk was interrupted by a shout of delight from Teddy, who, to the surprise of every one, did actually catch a trout where no trout had been seen for years. He was so enchanted with his splendid success that he insisted on showing his prize to the family before Asia cooked it for supper; so the three descended and went happily away together, all satisfied with the work of that half hour.

Ned was the next visitor to the tree, but he only made a short stay, sitting there at his ease while Dick and Dolly caught a pailful of grasshoppers and crickets for him. He wanted to play a joke on Tommy, and intended to tuck up a few dozen of the lively creatures in his bed, so that when Bangs got in he would speedily tumble out again, and pass a portion of the night in chasing "hopper-grasses" round the room. The hunt was soon over, and having paid the hunters with a few peppermints apiece Ned retired to make Tommy's bed.

For an hour the old willow sighed and sung to itself, talked with the brook, and watched the lengthening shadows as the sun went down. The first rosy color was touching its graceful branches when a boy came stealing up the avenue, across the lawn, and, spying Billy by the brook-side, went to him, saying, in a mysterious tone,

"Go and tell Mr. Bhaer I want to see him down here, please. Don't let any one hear."

Billy nodded and ran off, while the boy swung himself up into the tree, and sat there looking anxious, yet evidently feeling the charm of the place and hour. In five minutes, Mr. Bhaer appeared, and, stepping up on the fence, leaned into the nest, saying, kindly,

"I am glad to see you, Jack; but why not come in and meet us all at once?"

"I wanted to see you first, please, sir. Uncle made me come back. I know I don't deserve any thing, but I hope the fellows won't be hard upon me."

Poor Jack did not get on very well, but it was evident that he was sorry and ashamed, and wanted to be received as easily as possible; for his Uncle had thrashed him well and scolded him soundly for following the example he himself set. Jack had begged not to be sent back, but the school was cheap, and Mr. Ford insisted, so the boy returned as quietly as possible, and took refuge behind Mr. Bhaer.

"I hope not, but I can't answer for them, though I will see that they are not unjust. I think, as Dan and Nat have suffered so much, being innocent, you should suffer something, being guilty. Don't you?" asked Mr. Bhaer, pitying Jack, yet feeling he deserved punishment for a fault which had so little excuse.

"I suppose so, but I sent Tommy's money back, and I said I was sorry, isn't that enough?" said Jack, rather sullenly; for the boy who could do so mean a thing was not brave enough to bear the consequences well.

"No; I think you should ask pardon of all three boys, openly and honestly. You cannot expect them to respect and trust you for a time, but you can live down this disgrace if you try, and I will help you. Stealing and lying are detestable sins, and I hope this will be a lesson to you. I am glad you are ashamed, it is a good sign; bear it patiently, and do your best to earn a better reputation."

"I'll have an auction, and sell off all my goods dirt cheap," said Jack, showing his repentance in the most characteristic way.

"I think it would be better to give them away, and begin on a new foundation. Take 'Honesty is the best policy' for your motto, and live up to it in act, and word, and thought, and though you don't make a cent of money this summer, you will be a rich boy in the autumn," said Mr. Bhaer, earnestly.

It was hard, but Jack consented, for he really felt that cheating didn't pay, and wanted to win back the friendship of the boys. His heart clung to his possessions, and he groaned inwardly at the thought of actually giving away certain precious things. Asking pardon publicly was easy compared to this; but then he began to discover that certain other things, invisible, but most valuable, were better property than knives, fish-hooks, or even money itself. So he decided to buy up a little integrity, even at a high price, and secure the respect of his playmates, though it was not a salable article.

"Well, I'll do it," he said, with a sudden air of resolution, which pleased Mr. Bhaer.

"Good! and I'll stand by you. Now come and begin at once."

And Father Bhaer led the bankrupt boy back into the little world, which received him coldly at first, but slowly warmed to him, when he showed that he had profited by the lesson, and was sincerely anxious to go into a better business with a new stock-in-trade.

Lesson 121

1. While you are reading, look for the word coaxing. Do you remember what it means? Copy the sentence with coaxing in it. (Practice neat handwriting.) What is the subject? The predicate?
2. Read the title of Chapter 16. What do you know about taming an animal?
3. Read chapter 16.
4. Dan tames a colt in this chapter.
5. Mrs. Jo says that she is taming a colt too. What does she mean? (Answers)
6. What are you thinking at the end of the chapter?

Vocabulary

1. Read over the vocabulary list carefully.
2. What other in-, ir- and -able words can you think of?

magnanimous: showing a noble, generous spirit

inexplicable: unable to be explained; explicable: able to be explained
> in – as a prefix means not
> in-explicable means not able to be explained

gratitude: showing thanks; ingratitude means not grateful

perversity: This is a noun. Perverse is an adjective. Perverse means to be corrupt or having turned from good to bad. Changing the end of the word changes it into a noun with the same meaning.

indignant: feeling or showing anger because of an injustice

irrepressible: impossible to repress, control; Repress means to hold back or subdue.
> -ible or -able as a suffix means able to.
> -ir as a prefix means not.
> So, put them all together and it means not able to hold back.

salver: a flat metal serving tray (This is not important to learn, but it's in the story, and I thought you would like to know what it is talking about.)

salable: suitable for sale; pronounced (sale-able)
-able as a suffix means able to. So, this means able to be sold.

vaguely: not clearly or precisely
> What part of speech is this word? (Hint: It ends in -ly.)
> Vague is the adjective form of this adverb.

Chapter XVI. Taming the Colt

"What in the world is that boy doing?" said Mrs. Jo to herself, as she watched Dan running round the half-mile triangle as if for a wager. He was all alone, and seemed possessed by some strange desire to run himself into a fever, or break his neck; for, after several rounds, he tried leaping walls, and turning somersaults up the avenue, and finally dropped down on the grass before the door as if exhausted.

"Are you training for a race, Dan?" asked Mrs. Jo, from the window where she sat.

He looked up quickly, and stopped panting to answer, with a laugh,

"No; I'm only working off my steam."

"Can't you find a cooler way of doing it? You will be ill if you tear about so in such warm weather," said Mrs. Jo, laughing also, as she threw him out a great palm-leaf fan.

"Can't help it. I must run somewhere," answered Dan, with such an odd expression in his restless eyes, that Mrs. Jo was troubled, and asked, quickly,

"Is Plumfield getting too narrow for you?"

"I wouldn't mind if it was a little bigger. I like it though; only the fact is the devil gets into me sometimes, and then I do want to bolt."

The words seemed to come against his will, for he looked sorry the minute they were spoken, and seemed to think he deserved a reproof for his ingratitude. But Mrs. Jo understood the feeling, and though sorry to see it, she could not blame the boy for confessing it. She looked at him anxiously, seeing how tall and strong he had grown, how full of energy his face was, with its eager eyes and resolute mouth; and remembering the utter freedom he had known for years before, she felt how even the gentle restraint of this home would weigh upon him at times when the old lawless spirit stirred in him. "Yes," she said to herself, "my wild hawk needs a larger cage; and yet, if I let him go, I am afraid he will be lost. I must try and find some lure strong enough to keep him safe."

"I know all about it," she added, aloud. "It is not 'the devil,' as you call it, but the very natural desire of all young people for liberty. I used to feel just so, and once, I really did think for a minute that I would bolt."

"Why didn't you?" said Dan, coming to lean on the low window-ledge, with an evident desire to continue the subject.

"I knew it was foolish, and love for my mother kept me at home."

"I haven't got any mother," began Dan.
"I thought you had now," said Mrs. Jo, gently stroking the rough hair off his hot forehead.

"You are no end good to me, and I can't ever thank you enough, but it just isn't the same, is it?" and Dan looked up at her with a wistful, hungry look that went to her heart.

"No, dear, it is not the same, and never can be. I think an own mother would have been a great deal to you. But as that cannot be, you must try to let me fill her place. I fear I have not done all I ought, or you would not want to leave me," she added, sorrowfully.

"Yes, you have!" cried Dan, eagerly. "I don't want to go, and I won't go, if I can help it; but every now and then I feel as if I must burst out somehow. I want to run straight ahead somewhere, to smash something, or pitch into somebody. Don't know why, but I do, and that's all about it."

Dan laughed as he spoke, but he meant what he said, for he knit his black brows, and brought down his fist on the ledge with such force, that Mrs. Jo's thimble flew off into the grass. He brought it back, and as she took it she held the big, brown hand a minute, saying, with a look that showed the words cost her something

"Well, Dan, run if you must, but don't run very far; and come back to me soon, for I want you very much."

He was rather taken aback by this unexpected permission to play truant, and somehow it seemed to lessen his desire to go. He did not understand why, but Mrs. Jo did, and, knowing the natural perversity of the human mind, counted on it to help her now. She felt instinctively that the more the boy was restrained the more he would fret against it; but leave him free, and the mere sense of liberty would content him, joined to the knowledge that his presence was dear to those whom he loved best. It was a little experiment, but it succeeded, for Dan stood silent a moment, unconsciously picking the fan to pieces and turning the matter over in his mind. He felt that she appealed to his heart and his honor, and owned that he understood it by saying presently, with a mixture of regret and resolution in his face,

"I won't go yet awhile, and I'll give you fair warning before I bolt. That's fair, isn't it?"

"Yes, we will let it stand so. Now, I want to see if I can't find some way for you to work off your steam better than running about the place like a mad dog, spoiling my fans, or fighting with the boys. What can we invent?" and while Dan tried to repair the mischief he had done, Mrs. Jo racked her brain for some new device to keep her truant safe until he had learned to love his lessons better.

"How would you like to be my express-man?" she said, as a sudden thought popped into her head.

"Go into town, and do the errands?" asked Dan, looking interested at once.

"Yes; Franz is tired of it, Silas cannot be spared just now, and Mr. Bhaer has no time. Old Andy is a safe horse, you are a good driver, and know your way about the city as well as a postman. Suppose you try it, and see if it won't do most as well to drive away two or three times a week as to run away once a month."

"I'd like it ever so much, only I must go alone and do it all myself. I don't want any of the other fellows bothering round," said Dan, taking to the new idea so kindly that he began to put on business airs already.

"If Mr. Bhaer does not object you shall have it all your own way. I suppose Emil will growl, but he cannot be trusted with horses, and you can. By the way, to-morrow is market-day, and I must make out my list. You had better see that the wagon is in order, and tell Silas to have the fruit and vegetables ready for mother. You will have to be up early and get back in time for school, can you do that?"

"I'm always an early bird, so I don't mind," and Dan slung on his jacket with despatch.

"The early bird got the worm this time, I'm sure," said Mrs. Jo, merrily.

"And a jolly good worm it is," answered Dan, as he went laughing away to put a new lash to the whip, wash the wagon, and order Silas about with all the importance of a young express-man.

"Before he is tired of this I will find something else and have it ready when the next restless fit comes on," said Mrs. Jo to herself, as she wrote her list with a deep sense of gratitude that all her boys were not Dans.

Mr. Bhaer did not entirely approve of the new plan, but agreed to give it a trial, which put Dan on his mettle, and caused him to give up certain wild plans of his own, in which the new lash and the long hill were to have borne a part. He was up and away very early the next morning, heroically resisting the temptation to race with the milkmen going into town. Once there, he did his errands carefully, to Mr. Bhaer's surprise and Mrs. Jo's great satisfaction. The Commodore did growl at Dan's promotion, but was pacified by a superior padlock to his new boat-house, and the thought that seamen were meant for higher honors than driving market-wagons and doing family errands. So Dan filled his new office well and contentedly for weeks, and said no more about bolting. But one day Mr. Bhaer found him pummelling Jack, who was roaring for mercy under his knee.

"Why, Dan, I thought you had given up fighting," he said, as he went to the rescue.

"We ain't fighting, we are only wrestling," answered Dan, leaving off reluctantly.

"It looks very much like it, and feels like it, hey, Jack?" said Mr. Bhaer, as the defeated gentleman got upon his legs with difficulty.

"Catch me wrestling with him again. He's most knocked my head off," snarled Jack, holding on to that portion of his frame as if it really was loose upon his shoulders.

"The fact is, we began in fun, but when I got him down I couldn't help pounding him. Sorry I hurt you, old fellow," explained Dan, looking rather ashamed of himself.

"I understand. The longing to pitch into somebody was so strong you couldn't resist. You are a sort of Berserker, Dan, and something to tussle with is as necessary to you as music is to Nat," said Mr. Bhaer, who knew all about the conversation between the boy and Mrs. Jo.

"Can't help it. So if you don't want to be pounded you'd better keep out of the way," answered Dan, with a warning look in his black eyes that made Jack sheer off in haste.

"If you want something to wrestle with, I will give you a tougher specimen than Jack," said Mr. Bhaer; and, leading the way to the wood-yard, he pointed out certain roots of trees that had been grubbed up in the spring, and had been lying there waiting to be split.

"There, when you feel inclined to maltreat the boys, just come and work off your energies here, and I'll thank you for it."

"So I will;" and, seizing the axe that lay near Dan hauled out a tough root, and went at it so vigorously, that the chips flew far and wide, and Mr. Bhaer fled for his life.

To his great amusement, Dan took him at his word, and was often seen wrestling with the ungainly knots, hat and jacket off, red face, and wrathful eyes; for he got into royal rages over some of his adversaries, and swore at them under his breath till he had conquered them, when he exulted, and marched off to the shed with an armful of gnarled oak-wood in triumph. He blistered his hands, tired his back, and dulled the axe, but it did him good, and he got more comfort out of the ugly roots than any one dreamed, for with each blow he worked off some of the pent-up power that would otherwise have been expended in some less harmless way.

"When this is gone I really don't know what I shall do," said Mrs. Jo to herself, for no inspiration came, and she was at the end of her resources.

But Dan found a new occupation for himself, and enjoyed it some time before any one discovered the cause of his contentment. A fine young horse of Mr. Laurie's was kept at Plumfield that summer, running loose in a large pasture across the brook. The boys were all interested in the handsome, spirited creature, and for a time were fond of watching him gallop and frisk with his plumey tail flying, and his handsome head in the air. But they soon got tired of it, and left Prince Charlie to himself. All but Dan, he never tired of looking at the horse, and seldom failed to visit him each day with a lump of sugar, a bit of bread, or an apple to make him welcome. Charlie was grateful, accepted his friendship, and the two loved one another as if they felt some tie between them, inexplicable but strong. In whatever part of the wide field he might be, Charlie always came at full speed when Dan whistled at the bars, and the boy was never happier than when the beautiful, fleet creature put its head on his shoulder, looking up at him with fine eyes full of intelligent affection.

"We understand one another without any palaver, don't we, old fellow?" Dan would say, proud of the horse's confidence, and, so jealous of his regard, that he told no one how well the friendship prospered, and never asked anybody but Teddy to accompany him on these daily visits.

Mr. Laurie came now and then to see how Charlie got on, and spoke of having him broken to harness in the autumn.

"He won't need much taming, he is such a gentle, fine-tempered brute. I shall come out and try him with a saddle myself some day," he said, on one of these visits.

"He lets me put a halter on him, but I don't believe he will bear a saddle even if you put it on," answered Dan, who never failed to be present when Charlie and his master met.

"I shall coax him to bear it, and not mind a few tumbles at first. He has never been harshly treated, so, though he will be surprised at the new performance, I think he won't be frightened, and his antics will do no harm."

"I wonder what he would do," said Dan to himself, as Mr. Laurie went away with the Professor, and Charlie returned to the bars, from which he had retired when the gentlemen came up.

A daring fancy to try the experiment took possession of the boy as he sat on the topmost rail with the glossy back temptingly near him. Never thinking of danger, he obeyed the impulse, and while Charlie unsuspectingly nibbled at the apple he held, Dan quickly and quietly took his seat. He did not keep it long, however, for with an astonished snort, Charlie reared straight up, and deposited Dan on the ground. The fall did not hurt him, for the turf was soft, and he jumped up, saying, with a laugh,

"I did it anyway! Come here, you rascal, and I'll try it again."

But Charlie declined to approach, and Dan left him resolving to succeed in the end; for a struggle like this suited him exactly. Next time he took a halter, and having got it on, he played with the horse for a while, leading him to and fro, and putting him through various antics till he was a little tired; then Dan sat on the wall and gave him bread, but watched his chance, and getting a good grip of the halter, slipped on to his back. Charlie tried the old trick, but Dan held on, having had practice with Toby, who occasionally had an obstinate fit, and tried to shake off his rider. Charlie was both amazed and indignant; and after prancing for a minute, set off at a gallop, and away went Dan heels over head. If he had not belonged to the class of boys who go through all sorts of dangers unscathed, he would have broken his neck; as it was, he got a heavy fall, and lay still collecting his wits, while Charlie tore round the field tossing his head with every sign of satisfaction at the discomfiture of his rider. Presently it seemed to occur to him that something was wrong with Dan, and, being of a magnanimous nature, he went to see what the matter was. Dan let him sniff about and perplex himself for a few minutes; then he looked up at him, saying, as decidedly as if the horse could understand,

"You think you have beaten, but you are mistaken, old boy; and I'll ride you yet see if I don't."

He tried no more that day, but soon after attempted a new method of introducing Charlie to a burden. He strapped a folded blanket on his back, and then let him race, and rear, and roll, and fume as much as he liked. After a few fits of rebellion Charlie submitted, and in a few days permitted Dan to mount him, often stopped short to look round, as if he said, half patiently, half reproachfully, "I don't understand it, but I suppose you mean no harm, so I permit the liberty."

Dan patted and praised him, and took a short turn every day, getting frequent falls, but persisting in spite of them, and longing to try a saddle and bridle, but not daring to confess what he had done. He had his wish, however, for there had been a witness of his pranks who said a good word for him.

"Do you know what that chap has ben doin' lately?" asked Silas of his master, one evening, as he received his orders for the next day.

"Which boy?" said Mr. Bhaer, with an air of resignation, expecting some sad revelation.

"Dan, he's ben a breaking the colt, sir, and I wish I may die if he ain't done it," answered Silas, chuckling.

"How do you know?"

"Wal, I kinder keep an eye on the little fellers, and most gen'lly know what they're up to; so when Dan kep going off to the paster, and coming home black and blue, I mistrusted that suthing was goin' on. I didn't say nothin', but I crep up into the barn chamber, and from there I see him goin' through all manner of games with Charlie. Blest if he warn't throwed time and agin, and knocked round like a bag o' meal. But the pluck of that boy did beat all, and he 'peared to like it, and kep on as ef bound to beat."

"But, Silas, you should have stopped it the boy might have been killed," said Mr. Bhaer, wondering what freak his irrepressibles would take into their heads next.

"S'pose I oughter; but there warn't no real danger, for Charlie ain't no tricks, and is as pretty a tempered horse as ever I see. Fact was, I couldn't bear to spile sport, for ef there's any thing I do admire it's grit, and Dan is chock full on 't. But now I know he's hankerin' after a saddle, and yet won't take even the old one on the sly; so I just thought I'd up and tell, and may be you'd let him try what he can do. Mr. Laurie won't mind, and Charlie's all the better for 't."

"We shall see;" and off went Mr. Bhaer to inquire into the matter.

Dan owned up at once, and proudly proved that Silas was right by showing off his power over Charlie; for by dint of much coaxing, many carrots, and infinite perseverance, he really had succeeded in riding the colt with a halter and blanket. Mr. Laurie was much amused, and well pleased with Dan's courage and skill, and let him have a hand in all future performances; for he set about Charlie's education at once, saying that he was not going to be outdone by a slip of a boy. Thanks to Dan, Charlie took kindly to the saddle and bridle when he had once reconciled himself to the indignity of the bit; and after Mr. Laurie had trained him a little, Dan was permitted to ride him, to the great envy and admiration of the other boys.

"Isn't he handsome? and don't he mind me like a lamb?" said Dan one day as he dismounted and stood with his arm round Charlie's neck.

"Yes, and isn't he a much more useful and agreeable animal than the wild colt who spent his days racing about the field, jumping fences, and running away now and then?" asked Mrs. Bhaer from the steps where she always appeared when Dan performed with Charlie.

"Of course he is. See he won't run away now, even if I don't hold him, and he comes to me the minute I whistle; I have tamed him well, haven't I?" and Dan looked both proud and pleased, as well he might, for, in spite of their struggles together, Charlie loved him better than his master.

"I am taming a colt too, and I think I shall succeed as well as you if I am as patient and persevering," said Mrs. Jo, smiling so significantly at him, that Dan understood and answered, laughing, yet in earnest,

"We won't jump over the fence and run away, but stay and let them make a handsome, useful span of us, hey, Charlie?"

Lesson 122

1. Read the title of Chapter 17. What are you picturing?
2. Read the first part of chapter 17.
3. Write a one-sentence summary of what you read.

Chapter XVII. Composition Day
"Hurry up, boys, it's three o'clock, and Uncle Fritz likes us to be punctual, you know," said Franz one Wednesday afternoon as a bell rang, and a stream of literary-looking young gentlemen with books and paper in their hands were seen going toward the museum.

Tommy was in the school-room, bending over his desk, much bedaubed with ink, flushed with the ardor of inspiration, and in a great hurry as usual, for easy-going Bangs never was ready till the very last minute. As Franz passed the door looking up laggards, Tommy gave one last blot and flourish, and departed out the window, waving his paper to dry as he went. Nan followed, looking very important, with a large roll in her hand, and Demi escorted Daisy, both evidently brimful of some delightful secret.

The museum was all in order, and the sunshine among the hop-vines made pretty shadows on the floor as it peeped through the great window. On one side sat Mr. and Mrs. Bhaer, on the other was a little table on which the compositions were laid as soon as read, and in a large semicircle sat the children on camp-stools which occasionally shut up and let the sitter down, thus preventing any stiffness in the assembly. As it took too much time to have all read, they took turns, and on this Wednesday the younger pupils were the chief performers, while the elder ones listened with condescension and criticised freely.

"Ladies first; so Nan may begin," said Mr. Bhaer, when the settling of stools and rustling of papers had subsided.

Nan took her place beside the little table, and, with a preliminary giggle, read the following interesting essay on-

"THE SPONGE

"The sponge, my friends, is a most useful and interesting plant. It grows on rocks under the water, and is a kind of sea-weed, I believe. People go and pick it and dry it and wash it, because little fish and insects live in the holes of the sponge; I found shells in my new one, and sand. Some are very fine and soft; babies are washed with them. The sponge has many uses. I will relate some of them, and I hope my friends will remember what I say. One use is to wash the face; I don't like it myself, but I do it because I wish to be clean. Some people don't, and they are dirty." Here the eye of the reader rested sternly upon Dick and Dolly, who quailed under it, and instantly resolved to scrub themselves virtuously on all occasions. "Another use is to wake people up; I allude to boys par-tic -u-lar-ly." Another pause after the long word to enjoy the smothered laugh that went round the room. "Some boys do not get up when called, and Mary Ann squeezes the water out of a wet sponge on their faces, and it makes them so mad they wake up." Here the laugh broke out, and Emil said, as if he had been hit,

"Seems to me you are wandering from the subject."

"No, I ain't; we are to write about vegetables or animals, and I'm doing both: for boys are animals, aren't they?" cried Nan; and, undaunted by the indignant "No!" shouted at her, she calmly proceeded,

"One more interesting thing is done with sponges, and this is when doctors put ether on it, and hold it to people's noses when they have teeth out. I shall do this when I am bigger, and give ether to the sick, so they will go to sleep and not feel me cut off their legs and arms."

"I know somebody who killed cats with it," called out Demi, but was promptly crushed by Dan, who upset his camp-stool and put a hat over his face.

"I will not be interruckted," said Nan, frowning upon the unseemly scrimmagers. Order was instantly restored, and the young lady closed her remarks as follows:

"My composition has three morals, my friends." Somebody groaned, but no notice was taken of the insult. "First, is keep your faces clean; second, get up early; third, when the ether sponge is put over your nose, breathe hard and don't kick, and your teeth will come out easy. I have no more to say." And Miss Nan sat down amid tumultuous applause.

"That is a very remarkable composition; its tone is high, and there is a good deal of humor in it. Very well done, Nan. Now, Daisy," and Mr. Bhaer smiled at one young lady as he beckoned the other.

Daisy colored prettily as she took her place, and said, in her modest little voice,

"I'm afraid you won't like mine; it isn't nice and funny like Nan's. But I couldn't do any better."

"We always like yours, Posy," said Uncle Fritz, and a gentle murmur from the boys seemed to confirm the remark. Thus encouraged, Daisy read her little paper, which was listened to with respectful attention.

"THE CAT

"The cat is a sweet animal. I love them very much. They are clean and pretty, and catch rats and mice, and let you pet them, and are fond of you if you are kind. They are very wise, and can find their way anywhere. Little cats are called kittens, and are dear things. I have two, named Huz and Buz, and their mother is Topaz, because she has yellow eyes. Uncle told me a pretty story about a man named Ma-ho-met. He had a nice cat, and when she was asleep on his sleeve, and he wanted to go away, he cut off the sleeve so as not to wake her up. I think he was a kind man. Some cats catch fish."

"So do I!" cried Teddy, jumping up eager to tell about his trout.

"Hush!" said his mother, setting him down again as quickly as possible, for orderly Daisy hated to be "interruckted," as Nan expressed it.

"I read about one who used to do it very slyly. I tried to make Topaz, but she did not like the water, and scratched me. She does like tea, and when I play in my kitchen she pats the teapot with her paw, till I give her some. She is a fine cat, she eats apple-pudding and molasses. Most cats do not."

"That's a first-rater," called out Nat, and Daisy retired, pleased with the praise of her friend.

"Demi looks so impatient we must have him up at once or he won't hold out," said Uncle Fritz, and Demi skipped up with alacrity.

"Mine is a poem!" he announced in a tone of triumph, and read his first effort in a loud and solemn voice:

> "I write about the butterfly,
>   It is a pretty thing;
> And flies about like the birds,
>   But it does not sing.
>
> "First it is a little grub,
>   And then it is a nice yellow cocoon,
> And then the butterfly
>   Eats its way out soon.
>
> "They live on dew and honey,

> They do not have any hive,
> They do not sting like wasps, and bees, and hornets,
> And to be as good as they are we should strive.
>
> "I should like to be a beautiful butterfly,
>   All yellow, and blue, and green, and red;
> But I should not like
>   To have Dan put camphor on my poor little head."

This unusual burst of genius brought down the house, and Demi was obliged to read it again, a somewhat difficult task, as there was no punctuation whatever, and the little poet's breath gave out before he got to the end of some of the long lines.

"He will be a Shakespeare yet," said Aunt Jo, laughing as if she would die, for this poetic gem reminded her of one of her own, written at the age of ten, and beginning gloomily,

> "I wish I had a quiet tomb,
>   Beside a little rill;
> Where birds, and bees, and butterflies,
>   Would sing upon the hill."

"Come on, Tommy. If there is as much ink inside your paper as there is outside, it will be a long composition," said Mr. Bhaer, when Demi had been induced to tear himself from his poem and sit down.

"It isn't a composition, it's a letter. You see, I forgot all about its being my turn till after school, and then I didn't know what to have, and there wasn't time to read up; so I thought you wouldn't mind my taking a letter that I wrote to my Grandma. It's got something about birds in it, so I thought it would do."

With this long excuse, Tommy plunged into a sea of ink and floundered through, pausing now and then to decipher one of his own flourishes.

MY DEAR GRANDMA, I hope you are well. Uncle James sent me a pocket rifle. It is a beautiful little instrument of killing, shaped like this [Here Tommy displayed a remarkable sketch of what looked like an intricate pump, or the inside of a small steam-engine] 44 are the sights; 6 is a false stock that fits in at A; 3 is the trigger, and 2 is the cock. It loads at the breech, and fires with great force and straightness. I am going out shooting squirrels soon. I shot several fine birds for the museum. They had speckled breasts, and Dan liked them very much. He stuffed them tip-top, and they sit on the tree quite natural, only one looks a little tipsy. We had a Frenchman working here the other day, and Asia called his name so funnily that I will tell you about it. His name was Germain: first she called him Jerry, but we laughed at her, and she changed it to Jeremiah; but ridicule was the result, so it became Mr. Germany; but ridicule having been again resumed, it became Garrymon, which it has remained ever since. I do not write often, I am so busy; but I think of you often, and sympathize with you, and sincerely hope you get on as well as can be expected without me. Your affectionate grandson,

THOMAS BUCKMINSTER BANGS.

P.S. If you come across any postage-stamps, remember me.

N.B. Love to all, and a great deal to Aunt Almira. Does she make any nice plum-cakes now?

P.S. Mrs. Bhaer sends her respects.

P.S. And so would Mr. B, if he knew I was in act to write.

N.B. Father is going to give me a watch on my birthday. I am glad as at present I have no means of telling time, and am often late at school.

P.S. I hope to see you soon. Don't you wish to send for me?

T. B. B.

As each postscript was received with a fresh laugh from the boys, by the time he came to the sixth and last, Tommy was so exhausted that he was glad to sit down and wipe his ruddy face.

"I hope the dear old lady will live through it," said Mr. Bhaer, under cover of the noise.

"We won't take any notice of the broad hint given in that last P.S. The letter will be quite as much as she can bear without a visit from Tommy," answered Mrs. Jo, remembering that the old lady usually took to her bed after a visitation from her irrepressible grandson.

"Now, me," said Teddy, who had learned a bit of poetry, and was so eager to say it that he had been bobbing up and down during the reading, and could no longer be restrained.

"I'm afraid he will forget it if he waits; and I have had a deal of trouble teaching him," said his mother.

Teddy trotted to the rostrum, dropped a curtsey and nodded his head at the same time, as if anxious to suit every one; then, in his baby voice, and putting the emphasis on the wrong words, he said his verse all in one breath:

Little drops of water,
  Little drains of sand,
Mate a might okum (ocean),
  And a peasant land.

Little words of kindness,
  Pokin evvy day,
Make a home a hebbin,
  And hep us on a way.

Lesson 123

1. What do you predict will happen in the rest of the chapter?

2. Finish the chapter.

3. Had you remembered that the boys had planned to give Dan a gift?

4. Write or tell about a surprise gift that you received.

Chapter XVII. continued
Clapping his hands at the end, he made another double salutation, and then ran to hide his head in his mother's lap, quite overcome by the success of his "piece," for the applause was tremendous.

Dick and Dolly did not write, but were encouraged to observe the habits of animals and insects, and report what they saw. Dick liked this, and always had a great deal to say; so, when his name was called, he marched up, and, looking at the audience with his bright confiding eyes, told his little story so earnestly that no one smiled at his crooked body, because the "straight soul" shone through it beautifully.

"I've been watching dragonflies, and I read about them in Dan's book, and I'll try and tell you what I remember. There's lots of them flying round on the pond, all blue, with big eyes, and sort of lace wings, very pretty. I caught one, and looked at him, and I think he was the handsomest insect I ever saw. They catch littler creatures than they are to eat, and have a queer kind of hook thing that folds up when they ain't hunting. It likes the sunshine, and dances round all day. Let me see! what else was there to tell about? Oh, I know! The eggs are laid in the water, and go down to the bottom, and are hatched in the mud. Little ugly things come out of 'em; I can't say the name, but they are brown, and keep having new skins, and getting bigger and bigger. Only think! it takes them two years to be a dragonfly! Now this is the curiousest part of it, so you listen tight, for I don't believe you know it. When it is ready it knows somehow, and the ugly, grubby thing climbs up out of the water on a flag or a bulrush, and bursts open its back."

"Come, I don't believe that," said Tommy, who was not an observant boy, and really thought Dick was "making up."

"It does burst open its back, don't it?" and Dick appealed to Mr. Bhaer, who nodded a very decided affirmative, to the little speaker's great satisfaction.

"Well, out comes the dragonfly, all whole, and he sits in the sun sort of coming alive, you know; and he gets strong, and then he spreads his pretty wings, and flies away up in the air, and never is a grub any more. That's all I know; but I shall watch and try to see him do it, for I think it's splendid to turn into a beautiful dragonfly, don't you?"

Dick had told his story well, and, when he described the flight of the new-born insect, had waved his hands, and looked up as if he saw, and wanted to follow it. Something in his face suggested to the minds of the elder listeners the thought that some day little Dick would have his wish, and after years of helplessness and pain would climb up into the sun some happy day, and, leaving his poor little body behind him, find a new lovely shape in a fairer world than this. Mrs. Jo drew him to her side, and said, with a kiss on his thin cheek,

"That is a sweet little story, dear, and you remembered it wonderfully well. I shall write and tell your mother all about it;" and Dick sat on her knee, contentedly smiling at the praise, and resolving to watch well, and catch the dragonfly in the act of leaving its old body for the new, and see how he did it. Dolly had a few remarks to make upon the "Duck," and made them in a sing-song tone, for he had learned it by heart, and thought it a great plague to do it at all.

"Wild ducks are hard to kill; men hide and shoot at them, and have tame ducks to quack and make the wild ones come where the men can fire at them. They have wooden ducks made too, and they sail round, and the wild ones come to see them; they are stupid, I think. Our ducks are very tame. They eat a great deal, and go poking round in the mud and water. They don't take good care of their eggs, but them spoil, and-"

"Mine don't!" cried Tommy.

"Well, some people's do; Silas said so. Hens take good care of little ducks, only they don't like to have them go in the water, and make a great fuss. But the little ones don't care a bit. I like to eat ducks with stuffing in them and lots of apple-sauce."

"I have something to say about owls," began Nat, who had carefully prepared a paper upon this subject with some help from Dan.

"Owls have big heads, round eyes, hooked bills, and strong claws. Some are gray, some white, some black and yellowish. Their feathers are very soft, and stick out a great deal. They fly very quietly, and hunt bats, mice, little birds, and such things. They build nests in barns, hollow trees, and some take the nests of other birds. The great horned owl has two eggs bigger than a hen's and reddish brown. The tawny owl has five eggs, white and smooth; and this is the kind that hoots at night. Another kind sounds like a child crying. They eat mice and bats whole, and the parts that they cannot digest they make into little balls and spit out."

"My gracious! how funny!" Nan was heard to observe.

"They cannot see by day; and if they get out into the light, they go flapping round half blind, and the other birds chase and peck at them, as if they were making fun. The horned owl is very big, 'most as big as the eagle. It eats rabbits, rats, snakes, and birds; and lives in rocks and old tumble-down houses. They have a good many cries, and scream like a person being choked, and say, 'Waugh O! waugh O!' and it scares people at night in the woods. The white owl lives by the sea, and in cold places, and looks something like a hawk. There is a kind of owl that makes holes to live in like moles. It is called the burrowing owl, and is very small. The barn-owl is the commonest kind; and I have watched one sitting in a hole in a tree, looking like a little gray cat, with one eye shut and the other open. He comes out at dusk, and sits round waiting for the bats. I caught one, and here he is."

With that Nat suddenly produced from inside his jacket a little downy bird, who blinked and ruffled his feathers, looking very plump and sleepy and scared.

"Don't touch him! He is going to show off," said Nat, displaying his new pet with great pride. First he put a cocked hat on the bird's head, and the boys laughed at the funny effect; then he added a pair of paper spectacles, and that gave the owl such a wise look that they shouted with merriment. The performance closed with making the bird angry, and seeing him cling to a handkerchief upside down, pecking and "clucking," as Rob called it. He was allowed to fly after that, and settled himself on the bunch of pine-cones over the door, where he sat staring down at the company with an air of sleepy dignity that amused them very much.

"Have you anything for us, George?" asked Mr. Bhaer, when the room was still again.

"Well, I read and learned ever so much about moles, but I declare I've forgotten every bit of it, except that they dig holes to live in, that you catch them by pouring water down, and that they can't possibly live without eating very often;" and Stuffy sat down, wishing he had not been too lazy to write out his valuable observations, for a general smile went round when he mentioned the last of the three facts which lingered in his memory.

"Then we are done for to-day," began Mr. Bhaer, but Tommy called out in a great hurry,

"No we ain't. Don't you know? We must give the thing;" and he winked violently as he made an eye-glass of his fingers.

"Bless my heart, I forgot! Now is your time, Tom;" and Mr. Bhaer dropped into his seat again, while all the boys but Dan looked mightily tickled at something.

Nat, Tommy, and Demi left the room, and speedily returned with a little red morocco box set forth in state on Mrs. Jo's best silver salver. Tommy bore it, and, still escorted by Nat and Demi, marched up to unsuspecting Dan, who stared at them as if he thought they were going to make fun of him. Tommy had prepared an elegant and impressive speech for the occasion, but when the minute came, it all went out of his head, and he just said, straight from his kindly boyish heart,

"Here, old fellow, we all wanted to give you something to kind of pay for what happened awhile ago, and to show how much we liked you for being such a trump. Please take it, and have a jolly good time with it."

Dan was so surprised he could only get as red as the little box, and mutter, "Thanky, boys!" as he fumbled to open it. But when he saw what was inside, his face lighted up, and he seized the long desired treasure, saying so enthusiastically that every one was satisfied, though is language was anything but polished,

"What a stunner! I say, you fellows are regular bricks to give me this; it's just what I wanted. Give us your paw, Tommy."

Many paws were given, and heartily shaken, for the boys were charmed with Dan's pleasure, and crowded round him to shake hands and expatiate on the beauties of their gift. In the midst of this pleasant chatter, Dan's eye went to Mrs. Jo, who stood outside the group enjoying the scene with all her heart.

"No, I had nothing to do with it. The boys got it up all themselves," she said, answering the grateful look that seemed to thank her for that happy moment. Dan smiled, and said, in a tone that only she could understand,

"It's you all the same;" and making his way through the boys, he held out his hand first to her and then to the good Professor, who was beaming benevolently on his flock.

He thanked them both with the silent, hearty squeeze he gave the kind hands that had held him up, and led him into the safe refuge of a happy home. Not a word was spoken, but they felt all he would say, and little Teddy expressed his pleasure for them as he leaned from his father's arm to hug the boy, and say, in his baby way,

"My dood Danny! everybody loves him now."

"Come here, show off your spy-glass, Dan, and let us see some of your magnified pollywogs and annymalcumisms as you call 'em," said Jack, who felt so uncomfortable during this scene that he would have slipped away if Emil had not kept him.

"So I will, take a squint at that and see what you think of it," said Dan, glad to show off his precious microscope.

He held it over a beetle that happened to be lying on the table, and Jack bent down to take his squint, but looked up with an amazed face, saying,

"My eye! what nippers the old thing has got! I see now why it hurts so confoundedly when you grab a dorbug and he grabs back again."

"He winked at me," cried Nan, who had poked her head under Jack's elbow and got the second peep.

Every one took a look, and then Dan showed them the lovely plumage on a moth's wing, the four feathery corners to a hair, the veins on a leaf, hardly visible to the naked eye, but like a thick net through the wonderful little glass; the skin on their own fingers, looking like queer hills and valleys; a cobweb like a bit of coarse sewing silk, and the sting of a bee.

"It's like the fairy spectacles in my story-book, only more curious," said Demi, enchanted with the wonders he saw.

"Dan is a magician now, and he can show you many miracles going on all round you; for he has two things needful patience and a love of nature. We live in a beautiful and wonderful world, Demi, and the more you know about it the wiser and the better you will be. This little glass will give you a new set of teachers, and you may learn fine lessons from them if you will," said Mr. Bhaer, glad to see how interested the boys were in the matter.

"Could I see anybody's soul with this microscope if I looked hard?" asked Demi, who was much impressed with the power of the bit of glass.

"No, dear; it's not powerful enough for that, and never can be made so. You must wait a long while before your eyes are clear enough to see the most invisible of God's wonders. But looking at the lovely things you can see will help you to understand the lovelier things you can not see," answered Uncle Fritz, with his hand on the boy's head.

"Well, Daisy and I both think that if there are any angels, their wings look like that butterfly's as we see it through the glass, only more soft and gold."

"Believe it if you like, and keep your own little wings as bright and beautiful, only don't fly away for a long time yet."

"No, I won't," and Demi kept his word.

"Good-by, my boys; I must go now, but I leave you with our new Professor of Natural History;" and Mrs. Jo went away well pleased with that composition day.

Lesson 124

1. Read the title to Chapter 18. What are you picturing?
2. Read chapter 18.
3. Write a one-sentence summary of the chapter.
4. Tell or write a few sentences about a garden or a harvest feast that you have participated in. Which crops would you enjoy the most? Why?

Chapter XVIII. Crops

The gardens did well that summer, and in September the little crops were gathered in with much rejoicing. Jack and Ned joined their farms and raised potatoes, those being a good salable article. They got twelve bushels, counting little ones and all, and sold them to Mr. Bhaer at a fair price, for potatoes went fast in that house. Emil and Franz devoted themselves to corn, and had a jolly little husking in the barn, after which they took their corn to the mill, and came proudly home with meal enough to supply the family with hasty-pudding and Johnny-cake for a lone time. They would not take money for their crop; because, as Franz said, "We never can pay Uncle for all he has done for us if we raised corn for the rest of our days."

Nat had beans in such abundance that he despaired of ever shelling them, till Mrs. Jo proposed a new way, which succeeded admirably. The dry pods were spread upon the barn-floor, Nat fiddled, and the boys danced quadrilles on them, till they were thrashed out with much merriment and very little labor.

Tommy's six weeks' beans were a failure; for a dry spell early in the season hurt them, because he gave them no water; and after that he was so sure that they could take care of themselves, he let the poor things struggle with bugs and weeds till they were exhausted and died a lingering death. So Tommy had to dig his farm over again, and plant peas. But they were late; the birds ate many; the bushes, not being firmly planted, blew down, and when the poor peas came at last, no one cared for them, as their day was over, and spring-lamb had grown into mutton. Tommy consoled himself with a charitable effort; for he transplanted all the thistles he could find, and tended them carefully for Toby, who was fond of the prickly delicacy, and had eaten all he could find on the place. The boys had great fun over Tom's thistle bed; but he insisted that it was better to care for poor Toby than for himself, and declared that he would devote his entire farm next year to thistles, worms, and snails, that Demi's turtles and Nat's pet owl might have the food they loved, as well as the donkey. So like shiftless, kind-hearted, happy-go-lucky Tommy!

Demi had supplied his grandmother with lettuce all summer, and in the autumn sent his grandfather a basket of turnips, each one scrubbed up till it looked like a great white egg. His Grandma was fond of salad, and one of his Grandpa's favorite quotations was:

> Lucullus, whom frugality could charm,
> Ate roasted turnips at the Sabine farm.

Therefore these vegetable offerings to the dear domestic god and goddess were affectionate, appropriate, and classical.

Daisy had nothing but flowers in her little plot, and it bloomed all summer long with a succession of gay or fragrant posies. She was very fond of her garden, and delved away in it at all hours, watching over her roses, and pansies, sweet-peas, and mignonette, as faithfully and tenderly as she did over her dolls or her friends. Little nosegays were sent into town on all occasions, and certain vases about the house were her especial care. She had all sorts of pretty fancies about her flowers, and loved to tell the children the story of the pansy, and show them how the step-mother-leaf sat up in her green chair in purple and gold; how the two own children in gay yellow had each its little seat, while the step children, in dull colors, both sat on one small stool, and the poor little father in his red nightcap, was kept out of sight in the middle of the flower; that a monk's dark face looked out of the monk's-hood larkspur; that the flowers of the canary-vine were so like dainty birds fluttering their yellow wings, that one almost expected to see them fly away, and the snapdragons that went off like little pistol-shots when you cracked them. Splendid dollies did she make out of scarlet and white poppies, with ruffled robes tied round the waist with grass blade sashes, and astonishing hats of coreopsis on their green heads. Pea-pod boats, with rose-leaf sails, received these flower-people, and floated them about a placid pool in the most charming style; for finding that there were no elves, Daisy made her own, and loved the fanciful little friends who played their parts in her summer-life.

Nan went in for herbs, and had a fine display of useful plants, which she tended with steadily increasing interest and care. Very busy was she in September cutting, drying, and tying up her sweet harvest, and writing down in a little book how the different herbs are to be used. She had tried several experiments, and made several mistakes; so she wished to be particular lest she should give little Huz another fit by administering wormwood instead of catnip.

Dick, Dolly, and Rob each grubbed away on his small farm, and made more stir about it than all the rest put together. Parsnips and carrots were the crops of the two D.'s; and they longed for it to be late enough to pull up the precious vegetables. Dick did privately examine his carrots, and plant them again, feeling that Silas was right in saying it was too soon for them yet.

Rob's crop was four small squashes and one immense pumpkin. It really was a "bouncer," as every one said; and I assure you that two small persons could sit on it side by side. It seemed to have absorbed all the goodness of the little garden, and all the sunshine that shone down on it, and lay there a great round, golden ball, full of rich suggestions of pumpkin-pies for weeks to come. Robby was so proud of his mammoth vegetable that he took every one to see it, and, when frosts began to nip, covered it up each night with an old bedquilt, tucking it round as if the pumpkin was a well-beloved baby. The day it was gathered he would let no one touch it but himself, and nearly broke his back tugging it to the barn in his little wheelbarrow, with Dick and Dolly harnessed in front to give a heave up the path. His mother promised him that the Thanksgiving-pies should be made from it, and hinted vaguely that she had a plan in her head which would cover the prize pumpkin and its owner with glory.

Poor Billy had planted cucumbers, but unfortunately hoed them up and left the pig-weed. This mistake grieved him very much for tem minutes, then he forgot all about it, and sowed a handful of bright buttons which he had collected, evidently thinking in his feeble mind that they were money, and would come up and multiply, so that he might make many quarters, as Tommy did. No one disturbed him, and he did what he liked with his plot, which soon looked as if a series of small earthquakes had stirred it up. When the general harvest-day came, he would have had nothing but stones and weeds to show, if kind old Asia had not hung half-a-dozen oranges on the dead tree he stuck up in the middle. Billy was delighted with his crop; and no one spoiled his pleasure in the little miracle which pity wrought for him, by making withered branches bear strange fruit.

Stuffy had various trials with his melons; for, being impatient to taste them, he had a solitary revel before they were ripe, and made himself so ill, that for a day or two it seemed doubtful if he would ever eat any more. But he pulled through it, and served up his first cantaloupe without tasting a mouthful himself. They were excellent melons, for he had a warm slope for them, and they ripened fast. The last and best were lingering on the vines, and Stuffy had announced that he should sell them to a neighbor. This disappointed the boys, who had hoped to eat the melons themselves, and they expressed their displeasure in a new and striking manner. Going one morning to gaze upon the three fine watermelons which he had kept for the market, Stuffy was horrified to find the word "PIG" cut in white letters on the green rind, staring at him from every one. He was in a great rage, and flew to Mrs. Jo for redress. She listened, condoled with him, and then said,

"If you want to turn the laugh, I'll tell you how, but you must give up the melons."

"Well, I will; for I can't thrash all the boys, but I'd like to give them something to remember, the mean sneaks," growled Stuff, still in a fume.

Now Mrs. Jo was pretty sure who had done the trick, for she had seen three heads suspiciously near to one another in the sofa-corner the evening before; and when these heads had nodded with chuckles and whispers, this experienced woman knew mischief was afoot. A moonlight night, a rustling in the old cherry-tree near Emil's window, a cut on Tommy's finger, all helped to confirm her suspicions; and having cooled Stuffy's wrath a little, she bade him bring his maltreated melons to her room, and say not a word to any one of what had happened. He did so, and the three wags were amazed to find their joke so quietly taken. It spoilt the fun, and the entire disappearance of the melons made them uneasy. So did Stuffy's good-nature, for he looked more placid and plump than ever, and surveyed them with an air of calm pity that perplexed them very much.

At dinner-time they discovered why; for then Stuffy's vengeance fell upon them, and the laugh was turned against them. When the pudding was eaten, and the fruit was put on, Mary Ann re-appeared in a high state of giggle, bearing a large watermelon; Silas followed with another; and Dan brought up the rear with a third. One was placed before each of the three guilty lads; and they read on the smooth green skins this addition to their own work, "With the compliments of the PIG." Every one else read it also, and the whole table was in a roar, for the trick had been whispered about; so every one understood the sequel. Emil, Ned, and Tommy did not know where to look, and had not a word to say for themselves; so they wisely joined in the laugh, cut up the melons, and handed them round, saying, what all the rest agreed to, that Stuffy had taken a wise and merry way to return good for evil.

Dan had no garden, for he was away or lame the greater part of the summer; so he had helped Silas wherever he could, chopped wood for Asia, and taken care of the lawn so well, that Mrs. Jo always had smooth paths and nicely shaven turf before her door.

When the others got in their crops, he looked sorry that he had so little to show; but as autumn went on, he bethought himself of a woodland harvest which no one would dispute with him, and which was peculiarly his own. Every Saturday he was away alone to the forests, fields, and hills, and always came back loaded with spoils; for he seemed to know the meadows where the best flag-root grew, the thicket where the sassafras was spiciest, the haunts where the squirrels went for nuts, the white oak whose bark was most valuable, and the little gold-thread vine that Nursey liked to cure the canker with. All sorts of splendid red and yellow leaves did Dan bring home for Mrs. Jo to dress her parlor with, graceful-seeded grasses, clematis tassels, downy, soft, yellow wax-work berries, and mosses, red-brimmed, white, or emerald green.

"I need not sigh for the woods now, because Dan brings the woods to me," Mrs. Jo used to say, as she glorified the walls with yellow maple boughs and scarlet woodbine wreaths, or filled her vases with russet ferns, hemlock sprays full of delicate cones, and hardy autumn flowers; for Dan's crop suited her well.

The great garret was full of the children's little stores and for a time was one of the sights of the house. Daisy's flower seeds in neat little paper bags, all labelled, lay in a drawer of a three-legged table. Nan's herbs hung in bunches against the wall, filling the air with their aromatic breath. Tommy had a basket of thistle-down with the tiny seeds attached, for he meant to plant them next year, if they did not all fly away before that time. Emil had bunches of pop-corn hanging there to dry, and Demi laid up acorns and different sorts of grain for the pets. But Dan's crop made the best show, for fully one half of the floor was covered with the nuts he brought. All kinds were there, for he ranged the woods for miles round, climbed the tallest trees, and forced his way into the thickest hedges for his plunder. Walnuts, chestnuts, hazelnuts, and beechnuts lay in separate compartments, getting brown, and dry, and sweet, ready for winter revels.

There was one butternut-tree on the place, and Rob and Teddy called it theirs. It bore well this year, and the great dingy nuts came dropping down to hide among the dead leaves, where the busy squirrels found them better than the lazy Bhaers. Their father had told them (the boys, not the squirrels) they should have the nuts if they would pick them up, but no one was to help. It was easy work, and Teddy liked it, only he soon got tired, and left his little basket half full for another day. But the other day was slow to arrive, and, meantime, the sly squirrels were hard at work, scampering up and down the old elm-trees stowing the nuts away till their holes were full, then all about the crotches of the boughs, to be removed at their leisure. Their funny little ways amused the boys, till one day Silas said,

"Hev you sold them nuts to the squirrels?"

"No," answered Rob, wondering what Silas meant.

"Wal, then, you'd better fly round, or them spry little fellers won't leave you none."

"Oh, we can beat them when we begin. There are such lots of nuts we shall have a plenty."

"There ain't many more to come down, and they have cleared the ground pretty well, see if they hain't."

Robby ran to look, and was alarmed to find how few remained. He called Teddy, and they worked hard all one afternoon, while the squirrels sat on the fence and scolded.

"Now, Ted, we must keep watch, and pick up just as fast as they fall, or we shan't have more than a bushel, and every one will laugh at us if we don't."

"The naughty quillies tarn't have 'em. I'll pick fast and run and put 'em in the barn twick," said Teddy, frowning at little Frisky, who chattered and whisked his tail indignantly.

That night a high wind blew down hundreds of nuts, and when Mrs. Jo came to wake her little sons, she said, briskly,

"Come, my laddies, the squirrels are hard at it, and you will have to work well to-day, or they will have every nut on the ground."

"No, they won't," and Robby tumbled up in a great hurry, gobbled his breakfast, and rushed out to save his property.

Teddy went too, and worked like a little beaver, trotting to and fro with full and empty baskets. Another bushel was soon put away in the corn-barn, and they were scrambling among the leaves for more nuts when the bell rang for school.

"O father! let me stay out and pick. Those horrid squirrels will have my nuts if you don't. I'll do my lessons by and by," cried Rob, running into the school-room, flushed and tousled by the fresh cold wind and his eager work.

"If you had been up early and done a little every morning there would be no hurry now. I told you that, Rob, and you never minded. I cannot have the lessons neglected as the work has been. The squirrels will get more than their share this year, and they deserve it, for they have worked best. You may go an hour earlier, but that is all," and Mr. Bhaer led Rob to his place where the little man dashed at his books as if bent on making sure of the precious hour promised him.

It was almost maddening to sit still and see the wind shaking down the last nuts, and the lively thieves flying about, pausing now and then to eat one in his face, and flirt their tails, as if they said, saucily, "We'll have them in spite of you, lazy Rob." The only thing that sustained the poor child in this trying moment was the sight of Teddy working away all alone. It was really splendid the pluck and perseverance of the little lad. He picked and picked till his back ached; he trudged to and fro till his small legs were tired; and he defied wind, weariness, and wicked "quillies," till his mother left her work and did the carrying for him, full of admiration for the kind little fellow who tried to help his brother. When Rob was dismissed, he found Teddy reposing in the bushel-basket quite used up, but unwilling to quit the field; for he flapped his hat at the thieves with one grubby little hand, while he refreshed himself with the big apple held in the other.

Rob fell to work and the ground was cleared before two o'clock, the nuts safely in the corn-barn loft, and the weary workers exulted in their success. But Frisky and his wife were not to be vanquished so easily; and when Rob went up to look at his nuts a few days later he was amazed to see how many had vanished. None of the boys could have stolen them, because the door had been locked; the doves could not have eaten them, and there were no rats about. There was great lamentation among the young Bhaers till Dick said

"I saw Frisky on the roof of the corn-barn, may be he took them."

"I know he did! I'll have a trap, and kill him dead," cried Rob, disgusted with Frisky's grasping nature.

"Perhaps if you watch, you can find out where he puts them, and I may be able to get them back for you," said Dan, who was much amused by the fight between the boys and squirrels.

So Rob watched and saw Mr. and Mrs. Frisky drop from the drooping elm boughs on to the roof of the corn-barn, dodge in at one of the little doors, much to the disturbance of the doves, and come out with a nut in each mouth. So laden they could not get back the way they came, but ran down the low roof, along the wall, and leaping off at a corner they vanished a minute and re-appeared without their plunder. Rob ran to the place, and in a hollow under the leaves he found a heap of the stolen property hidden away to be carried off to the holes by and by.

"Oh, you little villains! I'll cheat you now, and not leave one," said Rob. So he cleared the corner and the corn-barn, and put the contested nuts in the garret, making sure that no broken window-pane could anywhere let in the unprincipled squirrels. They seemed to feel that the contest was over, and retired to their hole, but now and then could not resist throwing down nut-shells on Rob's head, and scolding violently as if they could not forgive him nor forget that he had the best of the battle.

Father and Mother Bhaer's crop was of a different sort, and not so easily described; but they were satisfied with it, felt that their summer work had prospered well, and by and by had a harvest that made them very happy.

Lesson 125

1. Read the title of Chapter 19. Make a prediction about who John Brooke is.

2. Read the first half of chapter 19.

3. What are you thinking?

Chapter XIX. John Brooke
"Wake up, Demi, dear! I want you."

"Why, I've just gone to bed; it can't be morning yet;" and Demi blinked like a little owl as he waked from his first sound sleep.

"It's only ten, but your father is ill, and we must go to him. O my little John! my poor little John!" and Aunt Jo laid her head down on the pillow with a sob that scared sleep from Demi's eyes and filled his heart with fear and wonder; for he dimly felt why Aunt Jo called him "John," and wept over him as if some loss had come that left him poor. He clung to her without a word, and in a minute she was quite steady again, and said, with a tender kiss as she saw his troubled face,

"We are going to say good-by to him, my darling, and there is no time to lose; so dress quickly and come to me in my room. I must go to Daisy."

"Yes, I will;" and when Aunt Jo was gone, little Demi got up quietly, dressed as if in a dream, and leaving Tommy fast asleep went away through the silent house, feeling that something new and sorrowful was going to happen something that set him apart from the other boys for a time, and made the world seem as dark and still and strange as those familiar rooms did in the night. A carriage sent by Mr. Laurie stood before the door. Daisy was soon ready, and the brother and sister held each other by the hand all the way into town, as they drove swiftly and silently with aunt and uncle through the shadowy roads to say good-by to father.

None of the boys but Franz and Emil knew what had happened, and when they came down next morning, great was their wonderment and discomfort, for the house seemed forlorn without its master and mistress. Breakfast was a dismal meal with no cheery Mrs. Jo behind the teapots; and when school-time came, Father Bhaer's place was empty. They wandered about in a disconsolate kind of way for an hour, waiting for news and hoping it would be all right with Demi's father, for good John Brooke was much beloved by the boys. Ten o'clock came, and no one arrived to relieve their anxiety. They did not feel like playing, yet the time dragged heavily, and they sat about listless and sober. All at once, Franz got up, and said, in his persuasive way,

"Look here, boys! let's go into school and do our lessons just as if Uncle was here. It will make the day go faster, and will please him, I know."

"But who will hear us say them?" asked Jack.

"I will; I don't know much more than you do, but I'm the oldest here, and I'll try to fill Uncle's place till he comes, if you don't mind."

Something in the modest, serious way Franz said this impressed the boys, for, though the poor lad's eyes were red with quiet crying for Uncle John in that long sad night, there was a new manliness about him, as if he had already begun to feel the cares and troubles of life, and tried to take them bravely.

"I will, for one," and Emil went to his seat, remembering that obedience to his superior officer is a seaman's first duty.

The others followed; Franz took his uncle's seat, and for an hour order reigned. Lessons were learned and said, and Franz made a patient, pleasant teacher, wisely omitting such lessons as he was not equal to, and keeping order more by the unconscious dignity that sorrow gave him than by any words of his own. The little boys were reading when a step was heard in the hall, and every one looked up to read the news in Mr. Bhaer's face as he came in. The kind face told them instantly that Demi had no father now, for it was worn and pale, and full of tender grief, which left him no words with which to answer Rob, as he ran to him, saying, reproachfully,

"What made you go and leave me in the night, papa?"

The memory of the other father who had left his children in the night, never to return, made Mr. Bhaer hold his own boy close, and, for a minute, hide his face in Robby's curly hair. Emil laid his head down on his arms, Franz, went to put his hand on his uncle's shoulder, his boyish face pale with sympathy and sorrow, and the others sat so still that the soft rustle of the falling leaves outside was distinctly heard.

Rob did not clearly understand what had happened, but he hated to see papa unhappy, so he lifted up the bent head, and said, in his chirpy little voice,

"Don't cry, mein Vater! we were all so good, we did our lessons, without you, and Franz was the master."

Mr. Bhaer looked up then, tried to smile, and said in a grateful tone that made the lads feel like saints, "I thank you very much, my boys. It was a beautiful way to help and comfort me. I shall not forget it, I assure you."

"Franz proposed it, and was a first-rate master, too," said Nat; and the others gave a murmur of assent most gratifying to the young dominie.

Mr. Bhaer put Rob down, and, standing up, put his arm round his tall nephew's shoulder, as he said, with a look of genuine pleasure,

"This makes my hard day easier, and gives me confidence in you all. I am needed there in town, and must leave you for some hours. I thought to give you a holiday, or send some of you home, but if you like to stay and go on as you have begun, I shall be glad and proud of my good boys."

"We'll stay;" "We'd rather;" "Franz can see to us;" cried several, delighted with the confidence shown in them.

"Isn't Marmar coming home?" asked Rob, wistfully; for home without "Marmar" was the world without the sun to him.

"We shall both come to-night; but dear Aunt Meg needs Mother more than you do now, and I know you like to lend her for a little while."

"Well, I will; but Teddy's been crying for her, and he slapped Nursey, and was dreadful naughty," answered Rob, as if the news might bring mother home.

"Where is my little man?" asked Mr. Bhaer.

"Dan took him out, to keep him quiet. He's all right now," said Franz, pointing to the window, through which they could see Dan drawing baby in his little wagon, with the dogs frolicking about him.

"I won't see him, it would only upset him again; but tell Dan I leave Teddy in his care. You older boys I trust to manage yourselves for a day. Franz will direct you, and Silas is here to over see matters. So good-by till to-night."

"Just tell me a word about Uncle John," said Emil, detaining Mr. Bhaer, as he was about hurrying away again.

"He was only ill a few hours, and died as he has lived, so cheerfully, so peacefully, that it seems a sin to mar the beauty of it with any violent or selfish grief. We were in time to say good-by: and Daisy and Demi were in his arms as he fell asleep on Aunt Meg's breast. No more now, I cannot bear it," and Mr. Bhaer went hastily away quite bowed with grief, for in John Brooke he had lost both friend and brother, and there was no one left to take his place.

All that day the house was very still; the small boys played quietly in the nursery; the others, feeling as if Sunday had come in the middle of the week, spent it in walking, sitting in the willow, or among their pets, all talking much of "Uncle John," and feeling that something gentle, just, and strong, had gone out of their little world, leaving a sense of loss that deepened every hour. At dusk, Mr. and Mrs. Bhaer came home alone, for Demi and Daisy were their mother's best comfort now, and could not leave her. Poor Mrs. Jo seemed quite spent, and evidently needed the same sort of comfort, for her first words, as she came up the stairs, were, "Where is my baby?"

"Here I is," answered a little voice, as Dan put Teddy into her arms, adding, as she hugged him close, "My Danny tooked tare of me all day, and I was dood."

Mrs. Jo turned to thank the faithful nurse, but Dan was waving off the boys, who had gathered in the hall to meet her, and was saying, in a low voice, "Keep back; she don't want to be bothered with us now."

"No, don't keep back. I want you all. Come in and see me, my boys. I've neglected you all day," and Mrs. Jo held out her hands to them as they gathered round and escorted her into her own room, saying little, but expressing much by affectionate looks and clumsy little efforts to show their sorrow and sympathy.

"I am so tired, I will lie here and cuddle Teddy, and you shall bring me in some tea," she said, trying to speak cheerfully for their sakes.

A general stampede into the dining-room followed, and the supper-table would have been ravaged if Mr. Bhaer had not interfered. It was agreed that one squad should carry in the mother's tea, and another bring it out. The four nearest and dearest claimed the first honor, so Franz bore the teapot, Emil the bread, Rob the milk, and Teddy insisted on carrying the sugar basin, which was lighter by several lumps when it arrived than when it started. Some women might have found it annoying at such a time to have boys creaking in and out, upsetting cups and rattling spoons in violent efforts to be quiet and helpful; but it suited Mrs. Jo, because just then her heart was very tender; and remembering that many of her boys were fatherless or motherless, she yearned over them, and found comfort in their blundering affection. It was the sort of food that did her more good than the very thick bread-and-butter that they gave her, and the rough Commodore's broken whisper,

"Bear up, Aunty, it's a hard blow; but we'll weather it somehow;" cheered her more than the sloppy cup he brought her, full of tea as bitter as if some salt tear of his own had dropped into it on the way. When supper was over, a second deputation removed the tray; and Dan said, holding out his arms for sleepy little Teddy,

"Let me put him to bed, you're so tired, Mother."

"Will you go with him, lovey?" asked Mrs. Jo of her small lord and master, who lay on her arm among the sofa-pillows.

"Torse I will;" and he was proudly carried off by his faithful bearer.

"I wish I could do something," said Nat, with a sigh, as Franz leaned over the sofa, and softly stroked Aunt Jo's hot forehead.

"You can, dear. Go and get your violin, and play me the sweet little airs Uncle Teddy sent you last. Music will comfort me better than any thing else to-night."

Nat flew for his fiddle, and, sitting just outside her door, played as he had never done before, for now his heart was in it, and seemed to magnetize his fingers. The other lads sat quietly upon the steps, keeping watch that no new-comer should disturb the house; Franz lingered at his post; and so, soothed, served, and guarded by her boys, poor Mrs. Jo slept at last, and forgot her sorrow for an hour.

Two quiet days, and on the third Mr. Bhaer came in just after school, with a note in his hand, looking both moved and pleased.

"I want to read you something, boys," he said; and as they stood round him he read this:

> DEAR BROTHER FRITZ, I hear that you do not mean to bring your flock today, thinking that I may not like it. Please do. The sight of his friends will help Demi through the hard hour, and I want the boys to hear what father says of my John. It will do them good, I know. If they would sing one of the sweet old hymns you have taught them so well, I

should like it better than any other music, and feel that it was beautifully suited to the occasion. Please ask them, with my love.

MEG.

Lesson 126

1. Finish chapter 19.
2. If you have ever attended a funeral, write or tell about your experience, or write a few sentences about someone in your life that you would consider "kind and good."

Vocabulary

1. Match the words to their definitions. These are the words from Lesson 121. Write your answers on a separate piece of paper. (Answers)

1.	corrupt or having turned from good to bad	A.	vaguely
2.	feeling or showing anger because of an injustice	B.	salable
3.	impossible to repress, control	C.	irrepressible
4.	not clearly or precisely	D.	indignant
5.	showing a noble, generous spirit	E.	inexplicable
6.	showing thanks	F.	perverse
7.	suitable for sale	G.	magnanimous
8.	unable to be explained	H.	gratitude

Chapter XIX. continued
"Will you go?" and Mr. Bhaer looked at the lads, who were greatly touched by Mrs. Brooke's kind words and wishes.

"Yes," they answered, like one boy; and an hour later they went away with Franz to bear their part in John Brooke's simple funeral.

The little house looked as quiet, sunny, and home-like as when Meg entered it as a bride, ten years ago, only then it was early summer, and rose blossomed everywhere; now it was early autumn, and dead leaves rustled softly down, leaving the branches bare. The bride was a widow now; but the same beautiful serenity shone in her face, and the sweet resignation of a truly pious soul made her presence a consolation to those who came to comfort her.

"O Meg! how can you bear it so?" whispered Jo, as she met them at the door with a smile of welcome, and no change in her gentle manner, except more gentleness.

"Dear Jo, the love that has blest me for ten happy years supports me still. It could not die, and John is more my own than ever," whispered Meg; and in her eyes the tender trust was so beautiful and bright, that Jo believed her, and thanked God for the immortality of love like hers.

They were all there father and mother, Uncle Teddy, and Aunt Amy, old Mr. Laurence, white-haired and feeble now, Mr. and Mrs. Bhaer, with their flock, and many friends, come to do honor to the dead. One would have said that modest John Brooke, in his busy, quiet, humble life, had had little time to make friends; but now they seemed to start up everywhere, old and young, rich and poor, high and low; for all unconsciously his influence had made itself widely felt, his virtues were remembered, and his hidden charities rose up to bless him. The group about his coffin was a far more eloquent eulogy than any Mr. March could utter. There were the rich men whom he had served faithfully for years; the poor old women whom he cherished with his little store, in memory of his mother; the wife to whom he had given such happiness that death could not mar it utterly; the brothers and sisters in whose hearts he had made a place for ever; the little son and daughter, who already felt the loss of his strong arm and tender voice; the young children, sobbing for their kindest playmate, and the tall lads, watching with softened faces a scene which they never could forget. A very simple service, and very short; for the fatherly voice that had faltered in the marriage-sacrament now failed entirely as Mr. March endeavored to pay his tribute of reverence and love to the son whom he most honored. Nothing but the soft coo of Baby Josy's voice up-stairs broke the long hush that followed the last Amen, till, at a sign from Mr. Bhaer, the well-trained boyish voices broke out in a hymn, so full of lofty cheer, that one by one all joined in it, singing with full hearts, and finding their troubled spirits lifted into peace on the wings of that brave, sweet psalm.

As Meg listened, she felt that she had done well; for not only did the moment comfort her with the assurance that John's last lullaby was sung by the young voices he loved so well, but in the faces of the boys she saw that they had caught a glimpse of the beauty of virtue in its most impressive form, and that the memory of the good man lying dead before them would live long and helpfully in their remembrance. Daisy's head lay in her lap, and Demi held her hand, looking often at her, with eyes so like his father's, and a little gesture that seemed to say, "Don't be troubled, mother; I am here;" and all about her were friends to lean upon and love; so patient, pious Meg put by her heavy grief, feeling that her best help would be to live for others, as her John had done.

That evening, as the Plumfield boys sat on the steps, as usual, in the mild September moonlight, they naturally fell to talking of the event of the day.

Emil began by breaking out, in his impetuous way, "Uncle Fritz is the wisest, and Uncle Laurie the jolliest, but Uncle John was the best; and I'd rather be like him than any man I ever saw."

"So would I. Did you hear what those gentlemen said to Grandpa to-day? I would like to have that said of me when I was dead;" and Franz felt with regret that he had not appreciated Uncle John enough.

"What did they say?" asked Jack, who had been much impressed by the scenes of the day.

"Why, one of the partners of Mr. Laurence, where Uncle John has been ever so long, was saying that he was conscientious almost to a fault as a business man, and above reproach in all things. Another gentleman said no money could repay the fidelity and honesty with which Uncle John had served him, and then Grandpa told them the best of all. Uncle John once had a place in the office of a man who cheated, and when this man wanted uncle to help him do it, uncle wouldn't, though he was offered a big salary. The man was angry and said, 'You will never get on in business with such strict principles;' and uncle answered back, 'I never will try to get on without them,' and left the place for a much harder and poorer one."

"Good!" cried several of the boys warmly, for they were in the mood to understand and value the little story as never before.

"He wasn't rich, was he?" asked Jack.

"No."

"He never did any thing to make a stir in the world, did he?"

"No."

"He was only good?"

"That's all;" and Franz found himself wishing that Uncle John had done something to boast of, for it was evident that Jack was disappointed by his replies.

"Only good. That is all and every thing," said Mr. Bhaer, who had overheard the last few words, and guessed what was going on the minds of the lads.

"Let me tell you a little about John Brooke, and you will see why men honor him, and why he was satisfied to be good rather than rich or famous. He simply did his duty in all things, and did it so cheerfully, so faithfully, that it kept him patient and brave, and happy through poverty and loneliness and years of hard work. He was a good son, and gave up his own plans to stay and live with his mother while she needed him. He was a good friend, and taught Laurie much beside his Greek and Latin, did it unconsciously, perhaps, by showing him an example of an upright man. He was a faithful servant, and made himself so valuable to those who employed him that they will find it hard to fill his place. He was a good husband and father, so tender, wise, and thoughtful, that

Laurie and I learned much of him, and only knew how well he loved his family, when we discovered all he had done for them, unsuspected and unassisted."

Mr. Bhaer stopped a minute, and the boys sat like statues in the moonlight until he went on again, in a subdued, but earnest voice: "As he lay dying, I said to him, 'Have no care for Meg and the little ones; I will see that they never want.' Then he smiled and pressed my hand, and answered, in his cheerful way, 'No need of that; I have cared for them.' And so he had, for when we looked among his papers, all was in order, not a debt remained; and safely put away was enough to keep Meg comfortable and independent. Then we knew why he had lived so plainly, denied himself so many pleasures, except that of charity, and worked so hard that I fear he shortened his good life. He never asked help for himself, though often for others, but bore his own burden and worked out his own task bravely and quietly. No one can say a word of complaint against him, so just and generous and kind was he; and now, when he is gone, all find so much to love and praise and honor, that I am proud to have been his friend, and would rather leave my children the legacy he leaves his than the largest fortune ever made. Yes! Simple, generous goodness is the best capital to found the business of this life upon. It lasts when fame and money fail, and is the only riches we can take out of this world with us. Remember that, my boys; and if you want to earn respect and confidence and love follow in the footsteps of John Brooke."

When Demi returned to school, after some weeks at home, he seemed to have recovered from his loss with the blessed elasticity of childhood, and so he had in a measure; but he did not forget, for his was a nature into which things sank deeply, to be pondered over, and absorbed into the soil where the small virtues were growing fast. He played and studied, worked and sang, just as before, and few suspected any change; but there was one and Aunt Jo saw it for she watched over the boy with her whole heart, trying to fill John's place in her poor way. He seldom spoke of his loss, but Aunt Jo often heard a stifled sobbing in the little bed at night; and when she went to comfort him, all his cry was, "I want my father! oh, I want my father!" for the tie between the two had been a very tender one, and the child's heart bled when it was broken. But time was kind to him, and slowly he came to feel that father was not lost, only invisible for a while, and sure to be found again, well and strong and fond as ever, even though his little son should see the purple asters blossom on his grave many, many times before they met. To this belief Demi held fast, and in it found both help and comfort, because it led him unconsciously through a tender longing for the father whom he had seen to a childlike trust in the Father whom he had not seen. Both were in heaven, and he prayed to both, trying to be good for love of them.

The outward change corresponded to the inward, for in those few weeks Demi seemed to have grown tall, and began to drop his childish plays, not as if ashamed of them, as some boys do, but as if he had outgrown them, and wanted something manlier. He took to the hated arithmetic, and held on so steadily that his uncle was charmed, though he could not understand the whim, until Demi said,

"I am going to be a bookkeeper when I grow up, like papa, and I must know about figures and things, else I can't have nice, neat ledgers like his."

At another time he came to his aunt with a very serious face, and said

"What can a small boy do to earn money?"

"Why do you ask, my deary?"

"My father told me to take care of mother and the little girls, and I want to, but I don't know how to begin."

"He did not mean now, Demi, but by and by, when you are large."

"But I wish to begin now, if I can, because I think I ought to make some money to buy things for the family. I am ten, and other boys no bigger than I earn pennies sometimes."

"Well, then, suppose you rake up all the dead leaves and cover the strawberry bed. I'll pay you a dollar for the job," said Aunt Jo.

"Isn't that a great deal? I could do it in one day. You must be fair, and no pay too much, because I want to truly earn it."

"My little John, I will be fair, and not pay a penny too much. Don't work too hard; and when that is done I will have something else for you to do," said Mrs. Jo, much touched by his desire to help, and his sense of justice, so like his scrupulous father.

When the leaves were done, many barrowloads of chips were wheeled from the wood to the shed, and another dollar earned. Then Demi helped cover the schoolbooks, working in the evenings under Franz's direction, tugging patiently away at each book, letting no one help, and receiving his wages with such satisfaction that the dingy bills became quite glorified in his sight.

"Now, I have a dollar for each of them, and I should like to take my money to mother all myself, so she can see that I have minded my father."

So Demi made a duteous pilgrimage to his mother, who received his little earnings as a treasure of great worth, and would have kept it untouched, if Demi had not begged her to buy some useful thing for herself and the women-children, whom he felt were left to his care.

This made him very happy, and, though he often forgot his responsibilities for a time, the desire to help was still there, strengthening with his years. He always uttered the words "my father" with an air of gentle pride, and often said, as if he claimed a title full of honor, "Don't call me Demi any more. I am John Brooke now." So, strengthened by a purpose and a hope, the little lad of ten bravely began the world, and entered into his inheritance, the memory of a wise and tender father, the legacy of an honest name.

Lesson 127

1. Read the title of Chapter 20. What activities do you picture happening "round the fire" at Plumfield? Think of two or three predictions.

2. Start reading chapter 20.

3. What are you thinking? If you have a choice, do you prefer true stories or fiction (made up) stories? Why?

Vocabulary

1. Review your words from Lesson 121 or use the matching activity on Lesson 126.

Chapter XX. Round the Fire

With the October frosts came the cheery fires in the great fireplaces; and Demi's dry pine-chips helped Dan's oak-knots to blaze royally, and go roaring up the chimney with a jolly sound. All were glad to gather round the hearth, as the evenings grew longer, to play games, read, or lay plans for the winter. But the favorite amusement was story-telling, and Mr. and Mrs. Bhaer were expected to have a store of lively tales always on hand. Their supply occasionally gave out, and then the boys were thrown upon their own resources, which were not always successful. Ghost-parties were the rage at one time; for the fun of the thing consisted in putting out the lights, letting the fire die down, and then sitting in the dark, and telling the most awful tales they could invent. As this resulted in scares of all sorts among the boys, Tommy's walking in his sleep on the shed roof, and a general state of nervousness in the little ones, it was forbidden, and they fell back on more harmless amusements.

One evening, when the small boys were snugly tucked in bed, and the older lads were lounging about the school-room fire, trying to decide what they should do, Demi suggested a new way of settling the question.

Seizing the hearth-brush, he marched up and down the room, saying, "Row, row, row;" and when the boys, laughing and pushing, had got into line, he said, "Now, I'll give you two minutes to think of a play." Franz was writing, and Emil reading the Life of Lord Nelson, and neither joined the party, but the others thought hard, and when the time was up were ready to reply.

"Now, Tom!" and the poker softly rapped him on the head.

"Blind-man's Buff."

"Jack!"

"Commerce; a good round game, and have cents for the pool."

"Uncle forbids our playing for money. Dan, what do you want?"

"Let's have a battle between the Greeks and Romans."

"Stuffy?"

"Roast apples, pop corn, and crack nuts."

"Good! good!" cried several; and when the vote was taken, Stuffy's proposal carried the day.

Some went to the cellar for apples, some to the garret for nuts, and others looked up the popper and the corn.

"We had better ask the girls to come in, hadn't we?" said Demi, in a sudden fit of politeness.

"Daisy pricks chestnuts beautifully," put in Nat, who wanted his little friend to share the fun.

"Nan pops corn tip-top, we must have her," added Tommy.

"Bring in your sweethearts then, we don't mind," said Jack, who laughed at the innocent regard the little people had for one another.

"You shan't call my sister a sweetheart; it is so silly!" cried Demi, in a way that made Jack laugh.

"She is Nat's darling, isn't she, old chirper?"

"Yes, if Demi don't mind. I can't help being fond of her, she is so good to me," answered Nat, with bashful earnestness, for Jack's rough ways disturbed him.

"Nan is my sweetheart, and I shall marry her in about a year, so don't you get in the way, any of you," said Tommy, stoutly; for he and Nan had settled their future, child-fashion, and were to live in the willow, lower down a basket for food, and do other charmingly impossible things.

Demi was quenched by the decision of Bangs, who took him by the arm and walked him off to get the ladies. Nan and Daisy were sewing with Aunt Jo on certain small garments, for Mrs. Carney's newest baby.

"Please, ma'am, could you lend us the girls for a little while? We'll be very careful of them," said Tommy, winking one eye to express apples, snapping his fingers to signify pop-corn, and gnashing his teeth to convey the idea of nut-cracking.

The girls understood this pantomime at once, and began to pull of their thimbles before Mrs. Jo could decide whether Tommy was going into convulsions or was brewing some unusual piece of mischief. Demi explained with elaboration, permission was readily granted, and the boys departed with their prize.

"Don't you speak to Jack," whispered Tommy, as he and Nan promenaded down the hall to get a fork to prick the apples.

"Why not?"

"He laughs at me, so I don't wish you to have any thing to do with him."

"Shall, if I like," said Nan, promptly resenting this premature assumption of authority on the part of her lord.

"Then I won't have you for my sweetheart."

"I don't care."

"Why, Nan, I thought you were fond of me!" and Tommy's voice was full of tender reproach.

"If you mind Jack's laughing I don't care for you one bit."

"Then you may take back your old ring; I won't wear it any longer;" and Tommy plucked off a horsehair pledge of affection which Nan had given him in return for one made of a lobster's feeler.

"I shall give it to Ned," was her cruel reply; for Ned liked Mrs. Giddy-gaddy, and had turned her clothespins, boxes, and spools enough to set up housekeeping with.

Tommy said, "Thunder turtles!" as the only vent equal to the pent-up anguish of the moment, and, dropping Nan's arm, retired in high dudgeon, leaving her to follow with the fork, a neglect which naughty Nan punished by proceeding to prick his heart with jealousy as if it were another sort of apple.

The hearth was swept, and the rosy Baldwins put down to roast. A shovel was heated, and the chestnuts danced merrily upon it, while the corn popped wildly in its wire prison. Dan cracked his best walnuts, and every one chattered and laughed, while the rain beat on the window-pane and the wind howled round the house.

"Why is Billy like this nut?" asked Emil, who was frequently inspired with bad conundrums.

"Because he is cracked," answered Ned.

"That's not fair; you mustn't make fun of Billy, because he can't hit back again. It's mean," cried Dan, smashing a nut wrathfully.

"To what family of insects does Blake belong?" asked peacemaker Franz, seeing that Emil looked ashamed and Dan lowering.

"Gnats," answered Jack.

"Why is Daisy like a bee?" cried Nat, who had been wrapt in thought for several minutes.

"Because she is queen of the hive," said Dan.

"No."

"Because she is sweet."

"Bees are not sweet."

"Give it up."

"Because she makes sweet things, is always busy, and likes flowers," said Nat, piling up his boyish compliments till Daisy blushed like a rosy clover.

"Why is Nan like a hornet?" demanded Tommy, glowering at her, and adding, without giving any one time to answer, "Because she isn't sweet, makes a great buzzing about nothing, and stings like fury."

"Tommy's mad, and I'm glad," cried Ned, as Nan tossed her head and answered quickly

"What thing in the china-closet is Tom like?"

"A pepper pot," answered Ned, giving Nan a nut meat with a tantalizing laugh that made Tommy feel as if he would like to bounce up like a hot chestnut and hit somebody.

Seeing that ill-humor was getting the better of the small supply of wit in the company, Franz cast himself into the breach again.

"Let's make a law that the first person who comes into the room shall tell us a story. No matter who it is, he must do it, and it will be fun to see who comes first."

The others agreed, and did not have to wait long, for a heavy step soon came clumping through the hall, and Silas appeared, bearing an armful of wood. He was greeted by a general shout, and stood staring about him with a bewildered grin on his big red face, till Franz explained the joke.

"Sho! I can't tell a story," he said, putting down his load and preparing to leave the room. But the boys fell upon him, forced him into a seat, and held him there, laughing, and clamoring for their story, till the good-natured giant was overpowered.

"I don't know but jest one story, and that's about a horse," he said, much flattered by the reception he received.

"Tell it! tell it!" cried the boys.

"Wal," began Silas, tipping his chair back against the wall, and putting his thumbs in the arm-holes of his waistcoat, "I jined a cavalry regiment durin' the war, and see a consid'able amount of fightin'. My horse, Major, was a fust-rate animal, and I was as fond on him as ef he'd ben a human critter. He warn't harnsome, but he was the best-tempered, stiddyest, lovenest brute I ever see. I fust battle we went into, he gave me a lesson that I didn't forgit in a hurry, and I'll tell you how it was. It ain't no use tryin' to picter the noise and hurry, and general horridness of a battle to you young fellers, for I ain't no words to do it in; but I'm free to confess that I got so sort of confused and upset at the fust on it, that I didn't know what I was about. We was ordered to charge, and went ahead like good ones, never stoppin' to pick up them that went down in the scrimmage. I got a shot in the arm, and was pitched out of the saddle don't know how, but there I was left behind with two or three others, dead and wounded, for the rest went on, as I say. Wal, I picked myself up and looked round for Major, feeling as ef I'd had about enough for that spell. I didn't see him nowhere, and was kinder walking back to camp, when I heard a whinny that sounded nateral. I looked round, and there was Major stopping for me a long way off, and lookin' as ef he didn't understand why I was loiterin' behind. I whistled, and he trotted up to me as I'd trained him to do. I mounted as well as I could with my left arm bleedin' and was for going on to camp, for I declare I felt as sick and wimbly as a woman; folks often do in their fust battle. But, no sir! Major was the bravest of the two, and he wouldn't go, not a peg; he jest rared up, and danced, and snorted, and acted as ef the smell of powder and the noise had drove him half wild. I done my best, but he wouldn't give in, so I did; and what do you think that plucky brute done? He wheeled slap round, and galloped back like a hurricane, right into the thickest of the scrimmage!"

"Good for him!" cried Dan excitedly, while the other boys forgot apples and nuts in their interest.

"I wish I may die ef I warn't ashamed of myself," continued Silas, warming up at the recollection of that day. "I was mad as a hornet, and I forgot my waound, and jest pitched in, rampagin' raound like fury till there come a shell into the midst of us, and in bustin' knocked a lot of us flat. I didn't know nothin' for a spell, and when I come-to, the fight was over just there, and I found myself layin' by a wall of poor Major long-side wuss wounded than I was. My leg was broke, and I had a ball in my shoulder, but he, poor old feller! was all tore in the side with a piece of that blasted shell."

"O Silas! what did you do?" cried Nan, pressing close to him with a face full of eager sympathy and interest.

"I dragged myself nigher, and tried to stop the bleedin' with sech rags as I could tear off of me with one hand. But it warn't no use, and he lay moanin' with horrid pain, and lookin' at me with them lovin' eyes of his, till I thought I couldn't bear it. I give him all the help I could, and when the sun got hotter and hotter, and he began to lap out his tongue, I tried to get to a brook that was a good piece away, but I couldn't do it, being stiff and faint, so I give it up and fanned him with my hat. Now you listen to this, and when you hear folks comin' down on the rebs, you jest remember what one on 'em did, and give him credit of it. I poor feller in gray laid not fur off, shot through the lungs and dyin' fast. I'd offered him my handkerchief to keep the sun off his face, and he'd thanked me kindly, for in sech times as that men don't stop to think on which side they belong, but jest buckle-to and help one another. When he see me mournin' over Major and tryin' to ease his pain, he looked up with his face all damp and white with sufferin', and sez he, 'There's water in my canteen; take it, for it can't help me,' and he flung it to me. I couldn't have took it ef I hadn't had a little brandy in a pocket flask, and I made him drink it. It done him good, and I felt as much set up as if I'd drunk it myself. It's surprisin' the good sech little things do folks sometime;" and Silas paused as if he felt again the comfort of that moment when he and his enemy forgot their feud, and helped one another like brothers.

"Tell about Major," cried the boys, impatient for the catastrophe.

"I poured the water over his poor pantin' tongue, and ef ever a dumb critter looked grateful, he did then. But it warn't of much use, for the dreadful waound kep on tormentin' him, till I couldn't bear it any longer. It was hard, but I done it in mercy, and I know he forgive me."

"What did you do?" asked Emil, as Silas stopped abruptly with a loud "hem," and a look in his rough face that made Daisy go and stand by him with her little hand on his knee.

"I shot him."

Quite a thrill went through the listeners as Silas said that, for Major seemed a hero in their eyes, and his tragic end roused all their sympathy.

"Yes, I shot him, and put him out of his misery. I patted him fust, and said, 'Good-by;' then I laid his head easy on the grass, give a last look into his lovin' eyes, and sent a bullet through his head. He hardly stirred, I aimed so true, and when I seen him quite still, with no more moanin' and pain, I was glad, and yet wal, I don't know as I need by ashamed on't I jest put my arms raound his neck and boo-hooed like a great baby. Sho! I didn't know I was sech a fool;" and Silas drew his sleeve across his eyes, as much touched by Daisy's sob, as by the memory of faithful Major.

No one spoke for a minute, because the boys were as quick to feel the pathos of the little story as tender-hearted Daisy, though they did not show it by crying.

"I'd like a horse like that," said Dan, half-aloud.

"Did the rebel man die, too?" asked Nan, anxiously.

"Not then. We laid there all day, and at night some of our fellers came to look after the missing ones. They nat'rally wanted to take me fust, but I knew I could wait, and the rebel had but one chance, maybe, so I made them carry him off right away. He had jest strength enough to hold out his hand to me and say, 'Thanky, comrade!' and them was the last words he spoke, for he died an hour after he got to the hospital-tent."

"How glad you must have been that you were kind to him!" said Demi, who was deeply impressed by this story.

"Wal, I did take comfort thinkin' of it, as I laid there alone for a number of hours with my head on Major's neck, and see the moon come up. I'd like to have buried the poor beast decent, but it warn't possible; so I cut off a bit of his mane, and I've kep it ever sence. Want to see it, sissy?"

"Oh, yes, please," answered Daisy, wiping away her tears to look.

Silas took out an old "wallet" as he called his pocket-book, and produced from an inner fold a bit of brown paper, in which was a rough lock of white horse-hair. The children looked at it silently, as it lay in the broad palm, and no one found any thing to ridicule in the love Silas bore his good horse Major.

"That is a sweet story, and I like it, though it did make me cry. Thank you very much, Si," and Daisy helped him fold and put away his little relic; while Nan stuffed a handful of pop-corn into his pocket, and the boys loudly expressed their flattering opinions of his story, feeling that there had been two heroes in it.

He departed, quite overcome by his honors, and the little conspirators talked the tale over, while they waited for their next victim. It was Mrs. Jo, who came in to measure Nan for some new pinafores she was making for her. They let her get well in, and then pounced upon her, telling her the law, and demanding the story. Mrs. Jo was very much amused at the new trap, and consented at once, for the sound of happy voices had been coming across the hall so pleasantly that she quite longed to join them, and forget her own anxious thoughts of Sister Meg.

"Am I the first mouse you have caught, you sly pussies-in-boots?" she asked, as she was conducted to the big chair, supplied with refreshments, and surrounded by a flock of merry-faced listeners.

They told her about Silas and his contribution, and she slapped her forehead in despair, for she was quite at her wits' end, being called upon so unexpectedly for a bran new tale.

"What shall I tell about?" she said.

"Boys," was the general answer.

"Have a party in it," said Daisy.

"And something good to eat," added Stuffy.

"That reminds me of a story, written years ago, by a dear old lady. I used to be very fond of it, and I fancy you will like it, for it has both boys, and 'something good to eat' in it."

"What is it called?" asked Demi.

"'The Suspected Boy.' "

Nat looked up from the nuts he was picking, and Mrs. Jo smiled at him, guessing what was in his mind.

"Miss Crane kept a school for boys in a quiet little town, and a very good school it was, of the old-fashioned sort. Six boys lived in her house, and four or five more came in from the town. Among those who lived with her was one named Lewis White. Lewis was not a bad boy, but rather timid, and now and then he told a lie. One day a neighbor sent Miss Crane a basket of gooseberries. There were not enough to go round, so kind Miss Crane, who liked to please her boys, went to work and made a dozen nice little gooseberry tarts."

"I'd like to try gooseberry tarts. I wonder if she made them as I do my raspberry ones," said Daisy, whose interest in cooking had lately revived.

"Hush," said Nat, tucking a plump pop-corn into her mouth to silence her, for he felt a particular interest in this tale, and thought it opened well.

"When the tarts were done, Miss Crane put them away in the best parlor closet, and said not a word about them, for she wanted to surprise the boys at tea-time. When the minute came and all were seated at table, she went to get her tarts, but came back looking much troubled, for what do you think had happened?"

"Somebody had hooked them!" cried Ned.

"No, there they were, but some one had stolen all the fruit out of them by lifting up the upper crust and then putting it down after the gooseberry had been scraped out."

Lesson 128

1. Who do you predict will be the next one to tell a story?
2. Finish reading chapter 20.
3. Aunt Jo calls the boys "insatiable Oliver Twists." Louisa Mae Alcott is expecting her readers to know Charles Dickens' story of Oliver Twist, a young orphan boy who got a lot of people mad at him by asking for "MORE" porridge when he was hungry. This use of another story in your story is called a "literary allusion." It is one way an author can give information without really telling it, by expecting the reader to make a connection in her mind with another story that they both know. "Insatiable" means "never satisfied." What did Jo's boys want more of? (Answers)
4. Write a one-sentence summary of the chapter.
5. What are you thinking?

Chapter XX. continued
"What a mean trick!" and Nan looked at Tommy, as if to imply that he would do the same.

"When she told the boys her plan and showed them the poor little patties all robbed of their sweetness, the boys were much grieved and disappointed, and all declared that they knew nothing about the matter. 'Perhaps the rats did it,' said Lewis, who was among the loudest to deny any knowledge of the tarts. 'No, rats would have nibbled crust and all, and never lifted it up and scooped out the fruit. Hands did that,' said Miss Crane, who was more troubled about the lie that some one must have told than about her lost patties. Well, they had supper and went to bed, but in the night Miss Crane heard some one groaning, and going to see who it was she found Lewis in great pain. He had evidently eaten something that disagreed with him, and was so sick that Miss Crane was alarmed, and was going to send for the doctor, when Lewis moaned out, 'It's the gooseberries; I ate them, and I must tell before I die,' for the thought of a doctor frightened him. 'If that is all, I'll give you an emetic and you will soon get over it,' said Miss Crane. So Lewis had a good dose, and by morning was quite comfortable. 'Oh, don't tell the boys; they will laugh at me so,' begged the invalid. Kind Miss Crane promised not to, but Sally, the girl, told the story, and poor Lewis had no peace for a long time. His mates called him Old Gooseberry, and were never tired of asking him the price of tarts."

"Served him right," said Emil.

"Badness always gets found out," added Demi, morally.

"No, it don't," muttered Jack, who was tending the apples with great devotion, so that he might keep his back to the rest and account for his red face.

"Is that all?" asked Dan.

"No, that is only the first part; the second part is more interesting. Some time after this a peddler came by one day and stopped to show his things to the boys, several of whom bought pocket-combs, jew's-harps, and various trifles of that sort. Among the knives was a little white-handled penknife that Lewis wanted very much, but he had spent all his pocket-money, and no one had any to lend him. He held the knife in his hand, admiring and longing for it, till the man packed up his goods to go, then he reluctantly laid it down, and the man went on his way. The next day, however, the peddler returned to say that he could not find that very knife, and thought he must have left it at Miss Crane's. It was a very nice one with a pearl handle, and he could not afford to lose it. Every one looked, and every one declared they knew nothing about it. 'This young gentleman had it last, and seemed to want it very much. Are you quite sure you put it back?' said the man to Lewis, who was much troubled at the loss, and vowed over and over again that he did return it. His denials seemed to do no good, however, for every one was sure he had taken it, and after a stormy scene Miss Crane paid for it, and the man went grumbling away."

"Did Lewis have it?" cried Nat, much excited.

"You will see. Now poor Lewis had another trial to bear, for the boys were constantly saying, 'Lend me your pearl-handled knife, Gooseberry,' and things of that sort, till Lewis was so unhappy he begged to be sent home. Miss Crane did her best to keep the boys quiet, but it was hard work, for they would tease, and she could not be with them all the time. That is one of the hardest things to teach boys; they won't 'hit a fellow when he is down,' as they say, but they will torment him in little ways till he would thank them to fight it out all round."

"I know that," said Dan.

"So do I," added Nat, softly.

Jack said nothing, but he quite agreed; for he knew that the elder boys despised him, and let him alone for that very reason.

"Do go on about poor Lewis, Aunt Jo. I don't believe he took the knife, but I want to be sure," said Daisy, in great anxiety.

"Well, week after week went on and the matter was not cleared up. The boys avoided Lewis, and he, poor fellow, was almost sick with the trouble he had brought upon himself. He resolved never to tell another lie, and tried so hard that Miss Crane pitied and helped him, and really came at last to believe that he did not take the knife. Two months after the peddler's first visit, he came again, and the first thing he said was-

"'Well, ma'am, I found that knife after all. It had slipped behind the lining of my valise, and fell out the other day when I was putting in a new stock of goods. I thought I'd call and let you know, as you paid for it, and maybe would like it, so here it is.'

"The boys had all gathered round, and at these words they felt much ashamed, and begged Lewis' pardon so heartily that he could not refuse to give it. Miss Crane presented the knife to him, and he kept it many years to remind him of the fault that had brought him so much trouble."

"I wonder why it is that things you eat on the sly hurt you, and don't when you eat them at table," observed Stuffy, thoughtfully.

"Perhaps your conscience affects your stomach," said Mrs. Jo, smiling at his speech.

"He is thinking of the cucumbers," said Ned, and a gale of merriment followed the words, for Stuffy's last mishap had been a funny one.

He ate two large cucumbers in private, felt very ill, and confided his anguish to Ned, imploring him to do something. Ned good-naturedly recommended a mustard plaster and a hot flat iron to the feet; only in applying these remedies he reversed the order of things, and put the plaster on the feet, the flat iron on the stomach, and poor Stuffy was found in the barn with blistered soles and a scorched jacket.

"Suppose you tell another story, that was such an interesting one," said Nat, as the laughter subsided.

Before Mrs. Jo could refuse these insatiable Oliver Twists, Rob walked into the room trailing his little bed-cover after him, and wearing an expression of great sweetness as he said, steering straight to his mother as a sure haven of refuge,

"I heard a great noise, and I thought sumfin dreffle might have happened, so I came to see."

"Did you think I would forget you, naughty boy?" asked his mother, trying to look stern.

"No; but I thought you'd feel better to see me right here," responded the insinuating little party.

"I had much rather see you in bed, so march straight up again, Robin."

"Everybody that comes in here has to tell a story, and you can't so you'd better cut and run," said Emil.

"Yes, I can! I tell Teddy lots of ones, all about bears and moons, and little flies that say things when they buzz," protested Rob, bound to stay at any price.

"Tell one now, then, right away," said Dan, preparing to shoulder and bear him off.

"Well, I will; let me fink a minute," and Rob climbed into his mother's lap, where he was cuddled, with the remark-

"It is a family failing, this getting out of bed at wrong times. Demi used to do it; and as for me, I was hopping in and out all night long. Meg used to think the house was on fire, and send me down to see, and I used to stay and enjoy myself, as you mean to, my bad son."

"I've finked now," observed Rob, quite at his ease, and eager to win the entree into this delightful circle.

Every one looked and listened with faces full of suppressed merriment as Rob, perched on his mother's knee and wrapped in the gay coverlet, told the following brief but tragic tale with an earnestness that made it very funny:

"Once a lady had a million children, and one nice little boy. She went up-stairs and said, 'You mustn't go in the yard.' But he wented, and fell into the pump, and was drowned dead."

"Is that all?" asked Franz, as Rob paused out of breath with this startling beginning.

"No, there is another piece of it," and Rob knit his downy eyebrows in the effort to evolve another inspiration.

"What did the lady do when he fell into the pump?" asked his mother, to help him on.

"Oh, she pumped him up, and wrapped him in a newspaper, and put him on a shelf to dry for seed."

A general explosion of laughter greeted this surprising conclusion, and Mrs. Jo patted the curly head, as she said, solemnly,

"My son, you inherit your mother's gift of story-telling. Go where glory waits thee."

"Now I can stay, can't I? Wasn't it a good story?" cried Rob, in high feather at his superb success.

"You can stay till you have eaten these twelve pop-corns," said his mother, expecting to see them vanish at one mouthful.

But Rob was a shrewd little man, and got the better of her by eating them one by one very slowly, and enjoying every minute with all his might.

"Hadn't you better tell the other story, while you wait for him?" said Demi, anxious that no time should be lost.

"I really have nothing but a little tale about a wood-box," said Mrs. Jo, seeing that Rob had still seven corns to eat.

"Is there a boy in it?"

"It is all boy."

"Is it true?" asked Demi.

"Every bit of it."

"Goody! tell on, please."

"James Snow and his mother lived in a little house, up in New Hampshire. They were poor, and James had to work to help his mother, but he loved books so well he hated work, and just wanted to sit and study all day long."

"How could he! I hate books, and like work," said Dan, objecting to James at the very outset.

"It takes all sorts of people to make a world; workers and students both are needed, and there is room for all. But I think the workers should study some, and the students should know how to work if necessary," answered Mrs. Jo, looking from Dan to Demi with a significant expression.

"I'm sure I do work," and Demi showed three small hard spots in his little palm, with pride.

"And I'm sure I study," added Dan, nodding with a groan toward the blackboard full of neat figures.

"See what James did. He did not mean to be selfish, but his mother was proud of him, and let him do as he liked, working by herself that he might have books and time to read them. One autumn James wanted to go to school, and went to the minister to see if he would help him, about decent clothes and books. Now the minister had heard the gossip about James's idleness, and was not inclined to do much for him, thinking that a boy who neglected his mother, and let her slave for him, was not likely to do very well even at school. But the good man felt more interested when he found how earnest James was, and being rather an odd man, he made this proposal to the boy, to try now sincere he was.

"'I will give you clothes and books on one condition, James.'

"'What is that, sir?' and the boy brightened up at once.

"'You are to keep your mother's wood-box full all winter long, and do it yourself. If you fail, school stops.' James laughed at the queer condition and readily agreed to it, thinking it a very easy one.

"He began school, and for a time got on capitally with the wood-box, for it was autumn, and chips and brushwood were plentiful. He ran out morning and evening and got a basket full, or chopped up the cat sticks for the little cooking stove, and as his mother was careful and saving, the task was not hard. But in November the frost came, the days were dull and cold, and wood went fast. His mother bought a load with her own earnings, but it seemed to melt away, and was nearly gone, before James remembered that he was to get the next. Mrs. Snow was feeble and lame with rheumatism, and unable to work as she had done, so James had to put down the books, and see what he could do.

"It was hard, for he was going on well, and so interested in his lessons that he hated to stop except for food and sleep. But he knew the minister would keep his word, and much against his will James set about earning money in his spare hours, lest the wood-box should get empty. He did all sorts of things, ran errands, took care of a neighbor's cow, helped the old sexton dust and warm the church on Sundays, and in these ways got enough to buy fuel in small quantities. But it was hard work; the days were short, the winter was bitterly cold, and precious time went fast, and the dear books were so fascinating, that it was sad to leave them, for dull duties that never seemed done.

"The minister watched him quietly, and seeing that he was in earnest helped him without his knowledge. He met him often driving the wood sleds from the forest, where the men were chopping and as James plodded beside the slow oxen, he read or studied, anxious to use every minute. 'The boy is worth helping, this lesson will do him good, and when he has learned it, I will give him an easier one,' said the minister to himself, and on Christmas eve a splendid load of wood was quietly dropped at the door of the little house, with a new saw and a bit of paper, saying only-

"'The Lord helps those who help themselves.'

"Poor James expected nothing, but when he woke on that cold Christmas morning, he found a pair of warm mittens, knit by his mother, with her stiff painful fingers. This gift pleased him very much, but her kiss and tender look as she called him her 'good son,' was better still. In trying to keep her warm, he had warmed his own heart, you see, and in filling the wood-box he had also filled those months with duties faithfully done. He began to see this, to feel that there was something better than books, and to try to learn the lessons God set him, as well as those his school-master gave.

"When he saw the great pile of oak and pine logs at his door, and read the little paper, he knew who sent it, and understood the minister's plan; thanked him for it, and fell to work with all his might. Other boys frolicked that day, but James sawed wood, and I think of all the lads in the town the happiest was the one in the new mittens, who whistled like a blackbird as he filled his mother's wood-box."

"That's a first rater!" cried Dan, who enjoyed a simple matter-of-face story better than the finest fairy tale; "I like that fellow after all."

"I could saw wood for you, Aunt Jo!" said Demi, feeling as if a new means of earning money for his mother was suggested by the story.

"Tell about a bad boy. I like them best," said Nan.

"You'd better tell about a naughty cross-patch of a girl," said Tommy, whose evening had been spoilt by Nan's unkindness. It made his apple taste bitter, his pop-corn was insipid, his nuts were hard to crack, and the sight of Ned and Nan on one bench made him feel his life a burden.

But there were no more stories from Mrs. Jo, for on looking down at Rob he was discovered to be fast asleep with his last corn firmly clasped in his chubby hand. Bundling him up in his coverlet, his mother carried him away and tucked him up with no fear of his popping out again.

"Now let's see who will come next," said Emil, setting the door temptingly ajar.

Mary Ann passed first, and he called out to her, but Silas had warned her, and she only laughed and hurried on in spite of their enticements. Presently a door opened, and a strong voice was heard humming in the hall:

> Ich weiss nicht was soll es bedeuten
> Dass ich so traurig bin.

"It's Uncle Fritz; all laugh loud and he will be sure to come in," said Emil.

A wild burst of laughter followed, and in came Uncle Fritz, asking, "What is the joke, my lads?"

"Caught! caught! you can't go out till you've told a story," cried the boys, slamming the door.

"So! that is the joke then? Well, I have no wish to go, it is so pleasant here, and I pay my forfeit at once," which he did by sitting down and beginning instantly:

"A long time ago your Grandfather, Demi, went to lecture in a great town, hoping to get some money for a home for little orphans that some good people were getting up. His lecture did well, and he put a considerable sum of money in his pocket, feeling very happy about it. As he was driving in a chaise to another town, he came to a lonely bit of road, late in the afternoon, and was just thinking what a good place it was for robbers when he saw a bad-looking man come out of the woods in front of him and go slowly along as if waiting till he came up. The thought of the money made Grandfather rather anxious, and at first he had a mind to turn round and drive away. But the horse was tired, and then he did not like to suspect the man, so he kept on, and when he got nearer and saw how poor and sick and ragged the stranger looked, his heart reproached him, and stopping, he said in a kind voice-

"'My friend, you look tired; let me give you a lift.' The man seemed surprised, hesitated a minute, and then got in. He did not seem inclined to talk, but Grandfather kept on in his wise, cheerful way, speaking of what a hard year it had been, how much the poor had suffered, and how difficult it was to get on sometimes. The man slowly softened a little, and won by the kind chat, told his story. How he had been sick, could get no work, had a family of children, and was almost in despair. Grandfather was so full of pity that he forgot his fear, and, asking the man his name, said he would try to get him work in the next town, as he had friends there. Wishing to get at pencil and paper to write down the address, Grandfather took out his plump pocket-book, and the minute he did so, the man's eye was on it. Then Grandfather remembered what was in it and trembled for his money, but said quietly-

"'Yes, I have a little sum here for some poor orphans. I wish it was my own, I would so gladly give you some of it. I am not rich, but I know many of the trials of the poor; this five dollars is mine, and I want to give it to you for your children.'

"The hard, hungry look in the man's eyes changed to a grateful one as he took the small sum, freely given, and left the orphans' money untouched. He rode on with Grandfather till they approached the town, then he asked to be set down. Grandpa shook hands with him, and was about to drive on, when the man said, as if something made him, 'I was desperate when we met, and I meant to rob you, but you were so kind I couldn't do it. God bless you, sir, for keeping me from it!' "

"Did Grandpa ever see him again?" asked Daisy, eagerly.

"No; but I believe the man found work, and did not try robbery any more."

"That was a curious way to treat him; I'd have knocked him down," said Dan.

"Kindness is always better than force. Try it and see," answered Mr. Bhaer, rising.

"Tell another, please," cried Daisy.

"You must, Aunt Jo did," added Demi.

"Then I certainly won't, but keep my others for next time. Too many tales are as bad as too many bonbons. I have paid my forfeit and I go," and Mr. Bhaer ran for his life, with the whole flock in full pursuit. He had the start, however, and escaped safely into his study, leaving the boys to go rioting back again.

They were so stirred up by the race that they could not settle to their former quiet, and a lively game of Blindman's Buff followed, in which Tommy showed that he had taken the moral of the last story to heart, for, when he caught Nan, he whispered in her ear, "I'm sorry I called you a cross-patch."

Nan was not to be outdone in kindness, so, when they played "Button, button, who's got the button?" and it was her turn to go round, she said, "Hold fast all I give you," with such a friendly smile at Tommy, that he was not surprised to find the horse-hair ring in his hand instead of the button. He only smiled back at her then, but when they were going to bed, he offered Nan the best bite of his last apple; she saw the ring on his stumpy little finger, accepted the bite, and peace was declared. Both were ashamed of the temporary coldness, neither was ashamed to say, "I was wrong, forgive me," so the childish friendship remained unbroken, and the home in the willow lasted long, a pleasant little castle in the air.

Lesson 129
1. What is the title of Chapter 21? Have you noticed that the structure of the book follows the seasons of one year? What do you picture happening in this chapter?
2. Start reading chapter 21.

Chapter XXI. Thanksgiving
This yearly festival was always kept at Plumfield in the good old-fashioned way, and nothing was allowed to interfere with it. For days beforehand, the little girls helped Asia and Mrs. Jo in store-room and kitchen, making pies and puddings, sorting fruit, dusting dishes, and being very busy and immensely important. The boys hovered on the outskirts of the forbidden ground, sniffing the savory odors, peeping in at the mysterious performances, and occasionally being permitted to taste some delicacy in the process of preparation.

Something more than usual seemed to be on foot this year, for the girls were as busy up-stairs as down, so were the boys in school-room and barn, and a general air of bustle pervaded the house.

There was a great hunting up of old ribbons and finery, much cutting and pasting of gold paper, and the most remarkable quantity of straw, gray cotton, flannel, and big black beads, used by Franz and Mrs. Jo. Ned hammered at strange machines in the workshop, Demi and Tommy went about murmuring to themselves as if learning something. A fearful racket was heard in Emil's room at intervals, and peals of laughter from the nursery when Rob and Teddy were sent for and hidden from sight whole hours at a time. But the thing that puzzled Mr. Bhaer the most was what became of Rob's big pumpkin. It had been borne in triumph to the kitchen, where a dozen golden-tinted pies soon after appeared. It would not have taken more than a quarter of the mammoth vegetable to make them, yet where was the rest? It disappeared, and Rob never seemed to care, only chuckled when it was mentioned, and told his father, "To wait and see," for the fun of the whole thing was to surprise Father Bhaer at the end, and not let him know a bit about what was to happen.

He obediently shut eyes, ears, and mouth, and went about trying not to see what was in plain sight, not to hear the tell-tale sounds that filled the air, not to understand any of the perfectly transparent mysteries going on all about him. Being a German, he loved these simple domestic festivals, and encouraged them with all his heart, for they made home so pleasant that the boys did not care to go elsewhere for fun.

When at last the day came, the boys went off for a long walk, that they might have good appetites for dinner; as if they ever needed them! The girls remained at home to help set the table, and give last touches to various affairs which filled their busy little souls with anxiety. The school-room had been shut up since the night before, and Mr. Bhaer was forbidden to enter it on pain of a beating from Teddy, who guarded the door like a small dragon, though he was dying to tell about it, and nothing but his father's heroic self-denial in not listening, kept him from betraying a grand secret.

"It's all done, and it's perfectly splendid," cried Nan, coming out at last with an air of triumph.

"The -you know- goes beautifully, and Silas knows just what to do now," added Daisy, skipping with delight at some unspeakable success.

"I'm blest if it ain't the 'cutest thing I ever see, them critters in particular," said Silas, who had been let into the secret, went off laughing like a great boy.

"They are coming; I hear Emil roaring 'Land lubbers lying down below,' so we must run and dress," cried Nan, and up-stairs they scampered in a great hurry.

The boys came trooping home with appetites that would have made the big turkey tremble, if it had not been past all fear. They also retired to dress; and for half-an-hour there was a washing, brushing, and prinking that would have done any tidy woman's heart good to see. When the bell rang, a troop of fresh-faced lads with shiny hair, clean collars, and Sunday jackets on, filed into the dining-room, where Mrs. Jo, in her one black silk, with a knot of her favorite white chrysanthemums in her bosom, sat at the head of the table, "looking splendid," as the boys said, whenever she got herself up. Daisy and Nan were as gay as a posy bed in their new winter dresses, with bright sashes and hair ribbons. Teddy was gorgeous to behold in a crimson merino blouse, and his best button boots, which absorbed and distracted him as much as Mr. Toot's wristbands did on one occasion.

As Mr. and Mrs. Bhaer glanced at each other down the long table, with those rows of happy faces on either side, they had a little thanksgiving all to themselves, and without a word, for one heart said to the other,

"Our work has prospered, let us be grateful and go on."

The clatter of knives and forks prevented much conversation for a few minutes, and Mary Ann with an amazing pink bow in her hair "flew round" briskly, handing plates and ladling out gravy. Nearly every one had contributed to the feast, so the dinner was a peculiarly interesting ones to the eaters of it, who beguiled the pauses by remarks on their own productions.

"If these are not good potatoes I never saw any," observed Jack, as he received his fourth big mealy one.

"Some of my herbs are in the stuffing of the turkey, that's why it's so nice," said Nan, taking a mouthful with intense satisfaction.

"My ducks are prime any way; Asia said she never cooked such fat ones," added Tommy.

"Well, our carrots are beautiful, ain't they, and our parsnips will be ever so good when we dig them," put in Dick, and Dolly murmured his assent from behind the bone he was picking.

"I helped make the pies with my pumpkin," called out Robby, with a laugh which he stopped by retiring into his mug.

"I picked some of the apples that the cider is made of," said Demi.

"I raked the cranberries for the sauce," cried Nat.

"I got the nuts," added Dan, and so it went on all round the table.

"Who made up Thanksgiving?" asked Rob, for being lately promoted to jacket and trousers he felt a new and manly interest in the institutions of his country.

"See who can answer that question," and Mr. Bhaer nodded to one or two of his best history boys.

"I know," said Demi, "the Pilgrims made it."

"What for?" asked Rob, without waiting to learn who the Pilgrims were.

"I forget," and Demi subsided.

"I believe it was because they were starved once, and so when they had a good harvest, they said, 'We will thank God for it,' and they had a day and called it Thanksgiving," said Dan, who liked the story of the brave men who suffered so nobly for their faith.

"Good! I didn't think you would remember any thing but natural history," and Mr. Bhaer tapped gently on the table as applause for his pupil.

Dan looked pleased; and Mrs. Jo said to her son, "Now do you understand about it, Robby?"

"No, I don't. I thought pil-grins were a sort of big bird that lived on rocks, and I saw pictures of them in Demi's book."

"He means penguins. Oh, isn't he a little goosey!" and Demi laid back in his chair and laughed aloud.

"Don't laugh at him, but tell him all about it if you can," said Mrs. Bhaer, consoling Rob with more cranberry sauce for the general smile that went round the table at his mistake.

"Well, I will;" and, after a pause to collect his ideas, Demi delivered the following sketch of the Pilgrim Fathers, which would have made even those grave gentlemen smile if they could have heard it.

"You see, Rob, some of the people in England didn't like the king, or something, so they got into ships and sailed away to this country. It was all full of Indians, and bears, and wild creatures, and they lived in forts, and had a dreadful time."

"The bears?" asked Robby, with interest.

"No; the Pilgrims, because the Indians troubled them. They hadn't enough to eat, and they went to church with guns, and ever so many died, and they got out of the ships on a rock, and it's called Plymouth Rock, and Aunt Jo saw it and touched it. The Pilgrims killed all the Indians, and got rich; and hung the witches, and were very good; and some of the greatest great-grandpas came in the ships. One was the Mayflower; and they made Thanksgiving, and we have it always, and I like it. Some more turkey, please."

"I think Demi will be an historian, there is such order and clearness in his account of events;" and Uncle Fritz's eyes laughed at Aunt Jo, as he helped the descendant of the Pilgrims to his third bit of turkey.

"I thought you must eat as much as ever you could on Thanksgiving. But Franz says you mustn't even then;" and Stuffy looked as if he had received bad news.

"Franz is right, so mind your knife and fork, and be moderate, or else you won't be able to help in the surprise by and by," said Mrs. Jo.

"I'll be careful; but everybody does eat lots, and I like it better than being moderate," said Stuffy, who leaned to the popular belief that Thanksgiving must be kept by coming as near apoplexy as possible, and escaping with merely a fit of indigestion or a headache.

"Now, my 'pilgrims' amuse yourselves quietly till tea-time, for you will have enough excitement this evening," said Mrs. Jo, as they rose from the table after a protracted sitting, finished by drinking every one's health in cider.

"I think I will take the whole flock for a drive, it is so pleasant; then you can rest, my dear, or you will be worn out this evening," added Mr. Bhaer; and as soon as coats and hats could be put on, the great omnibus was packed full, and away they went for a long gay drive, leaving Mrs. Jo to rest and finish sundry small affairs in peace.

An early and light tea was followed by more brushing of hair and washing of hands; then the flock waited impatiently for the company to come. Only the family was expected; for these small revels were strictly domestic, and such being the case, sorrow was not allowed to sadden the present festival. All came; Mr. and Mrs. March, with Aunt Meg, so sweet and lovely, in spite of her black dress and the little widow's cap that encircled her tranquil face. Uncle Teddy and Aunt Amy, with the Princess looking more fairy-like than ever, in a sky-blue gown, and a great bouquet of hot-house flowers, which she divided among the boys, sticking one in each button-hole, making them feel peculiarly elegant and festive. One strange face appeared, and Uncle Teddy led the unknown gentleman up to the Bhaers, saying-

"This is Mr. Hyde; he has been inquiring about Dan, and I ventured to bring him to-night, that he might see how much the boy has improved."

The Bhaers received him cordially, for Dan's sake, pleased that the lad had been remembered. But, after a few minutes' chat, they were glad to know Mr. Hyde for his own sake, so genial, simple, and interesting was he. It was pleasant to see the boy's face light up when he caught sight of his friend; pleasanter still to see Mr. Hyde's surprise and satisfaction in Dan's improved manners and appearance, and pleasantest of all to watch the two sit talking in a corner, forgetting the differences of age, culture, and position, in the one subject which interested both, as man and boy compared notes, and told the story of their summer life.

"The performance must begin soon, or the actors will go to sleep," said Mrs. Jo, when the first greetings were over.

So every one went into the school-room, and took seats before a curtain made of two bed-covers. The children had already vanished; but stifled laughter, and funny little exclamations from behind the curtain, betrayed their whereabouts. The entertainment began with a spirited exhibition of gymnastics, led by Franz. The six elder lads, in blue trousers and red shirts, made a fine display of muscle with dumb-bells, clubs, and weights, keeping time to the music of the piano, played by Mrs. Jo behind the scenes. Dan was so energetic in this exercise, that there was some danger of his knocking down his neighbors, like so many nine-pins, or sending his bean-bags whizzing among the audience; for he was excited by Mr. Hyde's presence, and a burning desire to do honor to his teachers.

"A fine, strong lad. If I go on my trip to South America, in a year or two, I shall be tempted to ask you to lend him to me, Mr. Bhaer," said Mr. Hyde, whose interest in Dan was much increased by the report he had just heard of him.

"You shall have him, and welcome, though we shall miss our young Hercules very much. It would do him a world of good, and I am sure he would serve his friend faithfully."

Dan heard both question and answer, and his heart leaped with joy at the thought of travelling in a new country with Mr. Hyde, and swelled with gratitude for the kindly commendation which rewarded his efforts to be all these friends desired to see him.

After the gymnastics, Demi and Tommy spoke the old school dialogue, "Money makes the mare go." Demi did very well, but Tommy was capital as the old farmer; for he imitated Silas in a way that convulsed the audience, and caused Silas himself to laugh so hard that Asia had to slap him on the back, as they stood in the hall enjoying the fun immensely.

Then Emil, who had got his breath by this time, gave them a sea-song in costume, with a great deal about "stormy winds," "lee shores," and a rousing chorus of "Luff, boys, luff," which made the room ring; after which Ned performed a funny Chinese dance, and hopped about like a large frog in a pagoda hat. As this was the only public exhibition ever held at Plumfield, a few exercises in lightning-arithmetic, spelling, and reading were given. Jack quite amazed the public by his rapid calculations on the blackboard. Tommy won in the spelling match, and Demi read a little French fable so well that Uncle Teddy was charmed.

"Where are the other children?" asked every one as the curtain fell, and none of the little ones appeared.

"Oh, that is the surprise. It's so lovely, I pity you because you don't know it," said Demi, who had gone to get his mother's kiss, and stayed by her to explain the mystery when it should be revealed.

Goldilocks had been carried off by Aunt Jo, to the great amazement of her papa, who quite outdid Mr. Bhaer in acting wonder, suspense, and wild impatience to know "what was going to happen."

Lesson 130

1. What would you like to find out before the book is ended? Why?

2. Finish chapter 21 and finish the book!

3. What are you thinking?

4. Is there anything you would still like to know about the "family" at Plumfield?

5. Would you recommend this book to a friend? Why or why not?

6. Write a book summary for *Little Men.* Write the setting, characters, problem, plot events, resolution to the problem. You can write these in a paragraph or you can list them and then write a paragraph summary of the book.

Chapter XXI. continued

At last, after much rustling, hammering, and very audible directions from the stage manager, the curtain rose to soft music, and Bess was discovered sitting on a stool beside a brown paper fire-place. A dearer little Cinderella was never seen; for the gray gown was very ragged, the tiny shoes all worn, the face so pretty under the bright hair, and the attitude so dejected, it brought tears, as well as smiles, to the fond eyes looking at the baby actress. She sat quite still, till a voice whispered, "Now!" then she sighed a funny little sigh, and said, "Oh I wish I tood go to the ball!" so naturally, that her father clapped frantically, and her mother called out, "Little darling!" These highly improper expressions of feeling caused Cinderella to forget herself, and shake her head at them, saying, reprovingly, "You mustn't 'peak to me."

Silence instantly prevailed, and three taps were heard on the wall. Cinderella looked alarmed, but before she could remember to say, "What is dat?" the back of the brown paper fire-place opened like a door, and, with some difficulty, the fairy godmother got herself and her pointed hat through. It was Nan, in a red cloak, a cap, and a wand, which she waved as she said decidedly,

"You shall go to the ball, my dear."

"Now you must pull and show my pretty dress," returned Cinderella, tugging at her brown gown.

"No, no; you must say, 'How can I go in my rags?' " said the godmother in her own voice.

"Oh yes, so I mus';" and the Princess said it, quite undisturbed by her forgetfulness.

"I change your rags into a splendid dress, because you are good," said the godmother in her stage tones; and deliberately unbuttoning the brown pinafore, she displayed a gorgeous sight.

The little Princess really was pretty enough to turn the heads of any number of small princes, for her mamma had dressed her like a tiny court lady, in a rosy silk train with satin under-skirt, and bits of bouquets here and there, quite lovely to behold. The godmother put a crown, with pink and white feathers drooping from it, on her head, and gave her a pair of silver paper slippers, which she put on, and then stood up, lifting her skirts to show them to the audience, saying, with pride, "My dlass ones, ain't they pitty?"

She was so charmed with them, that she was with difficulty recalled to her part, and made to say, "But I have no toach, Dodmother."

"Behold it!" and Nan waved her wand with such a flourish, that she nearly knocked off the crown of the Princess.

Then appeared the grand triumph of the piece. First, a rope was seen to flap on the floor, to tighten with a twitch as Emil's voice was heard to say, "Heave, ahoy!" and Silas's gruff one to reply, "Stiddy, now, stiddy!" A shout of laughter followed, for four large gray rats appeared, rather shaky as to their legs, and queer as to their tails, but quite fine about the head, where black beads shone in the most lifelike manner. They drew, or were intended to appear as if they did, a magnificent coach made of half the mammoth pumpkin, mounted on the wheels of Teddy's wagon, painted yellow to match the gay carriage. Perched on a seat in front sat a jolly little coachman in a white cotton-wool wig, cocked hat, scarlet breeches, and laced coat, who cracked a long whip and jerked the red reins so energetically, that the gray steeds reared finely. It was Teddy, and he beamed upon the company so affably that they gave him a round all to himself; and Uncle Laurie said, "If I could find as sober a coachman as that one, I would engage him on the spot." The coach stopped, the godmother lifted in the Princess, and she was trundled away in state, kissing her hand to the public, with her glass shoes sticking up in front, and her pink train sweeping the ground behind, for, elegant as the coach was, I regret to say that her Highness was rather a tight fit.

The next scene was the ball, and here Nan and Daisy appeared as gay as peacocks in all sorts of finery. Nan was especially good as the proud sister, and crushed many imaginary ladies as she swept about the palace-hall. The Prince, in solitary state upon a somewhat unsteady throne, sat gazing about him from under an imposing crown, as he played with his sword and admired the rosettes in his shoes. When Cinderella came in he jumped up, and exclaimed, with more warmth than elegance,

"My gracious! who is that?" and immediately led the lady out to dance, while the sisters scowled and turned up their noses in the corner.

The stately jig executed by the little couple was very pretty, for the childish faces were so earnest, the costumes so gay, and the steps so peculiar, that they looked like the dainty quaint figures painted on a Watteau fan. The Princess's train was very much in her way, and the sword of Prince Rob nearly tripped him up several times. But they overcame these obstacles remarkably well, and finished the dance with much grace and spirit, considering that neither knew what the other was about.

"Drop your shoe," whispered Mrs. Jo's voice as the lady was about to sit down.

"Oh, I fordot!" and, taking off one of the silvery slippers, Cinderella planted it carefully in the middle of the stage, said to Rob, "Now you must try and tatch me," and ran away, while the Prince, picking up the shoe, obediently trotted after her.

The third scene, as everybody knows, is where the herald comes to try on the shoe. Teddy, still in coachman's dress, came in blowing a tin fish-horn melodiously, and the proud sisters each tried to put on the slipper. Nan insisted on playing cut off her toe with a carving-knife, and performed that operation so well that the herald was alarmed, and begged her to be "welly keerful." Cinderella then was called, and came in with the pinafore half on, slipped her foot into the slipper, and announced, with satisfaction,

"I am the Pinsiss."

Daisy wept, and begged pardon; but Nan, who liked tragedy, improved upon the story, and fell in a fainting-fit upon the floor, where she remained comfortably enjoying the rest of the play. It was not long, for the Prince ran in, dropped upon his knees, and kissed the hand of Goldilocks with great ardor, while the herald blew a blast that nearly deafened the audience. The curtain had no chance to fall, for the Princess ran off the stage to her father, crying, "Didn't I do well?" while the Prince and herald had a fencing-match with the tin horn and wooden sword.

"It was beautiful!" said every one; and, when the raptures had a little subsided, Nat came out with his violin in his hand.

"Hush! hush!" cried all the children, and silence followed, for something in the boy's bashful manner and appealing eyes make every one listen kindly.

The Bhaers thought he would play some of the old airs he knew so well, but, to their surprise, they heard a new and lovely melody, so softly, sweetly played, that they could hardly believe it could be Nat. It was one of those songs without words that touch the heart, and sing of all tender home-like hopes and joys, soothing and cheering those who listen to its simple music. Aunt Meg leaned her head on Demi's shoulder, Grandmother wiped her eyes, and Mrs. Jo looked up at Mr. Laurie, saying, in a choky whisper,

"You composed that."

"I wanted your boy to do you honor, and thank you in his own way," answered Laurie, leaning down to answer her.

When Nat made his bow and was about to go, he was called back by many hands, and had to play again. He did so with such a happy face, that it was good to see him, for he did his best, and gave them the gay old tunes that set the feet to dancing, and made quietude impossible.

"Clear the floor!" cried Emil; and in a minute the chairs were pushed back, the older people put safely in corners and the children gathered on the stage.

"Show your manners!" called Emil; and the boys pranced up to the ladies, old and young; with polite invitations to "tread the mazy," as dear Dick Swiveller has it. The small lads nearly came to blows for the Princess, but she chose Dick, like a kind, little gentlewoman as she was, and let him lead her proudly to her place. Mrs. Jo was not allowed to decline; and Aunt Amy filled Dan with unspeakable delight by refusing Franz and taking him. Of course Nan and Tommy, Nat and Daisy paired off, while Uncle Teddy went and got Asia, who was longing to "jig it," and felt much elated by the honor done her. Silas and Mary Ann had a private dance in the hall; and for half-an-hour Plumfield was at its merriest.

The party wound up with a grand promenade of all the young folks, headed by the pumpkin-coach with the Princess and driver inside, and the rats in a wildly frisky state.

While the children enjoyed this final frolic, the elders sat in the parlor looking on as they talked together of the little people with the interest of parents and friends.

"What are you thinking of, all by yourself, with such a happy face, sister Jo?" asked Laurie, sitting down beside her on the sofa.

"My summer's work, Teddy, and amusing myself by imagining the future of my boys," she answered, smiling as she made room for him.

"They are all to be poets, painters, and statesmen, famous soldiers, or at least merchant princes, I suppose."

"No, I am not as aspiring as I once was, and I shall be satisfied if they are honest men. But I will confess that I do expect a little glory and a career for some of them. Demi is not a common child, and I think he will blossom into something good and great in the best sense of the word. The others will do well, I hope, especially my last two boys, for, after hearing Nat play to-night, I really think he has genius."

"Too soon to say; talent he certainly has, and there is no doubt that the boy can soon earn his bread by the work he loves. Build him up for another year or so, and then I will take him off your hands, and launch him properly."

"That is such a pleasant prospect for poor Nat, who came to me six months ago so friendless and forlorn. Dan's future is already plain to me. Mr. Hyde will want him soon, and I mean to give him a brave and faithful little servant. Dan is one who can serve well if the wages are love and confidence, and he has the energy to carve out his own future in his own way. Yes, I am very happy over our success with these boys one so weak, and one so wild; both so much better now, and so full of promise."

"What magic did you use, Jo?"

"I only loved them, and let them see it. Fritz did the rest."

"Dear soul! you look as if 'only loving' had been rather hard work sometimes," said Laurie, stroking her thin cheek with a look of more tender admiration than he had ever given her as a girl.

"I'm a faded old woman, but I'm a very happy one; so don't pity me, Teddy;" and she glanced about the room with eyes full of a sincere content.

"Yes, your plan seems to work better and better every year," he said, with an emphatic nod of approval toward the cheery scene before him.

"How can it fail to work well when I have so much help from you all?" answered Mrs. Jo, looking gratefully at her most generous patron.

"It is the best joke of the family, this school of yours and its success. So unlike the future we planned for you, and yet so suited to you after all. It was a regular inspiration, Jo," said Laurie, dodging her thanks as usual.

"Ah! but you laughed at it in the beginning, and still make all manner of fun of me and my inspirations. Didn't you predict that having girls with the boys would be a dead failure? Now see how well it works;" and she pointed to the happy group of lads and lassies dancing, singing, and chattering together with every sign of kindly good fellowship.

"I give in, and when my Goldilocks is old enough I'll send her to you. Can I say more than that?"

"I shall be so proud to have your little treasure trusted to me. But really, Teddy, the effect of these girls has been excellent. I know you will laugh at me, but I don't mind, I'm used to it; so I'll tell you that one of my favorite fancies is to look at my family as a small world, to watch the progress of my little men, and, lately, to see how well the influence of my little women works upon them. Daisy is the domestic element, and they all feel the charm of her quiet, womanly ways. Nan is the restless, energetic, strong-minded one; they admire her courage, and give her a fair chance to work out her will, seeing that she has sympathy as well as strength, and the power to do much in their small world. Your Bess is the lady, full of natural refinement, grace, and beauty. She polishes them unconsciously, and fills her place as any lovely woman may, using her gentle influence to lift and hold them above the coarse, rough things of life, and keep them gentlemen in the best sense of the fine old word."

"It is not always the ladies who do that best, Jo. It is sometimes the strong brave woman who stirs up the boy and makes a man of him;" and Laurie bowed to her with a significant laugh.

"No; I think the graceful woman, whom the boy you allude to married, has done more for him than the wild Nan of his youth; or, better still, the wise, motherly woman who watched over him, as Daisy watches over Demi, did more to make him what he is;" and Jo turned toward her mother, who sat a little apart with Meg, looking so full of the sweet dignity and beauty of old age, that Laurie gave her a glance of filial respect and love as he replied, in serious earnest,

"All three did much for him, and I can understand how well these little girls will help your lads."

"Not more than the lads help them; it is mutual, I assure you. Nat does much for Daisy with his music; Dan can manage Nan better than any of us; and Demi teaches your Goldilocks so easily and well that Fritz calls them Roger Ascham and Lady Jane Grey. Dear me! if men and women would only trust, understand, and help one another as my children do, what a capital place the world would be!" and Mrs. Jo's eyes grew absent, as if she was looking at a new and charming state of society in which people lived as happily and innocently as her flock at Plumfield.

"You are doing your best to help on the good time, my dear. Continue to believe in it, to work for it, and to prove its possibility by the success of her small experiment," said Mr. March, pausing as he passed to say an encouraging word, for the good man never lost his faith in humanity, and still hoped to see peace, good-will, and happiness reign upon the earth.

"I am not so ambitious as that, father. I only want to give these children a home in which they can be taught a few simple things which will help to make life less hard to them when they go out to fight their battles in the world. Honesty, courage, industry, faith in God, their fellow-creatures, and themselves; that is all I try for."

"That is every thing. Give them these helps, then let them go to work out their life as men and women; and whatever their success or failure is, I think they will remember and bless your efforts, my good son and daughter."

The Professor had joined them, and as Mr. March spoke he gave a hand to each, and left them with a look that was a blessing. As Jo and her husband stood together for a moment talking quietly, and feeling that their summer work had been well done if father approved, Mr. Laurie slipped into the hall, said a word to the children, and all of a sudden the whole flock pranced into the room, joined hands and danced about Father and Mother Bhaer, singing blithely:

Summer days are over,
Summer work is done;
Harvests have been gathered
Gayly one by one.

Now the feast is eaten,
Finished is the play;
But one rite remains for
Our Thanksgiving-day.

"Best of all the harvest
In the dear God's sight,
Are the happy children
In the home to-night;

And we come to offer
Thanks where thanks are due,
With grateful hearts and voices,
Father, mother, unto you.

With the last words the circle narrowed till the good Professor and his wife were taken prisoner by many arms, and half hidden by the bouquet of laughing young faces which surrounded them, proving that one plant had taken root and blossomed beautifully in all the little gardens. For love is a flower that grows in any soil, works its sweet miracles undaunted by autumn frost or winter snow, blooming fair and fragrant all the year, and blessing those who give and those who receive.

Lesson 131

1. Now you are going to be reading something very different. I wrote it!
2. Read the first chapter of *What I Learned Over Summer Vacation*.
3. Who is "the cackler?" (Answers)
4. What was the vocabulary word taught in the chapter?
5. How does the story show the word's meaning?

Balderdash

School started back this week, and my teacher said we each had to take a turn telling the class what we did over the summer. Sarah and Michael, the twins, told all about their trip to space camp. They're practically astronauts already. Randy told about skiing in Chile in July! I've never even been skiing in January. Julie flew in a hot air balloon, and Steve built a car, though I'm pretty sure his dad did most of the work. Their summers were all so exciting, so interesting, so unique, that I knew my summer vacation story had to be absolutely amazing. I wanted them to fall out of their seats for the sheer thrill of it! Do you want to hear my story? You might want to strap on a seat belt.

Summer started out in the usual way with a bus ride home. I'm the first one on and the last one off, so it was just me and bus driver Fran left on the bus when a hail storm ripped through the sky like my big brother opening a box of marshmallow cereal. The hail stones were so big that they tore right through the bus hood and crushed the engine. Well, the bus wouldn't go anywhere without an engine, but I got an idea. The hail was covering the road like marbles. I took off a bus tire and told bus driver Fran I could get myself home. I laid the tire down flat and sat in it like a sled. I shoved off and used my backpack as a paddle both to steer and to push my way along the rolling, marbley hailstones, and I started slipping and sledding down the road.

That worked for awhile until I started slipping and sledding down a big hill and lost grip of my paddle-backpack. I was careening down the steep hill, screaming at the top of my lungs and instead of trying to steer, I wrapped my arms around my face. I didn't stop screaming when I realized the ground wasn't underneath me anymore. I didn't even stop screaming when I felt myself splash down. I stopped screaming when my tire hit a big rock and spilled me into the water. That's when I realized I was drifting down a river.

Sputtering and spitting the water spurting into my mouth, I grabbed hold of something floating along with me and just focused on staying afloat. I was looking around me and just saw trees on both sides, and I was wishing I knew my geography because then maybe I would know where I was being carried. But then instead of worrying, I reminded myself I was on summer vacation and getting wet is a big part of summer vacation, so I figured I was getting off to a great start!

The water current slowed down and the river turned into a creek, and I found myself lying on the back of a baby elephant. I know you are thinking, what! Where did that elephant come from? I know that's what you are thinking because that's what I was thinking. I realized that the thing I grabbed hold of that was floating down the river was a baby elephant's trunk, not a branch or something. As the river thinned out, she rose up out of the water and took me with her.

This, of course, was an unexpected turn of events and required some quick thinking on my part. Unfortunately, in the last 180 days of school no one taught us anything about communicating with or controlling elephants, so I did my thinking while letting her carry me wherever she wanted to go. I had, however, read books and seen movies about animals who eventually found their way home, so I decided to trust that she was headed for her home, which I figured was probably the zoo since, how many people do you know have a baby elephant for a pet? Exactly.

The zoo wasn't our first stop though. The creek was surrounded by trees and I found myself on an elephant ride through the woods. I heard a cackling sound, you know, a really loud laugh that's not exactly contagious like a friendly, funny laugh is supposed to be. Then I heard yelling. Then I heard a squeal. It actually made me feel better that I was with Bucko, that's what I named the elephant. It just came out, "Hey, Bucko, where you taking me?" Like that. Bucko didn't seem fazed by the noises that I pretended not to be fazed by.

It wasn't long before the other noises stopped, probably because the crunching of the elephant's stomping was noise enough for everyone. Finally, we came into a small clearing in the woods and found the source of the cackle, yell and squeal. There was a horse, but the horse hadn't made any of those sounds. He was decorated with bright red and blue ropes and blinders and didn't pay any attention at all to me and Bucko. The dog had been the source of the squeal, and he repeated his squealy show when the cackler grabbed hold of him and wouldn't let him sniff or chase or whatever dog instinct had come over him in the moment.

The yeller was a boy, small compared to me, not that I told you how tall I am, but he wasn't taller than me and he wasn't a baby or toddler or anything either. I don't know what he had yelled about, but now his face was stone still, a looked-like-he-wasn't-breathing kind of still.

The cackler did it again, a sort of laugh-cough baring a mouth with four teeth left in it. Her hair was black or dyed but most of it was covered with a scarf that rivaled the horse's decorations for brightness of color. She asked me how I came to be riding Apara (*say a like the word a, the word par, then the word a again*). I asked if Bucko's name was really Apara and she said it was. She said the elephant was named that because she comes and goes as she pleases. She said she's like an apparition, she's there one minute and gone the next. Turns out my boy, Bucko, was a girl.

I mostly sat silent, which is not how I usually sit, but she knew Bucko, Apara, and she was talking like she's known her her whole life, which was impossible because I was the one riding her down the river. I had to quickly explain the whole river thing, and she explained that Apara wasn't from the zoo but from the circus. In fact her son and daughter-in-law, yeller's parents, were part of the circus. They were acrobats and the mom could do a head stand on the head of the father all while riding on the back of Apara's mother.

I displayed my excitement at the thought of a perilous headstand and was promptly invited to see the circus in action when we returned Apara. This is the part where we got to know each other, and I found out they are Gypsies and had always traveled with the circus, as in my father's-father's-father-before-me-was-in-the-circus kind of always. The cackler started telling me the most amazing stories, stories of circuses, of runaway trains, of renegade elephants, of robbers in the woods. They were the most amazing, unique, exciting and interesting stories that had ever been told. Well, I don't know that for a fact, but by my subjective opinion, they were!

As I sat next to the Gypsy grandmother on a log by the fire with a pot of something cooking over it, I asked her how she came to live and tell such marvelous, stupendous, outrageous stories. She told me she was the best story teller because she had lived a lot of life and had learned the secret ingredient to telling a story.

I'm curious even if curiosity did kill the cat, but I'm not a cat, so I don't have to worry about that, and I asked her right away what the secret story ingredient was. She looked at me like she was scrutinizing my thoughts that I thought I had hidden. Then she cackled. I liked the cackle a lot more up close, with those four teeth waggling in front of me, than when I didn't know whose teeth that cackle was behind. Then she told me that she couldn't tell me the secret ingredient. "Not yet," she said. Oooo, now isn't that tantalizing? Not yet. I wasn't going to run home with a *not yet* promising that *some time* a secret would be revealed.

The cackler served me goolash. I don't know if that's really what it was, but that's what it looked like. That's what my dad calls dinner when he empties everything leftover in the fridge into a pot and adds water. They didn't have a fridge, but same idea. Then I saddled up on Bucko, or you could say climbed up onto Apara's back, and we followed the cackler and yeller riding in the cart pulled by the horse of many colors. Did you see us in our mini parade? You probably heard about it if you didn't. I love a parade and started waving at the gaping gawkers along our route to the circus. One little girl asked for my autograph. I obliged, of course.

While I was signing my Hancock, Apara started sniffing into the wind. As I handed back the paper to the little girl, Apara took off charging in a direction almost opposite of the horse and cart. I didn't have time to call for help. I just grabbed on and went for a wild ride. Apara galloped through the streets. People dove to the right and to the left to get out of the way. Cars crashed, distracted by the site of a rampaging pachyderm.

Apara ran as the crow flies and didn't seem to want to bother with dodging obstacles. They dodged her or they got run over. She crashed over the flower pots in front of the *Stop and Smell the Roses* flower shop. She crashed into the *Five and Ten* which has been indestructible for the last century. She managed to bulldoze her way through the aisles and out the loading doors in the back. I managed to grab up a lollypop when we passed the front counter. I tossed a dollar from my pocket which I'm sure would cover the lollypop but certainly not the mess Apara made.

I popped the lollypop into my mouth and congratulated myself on snatching up a root beer flavored one. Apara wasn't slowing down, and I got to thinking about the circus acrobats, yeller's parents who rode on an elephant's back, his mother balancing upside-down on top of his father's head. I thought if they could do that, then I could probably ride standing up and sucking on a lollypop. I slowly got to my feet. I stood tall and threw my arms up in the air to signify my triumph. My left arm hit a traffic light post and knocked me off balance. I swung around the post and grabbed on with my lollypop still protruding from between my lips. I wrapped my legs tight around the pole and held on.

I didn't slide down right away because of the still-fresh memory of rope burn from gym class, but then I didn't dare slide down because two police dogs started barking at me and attacking the post as if that would somehow get me down. I went up. I made it all the way to the very top and sat on top of the traffic light. I guess my feet must have dangled down over the lights because cars started stopping instead of going, but maybe they were just distracted from driving because a kid was sitting on the traffic light.

Traffic came to a standstill, as they say. The police came out of their office to see what the dogs were yapping at and what all the cars were honking at, and what they saw was me! I waved. They called in a helicopter. It circled overhead, and I had to climb up a rope ladder they dangled from the helicopter for me. But before they could take me home, they got a call about an elephant that had barreled into the annual peanut festival.

My synapses were firing and I figured it must be Apara at the peanut festival. I figured that must be how she got away from the circus in the first place and then away from me. She had smelled those peanuts and just couldn't control herself. She is just a kid after all. You may think there's no way she could smell that festival a full ten miles away, but elephants can actually smell twelve miles away. If you don't believe me, Google it. I'm telling the truth.

I felt like a spy, flying over town in a helicopter, looking for the trouble-making elephant. We spotted her easy. It's not like we were looking for a needle in a haystack. We were looking for an elephant in a peanut pile which had been a peanut pyramid before the peanut-loving pachyderm pounced on it. (Mr. Johnson always builds a peanut pyramid for the peanut festival.)

I pointed to Apara and looked over at the helicopter pilot to see if he could see her too, but the pilot wasn't looking down. He was looking awful. He was wriggling like he was trying to scratch an itch that covered his whole body and his lips were looking puffy. In fact his whole face was looking splotchy, red and bumpy. Then I remembered seeing something just like that before when my dad accidently ate some shellfish and we had to rush him to the hospital. It's easy to remember because I have a memento. My brother and I took pictures of ourselves wearing bedpans as hats.

I gestured to the helicopter pilot that his face was red and puffy and that he should let me down with the rope ladder to go get the elephant. I think he understood or at least was too puffy to care because he didn't object when I kicked the ladder out the helicopter door. He hovered over the peanut festival and I climbed down and jumped off onto a pile of plush peanuts, prizes for the pick-the-winning peanut game where you reach into a barrel and pick up a peanut, and if it has a mark on its shell you get a stuffed peanut, you know, like a stuffed animal but legume instead. I learned about legumes from my elderly neighbor.

Once I was on the ground, I had to formulate a plan. Apara was not going to want to leave her peanut paradise. I remembered that carrot-on-a-stick trick where you dangle a carrot in front of a horse to get him to go forward to try and get it. But I was smart enough to know it wouldn't work with Apara since her trunk could reach farther than my stick would. I walked around surveying the scene and taking an inventory of my assets. I learned how to do that from television. I was hoping something would inspire a brilliant plan to free the festival of their four-legged intruder.

Brilliance had yet to strike, so I got some cotton candy and sat for a spell. That's an expression. I didn't spell anything. I started listing my options. I could push or pull or pick her up. They all sounded really hard and somewhat painful. Then it hit me like a bolt of lightning, figuratively speaking. Wheels would make pushing and pulling easier, right? That thought inspired two words: bumper cars. And air holds up planes, why not an elephant? That thought inspired one word: parachute. Can you figure out what my plan was?

I politely borrowed the canopy that Apara had partially knocked down anyway from the peanut pyramid pavilion. I tied the four corners onto the poles of three bumper cars. I made a trail of peanuts from Apara into the two back cars. She climbed in and stood with her two front feet in the one car and her two back feet in the other. I opened the door to the exit and then climbed into the first car. I stepped on the gas, which is an expression too, especially since it's an electric car and doesn't have any gas in it. I hurled my car toward the exit and pulled Apara behind me. I would have loved to have seen the look on her face, but I'm a serious driver and kept my eye on the road, which is another figure of speech. I wasn't on the street but in the middle of the peanut festival.

Just as I had hoped, we had built up enough momentum (I learned that word in school) that we made it to the hill and started rolling down toward the moon bounce. One bump later and we were airborne. We landed on the air-filled castle and bounced up high. The parachute caught us and I demonstrated to Apara how to blow hot air into our parachute. She started blowing through her trunk, sending hot air into the parachute, and it lifted us up. I knew that hot air rises. I learned that from my dad when I complained about how hot my bedroom was.

So there we were, flying. We had made it over the fence when lightning struck, literally, that wasn't an expression. The hail storm must have been following me because it found me again. The hail knocked down our parachute and us with it. The metal rods on the back of the bumper cars must have looked pretty attractive to the lightning because it kept striking the one on the back of my car. I figure it must have had the highest pole. It was just what I needed. The electricity in the lightning powered up my car which propelled down the road at lightning speed, pun intended. My car was still tied onto Apara's cars, and the lightning was enough power for us all.

At first I forgot that I was supposed to be getting Apara to the circus. It was so cool getting to drive a car so fast and on a real road too, but it didn't take long before I realized I had to figure out where I was going, or I was going to crash. I started turning right and then left at each chance I got. I figured at least that way I wouldn't go in a circle. The sun was a bit behind me, so I figured I was heading eastish. I learned that the sun sets in the west from my grandfather. The problem was that it didn't mean anything to me that I was heading east.

I was going too fast to think too much. Then I saw my school, turns out that I had gone in a circle. I was back where I had begun my summer vacation. The storm blew on ahead of us and the lightning stopped and so did we without our energizer. We rolled into the school parking lot. It was empty. I guess students aren't the only ones eager to head home on summer vacation. I got out of my car and encouraged Apara out of hers. A new plan flashed into my brain. I discretely picked some flowers and gave them to Apara to hold with her trunk. With her nose thus occupied I climbed onto her back and tried my hand at directing her steps, using her ears as reigns. She got the message.

I knew my way home from school so that's where we went. I don't think I need to go into what my mother said when she saw me riding into the driveway on the back of an elephant. She's very understanding though, and once all of her questions were answered she escorted us to the circus. She drove slowly with her hazard lights flashing, and Apara and I followed.

At the circus we met the yeller and cackler and Apara's mom. I was invited to ride Apara in the show and my mom bought a ticket to watch. The circus was great, but I suspect the highlight was my riding Apara standing up while sucking on a lollypop.

After the circus ended and I was about to head home, the Gypsy grandmother pulled me aside and told me her secret ingredient that she added to every story to make it amazingly fascinating and wonderfully exciting and that's what I learned from the cackler – balderdash.

Balderdash
senseless talk or writing; nonsense

Lesson 132

1. Read the second chapter of *What I Learned Over Summer Vacation,* "Lift/Thrust."

2. What are the main events of the chapter? (Answers)

3. What's "the lost pencil?" (Answers)

4. What words were taught in this chapter?

5. What do they mean?

6. How does the story show the words' meanings?

Lift/Thrust
Lift: An upward force that counteracts the force of gravity, produced by changing the direction and speed of a moving stream of air
Thrust: A force that increase the speed of an object

Thursday started out like any other morning-after-the-last-day-of-school. I slept until nine and didn't dress before I came downstairs, only to find all the marshmallow cereal was gone. I grumbled and grabbed the flakes. I cheered up when I saw a commercial for an F1000 remote control flyer. I wanted one and that got me thinking. I knew I wasn't going to be getting one because I don't have a job and my parents frown upon whim purchases. By the time my flakes stopped crunching and I was slurping down their soggy sweetness, I had my plan. I could build my own flyer, and if I was going to be building a plane anyway, why not build it big enough to fly with me in it?

I started out by drawing pictures of airplanes. You should always draw before you build. I learned that from the Wright brothers. They made a plane that could hold people, so I figured it was smart to imitate them. When I'm copying my older brother, my mom always says to him, "Imitation is the highest form of compliment." I'm hoping the Wright brothers feel flattered. My brother just seems to feel annoyed.

Once my drawing satisfied my snazz-o-meter, I started my scavenger hunt for building materials. I started in the basement with dad's supplies of handyman tools. He's not the handiest of men, but he has the basics—hammer, screwdriver, tape measure, and some other things I don't know what they do because I've never seen him use them. Maybe they had been presents like that sweater I have with the picture of a collie on it that my aunt thought was cute but that I keep in the darkest corner of my closest.

I carried everything outside and spread it out. I really had no idea how to turn my drawing into an actual airplane. I was thinking the Wright brothers' biographers could have shared with the rest of us a few more steps in the process. To boost my confidence I jumped around and did a few air punches. I knew my plane had to have a place for me to sit and it had to have wings. Beyond that I wasn't sure how it was going to work, but I decided just to start building it anyway. I mean, the day before I was flying with an elephant. This couldn't be any harder, right?

I had a cardboard box for my seat. I used duct tape to attach foam wings. I had this great huge packing foam from my mom's new freezer. The old one had a door that didn't like to shut, so it defrosted more than it froze. But don't feel bad because she got a new freezer, and I got wings that were light as a feather. Well, not exactly, that's just an expression, but they were really light. Finally, I duct taped my big brother's skateboard onto the box to give it wheels. My drawing had wheels. Real airplanes had wheels. I had to use it; it was a necessity. I couldn't worry that my brother threatened me with punishment of death if I ever used it.

That was all pretty easy. Then I had to figure out how to go up. I knew that air pushed up on a plane as the plane moved through it. That's called lift. I just had to figure out how to move through the air so it could lift the plane. Brilliance struck again. Nothing really hit me. (I just wanted to make sure you knew I was okay.) What was the brilliant idea? A sling shot. Now I just had to find elastic big enough to fling me, plane and all.

I asked my mom if I could clean out everyone's underwear drawer of anything holey, something with holes in it, not something used in religious ceremony. She gave me that look that means you-must-be-up-to-no-good-because-you-never-want-to-clean. I just smiled back and took off in a flash when she said okay. I didn't flash like a bulb, just ran off really fast. I gathered up any underwear that could pass as not perfect. It wasn't gross. They were clean. And anyway, desperate times call for desperate measures. I don't know where I learned that from.

I cut the elastic band out of each pair of underwear, cut open each one so that it stretched long, and stapled them all together into one long rubber band. I tied each end onto the railing on both sides of the porch steps. I was about eight feet off the ground, but I was hoping that lift would take me higher. I walked backward across our porch stretching the elastic with me. I had to sit backwards in the plane's box seat in order to stretch the elastic behind the box. I let go with a snap and off I went. I slid across the porch floor and then sledded down the porch steps. At the bottom of the steps I tipped and the back of my head hit the ground with a thud. I stared at the clouds and knew I had just learned an invaluable lesson: lift has to be greater than weight if you don't want to end up with a headache.

The sling shot hadn't worked exactly as I had hoped. Airplanes have lift because they cut through the air with their wings at high speeds. I needed better thrust, a better way to move forward faster. I decided to work on a car to perfect the forward thrust before trying to build another plane.

I dismantled my plane into its various parts and went back to the drawing board. I didn't really have a board, but I did draw a new design. I colored a lightning bolt onto the side of the car for a special touch, a memento. I learned from my grandma to remember the good times, and riding in a lightning-powered bumper car had been a blast, of the non-explosive kind. On the other side I wrote, "Thrust or Bust."

I took the wings off my box seat, thought of my brother and took off the skateboard, and then set off looking for a new set of wheels. I made a mental checklist of what counted as a wheel. It had to be round and big and strong enough to hold the weight of my box seat and I.

Round wasn't as easy to find as I had thought. Flower pots and cups had round edges, but they weren't the same round everywhere and couldn't roll forward. That was a problem if I expected to get anywhere. Lamp shades were too flimsy, light bulbs too fragile. I needed thin, round and strong. I sat down and chewed on my pencil while I thought it over. And that was my answer. My pencil. Thin. Round. Strong, well, strong enough. I thought about rolling on that hail and figured that I could roll on pencils just as well.

I went in search of *the lost pencil*. You know, that pencil you had a minute ago and now you can't find. I found three pencils in the couch, four under my bed, five in my backpack along with some jelly beans, though I don't remember having jelly beans. I found a pencil on my dad's desk and a full seventeen in my brother's room. I found six in our backyard which I had used to, well, never mind, that's another story. Thirty-six, an even number, so I could lay them side by side in two long rows under my box seat. As I rolled over them and they came out the back, I would pick them up and place them in front of my box. In the meantime I just taped them together two by two into eighteen long pencils.

Then I had one last problem. Or so I thought. Thrust. I had to have something that pushed me forward. What did regular cars use? Gas. Motor. I wasn't sure how they worked together. But I knew a little something about gas. Don't laugh. I mean carbon dioxide, CO_2. It's the stuff we breathe out. But it is also the stuff made when you build a volcano for science class and mix vinegar and baking soda. It's also what bubbles up in yeasty bread.

I raided the kitchen and got all the baking soda and yeast and vinegar and lemon juice I could find. I figured I could make gas and point it away from me. The gas would shoot one way and it should shoot me the other. I learned that from reading the book on rockets my friend got me for my birthday. I needed to get the gas in one place so it could shoot out some hole instead of just escaping into the sky. I grabbed a balloon that I had found under my bed along with some of those pencils. I duct taped a little box with a hole in it to my seat and set the balloon inside and filled it with the baking soda and yeast. I pulled the end of the balloon out the hole.

I grabbed up my box-seat and headed out to the street. In the driveway I almost broke my neck, literally, when I stepped on my brother's skateboard and my foot slipped right out from under me. I had a nasty bruise the next day, I won't mention where, but my spine stayed intact, and I decided that a skateboard's wheels were much better than a pencil conveyor belt. No harm, no foul, as they say. I'd just use the pencils some other way. There has to be another use for eighteen foot-long pencils, right?

In the middle of the road, I prepared for take off. I placed the box on the skateboard and climbed in. I had poured what was left of the vinegar and lemon juice into one empty water bottle. I stretched the lip of the balloon over the lip of the bottle. I tipped in the liquid and quick pulled out the bottle like a mouse stealing cheese from a trap.

I'm sure I must have produced some carbon dioxide gas, but I'm not sure how much because my big brother had been watching and waiting for his moment. He yelled like a madman, or maybe he yelled because he is a madman, and came charging at me. Maybe he was a little upset over my taking his skateboard. Maybe I should have tried the pencils first. He barreled into the box and started pushing me down the street at top speed, which was pretty fast, even for my brother. When he couldn't keep up any longer, he let me go, and I was flying down the street, figuratively speaking.

I ducked and crossed my arms over my head like they teach you to do on an airplane in case of an emergency landing. I was sure this was an emergency. I heard the crackling of branches and I fell out of the box. I had crash landed in a neighbor's blackberry bush. My left arm and left cheek were dyed purple from smooshing the berries. Lying there, I took a mental note of the lesson I learned. Thrust is good, but brakes are better.

I was stained beyond washing up, so when I got home, I just wiped my arm and cheek. The chunks and juice were gone, but I was stained. I guess I might have looked nice if I were glass. I parked the car in the garage, which means I threw it in the back along with the skateboard. Then I went back inside to regroup, as they say, even though there was just one of me.

I wasn't going to get up by going fast forward. Air might hold up an airplane, but I couldn't get going fast enough to get that kind of lift. If lift wasn't going to get me up, I needed a push upward. I decided to mull over my options for skyward thrust over a drink. I went to the fridge and poured myself a cup of lemonade. I topped it off with my favorite straw, the curly kind that's see-through and you can watch the lemonade go round and round before it disappears between your lips. I was sipping away and realized that I had my inspiration right in front of me. My curly straw!

I abandoned my lemonade and raced down the basement stairs, leaping off the fourth to the bottom step and landing with a crash at the bottom. I dug through the shelves until I found it. The pogo stick. Silver and blue in all its springy glory, I picked it up and dusted off a cobweb. Guess it had been awhile since I had bounced around on that thing. The pogo--thrust in a stick. If that didn't give me a push upward, what would?

I ran out to the yard and started bouncing. It was just like riding a bike, not that it had wheels or anything, but I hadn't forgotten how to balance and make it go. Boing! Boing! I bounced higher and higher. And then it happened. I landed on a tree stump and then from there I landed on the picnic table in our back yard and then from there on top of our shed and then from there on top of our neighbor's house. I started boinging from house to house and sometimes tree house in between. At first I was a little concerned getting so high and not knowing how to get down other than falling, but then I remembered I was on vacation, so I just stuck one hand in the air and swung it around like I was holding a lasso and riding a bucking bull instead of pogo stick.

The buildings started getting taller and taller and I realized that I was going into the city. That's when I heard a plane buzzing past. It was a small plane, a flying billboard. It was carrying a banner advertising some new kind of fizzy drink. The banner read, "Drink nothing but the best! Drink" and then it had a picture of the drink's logo. I can't tell you what it was or what it looked like because even though I got a close look at the plane and banner, I was really too close to see the end of it. And, well, not many people got a good look at the end of the banner because it fell off. Oh, okay, I confess. I ripped it off. It was an accident though!

I was bouncing, boinging along. I was at the top of a large building by then, higher and higher, like I said. The plane was passing close. And it was an instinct really. I boinged up by the banner and just grabbed on. The pogo stick crashed down on the roof of the building. I figured I would leave it there as a thank you, a thanks-for-letting-me-bounce-on-your-building gift.

When I grabbed onto the banner, the plane lost its balance and aimed up and then down, and I was struggling to just hang on. In the struggle, the banner ripped. I scrambled and managed to hang onto the front of the banner that was still attached to the plane. The pilot was shocked, of course, and headed right away to make an emergency landing. On the way to the airport, he inadvertently adverted to the following message: Drink nothing.

By the time we landed, the news crews had gathered. Did you see me on the evening news? If not, maybe you heard about it. Turns out that word had been spreading that the water supply was poisoned. As my feet hit the ground, Lisa Maloney from Channel 7 pointed the microphone at me and asked, "Why are you telling people not to drink anything? Is it true the city's water supply has been poisoned?"

I had no idea what she was talking about. I certainly didn't take the time to read the sign after it ripped; I was streaming through the air and holding on for dear life! She took my head shake to mean "no comment" and informed her viewing audience at home. Then she pointed the microphone at me again and said, "Did you have a reaction to drinking water?" Again I had no idea what she was talking about. She instructed the cameraman to zoom in on my face as she described the discoloration.

It dawned on me that she was talking about my blackberry stained cheek. I interrupted (I know that's rude, but she was saying it was a possible reaction to poisoned water) and told her it was just a blackberry stain. She stared at me like I was crazy. She then ignored me and interviewed the pilot. The story began to unfold. Lisa is quick on her feet and asked me to drink a glass of water in front of the viewing audience at home to show them the water really was safe to drink. I drank the whole cup without stopping for air. I wonder if there is a record for that?

Lisa gave me a ride home in Channel 7's news van. That was a first for me. After the initial thrill of it wore off, though, it was just like riding in a car. Riding an elephant is more fun over all. Did you see me on the news? Would I even ask if this were all balderdash?

Lesson 133

1. Read the third chapter of *What I Learned Over Summer Vacation,* "Obstreperous."

2. What word was taught in this chapter?

3. What does it mean?

4. How does the story show the word's meaning?

5. Do you think there's a bit of balderdash in every story?

6. Do you think the main character is obstreperous?

7. The idea I'm trying to get across is the meaning of the vocabulary word for each chapter. Do I get across my ideas? Do the stories show the meaning of the vocabulary words?

Obstreperous
Noisy and difficult to control

The next day our next-door neighbor Mrs. Carp stopped by to drop off some tomatoes from her garden. I heard her mention me. She called me obstreperous, ob-strep-er-ous! My very own neighbor calling me names. I'll tell you what happened and you tell me if I'm obstreperous.

When I woke up in the morning, the bruise I had gotten from my pre-car accident was still sore—I won't say where, so I chose a different creative outlet to explore. A safer outlet. As I was chomping my cereal, I envisioned myself on a big stage with flashing lights and ten thousand screaming fans. What was I doing up on stage? Don't worry, not singing. That's not going to happen. I was playing the drums. By the time I had slurped the last of my chocolate-colored milk from my bowl, I had a plan, a really good, not-at-all obstreperous plan. I was going to build a drum set.

I dropped my bowl and spoon in the dishwasher and got clean ones out. I tapped the one on the other and thought it sounded good. I got down on my hands and knees, opened all the cabinet doors and collected all the pots and bowls that I could find in the bowels of the kitchen. Then I opened all the drawers and collected all the long-handled utensils. I also found a hidden Reese's Peanut Butter Cup. I slipped it into my pocket to celebrate with later.

Now my mom has bruises. She says it's because I left every door and drawer open in the kitchen. I was an artist in the middle of creating a masterpiece. Could I really be blamed for not paying attention to such things?

I took everything down to the basement for some privacy because I wasn't that great yet, and I wasn't ready for an audience. That wasn't my fault; I just hadn't had a chance to practice. Before I could even do that, I first I had to set up my set. I experimented with combinations of each utensil on each pot and bowl. I tried plastic on plastic, metal on metal, wood on wood, plastic on metal, wood on plastic, well, you get the idea. Then I experimented with the bowls and pots on the floor, on a table, propped up slanted like they were a trap waiting for some innocent animal to sniff inside.

When I found my ideal sound, I got everything together that I wanted and piled aside all the rest. Then I started banging. How can I become a world-famous drummer if I don't practice, and how can I practice without banging? That does not qualify as obstreperous in my book. That was music!

My mom came down rather promptly and asked me what I was doing. She was rubbing her shin and shaking her head in dismay if I correctly read her expression. I explained my future as a rock and roll hall of fame drummer and told her this was just the beginning, a drop in the bucket, that I would save up for a drum set then join a band then become world-famous, of course. She said I could take my bucket outside before I dropped anything else into it. She thinks she's so funny.

I hauled my drum set outside and set up again. Then I got an idea. Have you seen *Mary Poppins*, the movie? The tall skinny chimney sweep slash sidewalk artist slash kite salesman is also a one man band. I started thinking maybe I could play more than just the drums. The problem was I couldn't play any instruments. Drums I just had to hit. That I could do. A whistle and kazoo I could blow. Bubble wrap and water I could stomp.

I rummaged through my closet until I found my whistle and through my desk drawers until I found my kazoo. I gave each a test blow. They worked great. Then I got the bubble wrap that came with the new freezer. Then I filled a wide bowl with water and took off my shoes.

I tied the whistle and kazoo to strings and hung them around my neck. I placed the bowl of water by my right foot and the bubble wrap by my left. I started practicing stomping and blowing and banging, and, if I do say so myself, I think I was making some pretty good progress when Mrs. Carp came over with her tomatoes. That was just a ruse. She wanted a reason to come over to complain. No irony there. That's when she used the O word and when I learned that my neighbor thought I was obstreperous.

I also learned she had tickets to the circus that afternoon. I begged to go with her to visit Apara. My mother gave her a sweet smile, and she agreed to let me come with her and her grandchildren. I didn't have a ticket, but I had already been in the show and didn't need to see it. I knew it wouldn't have been as good without me and my lollipop anyway. I just wanted to visit Apara. I didn't want her to forget me. I know they say an elephant never forgets, but I didn't want to take any chances.

When the time came, I squeezed into the backseat of the car with the little Carps. We weren't far from home when Mrs. Carp pulled over and stopped the car. She got out to speak to someone about something. I don't know who it was or what they talked about. I wasn't nosey and didn't ask. I did however take the opportunity to teach the little Carps a little something about the automobile. They were smaller than me, which made me older and wiser.

I pointed out the windows, the handles, the seats, the belts, the head and arm rests. I climbed up and over into the front seat. I taught them about the glove compartment, the dashboard and how to tell if you need gas or are going to get a speeding ticket. Then I showed them the horn. Well, I demonstrated the horn. The noise made Mrs. Carp jump and return immediately to her seat, out of which I dove in a jiffy. Did you know that a jiffy is an actual measurement of a really, really, really short period of time? Honest. Google it.

Mrs. Carp smoothed her ruffled feathers; just being expressive, she's not a bird. She asked me why I was always making noise. I said that wasn't noise that was education!

I put my hand down on the seat next to me and touched something warm and sticky and slimy. It smelled like peanut butter and chocolate. It tasted like peanut butter and chocolate. That's when I remembered I had slipped a peanut butter cup in my pocket. I licked my fingers, and it still tasted good all melty.

When we got to the circus, I followed the smell to the animal tent. I saw Apara with her mother, and it made me happy that I had helped her find her way home. The ring master recognized me and stopped by to say hello. He asked if I wanted to ride in the show again. I told him I didn't have a lollipop. He said, "Oh." But then I told him about my band I put together, the one-man one. He was interested. He said I could play in the show if I wanted.

I agreed right away even though I didn't have my band with me. I had to rethink the parts. I still had my kazoo and whistle around my neck, so the horn section was in place. For the percussion, I tied Apara's feed bowl to myself with a rope around it and my waist. I found a good stick for beating it. Then I tied a bucket onto each foot and filled them with water. I couldn't find bubble wrap.

While I was practicing, Apara and her family came over to me. They were strangely drawn to my melodies. I barely had time to practice when I was introduced. The animal's handler tried to pull them back as I started playing and marched out, but they were just too strong, too many, and too interested in me!

First Apara slipped away and followed me. Her mother followed her. Apara's brother followed too. Then for some reason the gorillas started following him. So instead of standing in the ring and putting on a one-man-band show, I put on a parade. I paraded in front of the elephants and gorillas, banging, sloshing and tooting.

I didn't want to steal the show again, so I just took one more lap around the tent and headed out, followed by Apara and her mother and her brother and the gorilla family. They followed me until I stopped and they all gathered around me and pressed close. Their trainer was frantic trying to figure out what had gotten into them all. I told him they must really like my music. Music does tame the savage beast, at least that's what someone once said. The trainer said I must make some pretty special music.

I thought they were probably waiting for an encore, but there are laws about how much kids and animals can work, and I didn't want to push it. I started thinking maybe I wanted to be in parades for a living. How much money do you think you can make parading? To help the handler out, I took off my music making equipment and headed over to the refreshments. Apara and her family and the gorilla family and now a rat followed me over.

I started thinking then about how I could *stop* leading a parade, and I started thinking about flying. How could I get up, up and away from my parade? I asked the balloon man if I could hold all of his balloons and see if I could fly. I learned that from Curious George. He said sure. Wasn't he nice? I gathered up all the balloons and jumped, my thrust up to get me going, and then I landed.

It turns out you need three helium balloons just to lift the amount of sugar in a can of soda pop. You would need 2000 balloons to lift me! I didn't have that many. I wasn't flying, but I felt like maybe I was jumping with ease, a little like the astronauts doing their version of the moon bounce.

It was fun pretending to bounce like the astronauts, so I ran and jumped and landed and ran and jumped and landed. Apara and family and gorilla and family and loner rat followed me. I headed toward the circus tent with leaps and bounds. I was supposed to meet Mrs. Carp after the show. The circus was ending, so I headed inside with my balloons and my parade.

Suddenly someone shrieked. I let go of the balloons because the scream startled me; it was so unexpected, so sudden, and so loud. It turns out a skunk had joined my parade. A few other women joined the shrieking and everyone else was just talking and shouting all at once. Then the balloons hit the hot lights at the top of the tent and started popping. The popping made Apara nervous and she started trumpeting. That agitated the gorillas, who started barking. Yes, barking. It was all rather, well, obstreperous. I think I was the only one who remained quiet and calm.

If I hadn't been still and calm, I might not have even noticed Apara's nose in my pocket. She reached her trunk right over and in. She brought it out all brown and sticky and slimy and it dawned on me. She, and probably all the others too, had smelled peanuts, my Reese's Peanut Butter cup. Oops.

That night when my mother was saying goodnight and I was lying in bed, I asked her if she thought I was obstreperous. My mother said that she told Mrs. Carp that a leopard can't change its spots. That means she's on my side or at least that she's given up trying to change me. I mean, you can't just take the spots off a leopard. And you can't take the noise out of an obstreperous kid, not that I am or ever will be obstreperous. You don't think so, do you?

Lesson 134

1. Read the fourth chapter of *What I Learned Over Summer Vacation,* "Salient/Inconspicuous."
2. What words were taught in this chapter?
3. What do they mean?
4. How does the story show the words' meanings?
5. What phrase does the main character say a lot? What are other things the main character says repeatedly? (Answers)

Salient/Inconspicuous
Salient: most noticeable or important; prominent; conspicuous
Inconspicuous: not clearly visible or attracting attention; not conspicuous

I admit that I may be a bit obstreperous when my creative energy explodes out into the world. But I knew I could be inconspicuous too, and I wanted to prove it to Mrs. Carp. I planned it all out that evening and slipped my notes under my pillow for safe keeping. Unfortunately, I don't sleep very soundly and in my stirring I seemed to have drooled on my notebook. But that was okay because my mind is like a steel trap; I don't forget a thing, unless it has to do with math facts or dates in history class.

I dressed all in black. I learned from movies that spies wear black, preferably leather. I don't know why they do that because aren't they supposed to be inconspicuous? Isn't it the point that people aren't supposed to notice them? But as soon as you see them all in black with their black sunglasses on, you know they are spies. It's their most salient feature. But who am I to buck tradition? I embraced conformity and dressed in black, settling for my black sweat suit because I don't own any leather.

I put on my brother's sunglasses and my red canvas sneakers. I wasn't about to paint them black. Not for Mrs. Carp, mission or not. My mission that I chose to accept was to prove to Mrs. Carp that I can be inconspicuous. She'll have to take back calling me obstreperous.

I casually walked around our yard, stopping to smell the roses, literally. I didn't want to appear like I was in a hurry to get anywhere. When I got to the fence that separates my yard from Mrs. Carp's, I slipped between the wooden posts. That had been a breeze, a snap, easy as pie. I don't know what's so easy about pie, but it was no problem sneaking into Mrs. Carp's yard. Not that this had been my first time in her yard. I've chased many a ball into her yard. I've chased our dog into her yard. I've chased my brother into her yard. And I've been chased out plenty of times. Not that day. I was inconspicuous. No one would notice me, and I would prove that my salient feature was not obstreperousness.

I slinked and slithered over to her tool shed in the backmost part of her back yard. I slid to the ground and pulled out my notebook. I wrote down the time and location. Check point one. I did a commando roll and crawled across to the azaleas. I pressed into the bush, snapping a few branches. They were a necessary casualty so that I could hide among the pink blooms.

I logged my time and location. I learned about keeping a log from reading a biography about a navigator named Nat. Google him if you don't know him. Or just take it from me that a log is for writing down what's going on and is named after a log they threw in the water to measure a ship's speed. My speed was zero. I was stone still. Now that's a figure of speech that means something. I didn't move. I was practicing my inconspicuous skills.

I sneezed. Blew my nose and my cover. I made a dash for the shed, opened the door and ran inside. I abruptly stopped because I knocked over something that knocked over something else with a boom and bang and a thwack and a tap. I have no idea what it all was. It was pitch black in there, as black as Mrs. Carp's pupils, as black as my brother's nose hair, as black as when you are asleep on a moonless night and the electricity goes out. I don't like the dark. I couldn't hear anything except my thoughts and my panting like a dog. I was thinking whether I would rather stay in the dark or face Mrs. Carp.

Before I could decide which was worse, some light was shed on the subject and on me. Mrs. Carp stood in the open door, shaking her head. She asked me what in the world I was doing in her shed. It's redundant to ask like that because obviously whatever I was doing I was doing in this world. I wasn't out in another galaxy or something.

I didn't answer. I had to think. A spy wouldn't reveal his mission, would he? What was I doing in the shed? "I sneezed" is what I told her. That was why I was in the shed. It was the catalyst that provided the thrust to propel me toward the shed. She didn't know what to say, so I took the moment of silence as a chance to make a quick getaway. Across the yard, through the fence, in the house, up the stairs, into bed I went with record speed, not that they have that as an entry in the *Guinness Book of World Records*. But if they did, my name would be there.

I needed a new plan. An inconspicuous plan. A plan that wouldn't end with me being in Mrs. Carp's shed. Thinking it over I realized that somehow Mrs. Carp needed to know that I was there so she would know that I'm not obstreperous. If she never knew I was there, how would she know how inconspicuous I could be?

I walked down to the kitchen to get something to suck on. I think better with something in my mouth, and this paradox had me stumped. She had to not know that I was there and she had to know that I was there. I started listing my options: taking pictures of myself there, leaving a note saying I was there, doing something that she would notice and realize that I was there. I was stumped. I put a popsicle in my mouth, cherry. And there it was, my idea.

Mrs. Carp had a cherry tree. I decided I would pick her cherries for her. I could leave the basket of cherries for her and let her figure out the rest. I left on my spy clothes and slipped back over to Mrs. Carp's yard. I had to stack up some pots from the shed to reach the bottom branch. After that I had no problem climbing up. I had decided to just pick the cherries and throw them down and then I would gather them into baskets.

I started picking and dropping. Some of them just popped right off the branch and some I had to pull really hard to get them off. I guess all that rattling of the leaves attracted some attention, despite my best efforts to remain inconspicuous. A flock of crows started landing on the branches. They started eating the cherries as fast as I was picking them, okay, maybe faster than I could pick them. At first, I tried to shoo them away, but then I realized I was camouflaged in all their blackness. I figured that would help with my inconspicuous mission.

With the help of the birds, I got that tree cleared off in no time. Unfortunately, I had failed to think the whole crow thing through. While I was camouflaged, the berries were not, and the birds had found them all. There weren't any left to put in baskets, not even one. Well, there were some smooshed on the ground. Those got smooshed onto my shoes.

I decided right then was a good time to end my mission. I had been inconspicuous, and it was the birds that had eaten all the cherries not me. Acting nonchalant, I slipped back into my house and remembered to slip off my cherry stained shoes. I raced upstairs, changed out of my spy clothes and worked at washing the cherry stains off my hands. Then I waited. Then I got bored. Then I got distracted making bubbles with dishwashing detergent and hangers.

I had the kitchen floor nice and slippery with popped bubbles when Mrs. Carp came by. She had zucchini. My mom invited her to come in and bring it into the kitchen. She hadn't known what

I'd been up to. Mrs. Carp slipped and fell. She didn't get hurt, but she did get a bit slimy. She didn't mention my being obstreperous, but words like slapdash and slipshod were coming out of her mouth. It was becoming more and more salient that she was upset. She went on and on about how I ruined her cherry tree.

I trudged up to my room and logged the last data into my notebook, writing across the page, "Mission failed." I had failed to prove my salient quality was inconspicuousness, not obstreperousness. One way or another I was going to prove to this woman what a dream kid I really am. But before that day came, I was sure she would be over to see my mom with more garden gifts, just as sure as I was that her salient trait was carpiness. Is that a word?

Lesson 135

1. Read the fifth chapter of *What I Learned Over Summer Vacation,* "Perimeter/Circumference."

2. What words were taught in this chapter?

3. What do they mean?

4. How does the story show the words' meanings?

Perimeter/Circumference
Perimeter: the outermost parts or boundary of an area or object
Circumference: the edge or region that entirely surrounds something

My mother suggested I spend the next day at home. She put it a little more strongly than that. I was forbidden to leave our yard. The good news was that I had a plan. Lying on the floor with one arm stuck under my bed trying to fish out a golf ball gone astray, I had come across my 18 foot-long pencils. I retrieved the three dozen pencils each strapped to another and headed out to the back yard. I had a most brilliant plan. I was going to dig a pool.

I knew my parents wouldn't be thrilled with half the yard missing, but I needed to make sure the pool was big enough to run and jump into while performing my famous front flip. I marked a spot by pushing one of the pencils into the ground. I ran and jumped and marked my landing spot with another pencil. I performed the feat in all directions. Having double jump distance in each direction I knew would allow for my famous front flip, flailing feet and all.

I found some string and tied it to the first pencil and then walked it around the circumference of my pool area, retying it to the first pencil when I finished my circumnavigation. It wasn't exactly round; I decided it was pool shaped. I got out a shovel and started to dig. I figured I would be finished when the pool was as deep as I am tall. I first dug carefully around the perimeter of the pool and then worked my way in, around and around, down and down.

Digging is back breaking work, and I had to take lots of breaks so that my back wouldn't break. It actually took me a few days to finish. I was so excited to finish that I ran immediately to get the hose to fill it up. It didn't take me long to realize I had a problem. A very muddy problem.

I turned off the hose and decided a cool mud bath might help me think through the problem. I splashed into my mud pit and let every bit of me sink into its gooiness. My father was the first to find me. He asked what I was doing and just nodded and turned back into the house. My mother, when she found me, made me get out and turned the hose on me to clean me off. That was kind of fun.

I realized that I needed a plastic tarp of some sort to cover the inside of the pool to hold the water away from the dirt. I visited our across-the-street neighbor who is a painter. He said he'd give me some used tarp, meaning already covered with paint splotches, if I could tell him exactly how much I needed. I told him I could and I would, but I really had no idea how to figure out how much I needed. I didn't know how big my pool was other than two jumps wide and one me high.

The dirt I had piled up from what I had taken out of the ground was the volume of my pool. That wasn't what I needed. I needed to find the area of the floor and walls of my pool. And I needed a drink. While I was trying to refresh, recharge and relax, my mom interrupted with a chore request. Except it was more of an order. I didn't get a chance to turn it down. I had to vacuum the living room and dining room and kitchen. Back on my feet, I started cleaning the downstairs of our house.

I had the pool problem on my mind and wasn't exactly paying full attention to the job. It's not that the lights were on and nobody was home. I wasn't day dreaming; I was trying to figure out a solution to my problem. That's the reason I didn't notice right away that I was vacuuming up the Legos I had left out. I must have sucked up one too many because the vacuum bag puffed up, filled to the brim and burst open like a bag of Orville Redenbacher's best.

A plume of smoke filled the air like Hiroshima, without the death and destruction. I coughed and sneezed out some dust and decided I needed some clean air. I fled the scene like a criminal and found a shady hiding place at the side of the house.

I still had not solved my problem, and I knew it was only a matter of time before I had the new chore of cleaning up after my first chore. I had been stumped before, but I was super stumped then and didn't know where to turn. Just then I saw one of the painters in the driveway, an employee of my neighbor, he was unloading the van after one of his jobs. I figured I could learn from him how he knew how much tarp he would need for a job. I ran over and put the question to him. He explained they knew the measurements of the room and used those.

I thanked him and ran back home. I had my next step. I needed measurements. I found my dad's tape measure and grabbed my log journal. I couldn't find a pencil or pen so I pulled up one of the pool boundary markers. I drew the shape of the pool in my notebook. I carefully marked and numbered each pencil location. Then I started to measure from pencil to pencil. I labeled each distance on my drawing. Then I jumped in and measured from top to bottom.

I had completed my next step and was again stumped as to what I was supposed to do next when my mom discovered the aftermath of my nuclear detonation, and I had to go back and vacuum up my vacuuming accident. When I was finished, I asked my mom how I was supposed to find the area of a pool shape. That's when I learned from her a valuable life lesson. She said, "Use what you know." That sounded simple enough because I already knew what I already know. It wouldn't require learning anything new or practicing or anything.

I chewed on the end of my foot-long pencil and stared at my pool diagram, trying to decide what it was I already knew. I had all the measurements for around the pool. I could add those all up and find the perimeter. But I needed the area of the bottom of the pool and the walls of the pool. I knew how to find the area of triangles, circles and rectangles, so I used what I knew. I drew triangles, circles and rectangles onto my paper filling in all the space between my pencil markers. Then I got all confused because I didn't know the real sizes of those shapes. Then I thought if I was going to have to figure out a scale to figure out the size of my pool, I would rather do it without doing math. So I got a new idea.

I climbed out onto the roof of the porch by going out my bedroom window. I held my hand up to block the pool from my sight. I went back and ran across the street and found my painter neighbor. I told him I knew how much tarp I needed. He asked how much and I told him two me's and as much as my hand covers from the top of my porch. He looked at me like I was crazy. He shook his head and fetched me a large tarp all folded up and told me I could try it to see if it was enough.

I hammered the pencils like spikes through the tarp to hold it in place. It was just the right size, two me's and a handful. My mom would say that two me's would be more than a handful. She thinks she's so funny. I drove in the last pencil, my golden spike, yellow number two. I had a pool.

I immediately filled the pool up with water and did at least forty-seven front flip flops into the water. Then I didn't know what else to do in my pool and started thinking about what else I could do. I started reminiscing about the day I spent with Apara. It was a lot of fun having a pet. I already knew that my parents would say no to any pet plea I presented. I knew I was never going to have my own pet until I owned my own home. That was too far into the future, so I knew I had to take matters into my own hands; if I wanted a pet, I was going to have to make one.

The next morning I convinced my mom to drop me off at the circus grounds. It wouldn't be long before the circus moved on, and I wanted to remember Apara. I wanted to keep her for myself. I was going to build an elephant robot. I talked to Apara's trainer and asked if Apara could spend the day with me. I told him I wanted to spend some time with her before they took off for their next city. He agreed and I rode her back to my house. Riding on an elephant has got to be one of the worst ways to try and be inconspicuous.

Once we got to my house, I set about taking measurements. I wanted my robot as life like as possible which meant life size as well. I measured her height and length and the circumference of her midsection. I even got her trunk measurement. My robot had to have a trunk; it's what is most salient on an elephant. She laid herself down for a nap while I went searching for parts to build my robot. I always think better with something in my mouth, so I headed for the fridge. It was that simple.

I started dumping everything out of the fridge. I know what you are thinking, but I wasn't completely thoughtless. I took all of the things from the freezer and moved them to my mom's new big freezer. It wouldn't have mattered anyway because once I got the refrigerator outside to start building my robot, Apara found her way inside (don't ask how she got in there) and ate up everything I had left out. She would have gotten the frozen foods before they spoiled.

When I realized what had happened, we made a hasty retreat. I trotted her off, but like I said, it's hard to be inconspicuous when you are with an elephant, and all I wanted to do was hide. At least I wasn't being obstreperous. Apara and I made our way to the local bowling alley. I thought it would be a good way to spend an hour before we headed back to the circus.

We rented a lane and they let Apara bowl without specially approved shoes. The owner decided it would probably be good publicity to have an elephant at his bowling alley. I'm sure it was because she had her picture taken a bunch of times, like I said, you can't be inconspicuous with an elephant. I bowled first to show Apara how it's done. Then she wrapped her trunk around the circumference of the ball and then let it fly like she was doing tricks with a yoyo.

She made a strike on her first attempt. I was so surprised I spit out my soda, which I wasn't supposed to have brought down to the bowling area with me, but I hadn't seen the sign until after I had bought it. I quickly looked around to see if anyone had seen. They were all too distracted by the elephant with the perfect bowling score. It was becoming salient that although an elephant may not be able to be inconspicuous, being near an elephant getting all of the attention can help you be just that.

My eyes scanned the perimeter of the room looking for a towel or rag or something to dry up my mess before I got in trouble. I spotted a wet/dry vac that had been left out near an "employees only" closet. I plugged it in and tried to roll it inconspicuously over to our lane. I was so glad I always pick the one on the end. I flicked the switch and it started sucking up the spill and immediately Apara became curious and started nosing around, literally. She stuck her nose right into the hose.

And now, I know you are going to think this is outright balderdash, but I've learned from scientists that our bodies are seventy-five percent water, so elephants probably are similar, and well, the wet dry vac must have been really powerful because it started sucking the water right out of her. The wet dry vac was dehydrating Apara, like that appliance they sell on TV. She started shrinking and shriveling like a grape turning into a raisin or a plum turning into a prune. I know elephants are always wrinkly, but this wasn't just came-out-of-the-suitcase wrinkly; this was balled up aluminum foil wrinkly.

I didn't do anything at first, I was too shocked. Wouldn't you be? But then the distressed look on her face knocked the sense into me, even though she just looked and didn't bop me upside my head or anything. I lunged for the vacuum and flicked the switch the other way, from suck to thrust. I was so relieved when she started blowing up again, and I'm pretty sure she got a little more than just water in her. She let out a big burp and I could smell my soda on her breath.

I thought that maybe it was a good time to make an exit. I took Apara back home, and we splashed into the pool to wash off our sticky feet from the soda. When we got out of the pool (Apara was quite nimble at getting out actually—must be all the circus training), we stopped inside so I could look up on the computer where Apara was traveling next.

Apara watched me Google her name and the circus, and I found her itinerary. I opened up Google Earth and started plotting a tour of the circus stops. Apara, it turns out, is a computer genius. She nudged me out of the way and started marking the tour herself. She knew her states and cities and was remarkably nimble at pressing the keys. I made a mental note to tell the ringmaster of her special talent. I was sure it would make a spectacular act for the show. I would bet the farm on it, not that I have a farm.

Lesson 136

1. Read the sixth chapter of *What I Learned Over Summer Vacation,* "Precipitous."
2. What word was taught in this chapter?
3. What does it mean?
4. How does the story show the word's meaning?

Precipitous
dangerously high or steep; sudden and dramatic change that worsens a situation

The ring master was pleased to hear of my discovery of Apara's hidden talent. He invited me to go on the road with the show. They were leaving the next day. I, of course, said I would have to ask my parents. I, of course, knew they would say no. There was no way I was going to run away with the circus. That would be cliché and I'm full of surprises. Cliché isn't my style.

I promised Apara I would follow the show's travels online, and we agreed to send emails. I can't tell you her email address. You can't be too careful with privacy concerns these days. I talked to my parents that night, however, and they agreed I could ride with Apara to the next town. My grandma lived there, and I could spend the night, and they would come and get me the next day.

Just for fun I packed a bandana with some snacks and some clean clothes and tied it to a stick like I was someone who ran away with the circus. The ringmaster was thrilled to see me and agreed to let me ride in Apara's car in the caravan. I don't mean that Apara was driving a car. Our bumper car driving days were over. I mean she was being pulled in this boxcar type thing, like a horse trailer.

At first it was great fun being in there with Apara. Then I realized just how much she smelled like an animal. Skunks weren't the only stinky animals. If skunks were bad because the odor stuck with you, Apara might as well have been a skunk because I was stuck with her and her smell.

I knew it was only about an hour's drive, but I couldn't take it any longer, and I hung my head out the top of the half door. (She wasn't closed in all the way. Animals have to breathe just like people do.) I know that sticking your head out of the window of a moving vehicle is not a smart thing to do. I learned that from the car makers who keep the backseat windows from rolling all the way down. I knew it was a bad idea, but I was desperate. I was even more desperate when precipitously my shirt got caught on a passing sign and I got pulled from the car. Oops.

The circus caravan kept on going without me. With each passing moment it was becoming more and more salient that no one noticed me, hanging out to dry on a speed limit sign. Too many other things to notice I guess. I was still hanging there when the last of the caravan drove out of sight. I realized too late that a bit of obstreperousness maybe could have helped my situation.

So there I was. Alone. Dangling from my precipitous location, I scanned the perimeter. It was barren. Empty. I repeat. I was alone. It was just me and the grasshoppers. I didn't even have my bandana knapsack. I was penniless. I didn't have any food. I didn't have anyone to help me. This precipitous turn of events had me all tied up in knots, figuratively speaking. I wasn't tied to the sign; I was hanging from it by my shirt.

I learned from the lady on the exercise videos to take deep breaths, so that's what I did. I breathed deeply. I guess the extra strain as my lungs expanded was more than my shirt could bare and it ripped. Now I looked as penniless as I was. Unfortunately, it didn't rip enough to release me.

I couldn't think of what to do, so I started thinking of new ways to create lift and thrust. I still had yet to create a real, flying machine. It seems I must have gotten lost in thought because cars started coming down the previously empty road. I started flailing my arms and yelling that I needed to get to the circus. I was being as not inconspicuous as I possibly could. I guess that means I was being conspicuous.

It turns out, though, that my conspicuous, obstreperous act had people thinking I was a living sign for the circus. They thought I was an advertisement, pointing the way to the rings of excitement, laughter, peanuts, and cotton candy. People honked and waved, but they didn't stop.

I gave up shouting about the circus. Someone stopped. I guess I finally looked like someone who needed help. When the person got out of the car, I realized it was Mrs. Carp. I was jumping for joy to see her. I wasn't really. Not that I could have jumped even if I weren't being sarcastic.

Mrs. Carp stood below me shaking her head. She didn't look surprised. She took me to the circus. She mentioned I smelled like I belonged there. I think the circus is full of wonderful smells, like the aforementioned peanuts and cotton candy, so I took it as a compliment.

I had trouble finding my grandma since I was so late. I decided to throw caution to the wind and climbed up onto the fence to see better. I didn't throw anything from there; I actually stepped out onto the top of a blue baseball cap. It was a little wobbly, so I stepped onto a brown cowboy hat. I stepped from hat to hat to hair to hat to hair to hair, you get the idea. I actually didn't see my grandma until after I heard her. In fact I happened to step on her head. Somehow she knew it was me. She called my name and I jumped down. She was surprised to see me. Well, she was surprised by how I looked. She bought me a circus t-shirt, so it turned out to be a pretty great day, and I have a memento to remember it by.

Lesson 137

1. Read the poems.

2. See if you can figure out what the idioms below mean. Write down any ones that you like that maybe you could use in a story. (Answers)

   - cream of the crop, hold down the fort, get your ducks in a row, in a pickle, deer in the headlights, hit the hay, bite someone's head off, hold your horses

The Sloth   By Oliver Herford

The Sloth en-joys a life of Ease;

He hangs in-vert-ed from the trees,

And views life up-side down.

If you, my child, are noth-ing loath

To live in In-dol-ence and Sloth,

Un-heed-ing the World's frown,

You, too, un-vexed by Toil and Strife,

May take a hu-mor-ous view of life.

I Heard a Bird Sing

I heard a bird sing

In the dark of December.

A magical thing

And sweet to remember.

"We are nearer to Spring

Than we were in September,"

I heard a bird sing

In the dark of December.

Lesson 138

1. Read "Brer Rabbit He's a Good Fisherman."

BRER RABBIT HE'S A GOOD FISHERMAN By Joel Chandler Harris

One day, when Brer Rabbit, and Brer Fox, and Brer Coon, and Brer Bear and a whole lot of them was clearing a new ground for to plant a roasting-pear patch, the sun began to get sort of hot, and Brer Rabbit, he got tired; but he didn't let on, 'cause he feared the others would call him lazy, and he keep on carrying away rubbish and piling it up, till by and by he holler out that he got a thorn in his hand, and then he take and slip off and hunt for a cool place to rest. After a while he come across a well with a bucket hanging in it.

"That looks cool," says Brer Rabbit, says he. "And cool I 'specs she is. I'll just about get in there and take a nap," and with that, in he jump, he did, and he ain't no sooner fix himself than the bucket begin to go down. Brer Rabbit, he was mighty scared. He know where he come from, but he don't know where he's going. Suddenly he feel the bucket hit the water, and there she sat, but Brer Rabbit, he keep mighty still, 'cause he don't know what minute's going to be the next. He just lay there and shook and shover.

Brer Fox always got one eye on Brer Rabbit, and when he slip off from the new ground, Brer Fox, he sneak after him. He knew Brer Rabbit was after some project or another, and he took and crope off, he did, and watch him. Brer Fox see Brer Rabbit come to the top of the well and stop, and then he see him jump in the bucket, and then, lo and behold! he see him go down out of sight. Brer Fox was the most 'stonished fox that you ever laid eyes on. He sat down in the bushes and thought and thought, but he don't make no head nor tails of this kind of business. Then he say to himself, says he:

"Well, if this don't beat everything!" says he. "Right down there in that well Brer Rabbit keep his money hid, and if it ain't that, he done gone and 'scovered a gold mine, and if it ain't that, then I'm a-going to see what's in there," says he.

Brer Fox crope up a little nearer, he did, and listen, but he don't hear no fuss, and he keep on getting nearer, and yet he don't hear nothing. By and by he get up close and peep down, but he don't see nothing, and he don't hear nothing. All this time Brer Rabbit was mighty near scared out of his skin, and he feared for to move 'cause the bucket might keel over and spill him out in the water. While he saying his prayers over and over, old Brer Fox holler out:

"Heyo, Brer Rabbit! Who you visitin' down there?" says he.

"Who? Me? Oh, I'm just a-fishing, Brer Fox," says Brer Rabbit, says he. "I just say to myself that I'd sort of s'prise you all with a mess of fishes, and so here I is, and there's the fishes. I'm a-fishing for supper, Brer Fox," says Brer Rabbit, says he. "Is there many of them down there, Brer Rabbit?"

says Brer Fox, says he. "Lots of them, Brer Fox; scores and scores of them. The water is naturally alive with them. Come down and help me haul them in, Brer Fox," says Brer Rabbit, says he.

"How I going to get down, Brer Rabbit?"

"Jump into the other bucket, Brer Fox. It'll fetch you down all safe and sound." Brer Rabbit talked so happy and talked so sweet that Brer Fox he jump in the bucket, he did, and so he went down, 'cause his weight pulled Brer Rabbit up. When they pass one another on the half-way ground, Brer Rabbit he sing out:

"Good-bye, Brer Fox, take care o' your clothes, For this is the way the world goes; Some goes up and some goes down, You'll get to the bottom all safe and soun'." When Brer Rabbit got out, he gallop off and told the folks what the well belonged to, that Brer Fox was down there muddying up the drinking water, and then he gallop back to the well, and holler down to Brer Fox:

"Here come a man with a great big gun—When he haul you up, you Jump and run." Well, soon enough Brer Fox was out of the well, and in just about half an hour both of them was back on the new ground working just as if they'd never heard of no well. But every now and then Brer Rabbit would burst out laughing, and old Brer Fox would scowl and say nothing.

Lesson 139

1. Read the first part of "How Boots Befooled the King" by Howard Pyle.

ONCE upon a time there was a king who was the wisest in all of the world. So wise was he that no one had ever befooled him, which is a rare thing, I can tell you. Now, this king had a daughter who was as pretty as a ripe apple, so that there was no end to the number of the lads who came asking to marry her. Every day there were two or three of them dawdling around the house, so that at last the old king grew tired of having them always about.

So he sent word far and near that whoever should befool him might have the princess and half of the kingdom to boot, for he thought that it would be a wise man indeed who could trick him. But the king also said, that whoever should try to befool him and should fail, should have a good whipping. This was to keep all foolish fellows away.

The princess was so pretty that there was no lack of lads who came to have a try for her and half of the kingdom, but every one of these went away with a sore back and no luck.

Now, there was a man who was well off in the world, and who had three sons; the first was named Peter, and the second was named Paul. Peter and Paul thought themselves as wise as anybody in all of the world, and their father thought as they did.

As for the youngest son, he was named Boots. Nobody thought anything of him except that he was silly, for he did nothing but sit poking in the warm ashes all of the day.

One morning Peter spoke up and said that he was going to the town to have a try at befooling the king, for it would be a fine thing to have a princess in the family. His father did not say no, for if anybody was wise enough to befool the king, Peter was the lad.

So, after Peter had eaten a good breakfast, off he set for the town, right foot foremost. After a while he came to the king's house and-rap! tap! tap!—he knocked at the door.

Well; what did he want?

Oh! he would only like to have a try at befooling the king.

Very good; he should have his try. He was not the first one who had been there that morning, early as it was.

So Peter was shown in to the king.

"Oh, look!" said he, "yonder are three black geese out in the court-yard!" But no, the king was not to be fooled so easily as all that. "One goose is enough to look at at a time," said he; "take him away and give him a whipping!"

And so they did, and Peter went home bleating like a sheep.

One day Paul spoke up. "I should like to go and have a try for the princess, too," said he.

Well, his father did not say no, for, after all, Paul was the more clever of the two.

So off Paul went as merrily as a duck in the rain. By and by he came to the castle, and then he too was brought before the king just as Peter had been. "Oh, look!" said he, "yonder is a crow sitting in the tree with three white stripes on his back!"

But the king was not so silly as to be fooled in that way. "Here is a Jack," said he, "who will soon have more stripes on his back than he will like. Take him away and give him his whipping!"

Then it was done as the king had said, and Paul went away home bawling like a calf.

One day up spoke Boots. "I should like to go and have a try for the pretty princess, too," said he.

At this they all stared and sniggered. What! he go where his clever brothers had failed, and had nothing to show for the trying but a good beating? What had come over the lout! Here was a pretty business, to be sure! That was what they all said.

But all of this rolled away from Boots like water from a duck's back. No matter, he would like to go and have a try like the others. So he begged and begged until his father was glad to let him go to be rid of his teasing, if nothing else.

Then Boots asked if he might have the old tattered hat that hung back of the chimney.

Oh, yes, he might have that if he wanted it, for nobody with good wits was likely to wear such a thing.

So Boots took the hat, and after he had brushed the ashes from his shoes set off for the town, whistling as he went.
The first body whom he met was an old woman with a great load of earthenware pots and crocks on her shoulders.

"Good-day, mother," said Boots.

"Good-day, son," said she.

"What will you take for all of your pots and crocks?" said Boots. "Three shillings," said she.

"I will give you five shillings if you will come and stand in front of the king's house, and do thus and so when I say this and that," said Boots.

Oh, yes! she would do that willingly enough.

So Boots and the old woman went on together, and presently came to the king's house. When they had come there, Boots sat down in front of the door and began bawling as loud as he could— "No, I will not! I will not do it, I say! No, I will not do it!"

So he kept on, bawling louder and louder until he made such a noise that, at last, the king himself came out to see what all of the hubbub was about. But when Boots saw him he only bawled out louder than ever. "No, I will not! I will not do it, I say!"

"Stop! stop!" cried the king, "what is all this about?"

"Why," said Boots, "everybody wants to buy my cap, but I will not sell it! I will not do it, I say!"

"But, why should anybody want to buy such a cap as that?" said the king. "Because," said Boots, "it is a fooling cap and the only one in all of the world."

"A fooling cap!" said the king. For he did not like to hear of such a cap as that coming into the town. "Hum-m-m-m! I should like to see you fool somebody with it. Could you fool that old body yonder with the pots and the crocks?"

"Oh, yes! That is easily enough done," said Boots, and without more ado he took off his tattered cap and blew into it. Then he put it on his head again and bawled out, "Break pots! break pots!"

Lesson 140

1. Read "How Boots Befooled the King" to the end.

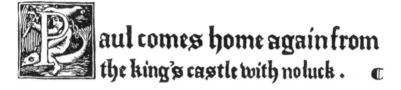

Paul comes home again from the king's castle with no luck.

…Then he put it on his head again and bawled out, "Break pots! break pots!"

No sooner had he spoken these words than the old woman jumped up and began breaking and smashing her pots and crocks as though she had gone crazy. That was what Boots had paid her five shillings for doing, but of it the king knew nothing. "Hui!" said he to himself, "I must buy that hat from the fellow or he will fool the princess away from me for sure and certain." Then he began talking to Boots as sweetly as though he had honey in his mouth. Perhaps Boots would sell the hat to him?

Oh, no! Boots could not think of such a thing as selling his fooling cap. Come, come; the king wanted that hat, and sooner than miss buying it he would give a whole bag of gold money for it.

At this Boots looked up and looked down, scratching his head. Well, he supposed he would have to sell the hat some time, and the king might as well have it as anybody else. But for all that he did not like parting with it. So the king gave Boots the bag of gold, and Boots gave the king the old tattered hat, and then he went his way.

After Boots had gone the king blew into the hat and blew into the hat, but though he blew enough breath into it to sail a big ship, he did not befool so much as a single titmouse. Then, at last, he began to see that the fooling cap was good on nobody else's head but Boots's; and he was none too pleased at that, you may be sure.

As for Boots, with his bag of gold he bought the finest clothes that were to be had in the town, and when the next morning had come he started away bright and early for the king's house. "I have come," said he, "to marry the princess, if you please."

At this the king hemmed and hawed and scratched his head. Yes; Boots had befooled him sure enough, but, after all, he could not give up the princess for such a thing as that. Still, he would give Boots another chance. Now, there was the high-councillor, who was the wisest man in all of the world. Did Boots think that he could fool him also?

Oh, yes! Boots thought that it might be done.

Very well; if he could befool the high-councillor so as to bring him to the castle the next morning against his will, Boots should have the princess and the half of the kingdom; if he did not do so he should have his beating.

Then Boots went away, and the king thought that he was rid of him now for good and all. As for the high-councillor, he was not pleased with the matter at all, for he did not like the thought of being fooled by a clever rogue, and taken here and there against his will. So when he had come home, he armed all of his servants with blunderbusses, and then waited to give Boots a welcome when he should come.

But Boots was not going to fall into any such trap as that! No indeed! not he! The next morning he went quietly and bought a fine large meal-sack. Then he put a black wig over his beautiful red hair, so that no one might know him.

After that he went to the place where the high-councillor lived, and when he had come there he crawled inside of the sack, and lay just beside the door of the house.

By and by came one of the maid servants to the door, and there lay the great meal-sack with somebody in it. "Ach!" cried she, "who is there?" But Boots only said, "Sh.h.h.h.h!"

Then the serving maid went back into the house, and told the high-- councillor that one lay outside in a great meal-sack, and that all that he said was, "Sh.h.h.hh!"

So the councillor went himself to see what it was all about. "What do you want here?" said he.

"Sh-h-h-h-h!" said Boots, "I am not to be talked to now. This is a wisdom - sack, and I am learning wisdom as fast as a drake can eat peas."

"And what wisdom have you learned?" said the councillor.

Oh! Boots had learned wisdom about everything in the world. He had learned that the clever scamp who had fooled the king yesterday was coming with seventeen tall men to take the high-councillor, willy-nilly, to the castle that morning.

When the high-councillor heard this he fell to trembling till his teeth rattled in his head. "And have you learned how I can get the better of this clever scamp?" said he.

Oh, yes! Boots had learned that easily enough.

So, good! then if the wise man in the sack would tell the high-councillor how to escape the clever rogue, the high-councillor would give the wise man twenty dollars.
But no, that was not to be done; wisdom was not bought so cheaply as the high-councillor seemed to think.

Well, the councillor would give him a hundred dollars then.

That was good! A hundred dollars were a hundred dollars. If the councillor would give him that much he might get into the sack himself, and then he could learn all the wisdom that he wanted, and more besides.

So Boots crawled out of the sack, and the councillor paid his hundred dollars and crawled in. As soon as he was in all snug and safe, Boots drew the mouth of the sack together and tied it tightly.

Then he flung sack, councillor, and all over his shoulder, and started away to the king's house, and anybody who met them could see with half an eye that the councillor was going against his will.

When Boots came to the king's castle he laid the councillor down in the goose-house, and then he went to the king.

When the king saw Boots again, he bit his lips with vexation. "Well," said he, "have you fooled the councillor?"

"Oh, yes!" says Boots, "I have done that." And where was the councillor now?

Oh, Boots had just left him down in the goose-house. He was tied up safe and sound in a sack, waiting till the king should send for him.

So the councillor was sent for, and when he came the king saw at once that he had been brought against his will.

"And now may I marry the princess?" said Boots.

But the king was not willing for him to marry the princess yet; no! no! Boots must not go so fast. There was more to be done yet. If he would come tomorrow morning he might have the princess and welcome, but he would have to pick her out from among fourscore other maids just like her; did he think that he could do that?

Oh, yes! Boots thought that that might be easy enough to do.

So, good! then come tomorrow; but he must understand that if he failed he should have a good whipping, and be sent packing from the town.

So off went Boots, and the king thought that he was rid of him now, for he had never seen the princess, and how could he pick her out from among eighty others?

But Boots was not going to give up so easily as all that! No, not he! He made a little box, and then he hunted up and down until he had caught a live mouse to put into it.

When the next morning came he started away to the king's house, taking his mouse along with him in the box.

There was the king, standing in the doorway, looking out into the street. When he saw Boots coming towards him he made a wry face. "What!" said he, "are you back again?"

Oh, yes! Boots was back again. And now if the princess was ready he would like to go and find her, for lost time was not to be gathered again like fallen apples.

So off they marched to a great room, and there stood eighty-and-one maidens, all as much alike as peas in the same dish.

Boots looked here and there, but, even if he had known the princess, he could not have told her from the others. But he was ready for all that. Before anyone knew what he was about, he opened the box, and out ran the little mouse among them all. Then what a screaming and a hubbub there was. Many looked as though they would have liked to swoon, but only one of them did so. As soon as the others saw what had happened, they forgot all about the mouse, and ran to her and fell to fanning her and slapping her hands and chafing her temples.

"This is the princess," said Boots. And so it was.

After that the king could think of nothing more to set Boots to do, so he let him marry the princess as he had promised, and have half of the kingdom to boot.

That is all of this story.

Only this: It is not always the silliest one that sits kicking his feet in the ashes at home.

Lesson 141

1. You are going to read one more book this year, just for fun. It's called *Pollyanna*.
2. Read these summaries.
3. Remember the parts of a book? List for this book the characters and setting.
4. Now for the plot. I know you haven't read it yet, but the summaries will help us.
5. There is always an incident toward the very beginning of a book that sets off the plot. What is the incident in this book that incites the plot? (gets it going) (Answers)
6. There is always a problem, a question to be resolved. What do you think the question is in this book? (Answers)
7. Then there is always some turning point, a climax. The question is about to be answered, but not quite yet. What big incident happens toward the end of the book? (Answers)
8. The plot ends with the resolution to the problem; the question has been answered. (And then you can make everyone feel good with a happy ending where everything is in its place.) What's the resolution in this book? (Answers)

Summary One (from Wikipedia)

The title character is named Pollyanna Whittier, a young orphan who goes to live in Beldingsville, Vermont, with her wealthy but stern and cold spinster Aunt Polly, who does not want to take in Pollyanna, but feels it is her duty to her late sister. Pollyanna's philosophy of life centers on what she calls "The Glad Game," an optimistic attitude she learned from her father. The game consists of finding something to be glad about in every situation. It originated in an incident one Christmas when Pollyanna, who was hoping for a doll in the missionary barrel, found only a pair of crutches inside. Making the game up on the spot, Pollyanna's father taught her to look at the good side of things—in this case, to be glad about the crutches because "we didn't need to use them!"

With this philosophy, and her own sunny personality and sincere, sympathetic soul, Pollyanna brings so much gladness to her aunt's dispirited New England town that she transforms it into a pleasant place to live. The Glad Game shields her from her aunt's stern attitude: when Aunt Polly puts her in a stuffy attic room without carpets or pictures, she exults at the beautiful view from the high window; when she tries to "punish" her niece for being late to dinner by sentencing her to a meal of bread and milk in the kitchen with the servant Nancy, Pollyanna thanks her rapturously because she likes bread and milk, and she likes Nancy.

Soon, Pollyanna teaches some of Beldingsville's most troubled inhabitants to "play the game" as well, from a querulous invalid named Mrs. Snow to a miserly bachelor, Mr. Pendleton, who lives all alone in a cluttered mansion. Aunt Polly, too—finding herself helpless before Pollyanna's buoyant refusal to be downcast—gradually begins to thaw, although she resists the glad game longer than anyone else.

Eventually, however, even Pollyanna's robust optimism is put to the test when she gets hit by a car and loses the use of her legs. At first she doesn't realize the seriousness of her situation, but her spirits plummet when she is told what happened to her. After that, she lies in bed, unable to find anything to be glad about. Then the townspeople begin calling at Aunt Polly's house, eager to let Pollyanna know how much her encouragement has improved their lives; and Pollyanna decides she can still be glad that she at least has had her legs. The novel ends with Aunt Polly marrying her former gentleman friend Dr. Chilton and Pollyanna being sent to a hospital where she learns to walk again and is able to appreciate the use of her legs far more as a result of being temporarily disabled.

Summary Two (excerpts from http:/www.bookrack.in/2010/06/pollyanna-by-eleanor-porter/)

Miss Polly is a stern disciplinarian who takes in Pollyanna, the child of her late Sister, in her care only as a duty. Miss Polly frowns upon open windows and banging doors, seldom smiles and is a classic case of a touch-me-not. Pollyanna breezes into Miss Polly's life and therein starts an adventure.Not just for Miss Polly, but also for the other folks in town.

Pollyanna's "Glad game" (a game that her father taught her to look at brighter side of everything) spreads like wild fire and starts making a difference to people's lives. Pollyanna's unbridled enthusiasm for life coupled with her innocent demeanor makes her the darling of the town. Pollyanna endears herself to the people in the town by teaching her glad game to them. She helps

Mrs Snow become less grouchy, makes a grouchy man, Mr Pendleton smile, rescues a stray cat, dog and a homeless boy, reunites a couple, makes her aunt "gladder" and causes several other minor miracles. However, a terrible accident threatens to ruin Pollyanna's game forever, and everyone wonders how they can teach her to be glad. This forms the rest of the plot.

Lesson 142

1. Read chapter 1.
2. Tell someone about the chapter.

Miss Polly Harrington entered her kitchen a little hurriedly this June morning. Miss Polly did not usually make hurried movements; she specially prided herself on her repose of manner. But to-day she was hurrying--actually hurrying.

Nancy, washing dishes at the sink, looked up in surprise. Nancy had been working in Miss Polly's kitchen only two months, but already she knew that her mistress did not usually hurry.

"Nancy!"

"Yes, ma'am." Nancy answered cheerfully, but she still continued wiping the pitcher in her hand.

"Nancy,"--Miss Polly's voice was very stern now--"when I'm talking to you, I wish you to stop your work and listen to what I have to say."

Nancy flushed miserably. She set the pitcher down at once, with the cloth still about it, thereby nearly tipping it over--which did not add to her composure.

"Yes, ma'am; I will, ma'am," she stammered, righting the pitcher, and turning hastily. "I was only keepin' on with my work 'cause you specially told me this mornin' ter hurry with my dishes, ye know."

Her mistress frowned.

"That will do, Nancy. I did not ask for explanations. I asked for your attention."

"Yes, ma'am." Nancy stifled a sigh. She was wondering if ever in any way she could please this woman. Nancy had never "worked out" before; but a sick mother suddenly widowed and left with three younger children besides Nancy herself, had forced the girl into doing something toward their support, and she had been so pleased when she found a place in the kitchen of the great house on the hill--Nancy had come from "The Corners," six miles away, and she knew Miss Polly Harrington only as the mistress of the old Harrington homestead, and one of the wealthiest residents of the town. That was two months before. She knew Miss Polly now as a stern, severe-faced woman who frowned if a knife clattered to the floor, or if a door banged--but who never thought to smile even when knives and doors were still.

"When you've finished your morning work, Nancy," Miss Polly was saying now, "you may clear the little room at the head of the stairs in the attic, and make up the cot bed. Sweep the room and clean it, of course, after you clear out the trunks and boxes."

"Yes, ma'am. And where shall I put the things, please, that I take out?"

"In the front attic." Miss Polly hesitated, then went on: "I suppose I may as well tell you now, Nancy. My niece, Miss Pollyanna Whittier, is coming to live with me. She is eleven years old, and will sleep in that room."

"A little girl--coming here, Miss Harrington? Oh, won't that be nice!" cried Nancy, thinking of the sunshine her own little sisters made in the home at "The Corners."

"Nice? Well, that isn't exactly the word I should use," rejoined Miss Polly, stiffly. "However, I intend to make the best of it, of course. I am a good woman, I hope; and I know my duty."

Nancy colored hotly.

"Of course, ma'am; it was only that I thought a little girl here might--might brighten things up for you," she faltered.

"Thank you," rejoined the lady, dryly. "I can't say, however, that I see any immediate need for that."

"But, of course, you--you'd want her, your sister's child," ventured Nancy, vaguely feeling that somehow she must prepare a welcome for this lonely little stranger.

Miss Polly lifted her chin haughtily.

"Well, really, Nancy, just because I happened to have a sister who was silly enough to marry and bring unnecessary children into a world that was already quite full enough, I can't see how I should particularly want to have the care of them myself. However, as I said before, I hope I know my duty. See that you clean the corners, Nancy," she finished sharply, as she left the room.

"Yes, ma'am," sighed Nancy, picking up the half-dried pitcher--now so cold it must be rinsed again.

In her own room, Miss Polly took out once more the letter which she had received two days before from the far-away Western town, and which had been so unpleasant a surprise to her. The letter was addressed to Miss Polly Harrington, Beldingsville, Vermont; and it read as follows:

> Dear Madam:--I regret to inform you that the Rev. John Whittier died two weeks ago, leaving one child, a girl eleven years old. He left practically nothing else save a few books; for, as you doubtless know, he was the pastor of this small mission church, and had a very meagre salary.
>
> I believe he was your deceased sister's husband, but he gave me to understand the families were not on the best of terms. He thought, however, that for your sister's sake you might wish to take the child and bring her up among her own people in the East. Hence I am writing to you.
>
> The little girl will be all ready to start by the time you get this letter; and if you can take her, we would appreciate it very much if you would write that she might come at once, as there is a man and his wife here who are going East very soon, and they would take her with them to Boston, and put her on the Beldingsville train. Of course you would be notified what day and train to expect Pollyanna on.
>
> Hoping to hear favorably from you soon, I remain,
> Respectfully yours,
> Jeremiah O. White.

With a frown Miss Polly folded the letter and tucked it into its envelope. She had answered it the day before, and she had said she would take the child, of course. She hoped she knew her duty well enough for that!--disagreeable as the task would be.

As she sat now, with the letter in her hands, her thoughts went back to her sister, Jennie, who had been this child's mother, and to the time when Jennie, as a girl of twenty, had insisted upon marrying the young minister, in spite of her family's remonstrances. There had been a man of wealth who had wanted her--and the family had much preferred him to the minister; but Jennie had not. The man of wealth had more years, as well as more money, to his credit, while the minister had only a young head full of youth's ideals and enthusiasm, and a heart full of love. Jennie had preferred these--quite naturally, perhaps; so she had married the minister, and had gone south with him as a home missionary's wife.

The break had come then. Miss Polly remembered it well, though she had been but a girl of fifteen, the youngest, at the time. The family had had little more to do with the missionary's wife. To be sure, Jennie herself had written, for a time, and had named her last baby "Pollyanna" for her two sisters, Polly and Anna--the other babies had all died. This had been the last time that Jennie had written; and in a few years there had come the news of her death, told in a short, but heart-broken little note from the minister himself, dated at a little town in the West.

Meanwhile, time had not stood still for the occupants of the great house on the hill. Miss Polly, looking out at the far-reaching valley below, thought of the changes those twenty-five years had brought to her.

She was forty now, and quite alone in the world. Father, mother, sisters--all were dead. For years, now, she had been sole mistress of the house and of the thousands left her by her father. There were people who had openly pitied her lonely life, and who had urged her to have some friend or companion to live with her; but she had not welcomed either their sympathy or their advice. She was not lonely, she said. She liked being by herself. She preferred quiet. But now--

Miss Polly rose with frowning face and closely-shut lips. She was glad, of course, that she was a good woman, and that she not only knew her duty, but had sufficient strength of character to perform it. But--Pollyanna!--what a ridiculous name!

Lesson 143

1. Read chapter 2.
2. How old is Miss Jennie's daughter? (Answers)
3. Tell someone about the chapter.

In the little attic room Nancy swept and scrubbed vigorously, paying particular attention to the corners. There were times, indeed, when the vigor she put into her work was more of a relief to her feelings than it was an ardor to efface dirt--Nancy, in spite of her frightened submission to her mistress, was no saint.

"I--just--wish--I could--dig--out the corners--of--her--soul!" she muttered jerkily, punctuating her words with murderous jabs of her pointed cleaning-stick. "There's plenty of 'em needs cleanin' all right, all right! The idea of stickin' that blessed child 'way off up here in this hot little room--with no fire in the winter, too, and all this big house ter pick and choose from! Unnecessary children, indeed! Humph!" snapped Nancy, wringing her rag so hard her fingers ached from the strain; "I guess it ain't *children* what is *most* unnecessary just now, just now!

For some time she worked in silence; then, her task finished, she looked about the bare little room in plain disgust.

"Well, it's done--my part, anyhow," she sighed. "There ain't no dirt here--and there's mighty little else. Poor little soul!--a pretty place this is ter put a homesick, lonesome child into!" she finished, going out and closing the door with a bang, "Oh!" she exclaimed, biting her lip. Then, doggedly: "Well, I don't care. I hope she did hear the bang,--I do, I do!"

In the garden that afternoon, Nancy found a few minutes in which to interview Old Tom, who had pulled the weeds and shovelled the paths about the place for uncounted years.

"Mr. Tom," began Nancy, throwing a quick glance over her shoulder to make sure she was unobserved; "did you know a little girl was comin' here ter live with Miss Polly?"

"A--what?" demanded the old man, straightening his bent back with difficulty.

"A little girl--to live with Miss Polly."

"Go on with yer jokin'," scoffed unbelieving Tom. "Why don't ye tell me the sun is a-goin' ter set in the east ter-morrer?"

"But it's true. She told me so herself," maintained Nancy. "It's her niece; and she's eleven years old."

The man's jaw fell.

"Sho!--I wonder, now," he muttered; then a tender light came into his faded eyes. "It ain't--but it must be--Miss Jennie's little gal! There wasn't none of the rest of 'em married. Why, Nancy, it must be Miss Jennie's little gal. Glory be ter praise! ter think of my old eyes a-seein' this!"

"Who was Miss Jennie?

"She was an angel straight out of Heaven," breathed the man, fervently; "but the old master and missus knew her as their oldest daughter. She was twenty when she married and went away from here long years ago. Her babies all died, I heard, except the last one; and that must be the one what's a-comin'."

"She's eleven years old."

"Yes, she might be," nodded the old man.

"And she's goin' ter sleep in the attic--more shame ter *her*!" scolded Nancy, with another glance over her shoulder toward the house behind her.

Old Tom frowned. The next moment a curious smile curved his lips.

I'm a-wonderin' what Miss Polly will do with a child in the house," he said.

"Humph! Well, I'm a-wonderin' what a child will do with Miss Polly in the house!" snapped Nancy.

The old man laughed.

"I'm afraid you ain't fond of Miss Polly," he grinned.

"As if ever anybody could be fond of her!" scorned Nancy.

Old Tom smiled oddly. He stooped and began to work again.

"I guess maybe you didn't know about Miss Polly's love affair," he said slowly.

"Love affair--*her*! No!--and I guess nobody else didn't, neither."

"Oh, yes they did," nodded the old man. "And the feller's livin' ter-day--right in this town, too."

"Who is he?"

"I ain't a-tellin' that. It ain't fit that I should." The old man drew himself erect. In his dim blue eyes, as he faced the house, there was the loyal servant's honest pride in the family he has served and loved for long years.

"But it don't seem possible--her and a gentleman friend," still maintained Nancy.

Old Tom shook his head.

"You didn't know Miss Polly as I did," he argued. "She used ter be real handsome--and she would be now, if she'd let herself be."

"Handsome! Miss Polly!"

"Yes. If she'd just let that tight hair of hern all out loose and careless-like, as it used ter be, and wear the sort of bunnits with posies in 'em, and the kind o' dresses all lace and white things--you'd see she'd be handsome! Miss Polly ain't old, Nancy."

"Ain't she, though? Well, then she's got an awfully good imitation of it--she has, she has!" sniffed Nancy.

"Yes, I know. It begun then--at the time of the trouble with her gentleman friend," nodded Old Tom; "and it seems as if she'd been feedin' on wormwood an' thistles ever since--she's that bitter an' prickly ter deal with."

"I should say she was," declared Nancy, indignantly. "There's no pleasin' her, nohow, no matter how you try! I wouldn't stay if 'twa'n't for the wages and the folks at home what's needin' 'em. But some day--some day I shall jest b'ile over; and when I do, of course it'll be good-by Nancy for me. It will, it will."

Old Tom shook his head.

"I know. I've felt it. It's nart'ral--but 'tain't best, child; 'tain't best. Take my word for it, 'tain't best." And again he bent his old head to the work before him.

"Nancy!" called a sharp voice.

"Y-yes, ma'am," stammered Nancy; and hurried toward the house.

Lesson 144

1. Read chapter 3.
2. Tell someone about the chapter.

In due time came the telegram announcing that Pollyanna would arrive in Beldingsville the next day, the twenty-fifth of June, at four o'clock. Miss Polly read the telegram, frowned, then climbed the stairs to the attic room. She still frowned as she looked about her.

The room contained a small bed, neatly made, two straight-backed chairs, a washstand, a bureau--without any mirror--and a small table. There were no drapery curtains at the dormer windows, no pictures on the wall. All day the sun had been pouring down upon the roof, and the little room was like an oven for heat. As there were no screens, the windows had not been raised. A big fly was buzzing angrily at one of them now, up and down, up and down, trying to get out.

Miss Polly killed the fly, swept it through the window (raising the sash an inch for the purpose), straightened a chair, frowned again, and left the room.

"Nancy," she said a few minutes later, at the kitchen door, "I found a fly up-stairs in Miss Pollyanna's room. The window must have been raised at some time. I have ordered screens, but until they come I shall expect you to see that the windows remain closed. My niece will arrive to-morrow at four o'clock. I desire you to meet her at the station. Timothy will take the open buggy and drive you over. The telegram says 'light hair, red-checked gingham dress, and straw hat.' That is all I know, but I think it is sufficient for your purpose."

"Yes, ma'am; but--you--"

Miss Polly evidently read the pause aright, for she frowned and said crisply:

"No, I shall not go. It is not necessary that I should, I think. That is all." And she turned away--Miss Polly's arrangements for the comfort of her niece, Pollyanna, were complete.

In the kitchen, Nancy sent her flatiron with a vicious dig across the dish-towel she was ironing.

"'Light hair, red-checked gingham dress, and straw hat'--all she knows, indeed! Well, I'd be ashamed ter own it up, that I would, I would--and her my onliest niece what was a-comin' from 'way across the continent!"

Promptly at twenty minutes to four the next afternoon Timothy and Nancy drove off in the open buggy to meet the expected guest. Timothy was Old Tom's son. It was sometimes said in the town that if Old Tom was Miss Polly's right-hand man, Timothy was her left.

Timothy was a good-natured youth, and a good-looking one, as well. Short as had been Nancy's stay at the house, the two were already good friends. To-day, however, Nancy was too full of her mission to be her usual talkative self; and almost in silence she took the drive to the station and alighted to wait for the train.

Over and over in her mind she was saying it "light hair, red-checked dress, straw hat." Over and over again she was wondering just what sort of child this Pollyanna was, anyway.

"I hope for her sake she's quiet and sensible, and don't drop knives nor bang doors," she sighed to Timothy, who had sauntered up to her.

"Well, if she ain't, nobody knows what'll become of the rest of us," grinned Timothy. "Imagine Miss Polly and a *noisy* kid! Gorry! there goes the whistle now!"

"Oh, Timothy, I--I think it was mean ter send me," chattered the suddenly frightened Nancy, as she turned and hurried to a point where she could best watch the passengers alight at the little station.

It was not long before Nancy saw her--the slender little girl in the red-checked gingham with two fat braids of flaxen hair hanging down her back. Beneath the straw hat, an eager, freckled little face turned to the right and to the left, plainly searching for some one.

Nancy knew the child at once, but not for some time could she control her shaking knees sufficiently to go to her. The little girl was standing quite by herself when Nancy finally did approach her.

"Are you Miss--Pollyanna?" she faltered. The next moment she found herself half smothered in the clasp of two gingham-clad arms.

"Oh, I'm so glad, *glad, glad* to see you," cried an eager voice in her ear. "Of course I'm Pollyanna, and I'm so glad you came to meet me! I hoped you would."

"You--you did?" stammered Nancy, vaguely wondering how Pollyanna could possibly have known her--and wanted her. "You--you did? she repeated, trying to straighten her hat.

"Oh, yes; and I've been wondering all the way here what you looked like," cried the little girl, dancing on her toes, and sweeping the embarrassed Nancy from head to foot, with her eyes. "And now I know, and I'm glad you look just like you do look."

Nancy was relieved just then to have Timothy come up. Pollyanna's words had been most confusing.

"This is Timothy. Maybe you have a trunk," she stammered.

"Yes, I have," nodded Pollyanna, importantly. "I've got a brand-new one. The Ladies' Aid bought it for me--and wasn't it lovely of them, when they wanted the carpet so? Of course I don't know how much red carpet a trunk could buy, but it ought to buy some, anyhow--much as half an aisle, don't you think? I've got a little thing here in my bag that Mr. Gray said was a check, and that I must give it to you before I could get my trunk. Mr. Gray is Mrs. Gray's husband. They're cousins of Deacon Carr's wife. I came East with them, and they're lovely! And--there, here 'tis," she finished, producing the check after much fumbling in the bag she carried.

Nancy drew a long breath. Instinctively she felt that some one had to draw one--after that speech. Then she stole a glance at Timothy. Timothy's eyes were studiously turned away.

The three were off at last, with Pollyanna's trunk in behind, and Pollyanna herself snugly ensconced between Nancy and Timothy. During the whole process of getting started, the little girl had kept up an uninterrupted stream of comments and questions, until the somewhat dazed Nancy found herself quite out of breath trying to keep up with her.

"There! Isn't this lovely? Is it far? I hope 'tis--I love to ride," sighed Pollyanna, as the wheels began to turn. "Of course, if 'tisn't far, I sha'n't mind, though, 'cause I'll be glad to get there all the sooner, you know. What a pretty street! I knew 'twas going to be pretty; father told me--"

She stopped with a little choking breath. Nancy, looking at her apprehensively, saw that her small chin was quivering, and that her eyes were full of tears. In a moment, however, she hurried on, with a brave lifting of her head.

"Father told me all about it. He remembered. And--and I ought to have explained before. Mrs. Gray told me to, at once--about this red gingham dress, you know, and why I'm not in black. She said you'd think 'twas queer. But there weren't any black things in the last missionary barrel, only a lady's velvet basque which Deacon Carr's wife said wasn't suitable for me at all; besides, it had white spots--worn, you know--on both elbows, and some other places. Part of the Ladies' Aid wanted to buy me a black dress and hat, but the other part thought the money ought to go toward the red carpet they're trying to get--for the church, you know. Mrs. White said maybe it was just as well, anyway, for she didn't like children in black--that is, I mean, she liked the children, of course, but not the black part."

Pollyanna paused for breath, and Nancy managed to stammer:

"Well, I'm sure it--it'll be all right."

"I'm glad you feel that way. I do, too," nodded Pollyanna, again with that choking little breath. "Of course, 'twould have been a good deal harder to be glad in black--"

"Glad!" gasped Nancy, surprised into an interruption.

"Yes--that father's gone to Heaven to be with mother and the rest of us, you know. He said I must be glad. But it's been pretty hard to--to do it, even in red gingham, because I--I wanted him, so; and I couldn't help feeling I *ought* to have him, specially as mother and the rest have God and all the angels, while I didn't have anybody but the Ladies' Aid. But now I'm sure it'll be easier because I've got you, Aunt Polly. I'm so glad I've got you!"

Nancy's aching sympathy for the poor little forlornness beside her turned suddenly into shocked terror.

"Oh, but--but you've made an awful mistake, d-dear," she faltered. "I'm only Nancy. I ain't your Aunt Polly, at all!"

"You--you *aren't?*" stammered the little girl, in plain dismay.

"No. I'm only Nancy. I never thought of your takin' me for her. We--we ain't a bit alike we ain't, we ain't!"

Timothy chuckled softly; but Nancy was too disturbed to answer the merry flash from his eyes.

"But who *are* you?" questioned Pollyanna. "You don't look a bit like a Ladies' Aider!"

Timothy laughed outright this time.

"I'm Nancy, the hired girl. I do all the work except the washin' an' hard ironin'. Mis' Durgin does that."

"But there *is* an Aunt Polly?" demanded the child, anxiously.

"You bet your life there is," cut in Timothy.

Pollyanna relaxed visibly.

"Oh, that's all right, then." There was a moment's silence, then she went on brightly: "And do you know? I'm glad, after all, that she didn't come to meet me; because now I've got *her* still coming, and I've got you besides."

Nancy flushed. Timothy turned to her with a quizzical smile.

"I call that a pretty slick compliment," he said. "Why don't you thank the little lady?"

"I--I was thinkin' about--Miss Polly," faltered Nancy.

Pollyanna sighed contentedly.

"I was, too. I'm so interested in her. You know she's all the aunt I've got, and I didn't know I had her for ever so long. Then father told me. He said she lived in a lovely great big house 'way on top of a hill."

"She does. You can see it now," said Nancy. "It's that big white one with the green blinds, 'way ahead."

"Oh, how pretty!--and what a lot of trees and grass all around it! I never saw such a lot of green grass, seems so, all at once. Is my Aunt Polly rich, Nancy?"

"Yes, Miss."

"I'm so glad. It must be perfectly lovely to have lots of money. I never knew any one that did have, only the Whites--they're some rich. They have carpets in every room and ice-cream Sundays. Does Aunt Polly have ice-cream Sundays?"

Nancy shook her head. Her lips twitched. She threw a merry look into Timothy's eyes.

"No, Miss. Your aunt don't like ice-cream, I guess; leastways I never saw it on her table."

Pollyanna's face fell.

"Oh, doesn't she? I'm so sorry! I don't see how she can help liking ice-cream. But--anyhow, I can be kinder glad about that, 'cause the ice-cream you don't eat can't make your stomach ache like Mrs. White's did--that is, I ate hers, you know, lots of it. Maybe Aunt Polly has got the carpets, though."

"Yes, she's got the carpets."

"In every room?"

"Well, in almost every room," answered Nancy, frowning suddenly at the thought of that bare little attic room where there was no carpet.

"Oh, I'm so glad," exulted Pollyanna. "I love carpets. We didn't have any, only two little rugs that came in a missionary barrel, and one of those had ink spots on it. Mrs. White had pictures, too, perfectly beautiful ones of roses and little girls kneeling and a kitty and some lambs and a lion--not together, you know--the lambs and the lion. Oh, of course the Bible says they will sometime, but they haven't yet--that is, I mean Mrs. White's haven't. Don't you just love pictures?"

"I--I don't know," answered Nancy in a half-stifled voice.

"I do. We didn't have any pictures. They don't come in the barrels much, you know. There did two come once, though. But one was so good father sold it to get money to buy me some shoes with; and the other was so bad it fell to pieces just as soon as we hung it up. Glass--it broke, you know. And I cried. But I'm glad now we didn't have any of those nice things, 'cause I shall like Aunt

Polly's all the better--not being used to 'em, you see. Just as it is when the *pretty* hair-ribbons come in the barrels after a lot of faded-out brown ones. My! but isn't this a perfectly beautiful house?" she broke off fervently, as they turned into the wide driveway.

It was when Timothy was unloading the trunk that Nancy found an opportunity to mutter low in his ear:

"Don't you never say nothin' ter me again about leavin', Timothy Durgin. You couldn't *hire* me ter leave!"

"Leave! I should say not," grinned the youth. "You couldn't drag me away. It'll be more fun here now, with that kid 'round, than movin'-picture shows, every day!"

"Fun!--fun!" repeated Nancy, indignantly, "I guess it'll be somethin' more than fun for that blessed child--when them two tries ter live tergether; and I guess she'll be a-needin' some rock ter fly to for refuge. Well, I'm a-goin' ter be that rock, Timothy; I am, I am!" she vowed, as she turned and led Pollyanna up the broad steps.

Lesson 145

1. Read chapter 4.
2. Tell someone about the chapter.

Miss Polly Harrington did not rise to meet her niece. She looked up from her book, it is true, as Nancy and the little girl appeared in the sitting-room doorway, and she held out a hand with "duty" written large on every coldly extended finger.

"How do you do, Pollyanna? I--" She had no chance to say more. Pollyanna, had fairly flown across the room and flung herself into her aunt's scandalized, unyielding lap.

"Oh, Aunt Polly, Aunt Polly, I don't know how to be glad enough that you let me come to live with you," she was sobbing. "You don't know how perfectly lovely it is to have you and Nancy and all this after you've had just the Ladies' Aid!"

"Very likely--though I've not had the pleasure of the Ladies' Aid's acquaintance," rejoined Miss Polly, stiffly, trying to unclasp the small, clinging fingers, and turning frowning eyes on Nancy in the doorway. "Nancy, that will do. You may go. Pollyanna, be good enough, please, to stand erect in a proper manner. I don't know yet what you look like."

Pollyanna drew back at once, laughing a little hysterically.

"No, I suppose you don't; but you see I'm not very much to look at, anyway, on account of the freckles. Oh, and I ought to explain about the red gingham and the black velvet basque with white spots on the elbows. I told Nancy how father said--"

"Yes; well, never mind now what your father said," interrupted Miss Polly, crisply. "You had a trunk, I presume?"

"Oh, yes, indeed, Aunt Polly. I've got a beautiful trunk that the Ladies' Aid gave me. I haven't got so very much in it--of my own, I mean. The barrels haven't had many clothes for little girls in them lately; but there were all father's books, and Mrs. White said she thought I ought to have those. You see, father--"

"Pollyanna," interrupted her aunt again, sharply, "there is one thing that might just as well be understood right away at once; and that is, I do not care to have you keep talking of your father to me."

The little girl drew in her breath tremulously.

"Why, Aunt Polly, you--you mean--" She hesitated, and her aunt filled the pause.

"We will go up-stairs to your room. Your trunk is already there, I presume. I told Timothy to take it up--if you had one. You may follow me, Pollyanna."

Without speaking, Pollyanna turned and followed her aunt from the room. Her eyes were brimming with tears, but her chin was bravely high.

"After all, I--I reckon I'm glad she doesn't want me to talk about father," Pollyanna was thinking. "It'll be easier, maybe--if I don't talk about him. Probably, anyhow, that is why she told me not to talk about him." And Pollyanna, convinced anew of her aunt's "kindness," blinked off the tears and looked eagerly about her.

She was on the stairway now. just ahead, her aunt's black silk skirt rustled luxuriously. Behind her an open door allowed a glimpse of soft-tinted rugs and satin-covered chairs. Beneath her feet a marvellous carpet was like green moss to the tread. On every side the gilt of picture frames or the glint of sunlight through the filmy mesh of lace curtains flashed in her eyes.

"Oh, Aunt Polly, Aunt Polly," breathed the little girl, rapturously; "what a perfectly lovely, lovely house! How awfully glad you must be you're so rich!"

"Poll*yanna*!" exclaimed her aunt, turning sharply about as she reached the head of the stairs. "I'm surprised at you--making a speech like that to me!"

"Why, Aunt Polly, *aren't* you?" queried Pollyanna, in frank wonder.

"Certainly not, Pollyanna. I hope I could not so far forget myself as to be sinfully proud of any gift the Lord has seen fit to bestow upon me," declared the lady; "certainly not, of *riches*!"

Miss Polly turned and walked down the hall toward the attic stairway door. She was glad, now, that she had put the child in the attic room. Her idea at first had been to get her niece as far away as possible from herself, and at the same time place her where her childish heedlessness would not destroy valuable furnishings. Now--with this evident strain of vanity showing thus early--it was all the more fortunate that the room planned for her was plain and sensible, thought Miss Polly.

Eagerly Pollyanna's small feet pattered behind her aunt. Still more eagerly her big blue eyes tried to look in all directions at once, that no thing of beauty or interest in this wonderful house might be passed unseen. Most eagerly of all her mind turned to the wondrously exciting problem about to be solved: behind which of all these fascinating doors was waiting now her room--the dear, beautiful room full of curtains, rugs, and pictures, that was to be her very own? Then, abruptly, her aunt opened a door and ascended another stairway.

There was little to be seen here. A bare wall rose on either side. At the top of the stairs, wide reaches of shadowy space led to far corners where the roof came almost down to the floor, and where were stacked innumerable trunks and boxes. It was hot and stifling, too. Unconsciously Pollyanna lifted her head higher--it seemed so hard to breathe. Then she saw that her aunt had thrown open a door at the right.

"There, Pollyanna, here is your room, and your trunk is here, I see. Have you your key?"

Pollyanna nodded dumbly. Her eyes were a little wide and frightened.

Her aunt frowned.

"When I ask a question, Pollyanna, I prefer that you should answer aloud not merely with your head."

"Yes, Aunt Polly."

"Thank you; that is better. I believe you have everything that you need here," she added, glancing at the well-filled towel rack and water pitcher. "I will send Nancy up to help you unpack. Supper is at six o'clock," she finished, as she left the room and swept down-stairs.

For a moment after she had gone Pollyanna stood quite still, looking after her. Then she turned her wide eyes to the bare wall, the bare floor, the bare windows. She turned them last to the little trunk that had stood not so long before in her own little room in the far-away Western home. The next moment she stumbled blindly toward it and fell on her knees at its side, covering her face with her hands.

Nancy found her there when she came up a few minutes later.

"There, there, you poor lamb," she crooned, dropping to the floor and drawing the little girl into her arms. "I was just a-fearin! I'd find you like this, like this."

Pollyanna shook her head.

"But I'm bad and wicked, Nancy--awful wicked," she sobbed. "I just can't make myself understand that God and the angels needed my father more than I did."

"No more they did, neither," declared Nancy, stoutly.

"Oh-h!--*Nancy*!" The burning horror in Pollyanna's eyes dried the tears.

Nancy gave a shamefaced smile and rubbed her own eyes vigorously.

"There, there, child, I didn't mean it, of course," she cried briskly. "Come, let's have your key and we'll get inside this trunk and take our your dresses in no time, no time."

Somewhat tearfully Pollyanna produced the key.

"There aren't very many there, anyway," she faltered.

"Then they're all the sooner unpacked," declared Nancy.

Pollyanna gave a sudden radiant smile.

"That's so! I can be glad of that, can't I?" she cried.

Nancy stared.

"Why, of--course," she answered a little uncertainly.

Nancy's capable hands made short work of unpacking the books, the patched undergarments, and the few pitifully unattractive dresses. Pollyanna, smiling bravely now, flew about, hanging the dresses in the closet, stacking the books on the table, and putting away the undergarments in the bureau drawers.

"I'm sure it--it's going to be a very nice room. Don't you think so?" she stammered, after a while.

There was no answer. Nancy was very busy, apparently, with her head in the trunk. Pollyanna, standing at the bureau, gazed a little wistfully at the bare wall above.

"And I can be glad there isn't any looking-glass here, too, 'cause where there *isn't* any glass I can't see my freckles."

Nancy made a sudden queer little sound with her mouth--but when Pollyanna turned, her head was in the trunk again. At one of the windows, a few minutes later, Pollyanna gave a glad cry and clapped her hands joyously.

"Oh, Nancy, I hadn't seen this before," she breathed. "Look--'way off there, with those trees and the houses and that lovely church spire, and the river shining just like silver. Why, Nancy, there doesn't anybody need any pictures with that to look at. Oh, I'm so glad now she let me have this room!"

To Pollyanna's surprise and dismay, Nancy burst into tears. Pollyanna hurriedly crossed to her side.

"Why, Nancy, Nancy--what is it?" she cried; then, fearfully: "This wasn't--*your* room, was it?"

"My room!" stormed Nancy, hotly, choking back the tears. "If you ain't a little angel straight from Heaven, and if some folks don't eat dirt before--Oh, land! there's her bell!" After which amazing speech, Nancy sprang to her feet, dashed out of the room, and went clattering down the stairs.

Left alone, Pollyanna went back to her "picture," as she mentally designated the beautiful view from the window. After a time she touched the sash tentatively. It seemed as if no longer could she endure the stifling heat. To her joy the sash moved under her fingers. The next moment the window was wide open, and Pollyanna was leaning far out, drinking in the fresh, sweet air.

She ran then to the other window. That, too, soon flew up under her eager hands. A big fly swept past her nose, and buzzed noisily about the room. Then another came, and another; but Pollyanna paid no heed. Pollyanna had made a wonderful discovery--against this window a huge tree flung great branches. To Pollyanna they looked like arms outstretched, inviting her. Suddenly she laughed aloud.

"I believe I can do it," she chuckled. The next moment she had climbed nimbly to the window ledge. From there it was an easy matter to step to the nearest tree-branch. Then, clinging like a monkey, she swung herself from limb to limb until the lowest branch was reached. The drop to the ground was--even for Pollyanna, who was used to climbing trees--a little fearsome. She took it, however, with bated breath, swinging from her strong little arms, and landing on all fours in the soft grass. Then she picked herself up and looked eagerly about her.

She was at the back of the house. Before her lay a garden in which a bent old man was working. Beyond the garden a little path through an open field led up a steep hill, at the top of which a lone pine tree stood on guard beside the huge rock. To Pollyanna, at the moment, there seemed to be just one place in the world worth being in--the top of that big rock.

With a run and a skilful turn, Pollyanna skipped by the bent old man, threaded her way between the orderly rows of green growing things, and--a little out of breath--reached the path that ran through the open field. Then, determinedly, she began to climb. Already, however, she was thinking what a long, long way off that rock must be, when back at the window it had looked so near!

Fifteen minutes later the great clock in the hallway of the Harrington homestead struck six. At precisely the last stroke Nancy sounded the bell for supper.

One, two, three minutes passed. Miss Polly frowned and tapped the floor with her slipper. A little jerkily she rose to her feet, went into the hall, and looked up-stairs, plainly impatient. For a minute she listened intently; then she turned and swept into the dining room.

"Nancy," she said with decision, as soon as the little serving-maid appeared; "my niece is late. No, you need not call her," she added severely, as Nancy made a move toward the hall door. "I told her what time supper was, and now she will have to suffer the consequences. She may as well begin at once to learn to be punctual. When she comes down she may have bread and milk in the kitchen."

"Yes, ma'am." It was well, perhaps, that Miss Polly did not happen to be looking at Nancy's face just then.

At the earliest possible moment after supper, Nancy crept up the back stairs and thence to the attic room.

"Bread and milk, indeed!--and when the poor lamb hain't only just cried herself to sleep," she was muttering fiercely, as she softly pushed open the door. The next moment she gave a frightened cry. "Where are you? Where've you gone? Where *have* you gone?" she panted, looking in the closet, under the bed, and even in the trunk and down the water pitcher. Then she flew down-stairs and out to Old Tom in the garden.

"Mr. Tom, Mr. Tom, that blessed child's gone," she wailed. "She's vanished right up into Heaven where she come from, poor lamb--and me told ter give her bread and milk in the kitchen--her what's eatin' angel food this minute, I'll warrant, I'll warrant!"

The old man straightened up.

"Gone? Heaven?" he repeated stupidly, unconsciously sweeping the brilliant sunset sky with his gaze. He stopped, stared a moment intently, then turned with a slow grin. "Well, Nancy, it do look like as if she'd tried ter get as nigh Heaven as she could, and that's a fact," he agreed, pointing with a crooked finger to where, sharply outlined against the reddening sky, a slender, wind-blown figure was poised on top of a huge rock.

"Well, she ain't goin' ter Heaven that way ter-night--not if I has my say," declared Nancy, doggedly. "If the mistress asks, tell her I ain't furgettin' the dishes, but I gone on a stroll," she flung back over her shoulder, as she sped toward the path that led through the open field.

Lesson 146

1. Read chapter 5 .
2. What is the game? (This is really important to the book.) (Answers)

"For the land's sake, Miss Pollyanna, what a scare you did give me," panted Nancy, hurrying up to the big rock, down which Pollyanna had just regretfully slid.

"Scare? Oh, I'm so sorry; but you mustn't, really, ever get scared about me, Nancy. Father and the Ladies' Aid used to do it, too, till they found I always came back all right."

"But I didn't even know you'd went," cried Nancy, tucking the little girl's hand under her arm and hurrying her down the hill. "I didn't see you go, and nobody didn't. I guess you flew right up through the roof; I do, I do."

Pollyanna skipped gleefully.

"I did, 'most--only I flew down instead of up. I came down the tree."

Nancy stopped short.

"You did--what?"

"Came down the tree, outside my window."

"My stars and stockings!" gasped Nancy, hurrying on again. "I'd like ter know what yer aunt would say ter that!"

"Would you? Well, I'll tell her, then, so you can find out," promised the little girl, cheerfully.

"Mercy!" gasped Nancy. "No--no!"

"Why, you don't mean she'd *care*!" cried Pollyanna, plainly disturbed.

"No--er--yes--well, never mind. I--I ain't so very particular about knowin' what she'd say, truly," stammered Nancy, determined to keep one scolding from Pollyanna, if nothing more. "But, say, we better hurry. I've got ter get them dishes done, ye know."

"I'll help," promised Pollyanna, promptly.

"Oh, Miss Pollyanna!" demurred Nancy.

For a moment there was silence. The sky was darkening fast. Pollyanna took a firmer hold of her friend's arm.

"I reckon I'm glad, after all, that you *did* get scared--a little, 'cause then you came after me," she shivered.

"Poor little lamb! And you must be hungry, too. I--I'm afraid you'll have ter have bread and milk in the kitchen with me. Yer aunt didn't like it--because you didn't come down ter supper, ye know."

"But I couldn't. I was up here."

"Yes; but--she didn't know that, you see!" observed Nancy, dryly, stifling a chuckle. "I'm sorry about the bread and milk; I am, I am."

"Oh, I'm not. I'm glad."

"Glad! Why?"

"Why, I like bread and milk, and I'd like to eat with you. I don't see any trouble about being glad about that."

"You don't seem ter see any trouble bein' glad about everythin'," retorted Nancy, choking a little over her remembrance of Pollyanna's brave attempts to like the bare little attic room.

Pollyanna laughed softly.

"Well, that's the game, you know, anyway."

"The--*game*?"

"Yes; the 'just being glad' game."

"Whatever in the world are you talkin' about?"

"Why, it's a game. Father told it to me, and it's lovely," rejoined Pollyanna. "We've played it always, ever since I was a little, little girl. I told the Ladies' Aid, and they played it--some of them."

"What is it? I ain't much on games, though."

Pollyanna laughed again, but she sighed, too; and in the gathering twilight her face looked thin and wistful.

"Why, we began it on some crutches that came in a missionary barrel."

"*Crutches*!"

"Yes. You see I'd wanted a doll, and father had written them so; but when the barrel came the lady wrote that there hadn't any dolls come in, but the little crutches had. So she sent 'em along as they might come in handy for some child, sometime. And that's when we began it."

"Well, I must say I can't see any game about that, about that," declared Nancy, almost irritably.

"Oh, yes; the game was to just find something about everything to be glad about--no matter what 'twas," rejoined Pollyanna, earnestly. "And we began right then--on the crutches."

"Well, goodness me! I can't see anythin' ter be glad about--gettin' a pair of crutches when you wanted a doll!"

Pollyanna clapped her hands.

"There is--there is," she crowed. "But *I* couldn't see it, either, Nancy, at first," she added, with quick honesty. "Father had to tell it to me."

"Well, then, suppose *you* tell *me*," almost snapped Nancy.

"Goosey! Why, just be glad because you don't--*need--'em*!" exulted Pollyanna, triumphantly. "You see it's just as easy--when you know how!"

"Well, of all the queer doin's!" breathed Nancy, regarding Pollyanna with almost fearful eyes.

"Oh, but it isn't queer--it's lovely," maintained Pollyanna enthusiastically. "And we've played it ever since. And the harder 'tis, the more fun 'tis to get 'em out; only--only sometimes it's almost too hard--like when your father goes to Heaven, and there isn't anybody but a Ladies' Aid left."

"Yes, or when you're put in a snippy little room 'way at the top of the house with nothin' in it," growled Nancy.

Pollyanna sighed.

"That was a hard one, at first," she admitted, "specially when I was so kind of lonesome. I just didn't feel like playing the game, anyway, and I *had* been wanting pretty things, so! Then I happened to think how I hated to see my freckles in the looking-glass, and I saw that lovely picture out the window, too; so then I knew I'd found the things to be glad about. You see, when you're hunting for the glad things, you sort of forget the other kind--like the doll you wanted, you know."

"Humph!" choked Nancy, trying to swallow the lump in her throat.

"Most generally it doesn't take so long," sighed Pollyanna; "and lots of times now I just think of them *without* thinking, you know. I've got so used to playing it. It's a lovely game. F-father and I used to like it so much," she faltered. "I suppose, though, it--it'll be a little harder now, as long as I haven't anybody to play it with. Maybe Aunt Polly will play it, though," she added, as an after-thought.

"My stars and stockings!--*her*!" breathed Nancy, behind her teeth. Then, aloud, she said doggedly: "See here, Miss Pollyanna, I ain't sayin' that I'll play it very well, and I ain't sayin' that I know how, anyway; but I'll play it with ye, after a fashion--I just will, I will!"

"Oh, Nancy!" exulted Pollyanna, giving her a rapturous hug. "That'll be splendid! Won't we have fun?"

"Er--maybe," conceded Nancy, in open doubt. "But you mustn't count too much on me, ye know. I never was no case fur games. but I'm a-goin' ter make a most awful old try on this one. You're goin' ter have some one ter play it with, anyhow," she finished, as they entered the kitchen together.

Pollyanna ate her bread and milk with good appetite; then, at Nancy's suggestion, she went into the sitting room, where her aunt sat reading. Miss Polly looked up coldly.

"Have you had your supper, Pollyanna?"

"Yes, Aunt Polly."

"I'm very sorry, Pollyanna, to have been obliged so soon to send you into the kitchen to eat bread and milk."

"But I was real glad you did it, Aunt Polly. I like bread and milk, and Nancy, too. You mustn't feel bad about that one bit."

Aunt Polly sat suddenly a little more erect in her chair.

"Pollyanna, it's quite time you were in bed. You have had a hard day, and to-morrow we must plan your hours and go over your clothing to see what it is necessary to get for you. Nancy will give you a candle. Be careful how you handle it. Breakfast will be at half-past seven. See that you are down to that. Good-night."

Quite as a matter of course, Pollyanna came straight to her aunt's side and gave her an affectionate hug.

"I've had such a beautiful time, so far," she sighed happily. I know I'm going to just love living with you but then, I knew I should before I came. Good-night," she called cheerfully, as she ran from the room.

"Well, upon my soul!" exclaimed Miss Polly, half aloud. "What a most extraordinary child!" Then she frowned. "She's 'glad' I punished her, and I 'mustn't feel bad one bit,' and she's going to 'love to live' with me! Well, upon my soul!" exclaimed Miss Polly again, as she took up her book.

Fifteen minutes later, in the attic room, a lonely little girl sobbed into the tightly-clutched sheet:

"I know, father-among-the-angels, I'm not playing the game one bit now--not one bit; but I don't believe even you could find anything to be glad about sleeping all alone 'way off up here in the dark--like this. If only I was near Nancy or Aunt Polly, or even a Ladies' Aider, it would be easier!"

Down-stairs in the kitchen, Nancy, hurrying with her belated work, jabbed her dish-mop into the milk pitcher, and muttered Jerkily:

"If playin' a silly-fool game--about bein' glad you've got crutches when you want dolls--is got ter be--my way--o' bein' that rock o' refuge--why, I'm a-goin' ter play it--I am, I am!"

Lesson 147

1. Read chapter 6 .
2. Tell someone about the chapter.

It was nearly seven o'clock when Pollyanna awoke that first day after her arrival. Her windows faced the south and the west, so she could not see the sun yet; but she could see the hazy blue of the morning sky, and she knew that the day promised to be a fair one.

The little room was cooler now, and the air blew in fresh and sweet. Outside, the birds were twittering joyously, and Pollyanna flew to the window to talk to them. She saw then that down in the garden her aunt was already out among the rosebushes. With rapid fingers, therefore, she made herself ready to join her.

Down the attic stairs sped Pollyanna, leaving both doors wide open. Through the hall, down the next flight, then bang through the front screened-door and around to the garden, she ran.

Aunt Polly, with the bent old man, was leaning over a rose-bush when Pollyanna, gurgling with delight, flung herself upon her.

"Oh, Aunt Polly, Aunt Polly, I reckon I am glad this morning just to be alive!"

"Poll*yanna*!" remonstrated the lady, sternly, pulling herself as erect as she could with a dragging weight of ninety pounds hanging about her neck. "Is this the usual way you say good morning?"

The little girl dropped to her toes, and danced lightly up and down.

"No, only when I love folks so I just can't help it! I saw you from my window, Aunt Polly, and I got to thinking how you *weren't* a Ladies' Aider, and you were my really truly aunt; and you looked so good I just had to come down and hug you!"

The bent old man turned his back suddenly. Miss Polly attempted a frown--with not her usual success.

"Pollyanna, you--I--Thomas, that will do for this morning. I think you understand--about those rose-bushes," she said stiffly. Then she turned and walked rapidly away.

"Do you always work in the garden, Mr.--Man?" asked Pollyanna, interestedly.

The man turned. His lips were twitching, but his eyes looked blurred as if with tears.

"Yes, Miss. I'm Old Tom, the gardener," he answered. Timidly, but as if impelled by an irresistible force, he reached out a shaking hand and let it rest for a moment on her bright hair. "You are so like your mother, little Miss! I used ter know her when she was even littler than you be. You see, I used ter work in the garden--then."

Pollyanna caught her breath audibly.

"You did? And you knew my mother, really--when she was just a little earth angel, and not a Heaven one? Oh, please tell me about her!" And down plumped Pollyanna in the middle of the dirt path by the old man's side.

A bell sounded from the house. The next moment Nancy was seen flying out the back door.

"Miss Pollyanna, that bell means breakfast--mornin's," she panted, pulling the little girl to her feet and hurrying her back to the house; "and other times it means other meals. But it always means that you're ter run like time when ye hear it, no matter where ye be. If ye don't--well, it'll take somethin' smarter'n we be ter find *anythin'* ter be glad about in that!" she finished, shooing Pollyanna into the house as she would shoo an unruly chicken into a coop.

Breakfast, for the first five minutes, was a silent meal; then Miss Polly, her disapproving eyes following the airy wings of two flies darting here and there over the table, said sternly:

"Nancy, where did those flies come from?"

"I don't know, ma'am. There wasn't one in the kitchen." Nancy had been too excited to notice Pollyanna's up-flung windows the afternoon before.

"I reckon maybe they're my flies, Aunt Polly," observed Pollyanna, amiably. "There were lots of them this morning having a beautiful time upstairs."

Nancy left the room precipitately, though to do so she had to carry out the hot muffins she had just brought in.

"Yours!" gasped Miss Polly. "What do you mean? Where did they come from?"

"Why, Aunt Polly, they came from out of doors of course, through the windows. I *saw* some of them come in."

"You saw them! You mean you raised those windows without any screens?"

"Why, yes. There weren't any screens there, Aunt Polly."

Nancy, at this moment, came in again with the muffins. Her face was grave, but very red.

"Nancy," directed her mistress, sharply, "you may set the muffins down and go at once to Miss Pollyanna's room and shut the windows. Shut the doors, also. Later, when your morning work is done, go through every room with the spatter. See that you make a thorough search."

To her niece she said:

"Pollyanna, I have ordered screens for those windows. I knew, of course, that it was my duty to do that. But it seems to me that you have quite forgotten *your* duty."

"My--duty?" Pollyanna's eyes were wide with wonder.

"Certainly. I know it is warm, but I consider it your duty to keep your windows closed till those screens come. Flies, Pollyanna, are not only unclean and annoying, but very dangerous to health. After breakfast I will give you a little pamphlet on this matter to read."

"To read? Oh, thank you, Aunt Polly. I love to read!"

Miss Polly drew in her breath audibly, then she shut her lips together hard. Pollyanna, seeing her stern face, frowned a little thoughtfully.

"Of course I'm sorry about the duty I forgot, Aunt Polly," she apologized timidly. "I won't raise the windows again."

Her aunt made no reply. She did not speak, indeed, until the meal was over. Then she rose, went to the bookcase in the sitting room, took out a small paper booklet, and crossed the room to her niece's side.

"This is the article I spoke of, Pollyanna. I desire you to go to your room at once and read it. I will be up in half an hour to look over your things."

Pollyanna, her eyes on the illustration of a fly's head, many times magnified, cried joyously:

"Oh, thank you, Aunt Polly!" The next moment she skipped merrily from the room, banging the door behind her.

Miss Polly frowned, hesitated, then crossed the room majestically and opened the door; but Pollyanna was already out of sight, clattering up the attic stairs.

Half an hour later when Miss Polly, her face expressing stern duty in every line, climbed those stairs and entered Pollyanna's room, she was greeted with a burst of eager enthusiasm.

"Oh, Aunt Polly, I never saw anything so perfectly lovely and interesting in my life. I'm so glad you gave me that book to read! Why, I didn't suppose flies could carry such a lot of things on their feet, and--"

"That will do," observed Aunt Polly, with dignity. "Pollyanna, you may bring out your clothes now, and I will look them over. What are not suitable for you I shall give to the Sullivans, of course."

With visible reluctance Pollyanna laid down the pamphlet and turned toward the closet.

"I'm afraid you'll think they're worse than the Ladies' Aid did--and *they* said they were shameful," she sighed. "But there were mostly things for boys and older folks in the last two or three barrels; and--did you ever have a missionary barrel, Aunt Polly?"

At her aunt's look of shocked anger, Pollyanna corrected herself at once.

"Why, no, of course you didn't, Aunt Polly!" she hurried on, with a hot blush. "I forgot; rich folks never have to have them. But you see sometimes I kind of forget that you are rich--up here in this room, you know."

Miss Polly's lips parted indignantly, but no words came. Pollyanna, plainly unaware that she had said anything in the least unpleasant, was hurrying on.

"Well, as I was going to say, you can't tell a thing about missionary barrels--except that you won't find in 'em what you think you're going to--even when you think you won't. It was the barrels every time, too, that were hardest to play the game on, for father and--"

Just in time Pollyanna remembered that she was not to talk of her father to her aunt. She dived into her closet then, hurriedly, and brought out all the poor little dresses in both her arms.

"They aren't nice, at all," she choked, "and they'd been black if it hadn't been for the red carpet for the church; but they're all I've got."

With the tips of her fingers Miss Polly turned over the conglomerate garments, so obviously made for anybody but Pollyanna. Next she bestowed frowning attention on the patched undergarments in the bureau drawers.

"I've got the best ones on," confessed Pollyanna, anxiously. "The Ladies' Aid bought me one set straight through all whole. Mrs. Jones--she's the president--told 'em I should have that if they had to clatter down bare aisles themselves the rest of their days. But they won't. Mr. White doesn't like the noise. He's got nerves, his wife says; but he's got money, too, and they expect he'll give a lot toward the carpet--on account of the nerves, you know. I should think he'd be glad that if he did have the nerves he'd got money, too; shouldn't you?"

Miss Polly did not seem to hear. Her scrutiny of the undergarments finished, she turned to Pollyanna somewhat abruptly.

"You have been to school, of course, Pollyanna?"

"Oh, yes, Aunt Polly. Besides, fath--I mean, I was taught at home some, too."

Miss Polly frowned.

"Very good. In the fall you will enter school here, of course. Mr. Hall, the principal, will doubtless settle in which grade you belong. Meanwhile, I suppose I ought to hear you read aloud half an hour each day."

"I love to read; but if you don't want to hear me I'd be just glad to read to myself--truly, Aunt Polly. And I wouldn't have to half try to be glad, either, for I like best to read to myself--on account of the big words, you know."

"I don't doubt it," rejoined Miss Polly, grimly. "Have you studied music?"

"Not much. I don't like my music--I like other people's, though. I learned to play on the piano a little. Miss Gray--she plays for church--she taught me. But I'd just as soon let that go as not, Aunt Polly. I'd rather, truly."

"Very likely," observed Aunt Polly, with slightly uplifted eyebrows. "Nevertheless I think it is my duty to see that you are properly instructed in at least the rudiments of music. You sew, of course."

"Yes, ma'am." Pollyanna sighed. The Ladies' Aid taught me that. But I had an awful time. Mrs. Jones didn't believe in holding your needle like the rest of 'em did on buttonholing, and Mrs. White thought backstitching ought to be taught you before hemming (or else the other way), and Mrs. Harriman didn't believe in putting you on patchwork ever, at all."

"Well, there will be no difficulty of that kind any longer, Pollyanna. I shall teach you sewing myself, of course. You do not know how to cook, I presume."

Pollyanna laughed suddenly.

"They were just beginning to teach me that this summer, but I hadn't got far. They were more divided up on that than they were on the sewing. They were *going* to begin on bread; but there wasn't two of 'em that made it alike, so after arguing it all one sewing-meeting, they decided to take turns at me one forenoon a week--in their own kitchens, you know. I'd only learned chocolate fudge and fig cake, though, when--when I had to stop." Her voice broke.

"Chocolate fudge and fig cake, indeed!" scorned Miss Polly. "I think we can remedy that very soon." She paused in thought for a minute, then went on slowly: "At nine o'clock every morning you will read aloud one half-hour to me. Before that you will use the time to put this room in order. Wednesday and Saturday forenoons, after half-past nine, you will spend with Nancy in the kitchen, learning to cook. Other mornings you will sew with me. That will leave the afternoons for your music. I shall, of course, procure a teacher at once for you," she finished decisively, as she arose from her chair.

Pollyanna cried out in dismay.

"Oh, but Aunt Polly, Aunt Polly, you haven't left me any time at all just to--to live."

"To live, child! What do you mean? As if you weren't living all the time!"

"Oh, of course I'd be *breathing* all the time I was doing those things, Aunt Polly, but I wouldn't be living. You breathe all the time you're asleep, but you aren't living. I mean living--doing the things you want to do: playing outdoors, reading (to myself, of course), climbing hills, talking to Mr. Tom in the garden, and Nancy, and finding out all about the houses and the people and everything everywhere all through the perfectly lovely streets I came through yesterday. That's what I call living, Aunt Polly. Just breathing isn't living!"

Miss Polly lifted her head irritably.

"Pollyanna, you *are* the most extraordinary child! You will be allowed a proper amount of playtime, of course. But, surely, it seems to me if I am willing to do my duty in seeing that you have proper care and instruction, *you* ought to be willing to do yours by seeing that that care and instruction are not ungratefully wasted."

Pollyanna looked shocked.

"Oh, Aunt Polly, as if I ever could be ungrateful--to *you*! Why, I *love you*--and you aren't even a Ladies' Aider; you're an aunt!"

"Very well; then see that you don't act ungrateful," vouchsafed Miss Polly, as she turned toward the door.

She had gone halfway down the stairs when a small, unsteady voice called after her:

"Please, Aunt Polly, you didn't tell me which of my things you wanted to--to give away."

Aunt Polly emitted a tired sigh--a sigh that ascended straight to Pollyanna's ears.

"Oh, I forgot to tell you, Pollyanna. Timothy will drive us into town at half-past one this afternoon. Not one of your garments is fit for my niece to wear. Certainly I should be very far from doing my duty by you if I should let you appear out in any one of them."

Pollyanna sighed now--she believed she was going to hate that word--duty.

"Aunt Polly, please," she called wistfully, "isn't there *any* way you can be glad about all that--duty business?"

"What?" Miss Polly looked up in dazed surprise; then, suddenly, with very red cheeks, she turned and swept angrily down the stairs. "Don't be impertinent, Pollyanna!"

In the hot little attic room Pollyanna dropped herself on to one of the straight-backed chairs. To her, existence loomed ahead one endless round of duty.

"I don't see, really, what there was impertinent about that," she sighed. "I was only asking her if she couldn't tell me something to be glad about in all that duty business."

For several minutes Pollyanna sat in silence, her rueful eyes fixed on the forlorn heap of garments on the bed. Then, slowly, she rose and began to put away the dresses.

"There just isn't anything to be glad about, that I can see," she said aloud; "unless--it's to be glad when the duty's done!" Whereupon she laughed suddenly.

Lesson 148

1. Read chapter 7.
2. Tell someone about the chapter.

At half-past one o'clock Timothy drove Miss Polly and her niece to the four or five principal dry goods stores, which were about half a mile from the homestead.

Fitting Pollyanna with a new wardrobe proved to be more or less of an exciting experience for all concerned. Miss Polly came out of it with the feeling of limp relaxation that one might have at finding oneself at last on solid earth after a perilous walk across the very thin crust of a volcano. The various clerks who had waited upon the pair came out of it with very red faces, and enough amusing stories of Pollyanna to keep their friends in gales of laughter the rest of the week. Pollyanna herself came out of it with radiant smiles and a heart content; for, as she expressed it to one of the clerks: "When you haven't had anybody but missionary barrels and Ladies' Aiders to dress you, it *is* perfectly lovely to just walk right in and buy clothes that are brand-new, and that don't have to be tucked up or let down because they don't fit!"

The shopping expedition consumed the entire afternoon; then came supper and a delightful talk with Old Tom in the garden, and another with Nancy on the back porch, after the dishes were done, and while Aunt Polly paid a visit to a neighbor.

Old Tom told Pollyanna wonderful things of her mother, that made her very happy indeed; and Nancy told her all about the little farm six miles away at "The Corners," where lived her own dear mother, and her equally dear brother and sisters. She promised, too, that sometime, if Miss Polly were willing, Pollyanna should be taken to see them.

"And *they've* got lovely names, too. You'll like *their* names," sighed Nancy. "They're 'Algernon,' and 'Florabelle' and 'Estelle.' I--I just hate 'Nancy'!"

"Oh, Nancy, what a dreadful thing to say! Why?"

"Because it isn't pretty like the others. You see, I was the first baby, and mother hadn't begun ter read so many stories with the pretty names in 'em, then."

"But I love 'Nancy,' just because it's you," declared Pollyanna.

"Humph! Well, I guess you could love 'Clarissa Mabelle' just as well," retorted Nancy, and it would be a heap happier for me. I think *that* name's just grand!"

Pollyanna laughed.

"Well, anyhow," she chuckled, "you can be glad it isn't 'Hephzibah.'

"Hephzibah!"

"Yes. Mrs. White's name is that. Her husband calls her 'Hep,' and she doesn't like it. She says when he calls out 'Hep--Hep!' she feels just as if the next minute he was going to yell 'Hurrah!' And she doesn't like to be hurrahed at."

Nancy's gloomy face relaxed into a broad smile.

"Well, if you don't beat the Dutch! Say, do you know?--I sha'n't never hear 'Nancy' now that I don't think o' that 'Hep--Hep!' and giggle. My, I guess I *am* glad--" She stopped short and turned amazed eyes on the little girl. "Say, Miss Pollyanna, do you mean--was you playin' that 'ere game *then*-- about my bein' glad I wa'n't named Hephzibah'?"

Pollyanna frowned; then she laughed.

"Why, Nancy, that's so! I *was* playing the game--but that's one of the times I just did it without thinking, I reckon. You see, you *do*, lots of times; you get so used to it--looking for something to be glad about, you know. And most generally there is something about everything that you can be glad about, if you keep hunting long enough to find it."

"Well, m-maybe," granted Nancy, with open doubt.

At half-past eight Pollyanna went up to bed. The screens had not yet come, and the close little room was like an oven. With longing eyes Pollyanna looked at the two fast-closed windows--but she did not raise them. She undressed, folded her clothes neatly, said her prayers, blew out her candle and climbed into bed.

Just how long she lay in sleepless misery, tossing from side to side of the hot little cot, she did not know; but it seemed to her that it must have been hours before she finally slipped out of bed, felt her way across the room and opened her door.

Out in the main attic all was velvet blackness save where the moon flung a path of silver half-way across the floor from the east dormer window. With a resolute ignoring of that fearsome darkness to the right and to the left, Pollyanna drew a quick breath and pattered straight into that silvery path, and on to the window.

She had hoped, vaguely, that this window might have a screen, but it did not. Outside, however, there was a wide world of fairy-like beauty, and there was, too, she knew, fresh, sweet air that would feel so good to hot cheeks and hands!

As she stepped nearer and peered longingly out, she saw something else: she saw, only a little way below the window, the wide, flat tin roof of Miss Polly's sun parlor built over the porte-cochere. The sight filled her with longing. If only, now, she were out there!

Fearfully she looked behind her. Back there, somewhere, were her hot little room and her still hotter bed; but between her and them lay a horrid desert of blackness across which one must feel one's way with outstretched, shrinking arms; while before her, out on the sun-parlor roof, were the moonlight and the cool, sweet night air.

If only her bed were out there! And folks did sleep out of doors. Joel Hartley at home, who was so sick with the consumption, *had* to sleep out of doors.

Suddenly Pollyanna remembered that she had seen near this attic window a row of long white bags hanging from nails. Nancy had said that they contained the winter clothing, put away for the summer. A little fearfully now, Pollyanna felt her way to these bags, selected a nice fat soft one (it contained Miss Polly's sealskin coat) for a bed; and a thinner one to be doubled up for a pillow, and still another (which was so thin it seemed almost empty) for a covering. Thus equipped, Pollyanna in high glee pattered to the moonlit window again, raised the sash, stuffed her burden through to the roof below, then let herself down after it, closing the window carefully behind her--Pollyanna had not forgotten those flies with the marvellous feet that carried things.

How deliciously cool it was! Pollyanna quite danced up and down with delight, drawing in long, full breaths of the refreshing air. The tin roof under her feet crackled with little resounding snaps that Pollyanna rather liked. She walked, indeed, two or three times back and forth from end to end--it gave her such a pleasant sensation of airy space after her hot little room; and the roof was so broad and flat that she had no fear of falling off. Finally, with a sigh of content, she curled herself up on the sealskin-coat mattress, arranged one bag for a pillow and the other for a covering, and settled herself to sleep.

"I'm so glad now that the screens didn't come," she murmured, blinking up at the stars; "else I couldn't have had this!"

Down-stairs in Miss Polly's room next the sun parlor, Miss Polly herself was hurrying into dressing gown and slippers, her face white and frightened. A minute before she had been telephoning in a shaking voice to Timothy:

"Come up quick!--you and your father. Bring lanterns. Somebody is on the roof of the sun parlor. He must have climbed up the rose-trellis or somewhere, and of course he can get right into the house through the east window in the attic. I have locked the attic door down here--but hurry, quick!"

Some time later, Pollyanna, just dropping off to sleep, was startled by a lantern flash, and a trio of amazed exclamations. She opened her eyes to find Timothy at the top of a ladder near her, Old Tom just getting through the window, and her aunt peering out at her from behind him.

"Pollyanna, what does this mean?" cried Aunt Polly then.

Pollyanna blinked sleepy eyes and sat up.

"Why, Mr. Tom--Aunt Polly!" she stammered. "Don't look so scared! It isn't that I've got the consumption, you know, like Joel Hartley. It's only that I was so hot--in there. But I shut the window, Aunt Polly, so the flies couldn't carry those germ-things in."

Timothy disappeared suddenly down the ladder. Old Tom, with almost equal precipitation, handed his lantern to Miss Polly, and followed his son. Miss Polly bit her lip hard--until the men were gone; then she said sternly:

"Pollyanna, hand those things to me at once and come in here. Of all the extraordinary children!" she exclaimed a little later, as, with Pollyanna by her side, and the lantern in her hand, she turned back into the attic.

To Pollyanna the air was all the more stifling after that cool breath of the out of doors; but she did not complain. She only drew a long quivering sigh.

At the top of the stairs Miss Polly jerked out crisply:

"For the rest of the night, Pollyanna, you are to sleep in my bed with me. The screens will be here to-morrow, but until then I consider it my duty to keep you where I know where you are."

Pollyanna drew in her breath.

"With you?--in your bed?" she cried rapturously. "Oh, Aunt Polly, Aunt Polly, how perfectly lovely of you! And when I've so wanted to sleep with some one sometime--some one that belonged to me, you know; not a Ladies' Aider. I've *had* them. My! I reckon I am glad now those screens didn't come! Wouldn't you be?"

There was no reply. Miss Polly was stalking on ahead. Miss Polly, to tell the truth, was feeling curiously helpless. For the third time since Pollyanna's arrival, Miss Polly was punishing Pollyanna--and for the third time she was being confronted with the amazing fact that her punishment was being taken as a special reward of merit. No wonder Miss Polly was feeling curiously helpless.

Lesson 149

1. Read chapter 8.
2. Tell someone about the chapter.

It was not long before life at the Harrington homestead settled into something like order--though not exactly the order that Miss Polly had at first prescribed. Pollyanna sewed, practised, read aloud, and studied cooking in the kitchen, it is true; but she did not give to any of these things quite so much time as had first been planned. She had more time, also, to "just live," as she expressed it, for almost all of every afternoon from two until six o'clock was hers to do with as she liked--provided she did not "like" to do certain things already prohibited by Aunt Polly.

It is a question, perhaps, whether all this leisure time was given to the child as a relief to Pollyanna from work--or as a relief to Aunt Polly from Pollyanna. Certainly, as those first July days passed, Miss Polly found occasion many times to exclaim "What an extraordinary child!" and certainly the reading and sewing lessons found her at their conclusion each day somewhat dazed and wholly exhausted.

Nancy, in the kitchen, fared better. She was not dazed nor exhausted. Wednesdays and Saturdays came to be, indeed, red-letter days to her.

There were no children in the immediate neighborhood of the Harrington homestead for Pollyanna to play with. The house itself was on the outskirts of the village, and though there were other houses not far away, they did not chance to contain any boys or girls near Pollyanna's age. This, however, did not seem to disturb Pollyanna in the least.

"Oh, no, I don't mind it at all," she explained to Nancy. "I'm happy just to walk around and see the streets and the houses and watch the people. I just love people. Don't you, Nancy?"

"Well, I can't say I do--all of 'em," retorted Nancy, tersely.

Almost every pleasant afternoon found Pollyanna begging for "an errand to run," so that she might be off for a walk in one direction or another; and it was on these walks that frequently she met the Man. To herself Pollyanna always called him "the Man," no matter if she met a dozen other men the same day.

The Man often wore a long black coat and a high silk hat--two things that the "just men" never wore. His face was clean shaven and rather pale, and his hair, showing below his hat, was somewhat gray. He walked erect, and rather rapidly, and he was always alone, which made Pollyanna vaguely sorry for him. Perhaps it was because of this that she one day spoke to him.

"How do you do, sir? Isn't this a nice day?" she called cheerily, as she approached him.

The man threw a hurried glance about him, then stopped uncertainly.

"Did you speak--to me?" he asked in a sharp voice.

"Yes, sir," beamed Pollyanna. "I say, it's a nice day, isn't it?"

"Eh? Oh! Humph!" he grunted; and strode on again.

Pollyanna laughed. He was such a funny man, she thought.

The next day she saw him again.

"'Tisn't quite so nice as yesterday, but it's pretty nice," she called out cheerfully.

"Eh? Oh! Humph!" grunted the man as before; and once again Pollyanna laughed happily.

When for the third time Pollyanna accosted him in much the same manner, the man stopped abruptly.

"See here, child, who are you, and why are you speaking to me every day?"

"I'm Pollyanna Whittier, and I thought you looked lonesome. I'm so glad you stopped. Now we're introduced--only I don't know your name yet."

"Well, of all the--" The man did not finish his sentence, but strode on faster than ever.

Pollyanna looked after him with a disappointed droop to her usually smiling lips.

"Maybe he didn't understand--but that was only half an introduction. I don't know *his* name, yet," she murmured, as she proceeded on her way.

Pollyanna was carrying calf's-foot jelly to Mrs. Snow to-day. Miss Polly Harrington always sent something to Mrs. Snow once a week. She said she thought that it was her duty, inasmuch as Mrs. Snow was poor, sick, and a member of her church--it was the duty of all the church members to look out for her, of course. Miss Polly did her duty by Mrs. Snow usually on Thursday afternoons--not personally, but through Nancy. To-day Pollyanna had begged the privilege, and Nancy had promptly given it to her in accordance with Miss Polly's orders.

"And it's glad that I am ter get rid of it," Nancy had declared in private afterwards to Pollyanna; "though it's a shame ter be tuckin' the job off on ter you, poor lamb, so it is, it is!"

"But I'd love to do it, Nancy."

"Well, you won't--after you've done it once," predicted Nancy, sourly.

"Why not?"

"Because nobody does. If folks wa'n't sorry for her there wouldn't a soul go near her from mornin' till night, she's that cantankerous. All is, I pity her daughter what *has* ter take care of her."

"But, why, Nancy?"

Nancy shrugged her shoulders.

"Well, in plain words, it's just that nothin' what ever has happened, has happened right in Mis' Snow's eyes. Even the days of the week ain't run ter her mind. If it's Monday she's bound ter say she wished 'twas Sunday; and if you take her jelly you're pretty sure ter hear she wanted chicken--but if you *did* bring her chicken, she'd be jest hankerin' for lamb broth!"

"Why, what a funny woman," laughed Pollyanna. "I think I shall like to go to see her. She must be so surprising and--and different. I love *different* folks."

"Humph! Well, Mis' Snow's 'different,' all right--I hope, for the sake of the rest of us!" Nancy had finished grimly.

Pollyanna was thinking of these remarks to-day as she turned in at the gate of the shabby little cottage. Her eyes were quite sparkling, indeed, at the prospect of meeting this "different" Mrs. Snow.

A pale-faced, tired-looking young girl answered her knock at the door.

"How do you do?" began Pollyanna politely. "I'm from Miss Polly Harrington, and I'd like to see Mrs. Snow, please."

"Well, if you would, you're the first one that ever 'liked' to see her," muttered the girl under her breath; but Pollyanna did not hear this. The girl had turned and was leading the way through the hall to a door at the end of it.

In the sick-room, after the girl had ushered her in and closed the door, Pollyanna blinked a little before she could accustom her eyes to the gloom. Then she saw, dimly outlined, a woman half-sitting up in the bed across the room. Pollyanna advanced at once.

"How do you do, Mrs. Snow? Aunt Polly says she hopes you are comfortable to-day, and she's sent you some calf's-foot jelly."

"Dear me! jelly?" murmured a fretful voice,

"Of course I'm very much obliged, but I was hoping 'twould be lamb broth to-day."

Pollyanna frowned a little.

"Why, I thought it was *chicken* you wanted when folks brought you jelly," she said.

"What?" The sick woman turned sharply.

"Why, nothing, much," apologized Pollyanna, hurriedly; "and of course it doesn't really make any difference. It's only that Nancy said it was chicken you wanted when we brought jelly, and lamb broth when we brought chicken--but maybe 'twas the other way, and Nancy forgot."

The sick woman pulled herself up till she sat erect in the bed--a most unusual thing for her to do, though Pollyanna did not know this.

"Well, Miss Impertinence, who are you?" she demanded.

Pollyanna laughed gleefully.

"Oh, *that* isn't my name, Mrs. Snow--and I'm so glad 'tisn't, too! That would be worse than 'Hephzibah,' wouldn't it? I'm Pollyanna Whittier, Miss Polly Harrington's niece, and I've come to live with her. That's why I'm here with the jelly this morning."

All through the first part of this sentence, the sick woman had sat interestedly erect; but at the reference to the jelly she fell back on her pillow listlessly.

"Very well; thank you. Your aunt is very kind, of course, but my appetite isn't very good this morning, and I was wanting lamb--" She stopped suddenly, then went on with an abrupt change of subject. "I never slept a wink last night--not a wink!"

"O dear, I wish *I* didn't," sighed Pollyanna, placing the jelly on the little stand and seating herself comfortably in the nearest chair. "You lose such a lot of time just sleeping! Don't you think so?"

"Lose time--sleeping!" exclaimed the sick woman.

"Yes, when you might be just living, you know. It seems such a pity we can't live nights, too."

Once again the woman pulled herself erect in her bed.

"Well, if you ain't the amazing young one!" she cried. "Here! do you go to that window and pull up the curtain," she directed. "I should like to know what you look like!"

Pollyanna rose to her feet, but she laughed a little ruefully.

"O dear! then you'll see my freckles, won't you?" she sighed, as she went to the window; "--and just when I was being so glad it was dark and you couldn't see 'em. There! Now you can--oh!" she broke off excitedly, as she turned back to the bed; "I'm so glad you wanted to see me, because now I can see you! They didn't tell me you were so pretty!"

"Me!--pretty!" scoffed the woman, bitterly.

"Why, yes. Didn't you know it?" cried Pollyanna.

"Well, no, I didn't," retorted Mrs. Snow, dryly. Mrs. Snow had lived forty years, and for fifteen of those years she had been too busy wishing things were different to find much time to enjoy things as they were.

"Oh, but your eyes are so big and dark, and your hair's all dark, too, and curly," cooed Pollyanna. "I love black curls. (That's one of the things I'm going to have when I get to Heaven.) And you've got two little red spots in your cheeks. Why, Mrs. Snow, you *are* pretty! I should think you'd know it when you looked at yourself in the glass."

"The glass!" snapped the sick woman, falling back on her pillow. "Yes, well, I hain't done much prinkin' before the mirror these days--and you wouldn't, if you was flat on your back as I am!"

"Why, no, of course not," agreed Pollyanna, sympathetically. "But wait--just let me show you," she exclaimed, skipping over to the bureau and picking up a small hand-glass.

On the way back to the bed she stopped, eyeing the sick woman with a critical gaze.

"I reckon maybe, if you don't mind, I'd like to fix your hair just a little before I let you see it," she proposed. "May I fix your hair, please?"

"Why, I--suppose so, if you want to," permitted Mrs. Snow, grudgingly; "but 'twon't stay, you know."

"Oh, thank you. I love to fix people's hair," exulted Pollyanna, carefully laying down the hand-glass and reaching for a comb. "I sha'n't do much to-day, of course--I'm in such a hurry for you to see how pretty you are; but some day I'm going to take it all down and have a perfectly lovely time with it, she cried, touching with soft fingers the waving hair above the sick woman's forehead.

For five minutes Pollyanna worked swiftly, deftly, combing a refractory curl into fluffiness, perking up a drooping ruffle at the neck, or shaking a pillow into plumpness so that the head might have a better pose. Meanwhile the sick woman, frowning prodigiously, and openly scoffing at the whole procedure, was, in spite of herself, beginning to tingle with a feeling perilously near to excitement.

"There!" panted Pollyanna, hastily plucking a pink from a vase near by and tucking it into the dark hair where it would give the best effect. "Now I reckon we're ready to be looked at!" And she held out the mirror in triumph.

"Humph!" grunted the sick woman, eyeing her reflection severely. "I like red pinks better than pink ones; but then, it'll fade, anyhow, before night, so what's the difference!"

"But I should think you'd be glad they did fade," laughed Pollyanna, " 'cause then you can have the fun of getting some more. I just love your hair fluffed out like that," she finished with a satisfied gaze. "Don't you?"

"Hm-m; maybe. Still--'twon't last, with me tossing back and forth on the pillow as I do."

"Of course not--and I'm glad, too," nodded Pollyanna, cheerfully, "because then I can fix it again. Anyhow, I should think you'd be glad it's black--black shows up so much nicer on a pillow than yellow hair like mine does."

"Maybe; but I never did set much store by black hair--shows gray too soon," retorted Mrs. Snow. She spoke fretfully, but she still held the mirror before her face.

"Oh, I love black hair! I should be so glad if I only had it," sighed Pollyanna.

Mrs. Snow dropped the mirror and turned irritably.

"Well, you wouldn't!--not if you were me. You wouldn't be glad for black hair nor anything else-- if you had to lie here all day as I do!"

Pollyanna bent her brows in a thoughtful frown.

"Why, 'twould be kind of hard--to do it then, wouldn't it?" she mused aloud.

"Do what?"

"Be glad about things."

"Be glad about things--when you're sick in bed all your days? Well, I should say it would," retorted Mrs. Snow. "If you don't think so, just tell me something to be glad about; that's all!"

To Mrs. Snow's unbounded amazement, Pollyanna sprang to her feet and clapped her hands.

"Oh, goody! That'll be a hard one--won't it? I've got to go, now, but I'll think and think all the way home; and maybe the next time I come I can tell it to you. Good-by. I've had a lovely time! Good- by," she called again, as she tripped through the doorway.

"Well, I never! Now, what does she mean by that?" exclaimed Mrs. Snow, staring after her visitor. By and by she turned her head and picked up the mirror, eyeing her reflection critically.

"That little thing *has* got a knack with hair and no mistake," she muttered under her breath. "I declare, I didn't know it could look so pretty. But then, what's the use?" she sighed, dropping the little glass into the bedclothes, and rolling her head on the pillow fretfully.

A little later, when Milly, Mrs. Snow's daughter, came in, the mirror still lay among the bedclothes- it had been carefully hidden from sight.

"Why, mother--the curtain is up!" cried Milly, dividing her amazed stare between the window and the pink in her mother's hair.

"Well, what if it is?" snapped the sick woman. "I needn't stay in the dark all my life, if I am sick, need I?"

"Why, n-no, of course not," rejoined Milly, in hasty conciliation, as she reached for the medicine bottle. "It's only--well, you know very well that I've tried to get you to have a lighter room for ages and you wouldn't."

There was no reply to this. Mrs. Snow was picking at the lace on her nightgown. At last she spoke fretfully.

"I should think *somebody* might give me a new nightdress--instead of lamb broth, for a change!

"Why--mother!"

No wonder Milly quite gasped aloud with bewilderment. In the drawer behind her at that moment lay two new nightdresses that Milly for months had been vainly urging her mother to wear.

Lesson 150

1. Read chapter 9.
2. Tell someone about the chapter.

It rained the next time Pollyanna saw the Man. She greeted him, however, with a bright smile.

"It isn't so nice to-day, is it?" she called blithesomely. "I'm glad it doesn't rain always, anyhow!"

The man did not even grunt this time, nor turn his head. Pollyanna decided that of course he did not hear her. The next time, therefore (which happened to be the following day), she spoke up louder. She thought it particularly necessary to do this, anyway, for the Man was striding along, his hands behind his back, and his eyes on the ground--which seemed, to Pollyanna, preposterous in the face of the glorious sunshine and the freshly-washed morning air: Pollyanna, as a special treat, was on a morning errand to-day.

"How do you do?" she chirped. "I'm so glad it isn't yesterday, aren't you?

The man stopped abruptly. There was an angry scowl on his face.

"See here, little girl, we might just as well settle this thing right now, once for all," he began testily. "I've got something besides the weather to think of. I don't know whether the sun shines or not." Pollyanna beamed joyously.

"No, sir; I thought you didn't. That's why I told you."

"Yes; well--Eh? What?" he broke off sharply, in sudden understanding of her words.

"I say, that's why I told you--so you would notice it, you know--that the sun shines, and all that. I knew you'd be glad it did if you only stopped to think of it--and you didn't look a bit as if you *were* thinking of it!"

"Well, of all the--" exclaimed the man, with an oddly impotent gesture. He started forward again, but after the second step he turned back, still frowning.

"See here, why don't you find some one your own age to talk to?"

"I'd like to, sir, but there aren't any 'round here, Nancy says. Still, I don't mind so very much. I like old folks just as well, maybe better, sometimes--being used to the Ladies' Aid, so."

"Humph! The Ladies' Aid, indeed! Is that what you took me for?" The man's lips were threatening to smile, but the scowl above them was still trying to hold them grimly stern.

Pollyanna laughed gleefully.

"Oh, no, sir. You don't look a mite like a Ladies' Aider--not but that you're just as good, of course-maybe better," she added in hurried politeness. "You see, I'm sure you're much nicer than you look!"

The man made a queer noise in his throat.

"Well, of all the--" he exclaimed again, as he turned and strode on as before.

The next time Pollyanna met the Man, his eyes were gazing straight into hers, with a quizzical directness that made his face look really pleasant, Pollyanna thought.

"Good afternoon," he greeted her a little stiffly. "Perhaps I'd better say right away that I *know* the sun is shining to-day."

"But you don't have to tell me," nodded Pollyanna, brightly. "I *knew* you knew it just as soon as I saw you."

"Oh, you did, did you?"

"Yes, sir; I saw it in your eyes, you know, and in your smile."

"Humph!" grunted the man, as he passed on.

The Man always spoke to Pollyanna after this, and frequently he spoke first, though usually he said little but "good afternoon." Even that, however, was a great surprise to Nancy, who chanced to be with Pollyanna one day when the greeting was given.

"Sakes alive, Miss Pollyanna," she gasped, "did that man *speak to you*?"

"Why, yes, he always does--now," smiled Pollyanna.

"'He always does'! Goodness! Do you know who--he--is?" demanded Nancy.

Pollyanna frowned and shook her head.

"I reckon he forgot to tell me one day. You see, I did my part of the introducing, but he didn't."

Nancy's eyes widened.

"But he never speaks ter anybody, child--he hain't for years, I guess, except when he just has to, for business, and all that. He's John Pendleton. He lives all by himself in the big house on Pendleton Hill. He won't even have any one 'round ter cook for him--comes down ter the hotel for his meals three times a day. I know Sally Miner, who waits on him, and she says he hardly opens his head enough ter tell what he wants ter eat. She has ter guess it more'n half the time--only it'll be somethin' *cheap*! She knows that without no tellin'."

Pollyanna nodded sympathetically.

"I know. You have to look for cheap things when you're poor. Father and I took meals out a lot. We had beans and fish balls most generally. We used to say how glad we were we liked beans-- that is, we said it specially when we were looking at the roast turkey place, you know, that was sixty cents. Does Mr. Pendleton like beans?"

"Like 'em! What if he does--or don't? Why, Miss Pollyanna, he ain't poor. He's got loads of money, John Pendleton has--from his father. There ain't nobody in town as rich as he is. He could eat dollar bills, if he wanted to--and not know it."

Pollyanna giggled.

"As if anybody *could* eat dollar bills and not know it, Nancy, when they come to try to chew 'em!"

"Ho! I mean he's rich enough ter do it," shrugged Nancy. "He ain't spendin' his money, that's all. He's a-savin' of it."

"Oh, for the heathen," surmised Pollyanna. "How perfectly splendid! That's denying yourself and taking up your cross. I know; father told me."

Nancy's lips parted abruptly, as if there were angry words all ready to come; but her eyes, resting on Pollyanna's jubilantly trustful face, saw something that prevented the words being spoken.

"Humph!" she vouchsafed. Then, showing her old-time interest, she went on: "But, say, it is queer, his speakin' to you, honestly, Miss Pollyanna. He don't speak ter no one; and he lives all alone in a great big lovely house all full of jest grand things, they say. Some says he's crazy, and some jest cross; and some says he's got a skeleton in his closet."

"Oh, Nancy!" shuddered Pollyanna. "How can he keep such a dreadful thing? I should think he'd throw it away!"

Nancy chuckled. That Pollyanna had taken the skeleton literally instead of figuratively, she knew very well; but, perversely, she refrained from correcting the mistake.

"And *everybody* says he's mysterious," she went on. "Some years he jest travels, week in and week out, and it's always in heathen countries--Egypt and Asia and the Desert of Sarah, you know."

"Oh, a missionary," nodded Pollyanna.

Nancy laughed oddly.

"Well, I didn't say that, Miss Pollyanna. When he comes back he writes books--queer, odd books, they say, about some gimcrack he's found in them heathen countries. But he don't never seem ter want ter spend no money here--leastways, not for jest livin'."

"Of course not--if he's saving it for the heathen," declared Pollyanna. "But he is a funny man, and he's different, too, just like Mrs. Snow, only he's a different different."

"Well, I guess he is--rather," chuckled Nancy.

"I'm gladder'n ever now, anyhow, that he speaks to me," sighed Pollyanna contentedly.

Lesson 151

1. Read chapter 10.
2. Tell someone about the chapter.

The next time Pollyanna went to see Mrs. Snow, she found that lady, as at first, in a darkened room.

"It's the little girl from Miss Polly's, mother," announced Milly, in a tired manner; then Pollyanna found herself alone with the invalid.

"Oh, it's you, is it?" asked a fretful voice from the bed. "I remember you. *Any*body'd remember you, I guess, if they saw you once. I wish you had come yesterday. I *wanted* you yesterday."

"Did you? Well, I'm glad 'tisn't any farther away from yesterday than to-day is, then," laughed Pollyanna, advancing cheerily into the room, and setting her basket carefully down on a chair. "My! but aren't you dark here, though? I can't see you a bit," she cried, unhesitatingly crossing to the window and pulling up the shade. "I want to see if you've fixed your hair like I did--oh, you haven't! But, never mind; I'm glad you haven't, after all, 'cause maybe you'll let me do it--later. But now I want you to see what I've brought you."

The woman stirred restlessly.

"Just as if how it looks would make any difference in how it tastes," she scoffed--but she turned her eyes toward the basket. "Well, what is it?"

"Guess! What do you want?" Pollyanna had skipped back to the basket. Her face was alight. The sick woman frowned.

"Why, I don't *want* anything, as I know of," she sighed. "After all, they all taste alike!"

Pollyanna chuckled.

"This won't. Guess! If you *did* want something, what would it be?"

The woman hesitated. She did not realize it herself, but she had so long been accustomed to wanting what she did not have, that to state off-hand what she *did* want seemed impossible--until she knew what she had. Obviously, however, she must say something. This extraordinary child was waiting.

"Well, of course, there's lamb broth--"

"I've got it!" crowed Pollyanna.

"But that's what I *didn't* want," sighed the sick woman, sure now of what her stomach craved. "It was chicken I wanted."

"Oh, I've got that, too," chuckled Pollyanna.

The woman turned in amazement.

"Both of them?" she demanded.

"Yes--and calf's-foot jelly," triumphed Pollyanna. "I was just bound you should have what you wanted for once; so Nancy and I fixed it. Oh, of course, there's only a little of each--but there's some of all of 'em! I'm so glad you did want chicken," she went on contentedly, as she lifted the three little bowls from her basket. "You see, I got to thinking on the way here--what if you should say tripe, or onions, or something like that, that I didn't have! Wouldn't it have been a shame--when I'd tried so hard?" she laughed merrily.

There was no reply. The sick woman seemed to be trying--mentally to find something she had lost.

"There! I'm to leave them all," announced Pollyanna, as she arranged the three bowls in a row on the table. "Like enough it'll be lamb broth you want to-morrow. How do you do to-day?" she finished in polite inquiry.

"Very poorly, thank you," murmured Mrs. Snow, falling back into her usual listless attitude. "I lost my nap this morning. Nellie Higgins next door has begun music lessons, and her practising drives me nearly wild. She was at it all the morning--every minute! I'm sure, I don't know what I shall do!"

Polly nodded sympathetically.

"I know. It *is* awful! Mrs. White had it once--one of my Ladies' Aiders, you know. She had rheumatic fever, too, at the same time, so she couldn't thrash 'round. She said 'twould have been easier if she could have. Can you?"

"Can I--what?"

"Thrash 'round--move, you know, so as to change your position when the music gets too hard to stand."

Mrs. Snow stared a little.

"Why, of course I can move--anywhere--in bed," she rejoined a little irritably.

"Well, you can be glad of that, then, anyhow, can't you?" nodded Pollyanna. "Mrs. White couldn't. You can't thrash when you have rheumatic fever--though you want to something awful, Mrs. White says. She told me afterwards she reckoned she'd have gone raving crazy if it hadn't been for Mr. White's sister's ears--being deaf, so."

"Sister's--*ears*! What do you mean?"

Pollyanna laughed.

"Well, I reckon I didn't tell it all, and I forgot you didn't know Mrs. White. You see, Miss White was deaf--awfully deaf; and she came to visit 'em and to help take care of Mrs. White and the house. Well, they had such an awful time making her understand *anything*, that after that, every time the piano commenced to play across the street, Mrs. White felt so glad she *could* hear it, that she didn't mind so much that she *did* hear it, 'cause she couldn't help thinking how awful 'twould be if she was deaf and couldn't hear anything, like her husband's sister. You see, she was playing the game, too. I'd told her about it."

"The--game?"

Pollyanna clapped her hands.

"There! I 'most forgot; but I've thought it up, Mrs. Snow--what you can be glad about."

"*Glad* about! What do you mean?"

"Why, I told you I would. Don't you remember? You asked me to tell you something to be glad about--glad, you know, even though you did have to lie here abed all day."

"Oh!" scoffed the woman. "*That*? Yes, I remember that; but I didn't suppose you were in earnest any more than I was."

"Oh, yes, I was," nodded Pollyanna, triumphantly; "and I found it, too. But '*twas* hard. It's all the more fun, though, always, when 'tis hard. And I will own up, honest to true, that I couldn't think of anything for a while. Then I got it."

"Did you, really? Well, what is it?" Mrs. Snow's voice was sarcastically polite.

Pollyanna drew a long breath.

"I thought--how glad you could be--that other folks weren't like you--all sick in bed like this, you know," she announced impressively. Mrs, Snow stared. Her eyes were angry.

"Well, really!" she exclaimed then, in not quite an agreeable tone of voice.

"And now I'll tell you the game," proposed Pollyanna, blithely confident. "It'll be just lovely for you to play--it'll be so hard. And there's so much more fun when it is hard! You see, it's like this." And she began to tell of the missionary barrel, the crutches, and the doll that did not come.

The story was just finished when Milly appeared at the door.

"Your aunt is wanting you, Miss Pollyanna," she said with dreary listlessness. "She telephoned down to the Harlows' across the way. She says you're to hurry--that you've got some practising to make up before dark."

Pollyanna rose reluctantly.

"All right," she sighed. "I'll hurry." Suddenly she laughed. "I suppose I ought to be glad I've got legs to hurry with, hadn't I, Mrs., Snow?"

There was no answer. Mrs. Snow's eyes were closed. But Milly, whose eyes were wide open with surprise, saw that there were tears on the wasted cheeks.

"Good-by," flung Pollyanna over her shoulder, as she reached the door. "I'm awfully sorry about the hair--I wanted to do it. But maybe I can next time!"

One by one the July days passed. To Pollyanna, they were happy days, indeed. She often told her aunt, joyously, how very happy they were. Whereupon her aunt would usually reply, wearily:

"Very well, Pollyanna. I am gratified, of course, that they are happy; but I trust that they are profitable, as well--otherwise I should have failed signally in my duty."

Generally Pollyanna would answer this with a hug and a kiss--a proceeding that was still always most disconcerting to Miss Polly; but one day she spoke. It was during the sewing hour.

"Do you mean that it wouldn't be enough then, Aunt Polly, that they should be just happy days?" she asked wistfully.

"That is what I mean, Pollyanna."

"They must be pro-fi-ta-ble as well?

"Certainly."

"What is being pro-fi-ta-ble?

"Why, it--it's just being profitable--having profit, something to show for it, Pollyanna. What an extraordinary child you are!"

"Then just being glad isn't pro-fi-ta-ble?" questioned Pollyanna, a little anxiously.

"Certainly not."

"O dear! Then you wouldn't like it, of course. I'm afraid, now, you won't ever play the game, Aunt Polly."

"Game? What game?"

"Why, that father--" Pollyanna clapped her hand to her lips. "N-nothing," she stammered. Miss Polly frowned.

"That will do for this morning, Pollyanna," she said tersely. And the sewing lesson was over.

It was that afternoon that Pollyanna, coming down from her attic room, met her aunt on the stairway.

"Why, Aunt Polly, how perfectly lovely!" she cried. "You were coming up to see me! Come right in. I love company," she finished, scampering up the stairs and throwing her door wide open.

Now Miss Polly had not been intending to call on her niece. She had been planning to look for a certain white wool shawl in the cedar chest near the east window. But to her unbounded surprise now, she found herself, not in the main attic before the cedar chest, but in Pollyanna's little room sitting in one of the straight-backed chairs--so many, many times since Pollyanna came, Miss Polly had found herself like this, doing some utterly unexpected, surprising thing, quite unlike the thing she had set out to do!

"I love company," said Pollyanna, again, flitting about as if she were dispensing the hospitality of a palace; "specially since I've had this room, all mine, you know. Oh, of course, I had a room, always, but 'twas a hired room, and hired rooms aren't half as nice as owned ones, are they? And of course I do own this one, don't I?"

"Why, y-yes, Pollyanna," murmured Miss Polly, vaguely wondering why she did not get up at once and go to look for that shawl.

"And of course *now* I just love this room, even if it hasn't got the carpets and curtains and pictures that I'd been want--" With a painful blush Pollyanna stopped short. She was plunging into an entirely different sentence when her aunt interrupted her sharply.

"What's that, Pollyanna?"

"N-nothing, Aunt Polly, truly. I didn't mean to say it."

"Probably not," returned Miss Polly, coldly; "but you did say it, so suppose we have the rest of it."

"But it wasn't anything only that I'd been kind of planning on pretty carpets and lace curtains and things, you know. But, of course--"

"*Planning* on them!" interrupted Miss Polly, sharply.

Pollyanna blushed still more painfully.

"I ought not to have, of course, Aunt Polly," she apologized. "It was only because I'd always wanted them and hadn't had them, I suppose. Oh, we'd had two rugs in the barrels, but they were little, you know, and one had ink spots, and the other holes; and there never were only those two pictures; the one fath--I mean the good one we sold, and the bad one that broke. Of course if it hadn't been for all that I shouldn't have wanted them, so--pretty things, I mean; and I shouldn't have got to planning all through the hall that first day how pretty mine would be here, and—and-- But, truly, Aunt Polly, it wasn't but just a minute--I mean, a few minutes--before I was being glad that the bureau *didn't* have a looking-glass, because it didn't show my freckles; and there couldn't be a nicer picture than the one out my window there; and you've been so good to me, that--"

Miss Polly rose suddenly to her feet. Her face was very red.

"That will do, Pollyanna," she said stiffly. "You have said quite enough, I'm sure." The next minute she had swept down the stairs--and not until she reached the first floor did it suddenly occur to her that she had gone up into the attic to find a white wool shawl in the cedar chest near the east window.

Less than twenty-four hours later, Miss Polly said to Nancy, crisply:

"Nancy, you may move Miss Pollyanna's things down-stairs this morning to the room directly beneath. I have decided to have my niece sleep there for the present."

"Yes, ma'am," said Nancy aloud.

"O glory!" said Nancy to herself.

To Pollyanna, a minute later, she cried joyously:

"And won't ye jest be listenin' ter this, Miss Pollyanna. You're ter sleep down-stairs in the room straight under this. You are--you are!"

Pollyanna actually grew white.

"You mean--why, Nancy, not really--really and truly?"

"I guess you'll think it's really and truly," prophesied Nancy, exultingly, nodding her head to Pollyanna over the armful of dresses she had taken from the closet. "I'm told ter take down yer things, and I'm goin' ter take 'em, too, 'fore she gets a chance ter change her mind."

Pollyanna did not stop to hear the end of this sentence. At the imminent risk of being dashed headlong, she was flying down-stairs, two steps at a time.

Bang went two doors and a chair before Pollyanna at last reached her goal--Aunt Polly.

"Oh, Aunt Polly, Aunt Polly, did you mean it, really? Why, that room's got *everything*--the carpet and curtains and three pictures, besides the one outdoors, too, 'cause the windows look the same way. Oh, Aunt Polly!"

"Very well, Pollyanna. I am gratified that you like the change, of course; but if you think so much of all those things, I trust you will take proper care of them; that's all. Pollyanna, please pick up that chair; and you have banged two doors in the last half-minute." Miss Polly spoke sternly, all the more sternly because, for some inexplicable reason, she felt inclined to cry--and Miss Polly was not used to feeling inclined to cry.

Pollyanna picked up the chair.

"Yes'm; I know I banged 'em--those doors," she admitted cheerfully. "You see I'd just found out about the room, and I reckon you'd have banged doors if--" Pollyanna stopped short and eyed her aunt with new interest. "Aunt Polly, *did* you ever bang doors?"

"I hope--not, Pollyanna!" Miss Polly's voice was properly shocked.

"Why, Aunt Polly, what a shame!" Pollyanna's face expressed only concerned sympathy.

"A shame!" repeated Aunt Polly, too dazed to say more.

"Why, yes. You see, if you'd felt like banging doors you'd have banged 'em, of course; and if you didn't, that must have meant that you weren't ever glad over anything--or you would have banged 'em. You couldn't have helped it. And I'm so sorry you weren't ever glad over anything!"

"Polly*anna*!" gasped the lady; but Pollyanna was gone, and only the distant bang of the attic-stairway door answered for her. Pollyanna had gone to help Nancy bring down "her things."

Miss Polly, in the sitting room, felt vaguely disturbed;--but then, of course she *had* been glad--over some things!

Lesson 152

1. Read chapter 11.
2. Tell someone about the chapter.

August came. August brought several surprises and some changes--none of which, however, were really a surprise to Nancy. Nancy, since Pollyanna's arrival, had come to look for surprises and changes.

First there was the kitten.

Pollyanna found the kitten mewing pitifully some distance down the road. When systematic questioning of the neighbors failed to find any one who claimed it, Pollyanna brought it home at once, as a matter of course.

"And I was glad I didn't find any one who owned it, too," she told her aunt in happy confidence; "'cause I wanted to bring it home all the time. I love kitties. I knew you'd be glad to let it live here."

Miss Polly looked at the forlorn little gray bunch of neglected misery in Pollyanna's arms, and shivered: Miss Polly did not care for cats--not even pretty, healthy, clean ones.

"Ugh! Pollyanna! What a dirty little beast! And it's sick, I'm sure, and all mangy and fleay."

"I know it, poor little thing," crooned Pollyanna, tenderly, looking into the little creature's frightened eyes. "And it's all trembly, too, it's so scared. You see it doesn't know, yet, that we're going to keep it, of course."

"No--nor anybody else," retorted Miss Polly, with meaning emphasis.

"Oh, yes, they do," nodded Pollyanna, entirely misunderstanding her aunt's words. "I told everybody we should keep it, if I didn't find where it belonged. I knew you'd be glad to have it--poor little lonesome thing!"

Miss Polly opened her lips and tried to speak; but in vain. The curious helpless feeling that had been hers so often since Pollyanna's arrival, had her now fast in its grip.

"Of course I knew," hurried on Pollyanna, gratefully, "that you wouldn't let a dear little lonesome kitty go hunting for a home when you'd just taken *me* in; and I said so to Mrs. Ford when she asked if you'd let me keep it. Why, I had the Ladies' Aid, you know, and kitty didn't have anybody. I knew you'd feel that way," she nodded happily, as she ran from the room.

"But, Pollyanna, Pollyanna," remonstrated Miss Polly. "I don't--" But Pollyanna was already halfway to the kitchen, calling:

"Nancy, Nancy, just see this dear little kitty that Aunt Polly is going to bring up along with me!" And Aunt Polly, in the sitting room--who abhorred cats--fell back in her chair with a gasp of dismay, powerless to remonstrate.

The next day it was a dog, even dirtier and more forlorn, perhaps, than was the kitten; and again Miss Polly, to her dumfounded amazement, found herself figuring as a kind protector and an angel of mercy--a role that Pollyanna so unhesitatingly thrust upon her as a matter of course, that the woman--who abhorred dogs even more than she did cats, if possible--found herself as before, powerless to remonstrate.

When, in less than a week, however, Pollyanna brought home a small, ragged boy, and confidently claimed the same protection for him, Miss Polly did have something to say. It happened after this wise.

On a pleasant Thursday morning Pollyanna had been taking calf's-foot jelly again to Mrs. Snow. Mrs. Snow and Pollyanna were the best of friends now. Their friendship had started from the third visit Pollyanna had made, the one after she had told Mrs. Snow of the game. Mrs. Snow herself was playing the game now, with Pollyanna. To be sure, she was not playing it very well--she had been sorry for everything for so long, that it was not easy to be glad for anything now. But under Pollyanna's cheery instructions and merry laughter at her mistakes, she was learning fast. To-day, even, to Pollyanna's huge delight, she had said that she was glad Pollyanna brought calf's-foot jelly, because that was just what she had been wanting--she did not know that Milly, at the front door, had told Pollyanna that the minister's wife had already that day sent over a great bowlful of that same kind of jelly.

Pollyanna was thinking of this now when suddenly she saw the boy.

The boy was sitting in a disconsolate little heap by the roadside, whittling half-heartedly at a small stick.

"Hullo," smiled Pollyanna, engagingly.

The boy glanced up, but he looked away again, at once.

"Hullo yourself," he mumbled.

Pollyanna laughed.

"Now you don't look as if you'd be glad even for calf's-foot jelly," she chuckled, stopping before him.

The boy stirred restlessly, gave her a surprised look, and began to whittle again at his stick, with the dull, broken-bladed knife in his hand.

Pollyanna hesitated, then dropped herself comfortably down on the grass near him. In spite of Pollyanna's brave assertion that she was "used to Ladies' Aiders," and "didn't mind," she had sighed at times for some companion of her own age. Hence her determination to make the most of this one.

"My name's Pollyanna Whittier," she began pleasantly. "What's yours?"

Again the boy stirred restlessly. He even almost got to his feet. But he settled back.

"Jimmy Bean," he grunted with ungracious indifference.

"Good! Now we're introduced. I'm glad you did your part--some folks don't, you know. I live at Miss Polly Harrington's house. Where do you live?"

"Nowhere."

"Nowhere! Why, you can't do that--everybody lives somewhere," asserted Pollyanna.

"Well, I don't--just now. I'm huntin' up a new place."

"Oh! Where is it?"

The boy regarded her with scornful eyes.

"Silly! As if I'd be a-huntin' for it--if I knew!"

Pollyanna tossed her head a little. This was not a nice boy, and she did not like to be called "silly." Still, he was somebody besides--old folks. Where did you live--before?" she queried.

"Well, if you ain't the beat'em for askin' questions!" sighed the boy impatiently.

"I have to be," retorted Pollyanna calmly, "else I couldn't find out a thing about you. If you'd talk more I wouldn't talk so much."

The boy gave a short laugh. It was a sheepish laugh, and not quite a willing one; but his face looked a little pleasanter when he spoke this time.

"All right then--here goes! I'm Jimmy Bean, and I'm ten years old goin' on eleven. I come last year ter live at the Orphans' Home; but they've got so many kids there ain't much room for me, an' I wa'n't never wanted, anyhow, I don't believe. So I've quit. I'm goin' ter live somewheres else--but I hain't found the place, yet. I'd *like* a home--jest a common one, ye know, with a mother in it, instead of a Matron. If ye has a home, ye has folks; an' I hain't had folks since--dad died. So I'm a-huntin' now. I've tried four houses, but--they didn't want me--though I said I expected ter work, 'course. There! Is that all you want ter know?" The boy's voice had broken a little over the last two sentences.

"Why, what a shame!" sympathized Pollyanna. "And didn't there anybody want you? O dear! I know just how you feel, because after--after my father died, too, there wasn't anybody but the Ladies' Aid for me, until Aunt Polly said she'd take--" Pollyanna stopped abruptly. The dawning of a wonderful idea began to show in her face.

"Oh, I know just the place for you," she cried. "Aunt Polly'll take you--I know she will! Didn't she take me? And didn't she take Fluffy and Buffy, when they didn't have any one to love them, or any place to go?--and they're only cats and dogs. Oh, come, I know Aunt Polly'll take you! You don't know how good and kind she is!"

Jimmy Bean's thin little face brightened.

"Honest Injun? Would she, now? I'd work, ye know, an' I'm real strong!" He bared a small, bony arm.

"Of course she would! Why, my Aunt Polly is the nicest lady in the world--now that my mama has gone to be a Heaven angel. And there's rooms--heaps of 'em," she continued, springing to her feet, and tugging at his arm. "It's an awful big house. Maybe, though," she added a little anxiously, as they hurried on, "maybe you'll have to sleep in the attic room. I did, at first. But there's screens there now, so 'twon't be so hot, and the flies can't get in, either, to bring in the germ-things on their feet. Did you know about that? It's perfectly lovely! Maybe she'll let you read the book if you're good--I mean, if you're bad. And you've got freckles, too,"--with a critical glance--"so you'll be glad there isn't any looking-glass; and the outdoor picture is nicer than any wall-one could be, so you won't mind sleeping in that room at all, I'm sure," panted Pollyanna, finding suddenly that she needed the rest of her breath for purposes other than talking.

"Gorry!" exclaimed Jimmy Bean tersely and uncomprehendingly, but admiringly. Then he added: "I shouldn't think anybody who could talk like that, runnin', would need ter ask no questions ter fill up time with!"

Pollyanna laughed.

"Well, anyhow, you can be glad of that," she retorted; "for when I'm talking, *you* don't have to!"

When the house was reached, Pollyanna unhesitatingly piloted her companion straight into the presence of her amazed aunt.

"Oh, Aunt Polly," she triumphed. "just look a-here! I've got something ever so much nicer, even, than Fluffy and Buffy for you to bring up. It's a real live boy. He won't mind a bit sleeping in the attic, at first, you know, and he says he'll work; but I shall need him the most of the time to play with, I reckon."

Miss Polly grew white, then very red. She did not quite understand; but she thought she understood enough.

"Pollyanna, what does this mean? Who is this dirty little boy? Where did you find him?" she demanded sharply.

The "dirty little boy" fell back a step and looked toward the door. Pollyanna laughed merrily.

"There, if I didn't forget to tell you his name! I'm as bad as the Man. And he is dirty, too, isn't he? --I mean, the boy is--just like Fluffy and Buffy were when you took them in. But I reckon he'll improve all right by washing, just as they did, and--Oh, I 'most forgot again," she broke off with a laugh. "This is Jimmy Bean, Aunt Polly."

"Well, what is he doing here?"

"Why, Aunt Polly, I just told you!" Pollyanna's eyes were wide with surprise. "He's for you. I brought him home--so he could live here, you know. He wants a home and folks. I told him how good you were to me, and to Fluffy and Buffy, and that I knew you would be to him, because of course he's even nicer than cats and dogs."

Miss Polly dropped back in her chair and raised a shaking hand to her throat. The old helplessness was threatening once more to overcome her. With a visible struggle, however, Miss Polly pulled herself suddenly erect.

"That will do, Pollyanna. This is a little the most absurd thing you've done yet. As if tramp cats and mangy dogs weren't bad enough but you must needs bring home ragged little beggars from the street, who--"

There was a sudden stir from the boy. His eyes flashed and his chin came up. With two strides of his sturdy little legs he confronted Miss Polly fearlessly.

"I ain't a beggar, marm, an' I don't want nothin' o' you. I was cal'latin' ter work, of course, fur my board an' keep. I wouldn't have come ter your old house, anyhow, if this 'ere girl hadn't 'a' made me, a-tellin' me how you was so good an' kind that you'd be jest dyin' ter take me in. So, there!" And he wheeled about and stalked from the room with a dignity that would have been absurd had it not been so pitiful.

"Oh, Aunt Polly," choked Pollyanna. "Why, I thought you'd be *glad* to have him here! I'm sure, I should think you'd be glad--"

Miss Polly raised her hand with a peremptory gesture of silence. Miss Polly's nerves had snapped at last. The "good and kind" of the boy's words were still ringing in her ears, and the old helplessness was almost upon her, she knew. Yet she rallied her forces with the last atom of her will power.

"Pollyanna," she cried sharply, "*will* you stop using that everlasting word 'glad'! It's 'glad'--'glad'--'glad' from morning till night until I think I shall grow wild!"

From sheer amazement Pollyanna's jaw dropped.

"Why, Aunt Polly," she breathed, "I should think you'd be glad to have me gl--Oh!" she broke off, clapping her hand to her lips and hurrying blindly from the room.

Before the boy had reached the end of the driveway, Pollyanna overtook him.

"Boy! Boy! Jimmy Bean, I want you to know how--how sorry I am," she panted, catching him with a detaining hand.

"Sorry nothin'! I ain't blamin' you," retorted the boy, sullenly. "But I ain't no beggar!" he added, with sudden spirit.

"Of course you aren't! But you mustn't blame auntie," appealed Pollyanna. "Probably I didn't do the introducing right, anyhow; and I reckon I didn't tell her much who you were. She is good and kind, really--she's always been; but I probably didn't explain it right. I do wish I could find some place for you, though!"

The boy shrugged his shoulders and half turned away.

"Never mind. I guess I can find one myself. I ain't no beggar, you know."

Pollyanna was frowning thoughtfully. Of a sudden she turned, her face illumined.

"Say, I'll tell you what I *will* do! The Ladies' Aid meets this afternoon. I heard Aunt Polly say so. I'll lay your case before them. That's what father always did, when he wanted anything--educating the heathen and new carpets, you know."

The boy turned fiercely.

"Well, I ain't a heathen or a new carpet. Besides--what is a Ladies' Aid?"

Pollyanna stared in shocked disapproval.

"Why, Jimmy Bean, wherever have you been brought up?--not to know what a Ladies' Aid is!"

"Oh, all right--if you ain't tellin'," grunted the boy, turning and beginning to walk away indifferently.

Pollyanna sprang to his side at once.

"It's--it's--why, it's just a lot of ladies that meet and sew and give suppers and raise money and--and talk; that's what a Ladies' Aid is. They're awfully kind--that is, most of mine was, back home. I haven't seen this one here, but they're always good, I reckon. I'm going to tell them about you this afternoon."

Again the boy turned fiercely.

"Not much you will! Maybe you think I'm goin' ter stand 'round an' hear a whole *lot* o' women call me a beggar, instead of jest *one*! Not much!"

"Oh, but you wouldn't be there," argued Pollyanna, quickly. "I'd go alone, of course, and tell them."

"You would?"

"Yes; and I'd tell it better this time," hurried on Pollyanna, quick to see the signs of relenting in the boy's face. "And there'd be some of 'em, I know, that would be glad to give you a home."

"I'd work--don't forget ter say that," cautioned the boy.

"Of course not," promised Pollyanna, happily, sure now that her point was gained. "Then I'll let you know to-morrow."

"Where?"

"By the road--where I found you to-day; near Mrs. Snow's house."

"All right. I'll be there." The boy paused before he went on slowly: "Maybe I'd better go back, then, for ter-night, ter the Home. You see I hain't no other place ter stay; and--and I didn't leave till this mornin'. I slipped out. I didn't tell 'em I wasn't comin' back, else they'd pretend I couldn't come-- though I'm thinkin' they won't do no worryin' when I don't show up sometime. They ain't like *folks*, ye know. They don't *care*!"

"I know," nodded Pollyanna, with understanding eyes. "But I'm sure, when I see you to-morrow, I'll have just a common home and folks that do care all ready for you. Good-by!" she called brightly, as she turned back toward the house.

In the sitting-room window at that moment, Miss Polly, who had been watching the two children, followed with sombre eyes the boy until a bend of the road hid him from sight. Then she sighed, turned, and walked listlesly up-stairs--and Miss Polly did not usually move listlessly. In her ears still was the boy's scornful "you was so good and kind." In her heart was a curious sense of desolation--as of something lost.

Lesson 153

1. Read chapter 12.
2. Tell someone about the chapter.

Dinner, which came at noon in the Harrington homestead, was a silent meal on the day of the Ladies' Aid meeting. Pollyanna, it is true, tried to talk; but she did not make a success of it, chiefly because four times she was obliged to break off a "glad" in the middle of it, much to her blushing discomfort. The fifth time it happened, Miss Polly moved her head wearily.

"There, there, child, say it, if you want to," she sighed. "I'm sure I'd rather you did than not if it's going to make all this fuss."

Pollyanna's puckered little face cleared.

"Oh, thank you. I'm afraid it would be pretty hard--not to say it. You see I've played it so long."

"You've--what?" demanded Aunt Polly.

"Played it--the game, you know, that father--" Pollyanna stopped with a painful blush at finding herself so soon again on forbidden ground.

Aunt Polly frowned and said nothing. The rest of the meal was a silent one.

Pollyanna was not sorry to hear Aunt Polly tell the minister's wife over the telephone, a little later, that she would not be at the Ladies' Aid meeting that afternoon, owing to a headache. When Aunt Polly went up-stairs to her room and closed the door, Pollyanna tried to be sorry for the headache; but she could not help feeling glad that her aunt was not to be present that afternoon when she laid the case of Jimmy Bean before the Ladies' Aid. She could not forget that Aunt Polly had called Jimmy Bean a little beggar; and she did not want Aunt Polly to call him that--before the Ladies' Aid.

Pollyanna knew that the Ladies' Aid met at two o'clock in the chapel next the church, not quite half a mile from home. She planned her going, therefore, so that she should get there a little before three.

"I want them all to be there," she said to herself; "else the very one that wasn't there might be the one who would be wanting to give Jimmy Bean a home; and, of course, two o'clock always means three, really--to Ladies' Aiders."

Quietly, but with confident courage, Pollyanna ascended the chapel steps, pushed open the door and entered the vestibule. A soft babel of feminine chatter and laughter came from the main room. Hesitating only a brief moment Pollyanna pushed open one of the inner doors.

The chatter dropped to a surprised hush. Pollyanna advanced a little timidly. Now that the time had come, she felt unwontedly shy. After all, these half-strange, half-familiar faces about her were not her own dear Ladies' Aid.

"How do you do, Ladies' Aiders?" she faltered politely. "I'm Pollyanna Whittier. I--I reckon some of you know me, maybe; anyway, I do *you*--only I don't know you all together this way."

The silence could almost be felt now. Some of the ladies did know this rather extraordinary niece of their fellow-member, and nearly all had heard of her; but not one of them could think of anything to say, just then.

"I--I've come to--to lay the case before you," stammered Pollyanna, after a moment, unconsciously falling into her father's familiar phraseology.

There was a slight rustle.

"Did--did your aunt send you, my dear?" asked Mrs. Ford, the minister's wife.

Pollyanna colored a little.

"Oh, no. I came all by myself. You see, I'm used to Ladies' Aiders. It was Ladies' Aiders that brought me up--with father."

Somebody tittered hysterically, and the minister's wife frowned.

"Yes, dear. What is it?"

"Well, it--it's Jimmy Bean," sighed Pollyanna. "He hasn't any home except the Orphan one, and they're full, and don't want him, anyhow, he thinks; so he wants another. He wants one of the common kind, that has a mother instead of a Matron in it--folks, you know, that'll care. He's ten years old going on eleven. I thought some of you might like him--to live with you, you know."

"Well, did you ever!" murmured a voice, breaking the dazed pause that followed Pollyanna's words.

With anxious eyes Pollyanna swept the circle of faces about her.

"Oh, I forgot to say; he will work," she supplemented eagerly.

Still there was silence; then, coldly, one or two women began to question her. After a time they all had the story and began to talk among themselves, animatedly, not quite pleasantly.

Pollyanna listened with growing anxiety. Some of what was said she could not understand. She did gather, after a time, however, that there was no woman there who had a home to give him, though every woman seemed to think that some of the others might take him, as there were several who had no little boys of their own already in their homes. But there was no one who agreed herself to take him. Then she heard the minister's wife suggest timidly that they, as a society, might perhaps assume his support and education instead of sending quite so much money this year to the little boys in far-away India.

A great many ladies talked then, and several of them talked all at once, and even more loudly and more unpleasantly than before. It seemed that their society was famous for its offering to Hindu missions, and several said they should die of mortification if it should be less this year. Some of what was said at this time Pollyanna again thought she could not have understood, too, for it sounded almost as if they did not care at all what the money *did*, so long as the sum opposite the name of their society in a certain "report" "headed the list"--and of course that could not be what they meant at all! But it was all very confusing, and not quite pleasant, so that Pollyanna was glad, indeed, when at last she found herself outside in the hushed, sweet air--only she was very sorry, too: for she knew it was not going to be easy, or anything but sad, to tell Jimmy Bean to-morrow that the Ladies' Aid had decided that they would rather send all their money to bring up the little

India boys than to save out enough to bring up one little boy in their own town, for which they would not get "a bit of credit in the report," according to the tall lady who wore spectacles.

"Not but that it's good, of course, to send money to the heathen, and I shouldn't want 'em not to send *some* there," sighed Pollyanna to herself, as she trudged sorrowfully along. "But they acted as if little boys *here* weren't any account--only little boys 'way off. I should *think*, though, they'd rather see Jimmy Bean grow--than just a report!"

Lesson 154

1. Read chapter 13.
2. Tell someone about the chapter.

Pollyanna had not turned her steps toward home, when she left the chapel. She had turned them, instead, toward Pendleton Hill. It had been a hard day, for all it had been a "vacation one" (as she termed the infrequent days when there was no sewing or cooking lesson), and Pollyanna was sure that nothing would do her quite so much good as a walk through the green quiet of Pendleton Woods. Up Pendleton Hill, therefore, she climbed steadily, in spite of the warm sun on her back.

"I don't have to get home till half-past five, anyway," she was telling herself; "and it'll be so much nicer to go around by the way of the woods, even if I do have to climb to get there."

It was very beautiful in the Pendleton Woods, as Pollyanna knew by experience. But to-day it seemed even more delightful than ever, notwithstanding her disappointment over what she must tell Jimmy Bean to-morrow.

"I wish they were up here--all those ladies who talked so loud," sighed Pollyanna to herself, raising her eyes to the patches of vivid blue between the sunlit green of the tree-tops. "Anyhow, if they were up here, I just reckon they'd change and take Jimmy Bean for their little boy, all right," she finished, secure in her conviction, but unable to give a reason for it, even to herself.

Suddenly Pollyanna lifted her head and listened. A dog had barked some distance ahead. A moment later he came dashing toward her, still barking.

"Hullo, doggie--hullo!" Pollyanna snapped her fingers at the dog and looked expectantly down the path. She had seen the dog once before, she was sure. He had been then with the Man, Mr. John Pendleton. She was looking now, hoping to see him. For some minutes she watched eagerly, but he did not appear. Then she turned her attention toward the dog.

The dog, as even Pollyanna could see, was acting strangely. He was still barking--giving little short, sharp yelps, as if of alarm. He was running back and forth, too, in the path ahead. Soon they reached a side path, and down this the little dog fairly flew, only to come back at once, whining and barking.

"Ho! That isn't the way home," laughed Pollyanna, still keeping to the main path.

The little dog seemed frantic now. Back and forth, back and forth, between Pollyanna and the side path he vibrated, barking and whining pitifully. Every quiver of his little brown body, and every glance from his beseeching brown eyes were eloquent with appeal--so eloquent that at last Pollyanna understood, turned, and followed him.

Straight ahead, now, the little dog dashed madly; and it was not long before Pollyanna came upon the reason for it all: a man lying motionless at the foot of a steep, overhanging mass of rock a few yards from the side path.

A twig cracked sharply under Pollyanna's foot, and the man turned his head. With a cry of dismay Pollyanna ran to his side.

"Mr. Pendleton! Oh, are you hurt?"

"Hurt? Oh, no! I'm just taking a siesta in the sunshine," snapped the man irritably. "See here, how much do you know? What can you do? Have you got any sense?"

Pollyanna caught her breath with a little gasp, but--as was her habit--she answered the questions literally, one by one.

"Why, Mr. Pendleton, I--I don't know so very much, and I can't do a great many things; but most of the Ladies' Aiders, except Mrs. Rawson, said I had real good sense. I heard 'em say so one day- they didn't know I heard, though."

The man smiled grimly.

"There, there, child, I beg your pardon, I'm sure; it's only this confounded leg of mine. Now listen." He paused, and with some difficulty reached his hand into his trousers pocket and brought out a bunch of keys, singling out one between his thumb and forefinger. "Straight through the path there, about five minutes' walk, is my house. This key will admit you to the side door under the porte-cochere. Do you know what a porte-cochere is?"

"Oh, yes, sir. Auntie has one with a sun parlor over it. That's the roof I slept on--only I didn't sleep, you know. They found me."

"Eh? Oh! Well, when you get into the house, go straight through the vestibule and hall to the door at the end. On the big, flat-topped desk in the middle of the room you'll find a telephone. Do you know how to use a telephone?"

"Oh, yes, sir! Why, once when Aunt Polly--"

"Never mind Aunt Polly now," cut in the man scowlingly, as he tried to move himself a little.

"Hunt up Dr. Thomas Chilton's number on the card you'll find somewhere around there--it ought to be on the hook down at the side, but it probably won't be. You know a telephone card, I suppose, when you see one!"

"Oh, yes, sir! I just love Aunt Polly's. There's such a lot of queer names, and--"

"Tell Dr. Chilton that John Pendleton is at the foot of Little Eagle Ledge in Pendleton Woods with a broken leg, and to come at once with a stretcher and two men. He'll know what to do besides that. Tell him to come by the path from the house."

"A broken leg? Oh, Mr. Pendleton, how perfectly awful!" shuddered Pollyanna. "But I'm so glad I came! Can't *I* do--"

"Yes, you can--but evidently you won't! *Will* you go and do what I ask and stop talking," moaned the man, faintly. And, with a little sobbing cry, Pollyanna went.

Pollyanna did not stop now to look up at the patches of blue between the sunlit tops of the trees. She kept her eyes on the ground to make sure that no twig nor stone tripped her hurrying feet.

It was not long before she came in sight of the house. She had seen it before, though never so near as this. She was almost frightened now at the massiveness of the great pile of gray stone with its pillared verandas and its imposing entrance. Pausing only a moment, however, she sped across the big neglected lawn and around the house to the side door under the porte-cochere. Her fingers, stiff from their tight clutch upon the keys, were anything but skilful in their efforts to turn the bolt in the lock; but at last the heavy, carved door swung slowly back on its hinges.

Pollyanna caught her breath. In spite of her feeling of haste, she paused a moment and looked fearfully through the vestibule to the wide, sombre hall beyond, her thoughts in a whirl. This was John Pendleton's house; the house of mystery; the house into which no one but its master entered; the house which sheltered, somewhere--a skeleton. Yet she, Pollyanna, was expected to enter alone these fearsome rooms, and telephone the doctor that the master of the house lay now--

With a little cry Pollyanna, looking neither to the right nor the left, fairly ran through the hall to the door at the end and opened it.

The room was large, and sombre with dark woods and hangings like the hall; but through the west window the sun threw a long shaft of gold across the floor, gleamed dully on the tarnished brass andirons in the fireplace, and touched the nickel of the telephone on the great desk in the middle of the room. It was toward this desk that Pollyanna hurriedly tiptoed.

The telephone card was not on its hook; it was on the floor. But Pollyanna found it, and ran her shaking forefinger down through the C's to "Chilton." In due time she had Dr. Chilton himself at the other end of the wires, and was tremblingly delivering her message and answering the doctor's terse, pertinent questions. This done, she hung up the receiver and drew a long breath of relief.

Only a brief glance did Pollyanna give about her; then, with a confused vision in her eyes of crimson draperies, book-lined walls, a littered floor, an untidy desk, innumerable closed doors (any one of which might conceal a skeleton), and everywhere dust, dust, dust, she fled back through the hall to the great carved door, still half open as she had left it.

In what seemed, even to the injured man, an incredibly short time, Pollyanna was back in the woods at the man's side.

"Well, what is the trouble? Couldn't you get in?" he demanded.

Pollyanna opened wide her eyes.

"Why, of course I could! I'm *here*," she answered. "As if I'd be here if I hadn't got in! And the doctor will be right up just as soon as possible with the men and things. He said he knew just where you were, so I didn't stay to show him. I wanted to be with you."

"Did you?" smiled the man, grimly. "Well, I can't say I admire your taste. I should think you might find pleasanter companions."

"Do you mean--because you're so--cross?"

"Thanks for your frankness. Yes."

Pollyanna laughed softly.

"But you're only cross *outside*--You aren't cross inside a bit!"

"Indeed! How do you know that?" asked the man, trying to change the position of his head without moving the rest of his body.

"Oh, lots of ways; there--like that--the way you act with the dog," she added, pointing to the long, slender hand that rested on the dog's sleek head near him. "It's funny how dogs and cats know the insides of folks better than other folks do, isn't it? Say, I'm going to hold your head," she finished abruptly.

The man winced several times and groaned once; softly while the change was being made; but in the end he found Pollyanna's lap a very welcome substitute for the rocky hollow in which his head had lain before.

"Well, that is--better," he murmured faintly.

He did not speak again for some time. Pollyanna, watching his face, wondered if he were asleep. She did not think he was. He looked as if his lips were tight shut to keep back moans of pain. Pollyanna herself almost cried aloud as she looked at his great, strong body lying there so helpless. One hand, with fingers tightly clenched, lay outflung, motionless. The other, limply open, lay on the dog's head. The dog, his wistful, eager eyes on his master's face, was motionless, too.

Minute by minute the time passed. The sun dropped lower in the west and the shadows grew deeper under the trees. Pollyanna sat so still she hardly seemed to breathe. A bird alighted fearlessly within reach of her hand, and a squirrel whisked his bushy tail on a tree-branch almost under her nose-- yet with his bright little eyes all the while on the motionless dog.

At last the dog pricked up his ears and whined softly; then he gave a short, sharp bark. The next moment Pollyanna heard voices, and very soon their owners appeared--three men carrying a stretcher and various other articles.

The tallest of the party--a smooth-shaven, kind-eyed man whom Pollyanna knew by sight as "Dr. Chilton"--advanced cheerily.

"Well, my little lady, playing nurse?"

"Oh, no, sir," smiled Pollyanna. "I've only held his head--I haven't given him a mite of medicine. But I'm glad I was here."

"So am I," nodded the doctor, as he turned his absorbed attention to the injured man.

Lesson 155

1. Read chapter 14.
2. Tell someone about the chapter.

Pollyanna was a little late for supper on the night of the accident to John Pendleton; but, as it happened, she escaped without reproof.

Nancy met her at the door.

"Well, if I ain't glad ter be settin' my two eyes on you," she sighed in obvious relief. "It's half-past six!"

"I know it," admitted Pollyanna anxiously; "but I'm not to blame--truly I'm not. And I don't think even Aunt Polly will say I am, either."

"She won't have the chance," retorted Nancy, with huge satisfaction. "She's gone."

"Gone!" gasped Pollyanna. "You don't mean that I've driven her away?" Through Pollyanna's mind at the moment trooped remorseful memories of the morning with its unwanted boy, cat, and dog, and its unwelcome "glad" and forbidden "father that would spring to her forgetful little tongue. "Oh, I *didn't* drive her away?"

"Not much you did," scoff ed Nancy. "Her cousin died suddenly down to Boston, and she had ter go. She had one o' them yeller telegram letters after you went away this afternoon, and she won't be back for three days. Now I guess we're glad all right. We'll be keepin' house tergether, jest you and me, all that time. We will, we will!"

Pollyanna looked shocked.

"Glad! Oh, Nancy, when it's a funeral?"

"Oh, but 'twa'n't the funeral I was glad for, Miss Pollyanna. It was--" Nancy stopped abruptly. A shrewd twinkle came into her eyes. "Why, Miss Pollyanna, as if it wa'n't yerself that was teachin' me ter play the game," she reproached her gravely.

Pollyanna puckered her forehead into a troubled frown.

"I can't help it, Nancy," she argued with a shake of her head. "It must be that there are some things that 'tisn't right to play the game on--and I'm sure funerals is one of them. There's nothing in a funeral to be glad about."

Nancy chuckled.

"We can be glad 'tain't our'n," she observed demurely. But Pollyanna did not hear. She had begun to tell of the accident; and in a moment Nancy, open-mouthed, was listening.

At the appointed place the next afternoon, Pollyanna met Jimmy Bean according to agreement. As was to be expected, of course, Jimmy showed keen disappointment that the Ladies' Aid preferred a little India boy to himself.

"Well, maybe 'tis natural," he sighed. "Of course things you don't know about are always nicer'n things you do, same as the pertater on 'tother side of the plate is always the biggest. But I wish I looked that way ter somebody 'way off. Wouldn't it be jest great, now, if only somebody over in India wanted *me*?"

Pollyanna clapped her hands.

"Why, of course! That's the very thing, Jimmy! I'll write to my Ladies' Aiders about you. They aren't over in India; they're only out West--but that's awful far away, just the same. I reckon you'd think so if you'd come all the way here as I did!"

Jimmy's face brightened.

"Do you think they would--truly--take me?" he asked.

"Of course they would! Don't they take little boys in India to bring up? Well, they can just play you are the little India boy this time. I reckon you're far enough away to make a report, all right. You wait. I'll write 'em. I'll write Mrs. White. No, I'll write Mrs. Jones. Mrs. White has got the most money, but Mrs. Jones gives the most--which is kind of funny, isn't it?--when you think of it. But I reckon some of the Aiders will take you."

"All right--but don't furgit ter say I'll work fur my board an' keep," put in Jimmy. "I ain't no beggar, an' biz'ness is biz'ness, even with Ladies' Aiders, I'm thinkin'." He hesitated, then added: "An' I s'pose I better stay where I be fur a spell yet--till you hear."

"Of course," nodded Pollyanna emphatically. "Then I'll know just where to find you. And they'll take you--I'm sure you're far enough away for that. Didn't Aunt Polly take--Say!" she broke off, suddenly, "*Do* you suppose I was Aunt Polly's little girl from India?"

"Well, if you ain't the queerest kid," grinned Jimmy, as he turned away.

It was about a week after the accident in Pendleton Woods that Pollyanna said to her aunt one morning:

"Aunt Polly, please would you mind very much if I took Mrs. Snow's calf's-foot jelly this week to some one else? I'm sure Mrs. Snow wouldn't--this once."

"Dear me, Pollyanna, what *are* you up to now?" sighed her aunt. "You *are* the most extraordinary child!"

Pollyanna frowned a little anxiously.

"Aunt Polly, please, what is extraordinary? If you're *ex*traordinary you can't be *or*dinary, can you?"

"You certainly can not."

"Oh, that's all right, then. I'm glad I'm *ex*traordinary," sighed Pollyanna, her face clearing. "You see, Mrs. White used to say Mrs. Rawson was a very ordinary woman--and she disliked Mrs. Rawson something awful. They were always fight--I mean, father had--that is, I mean, *we* had more trouble keeping peace between them than we did between any of the rest of the Aiders," corrected Pollyanna, a little breathless from her efforts to steer between the Scylla of her father's past commands in regard to speaking of church quarrels, and the Charybdis of her aunt's present commands in regard to speaking of her father.

"Yes, yes; well, never mind," interposed Aunt Polly, a trifle impatiently. "You do run on so, Pollyanna, and no matter what we're talking about you always bring up at those Ladies' Aiders!"

"Yes'm," smiled Pollyanna, cheerfully, "I reckon I do, maybe. But you see they used to bring me up, and--"

"That will do, Pollyanna," interrupted a cold voice. "Now what is it about this jelly?"

"Nothing, Aunt Polly, truly, that you would mind, I'm sure. You let me take jelly to *her*, so I thought you would to *him*--this once. You see, broken legs aren't like--like lifelong invalids, so his won't last forever as Mrs. Snow's does, and she can have all the rest of the things after just once or twice."

" 'Him'? 'He'? 'Broken leg'? What are you talking about, Pollyanna?"

Pollyanna stared; then her face relaxed.

"Oh, I forgot. I reckon you didn't know. You see, it happened while you were gone. It was the very day you went that I found him in the woods, you know; and I had to unlock his house and telephone for the men and the doctor, and hold his head, and everything. And of course then I came away and haven't seen him since. But when Nancy made the jelly for Mrs. Snow this week I thought how nice it would be if I could take it to him instead of her, just this once. Aunt Polly, may I?"

"Yes, yes, I suppose so," acquiesced Miss Polly, a little wearily. "Who did you say he was?"

"The Man. I mean, Mr. John Pendleton."

Miss Polly almost sprang from her chair.

"*John Pendleton!*"

"Yes. Nancy told me his name. Maybe you know him."

Miss Polly did not answer this. Instead she asked:

"Do *you* know him?"

Pollyanna nodded.

"Oh, yes. He always speaks and smiles--now. He's only cross *outside*, you know. I'll go and get the jelly. Nancy had it 'most fixed when I came in," finished Pollyanna, already halfway across the room.

"Pollyanna, wait!" Miss Polly's voice was suddenly very stern. I've changed my mind. I would prefer that Mrs. Snow had that jelly to-day--as usual. That is all. You may go now."

Pollyanna's face fell.

"Oh, but Aunt Polly, *hers* will last. She can always be sick and have things, you know; but his is just a broken leg, and legs don't last--I mean, broken ones. He's had it a whole week now."

"Yes, I remember. I heard Mr. John Pendleton had met with an accident," said Miss Polly, a little stiffly; "but--I do not care to be sending jelly to John Pendleton, Pollyanna."

"I know, he is cross--outside," admitted Pollyanna, sadly, "so I suppose you don't like him. But I wouldn't say 'twas you sent it. I'd say 'twas me. I like him. I'd be glad to send him jelly."

Miss Polly began to shake her head again. Then, suddenly, she stopped, and asked in a curiously quiet voice:

"Does he know who you--are, Pollyanna?"

The little girl sighed.

"I reckon not. I told him my name, once, but he never calls me it--never."

"Does he know where you--live?"

"Oh, no. I never told him that."

"Then he doesn't know you're my--niece?"

"I don't think so."

For a moment there was silence. Miss Polly was looking at Pollyanna with eyes that did not seem to see her at all. The little girl, shifting impatiently from one small foot to the other, sighed audibly. Then Miss Polly roused herself with a start.

"Very well, Pollyanna," she said at last , still in that queer voice, so unlike her own; "you may you may take the jelly to Mr. Pendleton as your own gift. But understand: I do not send it. Be very sure that he does not think I do!"

"Yes'm--no'm--thank you, Aunt Polly," exulted Pollyanna, as she flew through the door.

Lesson 156

1. Read chapter 15.
2. Tell someone about the chapter.

The great gray pile of masonry looked very different to Pollyanna when she made her second visit to the house of Mr. John Pendleton. Windows were open, an elderly woman was hanging out clothes in the back yard, and the doctor's gig stood under the porte-cochere.

As before Pollyanna went to the side door. This time she rang the bell--her fingers were not stiff to-day from a tight clutch on a bunch of keys.

A familiar-looking small dog bounded up the steps to greet her, but there was a slight delay before the woman who had been hanging out the clothes opened the door.

"If you please, I've brought some calf's-foot jelly for Mr. Pendleton," smiled Pollyanna.

"Thank you," said the woman, reaching for the bowl in the little girl's hand. "Who shall I say sent it? And it's calf's-foot jelly?"

The doctor, coming into the hall at that moment, heard the woman's words and saw the disappointed look on Pollyanna's face. He stepped quickly forward.

"Ah! Some calf's-foot jelly?" he asked genially. "That will be fine! Maybe you'd like to see our patient, eh?"

"Oh, yes, sir," beamed Pollyanna; and the woman, in obedience to a nod from the doctor, led the way down the hall at once, though plainly with vast surprise on her face.

Behind the doctor, a young man (a trained nurse from the nearest city) gave a disturbed exclamation.

"But, Doctor, didn't Mr. Pendleton give orders not to admit--any one?"

"Oh, yes," nodded the doctor, imperturbably. "But I'm giving orders now. I'll take the risk." Then he added whimsically: "You don't know, of course; but that little girl is better than a six-quart bottle of tonic any day. If anything or anybody can take the grouch out of Pendleton this afternoon, she can. That's why I sent her in."

"Who is she?"

For one brief moment the doctor hesitated.

"She's the niece of one of our best known residents. Her name is Pollyanna Whittier. I--I don't happen to enjoy a very extensive personal acquaintance with the little lady as yet; but lots of my patients do--I'm thankful to say!"

The nurse smiled.

"Indeed! And what are the special ingredients of this wonder-working--tonic of hers?"

The doctor shook his head.

"I don't know. As near as I can find out it is an overwhelming, unquenchable gladness for everything that has happened or is going to happen. At any rate, her quaint speeches are constantly being repeated to me, and, as near as I can make out, 'just being glad' is the tenor of most of them. All is," he added, with another whimsical smile, as he stepped out on to the porch, "I wish I could prescribe her--and buy her--as I would a box of pills;--though if there gets to be many of her in the world, you and I might as well go to ribbon-selling and ditch-digging for all the money we'd get out of nursing and doctoring," he laughed, picking up the reins and stepping into the gig.

Pollyanna, meanwhile, in accordance with the doctor's orders, was being escorted to John Pendleton's rooms.

Her way led through the great library at the end of the hall, and, rapid as was her progress through it, Pollyanna saw at once that great changes had taken place. The book-lined walls and the crimson curtains were the same; but there was no litter on the floor, no untidiness on the desk, and not so much as a grain of dust in sight. The telephone card hung in its proper place, and the brass andirons had been polished. One of the mysterious doors was open, and it was toward this that the maid led the way. A moment later Pollyanna found herself in a sumptuously furnished bedroom while the maid was saying in a frightened voice:

"If you please, sir, here--here's a little girl with some jelly. The doctor said I was to--to bring her in."

The next moment Pollyanna found herself alone with a very cross-looking man lying flat on his back in bed.

"See here, didn't I say--" began an angry voice. "Oh, it's you!" it broke off not very graciously, as Pollyanna advanced toward the bed.

"Yes, sir," smiled Pollyanna. "Oh, I'm so glad they let me in! You see, at first the lady 'most took my jelly, and I was so afraid I wasn't going to see you at all. Then the doctor came, and he said I might. Wasn't he lovely to let me see you?"

In spite of himself the man's lips twitched into a smile; but all he said was "Humph!"

"And I've brought you some jelly," resumed Pollyanna; "--calf's-foot. I hope you like it?" There was a rising inflection in her voice.

"Never ate it." The fleeting smile had gone, and the scowl had come back to the man's face.

For a brief instant Pollyanna's countenance showed disappointment; but it cleared as she set the bowl of jelly down.

"Didn't you? Well, if you didn't, then you can't know you *don't* like it, anyhow, can you? So I reckon I'm glad you haven't, after all. Now, if you knew--"

"Yes, yes; well, there's one thing I know all right, and that is that I'm flat on my back right here this minute, and that I'm liable to stay here--till doomsday, I guess."

Pollyanna looked shocked.

"Oh, no! It couldn't be till doomsday, you know, when the angel Gabriel blows his trumpet, unless it should come quicker than we think it will--oh, of course, I know the Bible says it may come quicker than we think, but I don't think it will--that is, of course I believe the Bible; but I mean I don't think it will come as much quicker as it would if it should come now, and--"

John Pendleton laughed suddenly--and aloud. The nurse, coming in at that moment, heard the laugh, and beat a hurried--but a very silent--retreat. He had the air of a frightened cook who, seeing the danger of a breath of cold air striking a half-done cake, hastily shuts the oven door.

"Aren't you getting a little mixed?" asked John Pendleton of Pollyanna.

The little girl laughed.

"Maybe. But what I mean is, that legs don't last--broken ones, you know--like lifelong invalids, same as Mrs. Snow has got. So yours won't last till doomsday at all. I should think you could be glad of that."

"Oh, I am," retorted the man grimly.

"And you didn't break but one. You can be glad 'twasn't two." Pollyanna was warming to her task.

"Of course! So fortunate," sniffed the man, with uplifted eyebrows; "looking at it from that standpoint, I suppose I might be glad I wasn't a centipede and didn't break fifty!"

Pollyanna chuckled.

"Oh, that's the best yet," she crowed. "I know what a centipede is; they've got lots of legs. And you can be glad--"

"Oh, of course," interrupted the man, sharply, all the old bitterness coming back to his voice; "I can be glad, too, for all the rest, I suppose--the nurse, and the doctor, and that confounded woman in the kitchen!"

"Why, yes, sir--only think how bad 'twould be if you *didn't* have them!"

"Well, I--eh?" he demanded sharply.

"Why, I say, only think how bad it would be if you didn't have 'em--and you lying here like this!"

"As if that wasn't the very thing that was at the bottom of the whole matter," retorted the man, testily, "because I am lying here like this! And yet you expect me to say I'm glad because of a fool woman who disarranges the whole house and calls it 'regulating,' and a man who aids and abets her in it, and calls it 'nursing,' to say nothing of the doctor who eggs 'em both on--and the whole bunch of them, meanwhile, expecting me to pay them for it, and pay them well, too!"

Pollyanna frowned sympathetically.

"Yes, I know. *That* part is too bad--about the money--when you've been saving it, too, all this time."

"When--eh?"

"Saving it--buying beans and fish balls, you know. Say, *do* you like beans?--or do you like turkey better, only on account of the sixty cents?"

"Look a-here, child, what are you talking about?"

Pollyanna smiled radiantly.

"About your money, you know--denying yourself, and saving it for the heathen. You see, I found out about it. Why, Mr. Pendleton, that's one of the ways I knew you weren't cross inside. Nancy told me."

The man's jaw dropped.

"Nancy told you I was saving money for the--Well, may I inquire who Nancy is?"

"Our Nancy. She works for Aunt Polly."

"Aunt Polly! Well, who is Aunt Polly?"

"She's Miss Polly Harrington. I live with her."

The man made a sudden movement.

"Miss--Polly--Harrington!" he breathed. "You live with--*her*!"

"Yes; I'm her niece. She's taken me to bring up--on account of my mother, you know," faltered Pollyanna, in a low voice. "She was her sister. And after father--went to be with her and the rest of us in Heaven, there wasn't any one left for me down here but the Ladies' Aid; so she took me."

The man did not answer. His face, as he lay back on the pillow now, was very white--so white that Pollyanna was frightened. She rose uncertainly to her feet.

"I reckon maybe I'd better go now," she proposed. "I--I hope you'll like--the jelly."

The man turned his head suddenly, and opened his eyes. There was a curious longing in their dark depths which even Pollyanna saw, and at which she marvelled.

"And so you are--Miss Polly Harrington's niece," he said gently.

"Yes, sir."

Still the man's dark eyes lingered on her face, until Pollyanna, feeling vaguely restless, murmured:

"I--I suppose you know--her."

John Pendleton's lips curved in an odd smile.

"Oh, yes; I know her." He hesitated, then went on, still with that curious smile. "But--you don't mean--you can't mean that it was Miss Polly Harrington who sent that jelly--to me?" he said slowly,

Pollyanna looked distressed.

"N-no, sir: she didn't. She said I must be very sure not to let you think she did send it. But I--"

"I thought as much," vouchsafed the man, shortly, turning away his head. And Pollyanna, still more distressed, tiptoed from the room.

Under the porte-cochere she found the doctor waiting in his gig. The nurse stood on the steps.

"Well, Miss Pollyanna, may I have the pleasure of seeing you home?" asked the doctor smilingly. "I started to drive on a few minutes ago; then it occurred to me that I'd wait for you."

"Thank you, sir. I'm glad you did. I just love to ride," beamed Pollyanna, as he reached out his hand to help her in.

"Do you?" smiled the doctor, nodding his head in farewell to the young man on the steps. "Well, as near as I can judge, there are a good many things you 'love' to do--eh?" he added, as they drove briskly away.

Pollyanna laughed.

"Why, I don't know. I reckon perhaps there are," she admitted. "I like to do 'most everything that's *living*. Of course I don't like the other things very well--sewing, and reading out loud, and all that. But *they* aren't *living*."

"No? What are they, then?"

"Aunt Polly says they're 'learning to live,'" sighed Pollyanna, with a rueful smile.

The doctor smiled now--a little queerly.

"Does she? Well, I should think she might say--just that."

"Yes," responded Pollyanna. "But I don't see it that way at all. I don't think you have to *learn* how to live. I didn't, anyhow."

The doctor drew a long sigh.

"After all, I'm afraid some of us--do have to, little girl," he said. Then, for a time he was silent. Pollyanna, stealing a glance at his face, felt vaguely sorry for him. He looked so sad. She wished, uneasily, that she could "do something." It was this, perhaps, that caused her to say in a timid voice:

"Dr. Chilton, I should think being a doctor would be the very gladdest kind of a business there was."

The doctor turned in surprise.

"'Gladdest'!--when I see so much suffering always, everywhere I go?" he cried.

She nodded.

"I know; but you're *helping* it--don't you see?--and of course you're glad to help it! And so that makes you the gladdest of any of us, all the time."

The doctor's eyes filled with sudden hot tears. The doctor's life was a singularly lonely one. He had no wife and no home save his two-room office in a boarding house. His profession was very dear to him. Looking now into Pollyanna's shining eyes, he felt as if a loving hand had been suddenly laid on his head in blessing. He knew, too, that never again would a long day's work or a long night's weariness be quite without that new-found exaltation that had come to him through Pollyanna's eyes.

"God bless you, little girl," he said unsteadily. Then, with the bright smile his patients knew and loved so well, he added: "And I'm thinking, after all, that it was the doctor, quite as much as his patients, that needed a draft of that tonic!" All of which puzzled Pollyanna very much--until a chipmunk, running across the road, drove the whole matter from her mind.

The doctor left Pollyanna at her own door, smiled at Nancy, who was sweeping off the front porch, then drove rapidly away.

"I've had a perfectly beautiful ride with the doctor," announced Pollyanna, bounding up the steps. "He's lovely, Nancy!"

"Is he?"

"Yes. And I told him I should think his business would be the very gladdest one there was."

"What!--goin' ter see sick folks--an' folks what ain't sick but thinks they is, which is worse?" Nancy's face showed open skepticism.

Pollyanna laughed gleefully.

"Yes. That's 'most what he said, too; but there is a way to be glad, even then. Guess!"

Nancy frowned in meditation. Nancy was getting so she could play this game of "being glad" quite successfully, she thought. She rather enjoyed studying out Pollyanna's "posers," too, as she called some of the little girl's questions.

"Oh, I know," she chuckled. "It's just the opposite from what you told Mis' Snow."

"Opposite?" repeated Pollyanna, obviously puzzled.

"Yes. You told her she could be glad because other folks wasn't like her--all sick, you know."

"Yes," nodded Pollyanna.

"Well, the doctor can be glad because he isn't like other folks--the sick ones, I mean, what he doctors," finished Nancy in triumph.

It was Pollyanna's turn to frown.

"Why, y-yes," she admitted. "Of course that *is* one way, but it isn't the way I said; and--someway, I don't seem to quite like the sound of it. It isn't exactly as if he said he was glad they *were* sick, but--You do play the game so funny, sometimes Nancy," she sighed, as she went into the house.

Pollyanna found her aunt in the sitting room.

"Who was that man--the one who drove into the yard, Pollyanna?" questioned the lady a little sharply.

"Why, Aunt Polly, that was Dr. Chilton! Don't you know him?"

"Dr. Chilton! What was he doing--here?"

"He drove me home. Oh, and I gave the jelly to Mr. Pendleton, and--"

Miss Polly lifted her head quickly.

"Pollyanna, he did not think I sent it?"

"Oh, no, Aunt Polly. I told him you didn't."

Miss Polly grew a sudden vivid pink.

"You *told* him I didn't!"

Pollyanna opened wide her eyes at the remonstrative dismay in her aunt's voice.

"Why, Aunt Polly, you *said* to!"

Aunt Polly sighed.

"I *said*, Pollyanna, that I did not send it, and for you to be very sure that he did not think I *did*!--which is a very different matter from *telling* him outright that I did not send it." And she turned vexedly away.

"Dear me! Well, I don't see where the difference is," sighed Pollyanna, as she went to hang her hat on the one particular hook in the house upon which Aunt Polly had said that it must be hung.

Lesson 157

1. Read chapter 16.
2. Tell someone about the chapter.

It was on a rainy day about a week after Pollyanna's visit to Mr. John Pendleton, that Miss Polly was driven by Timothy to an early afternoon committee meeting of the Ladies' Aid Society. When she returned at three o'clock, her cheeks were a bright, pretty pink, and her hair, blown by the damp wind, had fluffed into kinks and curls wherever the loosened pins had given leave.

Pollyanna had never before seen her aunt look like this.

"Oh--oh--oh! Why, Aunt Polly, you've got 'em, too," she cried rapturously, dancing round and round her aunt, as that lady entered the sitting room.

"Got what, you impossible child?"

Pollyanna was still revolving round and round her aunt.

"And I never knew you had 'em! Can folks have 'em when you don't know they've got 'em? *Do* you suppose I could?--'fore I get to Heaven, I mean," she cried, pulling out with eager fingers the straight locks above her ears. "But then, they wouldn't be black, if they did come. You can't hide the black part."

"Pollyanna, what does all this mean?" demanded Aunt Polly, hurriedly removing her hat, and trying to smooth back her disordered hair.

"No, no--please, Aunt Polly!" Pollyanna's jubilant voice turned to one of distressed appeal. "Don't smooth 'em out! It's those that I'm talking about--those darling little black curls. Oh, Aunt Polly, they're so pretty!"

"Nonsense! What do you mean, Pollyanna, by going to the Ladies' Aid the other day in that absurd fashion about that beggar boy?"

"But it isn't nonsense," urged Pollyanna, answering only the first of her aunt's remarks. "You don't know how pretty you look with your hair like that! Oh, Aunt Polly, please, mayn't I do your hair like I did Mrs. Snow's, and put in a flower? I'd so love to see you that way! Why, you'd be ever so much prettier than she was!"

"Pollyanna!" (Miss Polly spoke very sharply--all the more sharply because Pollyanna's words had given her an odd throb of joy: when before had anybody cared how she, or her hair looked? When before had anybody "loved" to see her "pretty"?) "Pollyanna, you did not answer my question. Why did you go to the Ladies' Aid in that absurd fashion?"

"Yes'm, I know; but, please, I didn't know it was absurd until I went and found out they'd rather see their report grow than Jimmy. So then I wrote to *my* Ladies' Aiders--'cause Jimmy is far away from them, you know; and I thought maybe he could be their little India boy same as--Aunt Polly, *was* I your little India girl? And, Aunt Polly, you *will* let me do your hair, won't you?"

Aunt Polly put her hand to her throat--the old, helpless feeling was upon her, she knew.

"But, Pollyanna, when the ladies told me this afternoon how you came to them, I was so ashamed! I--"

Pollyanna began to dance up and down lightly on her toes.

"You didn't!--You didn't say I *couldn't* do your hair," she crowed triumphantly; "and so I'm sure it means just the other way 'round, sort of--like it did the other day about Mr. Pendleton's jelly that you didn't send, but didn't want me to say you didn't send, you know. Now wait just where you are. I'll get a comb."

"But Pollyanna, Pollyanna," remonstrated Aunt Polly, following the little girl from the room and panting up-stairs after her.

"Oh, did you come up here?" Pollyanna greeted her at the door of Miss Polly's own room. "That'll be nicer yet! I've got the comb. Now sit down, please, right here. Oh, I'm so glad you let me do it!"

"But, Pollyanna, I—I--"

Miss Polly did not finish her sentence. To her helpless amazement she found herself in the low chair before the dressing table, with her hair already tumbling about her ears under ten eager, but very gentle fingers.

"Oh, my! what pretty hair you've got," prattled Pollyanna; "and there's so much more of it than Mrs. Snow has, too! But, of course, you need more, anyhow, because you're well and can go to places where folks can see it. My! I reckon folks'll be glad when they do see it--and surprised, too, 'cause you've hid it so long. Why, Aunt Polly, I'll make you so pretty everybody'll just love to look at you!"

"Pollyanna!" gasped a stifled but shocked voice from a veil of hair. "I--I'm sure I don't know why I'm letting you do this silly thing."

"Why, Aunt Polly, I should think you'd be glad to have folks like to look at you! Don't you like to look at pretty things? I'm ever so much happier when I look at pretty folks, 'cause when I look at the other kind I'm so sorry for them."

"But--but--"

"And I just love to do folks' hair," purred Pollyanna, contentedly. "I did quite a lot of the Ladies' Aiders'--but there wasn't any of them so nice as yours. Mrs. White's was pretty nice, though, and she looked just lovely one day when I dressed her up in--Oh, Aunt Polly, I've just happened to think of something! But it's a secret, and I sha'n't tell. Now your hair is almost done, and pretty quick I'm going to leave you just a minute; and you must promise--promise--*promise* not to stir nor peek, even, till I come back. Now remember!" she finished, as she ran from the room.

Aloud Miss Polly said nothing. To herself she said that of course she should at once undo the absurd work of her niece's fingers, and put her hair up properly again. As for "peeking" just as if she cared how--

At that moment--unaccountably--Miss Polly caught a glimpse of herself in the mirror of the dressing table. And what she saw sent such a flush of rosy color to her cheeks that--she only flushed the more at the sight.

She saw a face--not young, it is true--but just now alight with excitement and surprise. The cheeks were a pretty pink. The eyes sparkled. The hair, dark, and still damp from the outdoor air, lay in loose waves about the forehead and curved back over the ears in wonderfully becoming lines, with softening little curls here and there.

So amazed and so absorbed was Miss Polly with what she saw in the glass that she quite forgot her determination to do over her hair, until she heard Pollyanna enter the room again. Before she could move, then, she felt a folded something slipped across her eyes and tied in the back.

"Pollyanna, Pollyanna! What are you doing?" she cried.

Pollyanna chuckled.

"That's just what I don't want you to know, Aunt Polly, and I was afraid you *would* peek, so I tied on the handkerchief. Now sit still. It won't take but just a minute, then I'll let you see."

"But, Pollyanna," began Miss Polly, struggling blindly to her feet, "you must take this off! You-- child, child! what *are* you doing?" she gasped, as she felt a soft something slipped about her shoulders.

Pollyanna only chuckled the more gleefully. With trembling fingers she was draping about her aunt's shoulders the fleecy folds of a beautiful lace shawl, yellowed from long years of packing away, and fragrant with lavender. Pollyanna had found the shawl the week before when Nancy had been regulating the attic; and it had occurred to her to-day that there was no reason why her aunt, as well as Mrs. White of her Western home, should not be "dressed up."

Her task completed, Pollyanna surveyed her work with eyes that approved, but that saw yet one touch wanting. Promptly, therefore, she pulled her aunt toward the sun parlor where she could see a belated red rose blooming on the trellis within reach of her hand.

"Pollyanna, what are you doing? Where are you taking me to?" recoiled Aunt Polly, vainly trying to hold herself back. "Pollyanna, I shall not--"

"It's just to the sun parlor--only a minute! I'll have you ready now quicker'n no time," panted Pollyanna, reaching for the rose and thrusting it into the soft hair above Miss Polly's left ear. "There!" she exulted, untying the knot of the handkerchief and flinging the bit of linen far from her. "Oh, Aunt Polly, now I reckon you'll be glad I dressed you up!"

For one dazed moment Miss Polly looked at her bedecked self, and at her surroundings; then she gave a low cry and fled to her room. Pollyanna, following the direction of her aunt's last dismayed gaze, saw, through the open windows of the sun parlor, the horse and gig turning into the driveway. She recognized at once the man who held the reins. Delightedly she leaned forward.

"Dr. Chilton, Dr. Chilton! Did you want to see me? I'm up here."

"Yes," smiled the doctor, a little gravely. "Will you come down, please?"

In the bedroom Pollyanna found a flushed-faced, angry-eyed woman plucking at the pins that held a lace shawl in place.

"Pollyanna, how could you?" moaned the woman. "To think of your rigging me up like this, and then letting me--*be seen*!"

Pollyanna stopped in dismay.

"But you looked lovely--perfectly lovely, Aunt Polly; and--"

"'Lovely'!" scorned the woman, flinging the shawl to one side and attacking her hair with shaking fingers.

"Oh, Aunt Polly, please, please let the hair stay!"

"Stay? Like this? As if I would!" And Miss Polly pulled the locks so tightly back that the last curl lay stretched dead at the ends of her fingers.

"O dear! And you did look so pretty," almost sobbed Pollyanna, as she stumbled through the door.

Down-stairs Pollyanna found the doctor waiting in his gig.

"I've prescribed you for a patient, and he's sent me to get the prescription filled," announced the doctor. "Will you go?"

"You mean--an errand--to the drug store?" asked Pollyanna, a little uncertainly. "I used to go some--for the Ladies' Aiders."

The doctor shook his head with a smile.

"Not exactly. It's Mr. John Pendleton. He would like to see you to-day, if you'll be so good as to come. It's stopped raining, so I drove down after you. Will you come? I'll call for you and bring you back before six o'clock."

"I'd love to!" exclaimed Pollyanna. "Let me ask Aunt Polly."

In a few moments she returned, hat in hand, but with rather a sober face.

"Didn't--your aunt want you to go?" asked the doctor, a little diffidently, as they drove away.

"Y-yes," sighed Pollyanna. "She--she wanted me to go *too* much, I'm afraid."

"Wanted you to go *too much*!"

Pollyanna sighed again.

"Yes. I reckon she meant she didn't want me there. You see, she said: 'Yes, yes, run along, run along--do! I wish you'd gone before.' "

The doctor smiled--but with his lips only. His eyes were very grave. For some time he said nothing; then, a little hesitatingly, he asked:

"Wasn't it--your aunt I saw with you a few minutes ago--in the window of the sun parlor?"

Pollyanna drew a long breath.

"Yes; that's what's the whole trouble, I suppose. You see I'd dressed her up in a perfectly lovely lace shawl I found up-stairs, and I'd fixed her hair and put on a rose, and she looked so pretty. Didn't *you* think she looked just lovely?"

For a moment the doctor did not answer. When he did speak his voice was so low Pollyanna could but just hear the words.

"Yes, Pollyanna, I--I thought she did look--just lovely."

"Did you? I'm so glad! I'll tell her," nodded the little girl, contentedly.

To her surprise the doctor gave a sudden exclamation.

"Never! Pollyanna, I--I'm afraid I shall have to ask you not to tell her--that."

"Why, Dr. Chilton! Why not? I should think you'd be glad--"

"But she might not be," cut in the doctor.

Pollyanna considered this for a moment.

"That's so--maybe she wouldn't," she sighed. "I remember now; 'twas 'cause she saw you that she ran. And she--she spoke afterwards about her being seen in that rig."

"I thought as much," declared the doctor, under his breath.

"Still, I don't see why," maintained Pollyanna, "--when she looked so pretty!"

The doctor said nothing. He did not speak again, indeed, until they were almost to the great stone house in which John Pendleton lay with a broken leg.

Lesson 158

1. Read chapter 17.
2. Tell someone about the chapter.

John Pendleton greeted Pollyanna to-day with a smile.

"Well, Miss Pollyanna, I'm thinking you must be a very forgiving little person, else you wouldn't have come to see me again to-day."

"Why, Mr. Pendleton, I was real glad to come, and I'm sure I don't see why I shouldn't be, either."

"Oh, well, you know, I was pretty cross with you, I'm afraid, both the other day when you so kindly brought me the jelly, and that time when you found me with the broken leg at first. By the way, too, I don't think I've ever thanked you for that. Now I'm sure that even you would admit that you were very forgiving to come and see me, after such ungrateful treatment as that!"

Pollyanna stirred uneasily.

"But I was glad to find you--that is, I don't mean I was glad your leg was broken, of course," she corrected hurriedly.

John Pendleton smiled.

"I understand. Your tongue does get away with you once in a while, doesn't it, Miss Pollyanna? I do thank you, however; and I consider you a very brave little girl to do what you did that day. I thank you for the jelly, too," he added in a lighter voice.

"Did you like it?" asked Pollyanna with interest.

"Very much. I suppose--there isn't any more to-day that--that Aunt Polly *didn't* send, is there?" he asked with an odd smile.

His visitor looked distressed.

"N-no, sir." She hesitated, then went on with heightened color. "Please, Mr. Pendleton, I didn't mean to be rude the other day when I said Aunt Polly did *not* send the jelly."

There was no answer. John Pendleton was not smiling now. He was looking straight ahead of him with eyes that seemed to be gazing through and beyond the object before them. After a time he drew a long sigh and turned to Pollyanna. When he spoke his voice carried the old nervous fretfulness.

"Well, well, this will never do at all! I didn't send for you to see me moping this time. Listen! Out in the library--the big room where the telephone is, you know--you will find a carved box on the lower shelf of the big case with glass doors in the corner not far from the fireplace. That is, it'll be there if that confounded woman hasn't 'regulated' it to somewhere else! You may bring it to me. It is heavy, but not too heavy for you to carry, I think."

"Oh, I'm awfully strong," declared Pollyanna, cheerfully, as she sprang to her feet. In a minute she had returned with the box.

It was a wonderful half-hour that Pollyanna spent then. The box was full of treasures--curios that John Pendleton had picked up in years of travel--and concerning each there was some entertaining story, whether it were a set of exquisitely carved chessmen from China, or a little jade idol from India.

It was after she had heard the story about the idol that Pollyanna murmured wistfully:

"Well, I suppose it *would* be better to take a little boy in India to bring up--one that didn't know any more than to think that God was in that doll-thing--than it would be to take Jimmy Bean, a little boy who knows God is up in the sky. Still, I can't help wishing they had wanted Jimmy Bean, too, besides the India boys."

John Pendleton did not seem to hear. Again his, eyes were staring straight before him, looking at nothing. But soon he had roused himself, and had picked up another curio to talk about.

The visit, certainly, was a delightful one, but before it was over, Pollyanna was realizing that they were talking about something besides the wonderful things in the beautiful carved box. They were talking of herself, of Nancy, of Aunt Polly, and of her daily life. They were talking, too, even of the life and home long ago in the far Western town.

Not until it was nearly time for her to go, did the man say, in a voice Pollyanna had never before heard from stern John Pendleton:

"Little girl, I want you to come to see me often. Will you? I'm lonesome, and I need you. There's another reason--and I'm going to tell you that, too. I thought, at first, after I found out who you were, the other day, that I didn't want you to come any more. You reminded me of--of something I have tried for long years to forget. So I said to myself that I never wanted to see you again; and every day, when the doctor asked if I wouldn't let him bring you to me, I said no.

"But after a time I found I was wanting to see you so much that--that the fact that I *wasn't* seeing you was making me remember all the more vividly the thing I was so wanting to forget. So now I want you to come. Will you--little girl?"

"Why, yes, Mr. Pendleton," breathed Pollyanna, her eyes luminous with sympathy for the sad-faced man lying back on the pillow before her. "I'd love to come!"

"Thank you," said John Pendleton, gently.

After supper that evening, Pollyanna, sitting on the back porch, told Nancy all about Mr. John Pendleton's wonderful carved box, and the still more wonderful things it contained.

"And ter think," sighed Nancy, "that he *showed* ye all them things, and told ye about 'em like that--him that's so cross he never talks ter no one--no one!"

"Oh, but he isn't cross, Nancy, only outside," demurred Pollyanna, with quick loyalty. "I don't see why everybody thinks he's so bad, either. They wouldn't, if they knew him. But even Aunt Polly doesn't like him very well. She wouldn't send the jelly to him, you know, and she was so afraid he'd think she did send it!"

"Probably she didn't call him no duty," shrugged Nancy. "But what beats me is how he happened ter take ter you so, Miss Pollyanna--meanin' no offence ter you, of course--but he ain't the sort o' man what gen'rally takes ter kids; he ain't, he ain't."

Pollyanna smiled happily.

"But he did, Nancy," she nodded, "only I reckon even he didn't want to--*all* the time. Why, only to-day he owned up that one time he just felt he never wanted to see me again, because I reminded him of something he wanted to forget. But afterwards--"

"What's that?" interrupted Nancy, excitedly. "He said you reminded him of something he wanted to forget?"

"Yes. But afterwards--"

"What was it?" Nancy was eagerly insistent.

"He didn't tell me. He just said it was something."

"*The mystery*!" breathed Nancy, in an awestruck voice. "That's why he took to you in the first place. Oh, Miss Pollyanna! Why, that's just like a book--I've read lots of 'em; 'Lady Maud's Secret,' and 'The Lost Heir,' and 'Hidden for Years'--all of 'em had mysteries and things just like this. My stars and stockings! Just think of havin' a book lived right under yer nose like this an' me not knowin' it all this time! Now tell me everythin'--everythin' he said, Miss Pollyanna, there's a dear! No wonder he took ter you; no wonder--no wonder!"

"But he didn't," cried Pollyanna, "not till *I* talked to *him*, first. And he didn't even know who I was till I took the calf's-foot jelly, and had to make him understand that Aunt Polly didn't send it, and--"

Nancy sprang to her feet and clasped her hands together suddenly.

"Oh, Miss Pollyanna, I know, I know--I *know* I know!" she exulted rapturously. The next minute she was down at Pollyanna's side again. "Tell me--now think, and answer straight and true," she urged excitedly. "It was after he found out you was Miss Polly's niece that he said he didn't ever want ter see ye again, wa'n't it?"

"Oh, yes. I told him that the last time I saw him, and he told me this to-day."

"I thought as much," triumphed Nancy. "And Miss Polly wouldn't send the jelly herself, would she?"

"No."

"And you told him she didn't send it?"

"Why, yes; I--"

"And he began ter act queer and cry out sudden after he found out you was her niece. He did that, didn't he?"

"Why, y-yes; he did act a little queer--over that jelly," admitted Pollyanna, with a thoughtful frown.

Nancy drew a long sigh.

"Then I've got it, sure! Now listen. *Mr. John Pendleton was Miss Polly Harrington's gentleman friend!*" she announced impressively, but with a furtive glance over her shoulder.

"Why, Nancy, he couldn't be! She doesn't like him," objected Pollyanna.

Nancy gave her a scornful glance.

"Of course she don't! *That's* the quarrel!

Pollyanna still looked incredulous, and with another long breath Nancy happily settled herself to tell the story.

"It's like this. Just before you come, Mr. Tom told me Miss Polly had had a gentleman friend once. I didn't believe it. I couldn't--her and a gentleman friend! But Mr. Tom said she had, and that he was livin' now right in this town. And *now* I know, of course. It's John Pendleton. Hain't he got a mystery in his life? Don't he shut himself up in that grand house alone, and never speak ter no one? Didn't he act queer when he found out you was Miss Polly's niece? And now hain't he owned up that you remind him of somethin' he wants ter forget? Just as if *anybody* couldn't see 'twas Miss Polly!--an' her sayin' she wouldn't send him no jelly, too. Why, Miss Pollyanna, it's as plain as the nose on yer face; it is, it is!"

"Oh-h!" breathed Pollyanna, in wide-eyed amazement. "But, Nancy, I should think if they loved each other they'd make up some time. Both of 'em all alone, so, all these years. I should think they'd be glad to make up!"

Nancy sniffed disdainfully.

"I guess maybe you don't know much about love, Miss Pollyanna. You ain't big enough yet, anyhow. But if there *is* a set o' folks in the world that wouldn't have no use for that 'ere 'glad game' o' your'n, it'd be a quarrelin' couple; and that's what they be. Ain't he cross as sticks, most gen'rally?--and ain't she--"

Nancy stopped abruptly, remembering just in time to whom, and about whom, she was speaking. Suddenly, however, she chuckled.

"I ain't sayin', though, Miss Pollyanna, but what it would be a pretty slick piece of business if you could *get* 'em ter playin' it--so they *would* be glad ter make up. But, my land! wouldn't folks stare some--Miss Polly and him! I guess, though, there ain't much chance, much chance!"

Pollyanna said nothing; but when she went into the house a little later, her face was very thoughtful.

Lesson 159

1. Read chapter 18.
2. Tell someone about the chapter.

As the warm August days passed, Pollyanna went very frequently to the great house on Pendleton Hill. She did not feel, however, that her visits were really a success. Not but that the man seemed to want her there--he sent for her, indeed, frequently; but that when she was there, he seemed scarcely any the happier for her presence--at least, so Pollyanna thought.

He talked to her, it was true, and be showed her many strange and beautiful things--books, pictures, and curios. But he still fretted audibly over his own helplessness, and he chafed visibly under the rules and "regulatings" of the unwelcome members of his household. He did, indeed, seem to like to hear Pollyanna talk, however, and Pollyanna talked, Pollyanna liked to talk--but she was never sure that she would not look up and find him lying back on his pillow with that white, hurt look that always pained her; and she was never sure which--if any--of her words had brought it there. As for telling him the "glad game," and trying to get him to play it--Pollyanna had never seen the time yet when she thought he would care to hear about it. She had twice tried to tell him; but neither time had she got beyond the beginning of what her father had said--John Pendleton had on each occasion turned the conversation abruptly to another subject.

Pollyanna never doubted now that John Pendleton was her Aunt Polly's one-time gentleman friend; and with all the strength of her loving, loyal heart, she wished she could in some way bring happiness into their--to her mind--miserably lonely lives.

Just how she was to do this, however, she could not see. She talked to Mr. Pendleton about her aunt; and he listened, sometimes politely, sometimes irritably, frequently with a quizzical smile on his usually stern lips. She talked to her aunt about Mr. Pendleton--or rather, she tried to talk to her about him. As a general thing, however, Miss Polly would not listen--long. She always found something else to talk about. She frequently did that, however, when Pollyanna was talking of others--of Dr. Chilton, for instance. Pollyanna laid this, though, to the fact that it had been Dr. Chilton who had seen her in the sun parlor with the rose in her hair and the lace shawl draped about her shoulders. Aunt Polly, indeed, seemed particularly bitter against Dr. Chilton, as Pollyanna found out one day when a hard cold shut her up in the house.

"If you are not better by night I shall send for the doctor," Aunt Polly said.

"Shall you? Then I'm going to be worse," gurgled Pollyanna. "I'd love to have Dr. Chilton come to see me!"

She wondered, then, at the look that came to her aunt's face.

"It will not be Dr. Chilton, Pollyanna," Miss Polly said sternly. "Dr. Chilton is not our family physician. I shall send for Dr. Warren--if you are worse."

Pollyanna did not grow worse, however, and Dr. Warren was not summoned.

"And I'm so glad, too," Pollyanna said to her aunt that evening. "Of course I like Dr. Warren, and all that; but I like Dr. Chilton better, and I'm afraid he'd feel hurt if I didn't have him. You see, he wasn't really to blame, after all, that he happened to see you when I'd dressed you up so pretty that day, Aunt Polly," she finished wistfully.

"That will do, Pollyanna. I really do not wish to discuss Dr. Chilton--or his feelings," reproved Miss Polly, decisively.

Pollyanna looked at her for a moment with mournfully interested eyes; then she sighed:

"I just love to see you when your cheeks are pink like that, Aunt Polly; but I would so like to fix your hair. If--Why, Aunt Polly!" But her aunt was already out of sight down the hall.

It was toward the end of August that Pollyanna, making an early morning call on John Pendleton, found the flaming band of blue and gold and green edged with red and violet lying across his pillow. She stopped short in awed delight.

"Why, Mr. Pendleton, it's a baby rainbow--a real rainbow come in to pay you a visit!" she exclaimed, clapping her hands together softly. "Oh--oh--oh, how pretty it is! But how *did* it get in?" she cried.

The man laughed a little grimly: John Pendleton was particularly out of sorts with the world this morning.

"Well, I suppose it 'got in' through the bevelled edge of that glass thermometer in the window," he said wearily. "The sun shouldn't strike it at all but it does in the morning."

"Oh, but it's so pretty, Mr. Pendleton! And does just the sun do that? My! if it was mine I'd have it hang in the sun all day long!"

"Lots of good you'd get out of the thermometer, then," laughed the man. "How do you suppose you could tell how hot it was, or how cold it was, if the thermometer hung in the sun all day?"

"I shouldn't care," breathed Pollyanna, her fascinated eyes on the brilliant band of colors across the pillow. "Just as if anybody'd care when they were living all the time in a rainbow!"

The man laughed. He was watching Pollyanna's rapt face a little curiously. Suddenly a new thought came to him. He touched the bell at his side.

"Nora," he said, when the elderly maid appeared at the door, "bring me one of the big brass candle-sticks from the mantel in the front drawing-room."

"Yes, sir," murmured the woman, looking slightly dazed. In a minute she had returned. A musical tinkling entered the room with her as she advanced wonderingly toward the bed. It came from the prism pendants encircling the old-fashioned candelabrum in her hand.

"Thank you. You may set it here on the stand," directed the man. "Now get a string and fasten it to the sash-curtain fixtures of that window there. Take down the sash-curtain, and let the string reach straight across the window from side to side. That will be all. Thank you," he said, when she had carried out his directions.

As she left the room he turned smiling eyes toward the wondering Pollyanna.

"Bring me the candlestick now, please, Pollyanna."

With both hands she brought it; and in a moment he was slipping off the pendants, one by one, until they lay, a round dozen of them, side by side, on the bed.

"Now, my dear, suppose you take them and hook them to that little string Nora fixed across the window. If you really *want* to live in a rainbow--I don't see but we'll have to have a rainbow for you to live in!"

Pollyanna had not hung up three of the pendants in the sunlit window before she saw a little of what was going to happen. She was so excited then she could scarcely control her shaking fingers enough to hang up the rest. But at last her task was finished, and she stepped back with a low cry of delight.

It had become a fairyland--that sumptuous, but dreary bedroom. Everywhere were bits of dancing red and green, violet and orange, gold and blue. The wall, the floor, and the furniture, even to the bed itself, were aflame with shimmering bits of color.

"Oh, oh, oh, how lovely!" breathed Pollyanna; then she laughed suddenly. "I just reckon the sun himself is trying to play the game now, don't you?" she cried, forgetting for the moment that Mr. Pendleton could not know what she was talking about. "Oh, how I wish I had a lot of those things! How I would like to give them to Aunt Polly and Mrs. Snow and--lots of folks. I reckon *then* they'd be glad all right! Why, I think even Aunt Polly'd get so glad she couldn't help banging doors if she lived in a rainbow like that. Don't you?"

Mr. Pendleton laughed.

"Well, from my remembrance of your aunt, Miss Pollyanna, I must say I think it would take something more than a few prisms in the sunlight to--to make her bang many doors--for gladness. But come, now, really, what do you mean?"

Pollyanna stared slightly; then she drew a long breath.

"Oh, I forgot. You don't know about the game. I remember now."

"Suppose you tell me, then."

And this time Pollyanna told him. She told him the whole thing from the very first--from the crutches that should have been a doll. As she talked, she did not look at his face. Her rapt eyes were still on the dancing flecks of color from the prism pendants swaying in the sunlit window.

"And that's all," she sighed, when she had finished. "And now you know why I said the sun was trying to play it--that game."

For a moment there was silence. Then a low voice from the bed said unsteadily:

"Perhaps; but I'm thinking that the very finest prism of them all is yourself, Pollyanna."

"Oh, but I don't show beautiful red and green and purple when the sun shines through me, Mr. Pendleton!"

"Don't you?" smiled the man. And Pollyanna, looking into his face, wondered why there were tears in his eyes.

"No," she said. Then, after a minute she added mournfully: "I'm afraid, Mr. Pendleton, the sun doesn't make anything but freckles out of me. Aunt Polly says it *does* make them!"

The man laughed a little; and again Pollyanna looked at him: the laugh had sounded almost like a sob.

Lesson 160

1. Read chapter 19.
2. Tell someone about the chapter.

Pollyanna entered school in September. Preliminary examinations showed that she was well advanced for a girl of her years, and she was soon a happy member of a class of girls and boys her own age.

School, in some ways, was a surprise to Pollyanna; and Pollyanna, certainly, in many ways, was very much of a surprise to school. They were soon on the best of terms, however, and to her aunt Pollyanna confessed that going to school *was* living, after all--though she had had her doubts before.

In spite of her delight in her new work, Pollyanna did not forget her old friends. True, she could not give them quite so much time now, of course; but she gave them what time she could. Perhaps John Pendleton, of them all, however, was the most dissatisfied.

One Saturday afternoon he spoke to her about it.

"See here, Pollyanna, how would you like to come and live with me?" he asked, a little impatiently. "I don't see anything of you, nowadays."

Pollyanna laughed--Mr. Pendleton was such a funny man!

"I thought you didn't like to have folks 'round," she said.

He made a wry face.

"Oh, but that was before you taught me to play that wonderful game of yours. Now I'm glad to be waited on, hand and foot! Never mind, I'll be on my own two feet yet, one of these days; then I'll see who steps around," he finished, picking up one of the crutches at his side and shaking it playfully at the little girl. They were sitting in the great library to-day.

"Oh, but you aren't really glad at all for things; you just *say* you are," pouted Pollyanna, her eyes on the dog, dozing before the fire. "You know you don't play the game right *ever*, Mr. Pendleton-- you know you don't!"

The man's face grew suddenly very grave.

"That's why I want you, little girl--to help me play it. Will you come?"

Pollyanna turned in surprise.

"Mr. Pendleton, you don't really mean--that?"

"But I do. I want you. Will you come?"

Pollyanna looked distressed.

"Why, Mr. Pendleton, I can't--you know I can't. Why, I'm--Aunt Polly's!"

A quick something crossed the man's face that Pollyanna could not quite understand. His head came up almost fiercely.

"You're no more hers than--Perhaps she would let you come to me," he finished more gently. "Would you come--if she did?"

Pollyanna frowned in deep thought.

"But Aunt Polly has been so--good to me," she began slowly; "and she took me when I didn't have anybody left but the Ladies' Aid, and--"

Again that spasm of something crossed the man's face; but this time, when he spoke, his voice was low and very sad.

"Pollyanna, long years ago I loved somebody very much. I hoped to bring her, some day, to this house. I pictured how happy we'd be together in our home all the long years to come."

"Yes," pitied Pollyanna, her eyes shining with sympathy.

"But--well, I didn't bring her here. Never mind why. I just didn't that's all. And ever since then this great gray pile of stone has been a house--never a home. It takes a woman's hand and heart, or a child's presence, to make a home, Pollyanna; and I have not had either. Now will you come, my dear?"

Pollyanna sprang to her feet. Her face was fairly illumined.

"Mr. Pendleton, you--you mean that you wish you--you had had that woman's hand and heart all this time?"

"Why, y-yes, Pollyanna."

"Oh, I'm so glad! Then it's all right," sighed the little girl. "Now you can take us both, and everything will be lovely."

"Take--you--both?" repeated the man, dazedly.

A faint doubt crossed Pollyanna's countenance.

"Well, of course, Aunt Polly isn't won over, yet; but I'm sure she will be if you tell it to her just as you did to me, and then we'd both come, of course."

A look of actual terror leaped to the man's eyes.

"Aunt Polly come--*here*!"

Pollyanna's eyes widened a little.

"Would you rather go *there*?" she asked. "Of course the house isn't quite so pretty, but it's nearer-"

"Pollyanna, what *are* you talking about?" asked the man, very gently now.

"Why, about where we're going to live, of course," rejoined Pollyanna, in obvious surprise. "I *thought* you meant here, at first. You said it was here that you had wanted Aunt Polly's hand and heart all these years to make a home, and--"

An inarticulate cry came from the man's throat. He raised his hand and began to speak; but the next moment he dropped his hand nervelessly at his side.

"The doctor, sir," said the maid in the doorway.

Pollyanna rose at once.

John Pendleton turned to her feverishly.

"Pollyanna, for Heaven's sake, say nothing of what I asked you--yet," he begged, in a low voice. Pollyanna dimpled into a sunny smile.

"Of course not! Just as if I didn't know you'd rather tell her yourself!" she called back merrily over her shoulder.

John Pendleton fell limply back in his chair.

"Why, what's up?" demanded the doctor, a minute later, his fingers on his patient's galloping pulse.

A whimsical smile trembled on John Pendleton's lips.

"Overdose of your--tonic, I guess," he laughed, as he noted the doctor's eyes following Pollyanna's little figure down the driveway.

Lesson 161

1. Read chapter 20.
2. Tell someone about the chapter.

Sunday mornings Pollyanna usually attended church and Sunday school. Sunday afternoons she frequently went for a walk with Nancy. She had planned one for the day after her Saturday afternoon visit to Mr. John Pendleton; but on the way home from Sunday school Dr. Chilton overtook her in his gig, and brought his horse to a stop.

"Suppose you let me drive you home, Pollyanna," he suggested. "I want to speak to you a minute. I, was just driving out to your place to tell you," he went on, as Pollyanna settled herself at his side. "Mr. Pendleton sent a special request for you to go to see him this afternoon, sure. He says it's very important."

Pollyanna nodded happily.

"Yes, it is, I know. I'll go."

The doctor eyed her with some surprise.

"I'm not sure I shall let you, after all," he declared, his eyes twinkling. "You seemed more upsetting than soothing yesterday, young lady."

Pollyanna laughed.

"Oh, it wasn't me, truly--not really, you know; not so much as it was Aunt Polly."

The doctor turned with a quick start.

"Your--aunt!" he exclaimed.

Pollyanna gave a happy little bounce in her seat.

"Yes. And it's so exciting and lovely, just like a story, you know. I--I'm going to tell you," she burst out, with sudden decision. "He said not to mention it; but he wouldn't mind your knowing, of course. He meant not to mention it to her."

"Her?"

"Yes; Aunt Polly. And, of course he would want to tell her himself instead of having me do it—in love, so!"

"In love!" As the doctor said the word, the horse started violently, as if the hand that held the reins had given them a sharp jerk.

"Yes," nodded Pollyanna, happily. "That's the story-part, you see. I didn't know it till Nancy told me. She said Aunt Polly had a gentleman friend years ago, and they quarrelled. She didn't know who it was at first. But we've found out now. It's Mr. Pendleton, you know."

The doctor relaxed suddenly, The hand holding the reins fell limply to his lap.

"Oh! No; I--didn't know," he said quietly.

Pollyanna hurried on--they were nearing the Harrington homestead.

"Yes; and I'm so glad now. It's come out lovely. Mr. Pendleton asked me to come and live with him, but of course I wouldn't leave Aunt Polly like that--after she'd been so good to me. Then he told me all about the woman's hand and heart that he used to want, and I found out that he wanted it now; and I was so glad! For of course if he wants to make up the quarrel, everything will be all right now, and Aunt Polly and I will both go to live there, or else he'll come to live with us. Of course Aunt Polly doesn't know yet, and we haven't got everything settled; so I suppose that is why he wanted to see me this afternoon, sure."

The doctor sat suddenly erect. There was an odd smile on his lips.

"Yes; I can well imagine that Mr. John Pendleton does--want to see you, Pollyanna," he nodded, as he pulled his horse to a stop before the door.

"There's Aunt Polly now in the window," cried Pollyanna; then, a second later: "Why, no, she isn't--but I thought I saw her!"

"No; she isn't there--now," said the doctor. His lips had suddenly lost their smile.

Pollyanna found a very nervous John Pendleton waiting for her that afternoon.

"Pollyanna," he began at once. "I've been trying all night to puzzle out what you meant by all that, yesterday--about my wanting your Aunt Polly's hand and heart here all those years. What did you mean?"

"Why, because you were in love, you know once; and I was so glad you still felt that way now."

"In love!--your Aunt Polly and I?"

At the obvious surprise in the man's voice, Pollyanna opened wide her eyes.

"Why, Mr. Pendleton, Nancy said you were!"

The man gave a short little laugh.

"Indeed! Well, I'm afraid I shall have to say that Nancy--didn't know."

"Then you--weren't in love?" Pollyanna's voice was tragic with dismay.

"Never!"

"And it isn't all coming out like a book?"

There was no answer. The man's eyes were moodily fixed out the window.

"O dear! And it was all going so splendidly," almost sobbed Pollyanna. "I'd have been so glad to come--with Aunt Polly."

"And you won't--now?" The man asked the question without turning his head.

"Of course not! I'm Aunt Polly's."

The man turned now, almost fiercely.

"Before you were hers, Pollyanna, you were--your mother's. And--it was your mother's hand and heart that I wanted long years ago."

"My mother's!"

"Yes. I had not meant to tell you, but perhaps it's better, after all, that I do--now." John Pendleton's face had grown very white. He was speaking with evident difficulty. Pollyanna, her eyes wide and frightened, and her lips parted, was gazing at him fixedly. "I loved your mother; but she--didn't love me. And after a time she went away with--your father. I did not know until then how much I did--care. The whole world suddenly seemed to turn black under my fingers, and--But, never mind. For long years I have been a cross, crabbed, unlovable, unloved old man--though I'm not nearly sixty, yet, Pollyanna. Then, one day, like one of the prisms that you love so well, little girl, you danced into my life, and flecked my dreary old world with dashes of the purple and gold and scarlet of your own bright cheeriness. I found out, after a time, who you were, and--and I thought then I never wanted to see you again. I didn't want to be reminded of--your mother. But--you know how that came out. I just had to have you come. And now I want you always. Pollyanna, won't you come now?"

"But, Mr. Pendleton, I--There's Aunt Polly!" Pollyanna's eyes were blurred with tears.

The man made an impatient gesture.

"What about me? How do you suppose I'm going to be 'glad' about anything--without you? Why, Pollyanna, it's only since you came that I've been even half glad to live! But if I had you for my own little girl, I'd be glad for--anything; and I'd try to make you glad, too, my dear. You shouldn't have a wish ungratified. All my money, to the last cent, should go to make you happy."

Pollyanna looked shocked.

"Why, Mr. Pendleton, as if I'd let you spend it on me--all that money you've saved for the heathen!"

A dull red came to the man's face. He started to speak, but Pollyanna was still talking.

"Besides, anybody with such a lot of money as you have doesn't need me to make you glad about things. You're making other folks so glad giving them things that you just can't help being glad yourself! Why, look at those prisms you gave Mrs. Snow and me, and the gold piece you gave Nancy on her birthday, and--"

"Yes, yes--never mind about all that," interrupted the man. His face was very, very red now--and no wonder, perhaps: it was not for "giving things" that John Pendleton had been best known in the past. "That's all nonsense. 'Twasn't much, anyhow--but what there was, was because of you. You gave those things; not I! Yes, you did," he repeated, in answer to the shocked denial in her face. "And that only goes to prove all the more how I need you, little girl," he added, his voice softening into tender pleading once more. "If ever, ever I am to play the 'glad game,' Pollyanna, you'll have to come and play it with me."

The little girl's forehead puckered into a wistful frown.

"Aunt Polly has been so good to me," she began; but the man interrupted her sharply. The old irritability had come back to his face. Impatience which would brook no opposition had been a part of John Pendleton's nature too long to yield very easily now to restraint.

"Of course she's been good to you! But she doesn't want you, I'll warrant, half so much as I do," he contested.

"Why, Mr. Pendleton, she's glad, I know, to have--"

"Glad!" interrupted the man, thoroughly losing his patience now. "I'll wager Miss Polly doesn't know how to be glad--for anything! Oh, she does her duty, I know. She's a very dutiful woman. I've had experience with her 'duty,' before. I'll acknowledge we haven't been the best of friends for the last fifteen or twenty years. But I know her. Every one knows her--and she isn't the 'glad' kind, Pollyanna. She doesn't know how to be. As for your coming to me--you just ask her and see if she won't let you come. And, oh, little girl, little girl, I want you so!" he finished brokenly.

Pollyanna rose to her feet with a long sigh.

"All right. I'll ask her," she said wistfully. "Of course I don't mean that I wouldn't like to live here with you, Mr. Pendleton, but--" She did not complete her sentence. There was a moment's silence, then she added: "Well, anyhow, I'm glad I didn't tell her yesterday;--'cause then I supposed she was wanted, too."

John Pendleton smiled grimly.

"Well, yes, Pollyanna; I guess it is just as well you didn't mention it--yesterday."

"I didn't--only to the doctor; and of course he doesn't count."

"The doctor!" cried John Pendleton, turning quickly. "Not--Dr.--Chilton?"

"Yes; when he came to tell me you wanted to see me to-day, you know."

"Well, of all the--" muttered the man, falling back in his chair. Then he sat up with sudden interest. "And what did Dr. Chilton say?" he asked.

Pollyanna frowned thoughtfully.

"Why, I don't remember. Not much, I reckon. Oh, he did say he could well imagine you did want to see me."

"Oh, did he, indeed!" answered John Pendleton. And Pollyanna wondered why he gave that sudden queer little laugh.

Lesson 162

1. Read chapter 21.
2. Tell someone about the chapter.

The sky was darkening fast with what appeared to be an approaching thunder shower when Pollyanna hurried down the hill from John Pendleton's house. Half-way home she met Nancy with an umbrella. By that time, however, the clouds had shifted their position and the shower was not so imminent.

"Guess it's goin' 'round ter the north," announced Nancy, eyeing the sky critically. "I thought 'twas, all the time, but Miss Polly wanted me ter come with this. She was *worried* about ye!"

"Was she?" murmured Pollyanna abstractedly, eyeing the clouds in her turn.

Nancy sniffed a little.

"You don't seem ter notice what I said," she observed aggrievedly. "I said yer aunt was *worried* about ye!"

"Oh," sighed Pollyanna, remembering suddenly the question she was so soon to ask her aunt. "I'm sorry. I didn't mean to scare her."

"Well, I'm glad," retorted Nancy, unexpectedly. "I am, I am."

Pollyanna stared.

"*Glad* that Aunt Polly was scared about me! Why, Nancy, *that* isn't the way to play the game--to be glad for things like that!" she objected.

"There wa'n't no game in it," retorted Nancy. "Never thought of it. *You* don't seem ter sense what it means ter have Miss Polly *worried* about ye, child!"

"Why, it means worried--and worried is horrid--to feel," maintained Pollyanna. "What else can it mean?"

Nancy tossed her head.

"Well, I'll tell ye what it means. It means she's at last gettin' down somewheres near human--like folks; an' that she ain't jest doin' her duty by ye all the time."

"Why, Nancy," demurred the scandalized Pollyanna, "Aunt Polly always does her duty. She--she's a very dutiful woman!" Unconsciously Pollyanna repeated John Pendleton's words of half an hour before.

Nancy chuckled.

"You're right she is--and she always was, I guess! But she's somethin' more, now, since you came."

Pollyanna's face changed. Her brows drew into a troubled frown.

"There, that's what I was going to ask you, Nancy," she sighed. "Do you think Aunt Polly likes to have me here? Would she mind--if if I wasn't here any more?"

Nancy threw a quick look into the little girl's absorbed face. She had expected to be asked this question long before, and she had dreaded it. She had wondered how she should answer it--how she could answer it honestly without cruelly hurting the questioner. But now, *now*, in the face of the new suspicions that had become convictions by the afternoon's umbrella-sending--Nancy only welcomed the question with open arms. She was sure that, with a clean conscience to-day, she could set the love-hungry little girl's heart at rest.

"Likes ter have ye here? Would she miss ye if ye wa'n't here?" cried Nancy, indignantly. "As if that wa'n't jest what I was tellin' of ye! Didn't she send me posthaste with an umbrella 'cause she see a little cloud in the sky? Didn't she make me tote yer things all down-stairs, so you could have the pretty room you wanted? Why, Miss Pollyanna, when ye remember how at first she hated ter have--"

With a choking cough Nancy pulled herself up just in time.

"And it ain't jest things I can put my fingers on, neither," rushed on Nancy, breathlessly. "It's little ways she has, that shows how you've been softenin' her up an' mellerin' her down--the cat, and the dog, and the way she speaks ter me, and oh, lots o' things. Why, Miss Pollyanna, there ain't no tellin' how she'd miss ye--if ye wa'n't here," finished Nancy, speaking with an enthusiastic certainty that was meant to hide the perilous admission she had almost made before. Even then she was not quite prepared for the sudden joy that illumined Pollyanna's face.

"Oh, Nancy, I'm so glad--glad--glad! You don't know how glad I am that Aunt Polly--wants me!"

"As if I'd leave her now!" thought Pollyanna, as she climbed the stairs to her room a little later. "I always knew I wanted to live with Aunt Polly--but I reckon maybe I didn't know quite how much I wanted Aunt Polly--to want to live with *me*!"

The task of telling John Pendleton of her decision would not be an easy one, Pollyanna knew, and she dreaded it. She was very fond of John Pendleton, and she was very sorry for him--because he seemed to be so sorry for himself. She was sorry, too, for the long, lonely life that had made him so unhappy; and she was grieved that it had been because of her mother that he had spent those dreary years. She pictured the great gray house as it would be after its master was well again, with its silent rooms, its littered floors, its disordered desk; and her heart ached for his loneliness. She wished that somewhere, some one might be found who--And it was at this point that she sprang to her feet with a little cry of joy at the thought that had come to her.

As soon as she could, after that, she hurried up the hill to John Pendleton's house; and in due time she found herself in the great dim library, with John Pendleton himself sitting near her, his long, thin hands lying idle on the arms of his chair, and his faithful little dog at his feet.

"Well, Pollyanna, is it to be the 'glad game' with me, all the rest of my life?" asked the man, gently.

"Oh, yes," cried Pollyanna. "I've thought of the very gladdest kind of a thing for you to do, and--"

"With--*you*?" asked John Pendleton, his mouth growing a little stern at the corners.

"N-no; but--"

"Pollyanna, you aren't going to say no!" interrupted a voice deep with emotion.

"I--I've got to, Mr. Pendleton; truly I have. Aunt Polly--"

"Did she *refuse*--to let you--come?"

"I--I didn't ask her," stammered the little girl, miserably.

"Pollyanna!"

Pollyanna turned away her eyes. She could not meet the hurt, grieved gaze of her friend.

"So you didn't even ask her!"

"I couldn't, sir--truly," faltered Pollyanna. "You see, I found out--without asking. Aunt Polly *wants* me with her, and--and I want to stay, too," she confessed bravely. "You don't know how good she's been to me; and--and I think, really, sometimes she's beginning to be glad about things-lots of things. And you know she never used to be. You said it yourself. Oh, Mr. Pendleton, I *couldn't* leave Aunt Polly--now!"

There was a long pause. Only the snapping of the wood fire in the grate broke the silence. At last, however, the man spoke.

"No, Pollyanna; I see. You couldn't leave her--now," he said. "I won't ask you--again." The last word was so low it was almost inaudible; but Pollyanna heard.

"Oh, but you don't know about the rest of it," she reminded him eagerly. "There's the very gladdest thing you *can* do--truly there is!"

"Not for me, Pollyanna."

"Yes, sir, for you. You *said* it. You said only a--a woman's hand and heart or a child's presence could make a home. And I can get it for you--a child's presence;--not me, you know, but another one."

"As if I would have any but you!" resented an indignant voice.

"But you will--when you know; you're so kind and good! Why, think of the prisms and the gold pieces, and all that money you save for the heathen, and--"

"Pollyanna!" interrupted the man, savagely. "Once for all let us end that nonsense! I've tried to tell you half a dozen times before. There is no money for the heathen. I never sent a penny to them in my life. There!"

He lifted his chin and braced himself to meet what he expected--the grieved disappointment of Pollyanna's eyes. To his amazement, however, there was neither grief nor disappointment in Pollyanna's eyes. There was only surprised joy.

"Oh, oh!" she cried, clapping her hands. "I'm so glad! That is," she corrected, coloring distressfully, "I don't mean that I'm not sorry for the heathen, only just now I can't help being glad that you don't want the little India boys, because all the rest have wanted them. And so I'm glad you'd rather have Jimmy Bean. Now I know you'll take him!"

"Take--*who*?"

"Jimmy Bean. He's the 'child's presence,' you know; and he'll be so glad to be it. I had to tell him last week that even my Ladies' Aid out West wouldn't take him, and he was so disappointed. But now--when he hears of this--he'll be so glad!"

"Will he? Well, I won't," exclaimed the man, decisively. "Pollyanna, this is sheer nonsense!"

"You don't mean--you won't take him?"

"I certainly do mean just that."

"But he'd be a lovely child's presence," faltered Pollyanna. She was almost crying now. "And you *couldn't* be lonesome--with Jimmy 'round."

"I don't doubt it," rejoined the man; "but--I think I prefer the lonesomeness."

It was then that Pollyanna, for the first time in weeks, suddenly remembered something Nancy had once told her. She raised her chin aggrievedly.

"Maybe you think a nice live little boy wouldn't be better than that old dead skeleton you keep somewhere; but I think it would!"

"*Skeleton*?"

"Yes. Nancy said you had one in your closet, somewhere."

"Why, what--" Suddenly the man threw back his head and laughed. He laughed very heartily indeed--so heartily that Pollyanna began to cry from pure nervousness. When he saw that, John Pendleton sat erect very promptly. His face grew grave at once.

"Pollyanna, I suspect you are right--more right than you know," he said gently. "In fact, I *know* that a 'nice live little boy' would be far better than--my skeleton in the closet; only--we aren't always willing to make the exchange. We are apt to still cling to--our skeletons, Pollyanna. However, suppose you tell me a little more about this nice little boy." And Pollyanna told him.

Perhaps the laugh cleared the air; or perhaps the pathos of Jimmy Bean's story as told by Pollyanna's eager little lips touched a heart already strangely softened. At all events, when Pollyanna went home that night she carried with her an invitation for Jimmy Bean himself to call at the great house with Pollyanna the next Saturday afternoon.

"And I'm so glad, and I'm sure you'll like him," sighed Pollyanna, as she said good-by. "I do so want Jimmy Bean to have a home--and folks that care, you know."

Lesson 163

1. Read chapter 22.
2. Tell someone about the chapter.

On the afternoon that Pollyanna told John Pendleton of Jimmy Bean, the Rev. Paul Ford climbed the hill and entered the Pendleton Woods, hoping that the hushed beauty of God's out-of-doors would still the tumult that His children of men had wrought.

The Rev. Paul Ford was sick at heart. Month by month, for a year past, conditions in the parish under him had been growing worse and worse; until it seemed that now, turn which way he would, he encountered only wrangling, backbiting, scandal, and jealousy. He had argued, pleaded, rebuked, and ignored by turns; and always and through all he had prayed--earnestly, hopefully. But to-day miserably he was forced to own that matters were no better, but rather worse.

Two of his deacons were at swords' points over a silly something that only endless brooding had made of any account. Three of his most energetic women workers had withdrawn from the Ladies' Aid Society because a tiny spark of gossip had been fanned by wagging tongues into a devouring flame of scandal. The choir had split over the amount of solo work given to a fanciedly preferred singer. Even the Christian Endeavor Society was in a ferment of unrest owing to open criticism of two of its officers. As to the Sunday school--it had been the resignation of its superintendent and two of its teachers that had been the last straw, and that had sent the harassed minister to the quiet woods for prayer and meditation.

Under the green arch of the trees the Rev. Paul Ford faced the thing squarely. To his mind, the crisis had come. Something must be done--and done at once. The entire work of the church was at a standstill. The Sunday services, the week-day prayer meeting, the missionary teas, even the suppers and socials were becoming less and less well attended. True, a few conscientious workers were still left. But they pulled at cross purposes, usually; and always they showed themselves to be acutely aware of the critical eyes all about them, and of the tongues that had nothing to do but to talk about what the eyes saw.

And because of all this, the Rev. Paul Ford understood very well that he (God's minister), the church, the town, and even Christianity itself was suffering; and must suffer still more unless--

Clearly something must be done, and done at once. But what?

Slowly the minister took from his pocket the notes he had made for his next Sunday's sermon. Frowningly he looked at them. His mouth settled into stern lines, as aloud, very impressively, he read the verses on which he had determined to speak:

"'But woe unto you, scribes and Pharisees, hypocrites! for ye shut up the kingdom of heaven against men: for ye neither go in yourselves, neither suffer ye them that are entering to go in.'

"'Woe unto you, scribes and Pharisees, hypocrites! for ye devour widows' houses, and for a pretence make long prayer: therefore ye shall receive the greater damnation.'

"'Woe unto you, scribes and Pharisees, hypocrites! for ye pay tithe of mint and anise and cummin, and have omitted the weightier matters of the law, judgment, mercy, and faith: these ought ye to have done, and not to leave the other undone.' "

It was a bitter denunciation. In the green aisles of the woods, the minister's deep voice rang out with scathing effect. Even the birds and squirrels seemed hushed into awed silence. It brought to the minister a vivid realization of how those words would sound the next Sunday when he should utter them before his people in the sacred hush of the church.

His people!--they *were* his people. Could he do it? Dare he do it? Dare he not do it? It was a fearful denunciation, even without the words that would follow--his own words. He had prayed and prayed. He had pleaded earnestly for help, for guidance. He longed--oh, how earnestly he longed!--to take now, in this crisis, the right step. But was this--the right step?

Slowly the minister folded the papers and thrust them back into his pocket. Then, with a sigh that was almost a moan, he flung himself down at the foot of a tree, and covered his face with his hands.

It was there that Pollyanna, on her way home from the Pendleton house, found him. With a little cry she ran forward.

"Oh, oh, Mr. Ford! You--*you* haven't broken *your* leg or--or anything, have you?" she gasped.

The minister dropped his hands, and looked up quickly. He tried to smile.

"No, dear--no, indeed! I'm just--resting."

"Oh," sighed Pollyanna, falling back a little. "That's all right, then. You see, Mr. Pendleton *had* broken his leg when I found him--but he was lying down, though. And you are sitting up."

"Yes, I am sitting up; and I haven't broken anything--that doctors can mend."

The last words were very low, but Pollyanna heard them. A swift change crossed her face. Her eyes glowed with tender sympathy.

"I know what you mean--something plagues you. Father used to feel like that, lots of times. I reckon ministers do--most generally. You see there's such a lot depends on 'em, somehow."

The Rev. Paul Ford turned a little wonderingly.

"Was *your* father a minister, Pollyanna?"

"Yes, sir. Didn't you know? I supposed everybody knew that. He married Aunt Polly's sister, and she was my mother."

"Oh, I understand. But, you see, I haven't been here many years, so I don't know all the family histories."

"Yes, sir--I mean, no, sir," smiled Pollyanna.

There was a long pause. The minister, still sitting at the foot of the tree, appeared to have forgotten Pollyanna's presence. He had pulled some papers from his pocket and unfolded them; but he was not looking at them. He was gazing, instead, at a leaf on the ground a little distance away--and it was not even a pretty leaf. It was brown and dead. Pollyanna, looking at him, felt vaguely sorry for him.

"It--it's a nice day," she began hopefully.

For a moment there was no answer; then the minister looked up with a start.

"What? Oh!--yes, it is a very nice day."

"And 'tisn't cold at all, either, even if 'tis October," observed Pollyanna, still more hopefully. "Mr. Pendleton had a fire, but he said he didn't need it. It was just to look at. I like to look at fires, don't you?"

There was no reply this time, though Pollyanna waited patiently, before she tried again--by a new route.

"Do you like being a minister?"

The Rev. Paul Ford looked up now, very quickly.

"Do I like--Why, what an odd question! Why do you ask that, my dear?"

"Nothing--only the way you looked. It made me think of my father. He used to look like that--sometimes."

"Did he?" The minister's voice was polite, but his eyes had gone back to the dried leaf on the ground.

"Yes, and I used to ask him just as I did you if he was glad he was a minister."

The man under the tree smiled a little sadly.

"Well--what did he say?"

"Oh, he always said he was, of course, but 'most always he said, too, that he wouldn't *stay* a minister a minute if 'twasn't for the rejoicing texts."

"The--*what*?" The Rev. Paul Ford's eyes left the leaf and gazed wonderingly into Pollyanna's merry little face.

"Well, that's what father used to call 'em," she laughed. "Of course the Bible didn't name 'em that. But it's all those that begin 'Be glad in the Lord,' or 'Rejoice greatly,' or 'Shout for joy,' and all that, you know--such a lot of 'em. Once, when father felt specially bad, he counted 'em. There were eight hundred of 'em."

"Eight hundred!"

"Yes--that told you to rejoice and be glad, you know; that's why father named 'em the 'rejoicing texts.' "

"Oh!" There was an odd look on the minister's face. His eyes had fallen to the words on the top paper in his hands--"But woe unto you, scribes and Pharisees, hypocrites!" "And so your father-- liked those 'rejoicing texts,' " he murmured.

"Oh, yes," nodded Pollyanna, emphatically. "He said he felt better right away, that first day he thought to count 'em. He said if God took the trouble to tell us eight hundred times to be glad and rejoice, He must want us to do it--*some*. And father felt ashamed that he hadn't done it more. After that, they got to be such a comfort to him, you know, when things went wrong; when the Ladies' Aiders got to fight--I mean, when they *didn't agree* about something," corrected Pollyanna, hastily. "Why, it was those texts, too, father said, that made *him* think of the game--he began with *me* on the crutches--but he said 'twas the rejoicing texts that started him on it."

"And what game might that be?" asked the minister.

"About finding something in everything to be glad about, you know. As I said, he began with me on the crutches." And once more Pollyanna told her story--this time to a man who listened with tender eyes and understanding ears.

A little later Pollyanna and the minister descended the hill, hand in hand. Pollyanna's face was radiant. Pollyanna loved to talk, and she had been talking now for some time: there seemed to be so many, many things about the game, her father, and the old home life that the minister wanted to know.

At the foot of the hill their ways parted, and Pollyanna down one road, and the minister down another, walked on alone.

In the Rev. Paul Ford's study that evening the minister sat thinking. Near him on the desk lay a few loose sheets of paper--his sermon notes. Under the suspended pencil in his fingers lay other sheets of paper, blank--his sermon to be. But the minister was not thinking either of what he had written, or of what be intended to write. In his imagination he was far away in a little Western town with a missionary minister who was poor, sick, worried, and almost alone in the world--but who was poring over the Bible to find how many times his Lord and Master had told him to "rejoice and be glad."

After a time, with a long sigh, the Rev. Paul Ford roused himself, came back from the far Western town, and adjusted the sheets of paper under his hand.

"Matthew twenty-third; 13--14 and 23," he wrote; then, with a gesture of impatience, he dropped his pencil and pulled toward him a magazine left on the desk by his wife a few minutes before. Listlessly his tired eyes turned from paragraph to paragraph until these words arrested them:

"A father one day said to his son, Tom, who, he knew, had refused to fill his mother's woodbox that morning: 'Tom, I'm sure you'll be glad to go and bring in some wood for your mother.' And without a word Tom went. Why? Just because his father showed so plainly that he expected him to do the right thing. Suppose he had said: 'Tom, I overheard what you said to your mother this morning, and I'm ashamed of you. Go at once and fill that woodbox!' I'll warrant that woodbox, would be empty yet, so far as Tom was concerned!"

On and on read the minister--a word here, a line there, a paragraph somewhere else:

"What men and women need is encouragement. Their natural resisting powers should be strengthened, not weakened. . . . Instead of always harping on a man's faults, tell him of his virtues. Try to pull him out of his rut of bad habits. Hold up to him his better self, his *real* self that can dare and do and win out! . . . The influence of a beautiful, helpful, hopeful character is contagious, and may revolutionize a whole town. . . . People radiate what is in their minds and in their hearts. If a man feels kindly and obliging, his neighbors will feel that way, too, before long. But if he scolds and scowls and criticizes--his neighbors will return scowl for scowl, and add interest! . . . When you look for the bad, expecting it, you will get it. When you know you will find the good--you will get that. . . . Tell your son Tom you *know* he'll be glad to fill that woodbox--then watch him start, alert and interested!"

The minister dropped the paper and lifted his chin. In a moment he was on his feet, tramping the narrow room back and forth, back and forth. Later, some time later, he drew a long breath, and dropped himself in the chair at his desk.

"God helping me, I'll do it!" he cried softly. "I'll tell all my Toms I *know* they'll be glad to fill that woodbox! I'll give them work to do, and I'll make them so full of the very joy of doing it that they won't have *time* to look at their neighbors' woodboxes!" And he picked up his sermon notes, tore straight through the sheets, and cast them from him, so that on one side of his chair lay "But woe unto you," and on the other, "scribes and Pharisees, hypocrites!" while across the smooth white paper before him his pencil fairly flew--after first drawing one black line through "Matthew twenty-third; 13--14 and 23."

Thus it happened that the Rev. Paul Ford's sermon the next Sunday was a veritable bugle-call to the best that was in every man and woman and child that heard it; and its text was one of Pollyanna's shining eight hundred:

"Be glad in the Lord and rejoice, ye righteous, and shout for joy all ye that are upright in heart."

Lesson 164

1. Read chapter 23.
2. Tell someone about the chapter.

At Mrs. Snow's request, Pollyanna went one day to Dr. Chilton's office to get the name of a medicine which Mrs. Snow had forgotten. As it chanced, Pollyanna had never before seen the inside of Dr. Chilton's office.

"I've never been to your home before! This *is* your home, isn't it?" she said, looking interestedly about her.

The doctor smiled a little sadly.

"Yes--such as 'tis," he answered, as he wrote something on the pad of paper in his hand; "but it's a pretty poor apology for a home, Pollyanna. They're just rooms, that's all--not a home."

Pollyanna nodded her head wisely. Her eyes glowed with sympathetic understanding.

"I know. It takes a woman's hand and heart, or a child's presence to make a home," she said.

"Eh?" The doctor wheeled about abruptly.

"Mr. Pendleton told me," nodded Pollyanna, again; "about the woman's hand and heart, or the child's presence, you know. Why don't you get a woman's hand and heart, Dr. Chilton? Or maybe you'd take Jimmy Bean--if Mr. Pendleton doesn't want him."

Dr. Chilton laughed a little constrainedly.

"So Mr. Pendleton says it takes a woman's hand and heart to make a home, does he?" he asked evasively.

"Yes. He says his is just a house, too. Why don't you, Dr. Chilton?"

"Why don't I--what?" The doctor had turned back to his desk.

"Get a woman's hand and heart. Oh--and I forgot." Pollyanna's face showed suddenly a painful color. "I suppose I ought to tell you. It wasn't Aunt Polly that Mr. Pendleton loved long ago; and so we--we aren't going there to live. You see, I told you it was--but I made a mistake. I hope *you* didn't tell any one," she finished anxiously.

"No--I didn't tell any one, Pollyanna," replied the doctor, a little queerly.

"Oh, that's all right, then," sighed Pollyanna in relief. "You see you're the only one I told, and I thought Mr. Pendleton looked sort of funny when I said I'd told *you*."

"Did he?" The doctor's lips twitched.

"Yes. And of course he wouldn't want many people to know it--when 'twasn't true. But why don't you get a woman's hand and heart, Dr. Chilton?"

There was a moment's silence; then very gravely the doctor said:

"They're not always to be had--for the asking, little girl."

Pollyanna frowned thoughtfully.

"But I should think *you* could get 'em," she argued. The flattering emphasis was unmistakable.

"Thank you," laughed the doctor, with uplifted eyebrows. Then, gravely again: "I'm afraid some of your older sisters would not be quite so--confident. At least, they--they haven't shown themselves to be so--obliging," he observed.

Pollyanna frowned again. Then her eyes widened in surprise.

"Why, Dr. Chilton, you don't mean--you didn't try to get somebody's hand and heart once, like Mr. Pendleton, and--and couldn't, did you?"

The doctor got to his feet a little abruptly.

"There, there, Pollyanna, never mind about that now. Don't let other people's troubles worry your little head. Suppose you run back now to Mrs. Snow. I've written down the name of the medicine, and the directions how she is to take it. Was there anything else?"

Pollyanna shook her head.

"No, Sir; thank you, Sir," she murmured soberly, as she turned toward the door. From the little hallway she called back, her face suddenly alight: "Anyhow, I'm glad 'twasn't my mother's hand and heart that you wanted and couldn't get, Dr. Chilton. Good-by!"

*   *   *   *   *   *

It was on the last day of October that the accident occurred. Pollyanna, hurrying home from school, crossed the road at an apparently safe distance in front of a swiftly approaching motor car.

Just what happened, no one could seem to tell afterward. Neither was there any one found who could tell why it happened or who was to blame that it did happen. Pollyanna, however, at five o'clock, was borne, limp and unconscious, into the little room that was so dear to her. There, by a white-faced Aunt Polly and a weeping Nancy she was undressed tenderly and put to bed, while from the village, hastily summoned by telephone, Dr. Warren was hurrying as fast as another motor car could bring him.

"And ye didn't need ter more'n look at her aunt's face," Nancy was sobbing to Old Tom in the garden, after the doctor had arrived and was closeted in the hushed room; "ye didn't need ter more'n look at her aunt's face ter see that 'twa'n't no duty that was eatin' her. Yer hands don't shake, and yer eyes don't look as if ye was tryin' ter hold back the Angel o' Death himself, when you're jest doin' yer *duty*, Mr. Tom they don't, they don't!"

"Is she hurt--bad?" The old man's voice shook.

"There ain't no tellin'," sobbed Nancy. "She lay back that white an' still she might easy be dead; but Miss Polly said she wa'n't dead--an' Miss Polly had oughter know, if any one would--she kept up such a listenin' an' a feelin' for her heartbeats an' her breath!"

"Couldn't ye tell anythin' what it done to her?--that--that--" Old Tom's face worked convulsively.

Nancy's lips relaxed a little.

"I wish ye *would* call it somethin', Mr. Tom an' somethin' good an' strong, too. Drat it! Ter think of its runnin' down our little girl! I always hated the evil-smellin' things, anyhow--I did, I did!"

"But where is she hurt?"

"I don't know, I don't know," moaned Nancy. "There's a little cut on her blessed head, but 'tain't bad--that ain't--Miss Polly says. She says she's afraid it's infernally she's hurt."

A faint flicker came into Old Tom's eyes.

"I guess you mean internally, Nancy," he said dryly. "She's hurt infernally, all right--plague take that autymobile!--but I don't guess Miss Polly'd be usin' that word, all the same."

"Eh? Well, I don't know, I don't know," moaned Nancy, with a shake of her head as she turned away. "Seems as if I jest couldn't stand it till that doctor gits out o' there. I wish I had a washin' ter do--the biggest washin' I ever see, I do, I do!" she wailed, wringing her hands helplessly.

Even after the doctor was gone, however, there seemed to be little that Nancy could tell Mr. Tom. There appeared to be no bones broken, and the cut was of slight consequence; but the doctor had looked very grave, had shaken his head slowly, and had said that time alone could tell. After he had gone, Miss Polly had shown a face even whiter and more drawn looking than before. The patient had not fully recovered consciousness, but at present she seemed to be resting as comfortably as could be expected. A trained nurse had been sent for, and would come that night. That was all. And Nancy turned sobbingly, and went back to her kitchen.

It was sometime during the next forenoon that Pollyanna opened conscious eyes and realized where she was.

"Why, Aunt Polly, what's the matter? Isn't it daytime? Why don't I get up?" she cried. "Why, Aunt Polly, I can't get up," she moaned, falling back on the pillow, after an ineffectual attempt to lift herself.

"No, dear, I wouldn't try--just yet," soothed her aunt quickly, but very quietly.

"But what is the matter? Why can't I get up?"

Miss Polly's eyes asked an agonized question of the white-capped young woman standing in the window, out of the range of Pollyanna's eyes.

The young woman nodded.

"Tell her," the lips said.

Miss Polly cleared her throat, and tried to swallow the lump that would scarcely let her speak.

"You were hurt, dear, by the automobile last night. But never mind that now. Auntie wants you to rest and go to sleep again."

"Hurt? Oh, yes; I--I ran." Pollyanna's eyes were dazed. She lifted her hand to her forehead. "Why, it's--done up, and it--hurts!"

"Yes, dear; but never mind. Just--just rest."

"But, Aunt Polly, I feel so funny, and so bad! My legs feel so--so queer--only they don't *feel*--at all!"

With an imploring look into the nurse's face, Miss Polly struggled to her feet, and turned away. The nurse came forward quickly.

"Suppose you let me talk to you now," she began cheerily. "I'm sure I think it's high time we were getting acquainted, and I'm going to introduce myself. I am Miss Hunt, and I've come to help your aunt take care of you. And the very first thing I'm going to do is to ask you to swallow these little white pills for me."

Pollyanna's eyes grew a bit wild.

"But I don't want to be taken care of--that is, not for long! I want to get up. You know I go to school. Can't I go to school to-morrow?"

From the window where Aunt Polly stood now there came a half-stifled cry.

"Tomorrow?" smiled the nurse, brightly.

"Well, I may not let you out quite so soon as that, Miss Pollyanna. But just swallow these little pills for me, please, and we'll see what *they'll* do."

"All right," agreed Pollyanna, somewhat doubtfully; "but I *must* go to school day after to-morrow--there are examinations then, you know."

She spoke again, a minute later. She spoke of school, and of the automobile, and of how her head ached; but very soon her voice trailed into silence under the blessed influence of the little white pills she had swallowed.

Lesson 165

1. Read chapter 24.
2. Tell someone about the chapter.

Pollyanna did not go to school "to-morrow," nor the "day after to-morrow." Pollyanna, however, did not realize this, except momentarily when a brief period of full consciousness sent insistent questions to her lips. Pollyanna did not realize anything, in fact, very clearly until a week had passed; then the fever subsided, the pain lessened somewhat, and her mind awoke to full consciousness. She had then to be told all over again what had occurred.

"And so it's hurt that I am, and not sick," she sighed at last. "Well, I'm glad of that."

"G-glad, Pollyanna?" asked her aunt, who was sitting by the bed.

"Yes. I'd so much rather have broken legs like Mr. Pendleton's than life-long-invalids like Mrs. Snow, you know. Broken legs get well, and lifelong-invalids don't."

Miss Polly--who had said nothing whatever about broken legs--got suddenly to her feet and walked to the little dressing table across the room. She was picking up one object after another now, and putting each down, in an aimless fashion quite unlike her usual decisiveness. Her face was not aimless-looking at all, however; it was white and drawn.

On the bed Pollyanna lay blinking at the dancing band of colors on the ceiling, which came from one of the prisms in the window.

"I'm glad it isn't smallpox that ails me, too," she murmured contentedly. "That would be worse than freckles. And I'm glad 'tisn't whooping cough--I've had that, and it's horrid--and I'm glad 'tisn't appendicitis nor measles, 'cause they're catching--measles are, I mean--and they wouldn't let you stay here."

"You seem to--to be glad for a good many things, my dear," faltered Aunt Polly, putting her hand to her throat as if her collar bound.

Pollyanna laughed softly.

"I am. I've been thinking of 'em--lots of 'em--all the time I've been looking up at that rainbow. I love rainbows. I'm so glad Mr. Pendleton gave me those prisms! I'm glad of some things I haven't said yet. I don't know but I'm 'most glad I was hurt."

"Pollyanna!"

Pollyanna laughed softly again. She turned luminous eyes on her aunt. "Well, you see, since I have been hurt, you've called me 'dear' lots of times--and you didn't before. I love to be called 'dear'--by folks that belong to you, I mean. Some of the Ladies' Aiders did call me that; and of course that was pretty nice, but not so nice as if they had belonged to me, like you do. Oh, Aunt Polly, I'm so glad you belong to me!"

Aunt Polly did not answer. Her hand was at her throat again. Her eyes were full of tears. She had turned away and was hurrying from the room through the door by which the nurse had just entered.

It was that afternoon that Nancy ran out to Old Tom, who was cleaning harnesses in the barn. Her eyes were wild.

"Mr. Tom, Mr. Tom, guess what's happened," she panted. "You couldn't guess in a thousand years--you couldn't, you couldn't!"

"Then I cal'late I won't try," retorted the man, grimly, "specially as I hain't got more'n *ten* ter live, anyhow, probably. You'd better tell me first off, Nancy."

"Well, listen, then. Who do you s'pose is in the parlor now with the mistress? Who, I say?"

Old Tom shook his head.

"There's no tellin'," he declared.

"Yes, there is. I'm tellin'. It's--John Pendleton!"

"Sho, now! You're jokin', girl."

"Not much I am--an' me a-lettin' him in myself--crutches an' all! An' the team he come in a-waitin' this minute at the door for him, jest as if he wa'n't the cranky old crosspatch he is, what never talks ter no one! Jest think, Mr. Tom--*him* a-callin' on *her*!"

"Well, why not?" demanded the old man, a little aggressively.

Nancy gave him a scornful glance.

"As if you didn't know better'n me!" she derided.

"Eh?"

"Oh, you needn't be so innercent," she retorted with mock indignation; "--you what led me wildgoose chasin' in the first place!"

"What do ye mean?"

Nancy glanced through the open barn door toward the house, and came a step nearer to the old man.

"Listen! 'Twas you that was tellin' me Miss Polly had a gentleman friend in the first place, wa'n't it? Well, one day I thinks I finds two and two, and I puts 'em tergether an' makes four. But it turns out ter be five--an' no four at all, at all!"

With a gesture of indifference Old Tom turned and fell to work.

"If you're goin' ter talk ter me, you've got ter talk plain horse sense," he declared testily. "I never was no hand for figgers."

Nancy laughed.

"Well, it's this," she explained. "I heard somethin' that made me think him an' Miss Polly was in love."

"*Mr. Pendleton!*" Old Tom straightened up.

"Yes. Oh, I know now; he wasn't. It was that blessed child's mother he was in love with, and that's why he wanted--but never mind that part," she added hastily, remembering just in time her promise to Pollyanna not to tell that Mr. Pendleton had wished her to come and live with him. "Well, I've been askin' folks about him some, since, and I've found out that him an' Miss Polly hain't been friends for years, an' that she's been hatin' him like pizen owin' ter the silly gossip that coupled their names tergether when she was eighteen or twenty."

"Yes, I remember," nodded Old Tom. "It was three or four years after Miss Jennie give him the mitten and went off with the other chap. Miss Polly knew about it, of course, and was sorry for him. So she tried ter be nice to him. Maybe she overdid it a little--she hated that minister chap so who had took off her sister. At any rate, somebody begun ter make trouble. They said she was runnin' after him."

"Runnin' after any man--her!" interjected Nancy.

"I know it; but they did," declared Old Tom, "and of course no gal of any spunk'll stand that. Then about that time come her own gentleman friend an' the trouble with *him*. After that she shut up like an oyster an' wouldn't have nothin' ter do with nobody fur a spell. Her heart jest seemed to turn bitter at the core."

"Yes, I know. I've heard about that now," rejoined Nancy; "an' that's why you could 'a' knocked me down with a feather when I see *him* at the door--him, what she hain't spoke to for years! But I let him in an' went an' told her."

"What did she say?" Old Tom held his breath suspended.

"Nothin'--at first. She was so still I thought she hadn't heard; and I was jest goin' ter say it over when she speaks up quiet like: 'Tell Mr. Pendleton I will be down at once.' An' I come an' told him. Then I come out here an' told you," finished Nancy, casting another backward glance toward the house.

"Humph!" grunted Old Tom; and fell to work again.

In the ceremonious "parlor" of the Harrington homestead, Mr. John Pendleton did not have to wait long before a swift step warned him of Miss Polly's coming. As he attempted to rise, she made a gesture of remonstrance. She did not offer her hand, however, and her face was coldly reserved.

"I called to ask for--Pollyanna," he began at once, a little brusquely.

"Thank you. She is about the same," said Miss Polly.

"And that is--won't you tell me *how* she is? His voice was not quite steady this time."

A quick spasm of pain crossed the woman's face.

"I can't, I wish I could!"

"You mean--you don't know?"

"Yes."

"But--the doctor?"

"Dr. Warren himself seems--at sea. He is in correspondence now with a New York specialist. They have arranged for a consultation at once."

"But--but what *were* her injuries that you do know?"

"A slight cut on the head, one or two bruises, and--and an injury to the spine which has seemed to cause--paralysis from the hips down."

A low cry came from the man. There was a brief silence; then, huskily, he asked:

"And Pollyanna--how does she--take it?"

"She doesn't understand--at all--how things really are. And I *can't* tell her."

"But she must know--something!"

Miss Polly lifted her hand to the collar at her throat in the gesture that had become so common to her of late.

"Oh, yes. She knows she can't--move; but she thinks her legs are--broken. She says she's glad it's broken legs like yours rather than 'lifelong-invalids' like Mrs. Snow's; because broken legs get well, and the other--doesn't. She talks like that all the time, until it--it seems as if I should--die!"

Through the blur of tears in his own eyes, the man saw the drawn face opposite, twisted with emotion. Involuntarily his thoughts went back to what Pollyanna had said when he had made his final plea for her presence: "Oh, I couldn't leave Aunt Polly--now!"

It was this thought that made him ask very gently, as soon as he could control his voice:

"I wonder if you know, Miss Harrington, how hard I tried to get Pollyanna to come and live with me."

"With *you*!--Pollyanna!"

The man winced a little at the tone of her voice; but his own voice was still impersonally cool when he spoke again.

"Yes. I wanted to adopt her--legally, you understand; making her my heir, of course."

The woman in the opposite chair relaxed a little. It came to her, suddenly, what a brilliant future it would have meant for Pollyanna--this adoption; and she wondered if Pollyanna were old enough and mercenary enough--to be tempted by this man's money and position.

"I am very fond of Pollyanna," the man was continuing. "I am fond of her both for her own sake, and for--her mother's. I stood ready to give Pollyanna the love that had been twenty-five years in storage."

"*Love*." Miss Polly remembered suddenly why *she* had taken this child in the first place--and with the recollection came the remembrance of Pollyanna's own words uttered that very morning: "I

414

love to be called 'dear' by folks that belong to you!" And it was this love-hungry little girl that had been offered the stored-up affection of twenty-five years:--and she was old enough to be tempted by love! With a sinking heart Miss Polly realized that. With a sinking heart, too, she realized something else: the dreariness of her own future now without Pollyanna.

"Well?" she said. And the man, recognizing the self-control that vibrated through the harshness of the tone, smiled sadly.

"She would not come," he answered.

"Why?"

"She would not leave you. She said you had been so good to her. She wanted to stay with you--and she said she *thought* you wanted her to stay," he finished, as he pulled himself to his feet.

He did not look toward Miss Polly. He turned his face resolutely toward the door. But instantly he heard a swift step at his side, and found a shaking hand thrust toward him.

"When the specialist comes, and I know anything--definite about Pollyanna, I will let you hear from me," said a trembling voice. "Good-by--and thank you for coming. Pollyanna will be pleased."

Lesson 166

1. Read chapter 25.
2. Tell someone about the chapter.

On the day after John Pendleton's call at the Harrington homestead, Miss Polly set herself to the task of preparing Pollyanna for the visit of the specialist.

"Pollyanna, my dear," she began gently, "we have decided that we want another doctor besides Dr. Warren to see you. Another one might tell us something new to do--to help you get well faster, you know."

A joyous light came to Pollyanna's face.

"Dr. Chilton! Oh, Aunt Polly, I'd so love to have Dr. Chilton! I've wanted him all the time, but I was afraid you didn't, on account of his seeing you in the sun parlor that day, you know; so I didn't like to say anything. But I'm so glad you do want him!"

Aunt Polly's face had turned white, then red, then back to white again. But when she answered, she showed very plainly that she was trying to speak lightly and cheerfully.

"Oh, no, dear! It wasn't Dr. Chilton at all that I meant. It is a new doctor--a very famous doctor from New York, who--who knows a great deal about--about hurts like yours."

Pollyanna's face fell.

"I don't believe he knows half so much as Dr. Chilton."

"Oh, yes, he does, I'm sure, dear."

"But it was Dr. Chilton who doctored Mr. Pendleton's broken leg, Aunt Polly. If--if you don't mind *very* much, I *would like* to have Dr. Chilton--truly I would!"

A distressed color suffused Miss Polly's face. For a moment she did not speak at all; then she said gently--though yet with a touch of her old stern decisiveness:

"But I do mind, Pollyanna. I mind very much. I would do anything--almost anything for you, my dear; but I--for reasons which I do not care to speak of now, I don't wish Dr. Chilton called in on-- on this case. And believe me, he can *not* know so much about--about your trouble, as this great doctor does, who will come from New York to-morrow."

Pollyanna still looked unconvinced.

"But, Aunt Polly, if you *loved* Dr. Chilton--"

"*What*, Pollyanna?" Aunt Polly's voice was very sharp now. Her cheeks were very red, too.

"I say, if you loved Dr. Chilton, and didn't love the other one," sighed Pollyanna, "seems to me that would make some difference in the good he would do; and I love Dr. Chilton."

The nurse entered the room at that moment, and Aunt Polly rose to her feet abruptly, a look of relief on her face.

"I am very sorry, Pollyanna," she said, a little stiffly; "but I'm afraid you'll have to let me be the judge, this time. Besides, it's already arranged. The New York doctor is coming to-morrow."

As it happened, however, the New York doctor did not come "to-morrow." At the last moment a telegram told of an unavoidable delay owing to the sudden illness of the specialist himself. This led Pollyanna into a renewed pleading for the substitution of Dr. Chilton--"which would be so easy now, you know."

But as before, Aunt Polly shook her head and said "no, dear," very decisively, yet with a still more anxious assurance that she would do anything--anything but that--to please her dear Pollyanna.

As the days of waiting passed, one by one, it did indeed, seem that Aunt Polly was doing everything (but that) that she could do to please her niece.

"I wouldn't 'a' believed it--you couldn't 'a' made me believe it," Nancy said to Old Tom one morning. "There don't seem ter be a minute in the day that Miss Polly ain't jest hangin' 'round waitin' ter do somethin' for that blessed lamb if 'tain't more than ter let in the cat--an' her what wouldn't let Fluff nor Buff up-stairs for love nor money a week ago; an' now she lets 'em tumble all over the bed jest 'cause it pleases Miss Pollyanna!

"An' when she ain't doin' nothin' else, she's movin' them little glass danglers 'round ter diff'rent winders in the room so the sun'll make the 'rainbows dance,' as that blessed child calls it. She's sent Timothy down ter Cobb's greenhouse three times for fresh flowers--an' that besides all the posies fetched in ter her, too. An' the other day, if I didn't find her sittin' 'fore the bed with the nurse actually doin' her hair, an' Miss Pollyanna lookin' on an' bossin' from the bed, her eyes all shinin' an' happy. An' I declare ter goodness, if Miss Polly hain't wore her hair like that every day now-- jest ter please that blessed child!"

Old Tom chuckled.

"Well, it strikes me Miss Polly herself ain't lookin' none the worse--for wearin' them 'ere curls 'round her forehead," he observed dryly.

"Course she ain't," retorted Nancy, indignantly. "She looks like *folks*, now. She's actually almost-"

"Keerful, now, Nancy!" interrupted the old man, with a slow grin. "You know what you said when I told ye she was handsome once."

Nancy shrugged her shoulders.

"Oh, she ain't handsome, of course; but I will own up she don't look like the same woman, what with the ribbons an' lace jiggers Miss Pollyanna makes her wear 'round her neck."

"I told ye so," nodded the man. "I told ye she wa'n't--old."

Nancy laughed.

"Well, I'll own up she *hain't* got quite so good an imitation of it--as she did have, 'fore Miss Pollyanna come. Say, Mr. Tom, who *was* her gentleman friend? I hain't found that out, yet; I hain't, I hain't!"

"Hain't ye?" asked the old man, with an odd look on his face. "Well, I guess ye won't then from me."

"Oh, Mr. Tom, come on, now," wheedled the girl. "Ye see, there ain't many folks here that I *can* ask."

"Maybe not. But there's one, anyhow, that ain't answerin'," grinned Old Tom. Then, abruptly, the light died from his eyes. "How is she, ter-day--the little gal?"

Nancy shook her head. Her face, too, had sobered.

"Just the same, Mr. Tom. There ain't no special diff'rence, as I can see--or anybody, I guess. She jest lays there an' sleeps an' talks some, an' tries ter smile an' be 'glad' 'cause the sun sets or the moon rises, or some other such thing, till it's enough ter make yer heart break with achin'."

"I know; it's the 'game'--bless her sweet heart!" nodded Old Tom, blinking a little.

"She told *you*, then, too, about that 'ere--game?"

"Oh, yes. She told me long ago." The old man hesitated, then went on, his lips twitching a little. "I was growlin' one day 'cause I was so bent up and crooked; an' what do ye s'pose the little thing said?"

"I couldn't guess. I wouldn't think she could find *anythin'* about *that* ter be glad about!"

"She did. She said I could be glad, anyhow, that I didn't have ter *stoop so far ter do my weedin'* 'cause I was already bent part way over."

Nancy gave a wistful laugh.

"Well, I ain't surprised, after all. You might know she'd find somethin'. We've been playin' it--that game--since almost the first, 'cause there wa'n't no one else she could play it with--though she did speak of--her aunt."

"*Miss Polly!*"

Nancy chuckled.

"I guess you hain't got such an awful diff'rent opinion o' the mistress than I have," she bridled.

Old Tom stiffened.

"I was only thinkin' 'twould be--some of a surprise--to her," he explained with dignity.

"Well, yes, I guess 'twould be--*then*," retorted Nancy. "I ain't sayin' what 'twould be *now*. I'd believe anythin' o' the mistress now--even that she'd take ter playin' it herself!"

"But hain't the little gal told her--ever? She's told ev'ry one else, I guess. I'm hearin' of it ev'rywhere, now, since she was hurted," said Tom.

"Well, she didn't tell Miss Polly," rejoined Nancy. "Miss Pollyanna told me long ago that she couldn't tell her, 'cause her aunt didn't like ter have her talk about her father; an' 'twas her father's game, an' she'd have ter talk about him if she did tell it. So she never told her."

"Oh, I see, I see." The old man nodded his head slowly. "They was always bitter against the minister chap--all of 'em, 'cause he took Miss Jennie away from 'em. An' Miss Polly--young as she was-- couldn't never forgive him; she was that fond of Miss Jennie--in them days. I see, I see. 'Twas a bad mess," he sighed, as he turned away.

"Yes, 'twas--all 'round, all 'round," sighed Nancy in her turn, as she went back to her kitchen.

For no one were those days of waiting easy. The nurse tried to look cheerful, but her eyes were troubled. The doctor was openly nervous and impatient. Miss Polly said little; but even the softening waves of hair about her face, and the becoming laces at her throat, could not hide the fact that she was growing thin and pale. As to Pollyanna--Pollyanna petted the dog, smoothed the cat's sleek head, admired the flowers and ate the fruits and jellies that were sent in to her; and returned innumerable cheery answers to the many messages of love and inquiry that were brought to her bedside. But she, too, grew pale and thin; and the nervous activity of the poor little hands and arms only emphasized the pitiful motionlessness of the once active little feet and legs now lying so woefully quiet under the blankets.

As to the game--Pollyanna told Nancy these days how glad she was going to be when she could go to school again, go to see Mrs. Snow, go to call on Mr. Pendleton, and go to ride with Dr. Chilton nor did she seem to realize that all this "gladness" was in the future, not the present. Nancy, however, did realize it--and cry about it, when she was alone.

Lesson 167

1. Read chapter 26.
2. Tell someone about the chapter.

Just a week from the time Dr. Mead, the specialist, was first expected, he came. He was a tall, broad-shouldered man with kind gray eyes, and a cheerful smile. Pollyanna liked him at once, and told him so.

"You look quite a lot like *my* doctor, you see," she added engagingly.

"*Your* doctor?" Dr. Mead glanced in evident surprise at Dr. Warren, talking with the nurse a few feet away. Dr. Warren was a small, brown-eyed man with a pointed brown beard.

"Oh, *that* isn't my doctor," smiled Pollyanna, divining his thought. "Dr. Warren is Aunt Polly's doctor. My doctor is Dr. Chilton."

"Oh-h!" said Dr. Mead, a little oddly, his eyes resting on Miss Polly, who, with a vivid blush, had turned hastily away.

"Yes." Pollyanna hesitated, then continued with her usual truthfulness. "You see, *I* wanted Dr. Chilton all the time, but Aunt Polly wanted you. She said you knew more than Dr. Chilton, anyway about--about broken legs like mine. And of course if you do, I can be glad for that. Do you?"

A swift something crossed the doctor's face that Pollyanna could not quite translate.

"Only time can tell that, little girl," he said gently; then he turned a grave face toward Dr. Warren, who had just come to the bedside.

Every one said afterward that it was the cat that did it. Certainly, if Fluffy had not poked an insistent paw and nose against Pollyanna's unlatched door, the door would not have swung noiselessly open on its hinges until it stood perhaps a foot ajar; and if the door had not been open, Pollyanna would not have heard her aunt's words.

In the hall the two doctors, the nurse, and Miss Polly stood talking. In Pollyanna's room Fluffy had just jumped to the bed with a little purring "meow" of joy when through the open door sounded clearly and sharply Aunt Polly's agonized exclamation.

"Not that! Doctor, not that! You don't mean--the child--will *never walk* again!"

It was all confusion then. First, from the bedroom came Pollyanna's terrified "Aunt Polly--Aunt Polly!" Then Miss Polly, seeing the open door and realizing that her words had been heard, gave a low little moan and--for the first time in her life--fainted dead away.

The nurse, with a choking "She heard!" stumbled toward the open door. The two doctors stayed with Miss Polly. Dr. Mead had to stay--he had caught Miss Polly as she fell. Dr. Warren stood by, helplessly. It was not until Pollyanna cried out again sharply and the nurse closed the door, that the two men, with a despairing glance into each other's eyes, awoke to the immediate duty of bringing the woman in Dr. Mead's arms back to unhappy consciousness.

In Pollyanna's room, the nurse had found a purring gray cat on the bed vainly trying to attract the attention of a white-faced, wild-eyed little girl.

"Miss Hunt, please, I want Aunt Polly. I want her right away, quick, please!"

The nurse closed the door and came forward hurriedly. Her face was very pale.

"She--she can't come just this minute, dear. She will--a little later. What is it? Can't I--get it?"

Pollyanna shook her head.

"But I want to know what she said--just now. Did you hear her? I want Aunt Polly--she said something. I want her to tell me 'tisn't true--'tisn't true!"

The nurse tried to speak, but no words came. Something in her face sent an added terror to Pollyanna's eyes.

"Miss Hunt, you *did* hear her! It is true! Oh, it isn't true! You don't mean I can't ever--walk again?"

"There, there, dear--don't, don't!" choked the nurse. "Perhaps he didn't know. Perhaps he was mistaken. There's lots of things that could happen, you know."

"But Aunt Polly said he did know! She said he knew more than anybody else about--about broken legs like mine!"

"Yes, yes, I know, dear; but all doctors make mistakes sometimes. Just--just don't think any more about it now--please don't, dear."

Pollyanna flung out her arms wildly. "But I can't help thinking about it," she sobbed. "It's all there is now to think about. Why, Miss Hunt, how am I going to school, or to see Mr. Pendleton, or Mrs. Snow, or--or anybody?" She caught her breath and sobbed wildly for a moment. Suddenly she stopped and looked up, a new terror in her eyes. "Why, Miss Hunt, if I can't walk, how am I ever going to be glad for--*anything*?"

Miss Hunt did not know "the game;" but she did know that her patient must be quieted, and that at once. In spite of her own perturbation and heartache, her hands had not been idle, and she stood now at the bedside with the quieting powder ready.

"There, there, dear, just take this," she soothed; "and by and by we'll be more rested, and we'll see what can be done then. Things aren't half as bad as they seem, dear, lots of times, you know."

Obediently Pollyanna took the medicine, and sipped the water from the glass in Miss Hunt's hand.

"I know; that sounds like things father used to say," faltered Pollyanna, blinking off the tears. "He said there was always something about everything that might be worse; but I reckon he'd never just heard he couldn't ever walk again. I don't see how there *can* be anything about that, that could be worse--do you?"

Miss Hunt did not reply. She could not trust herself to speak just then.

Lesson 168

1. Read chapter 27.
2. Tell someone about the chapter.

It was Nancy who was sent to tell Mr. John Pendleton of Dr. Mead's verdict. Miss Polly had remembered her promise to let him have direct information from the house. To go herself, or to write a letter, she felt to be almost equally out of the question. It occurred to her then to send Nancy.

There had been a time when Nancy would have rejoiced greatly at this extraordinary opportunity to see something of the House of Mystery and its master. But to-day her heart was too heavy to rejoice at anything. She scarcely even looked about her at all, indeed, during the few minutes, she waited for Mr. John Pendleton to appear.

"I'm Nancy, sir," she said respectfully, in response to the surprised questioning of his eyes, when he came into the room. "Miss Harrington sent me to tell you about--Miss Pollyanna."

"Well?"

In spite of the curt terseness of the word, Nancy quite understood the anxiety that lay behind that short "well?"

"It ain't well, Mr. Pendleton," she choked.

"You don't mean--" He paused, and she bowed her head miserably.

"Yes, sir. He says--she can't walk again--never."

For a moment there was absolute silence in the room; then the man spoke, in a voice shaken with emotion.

"Poor--little--girl! Poor--little--girl!"

Nancy glanced at him, but dropped her eyes at once. She had not supposed that sour, cross, stern John Pendleton could look like that. In a moment he spoke again, still in the low, unsteady voice.

"It seems cruel--never to dance in the sunshine again! My little prism girl!"

There was another silence; then, abruptly, the man asked:

"She herself doesn't know yet--of course--does she?"

"But she does, sir," sobbed Nancy, "an' that's what makes it all the harder. She found out--drat that cat! I begs yer pardon," apologized the girl, hurriedly. "It's only that the cat pushed open the door an' Miss Pollyanna overheard 'em talkin'. She found out--that way."

"Poor--little--girl!" sighed the man again.

"Yes, sir. You'd say so, sir, if you could see her," choked Nancy. "I hain't seen her but twice since she knew about it, an' it done me up both times. Ye see it's all so fresh an' new to her, an' she keeps thinkin' all the time of new things she can't do--*now*. It worries her, too, 'cause she can't seem ter be glad--maybe you don't know about her game, though," broke off Nancy, apologetically.

"The 'glad game'?" asked the man. "Oh, yes; she told me of that."

"Oh, she did! Well, I guess she has told it generally ter most folks. But ye see, now she--she can't play it herself, an' it worries her. She says she can't think of a thing--not a thing about this not walkin' again, ter be glad about."

"Well, why should she?" retorted the man, almost savagely.

Nancy shifted her feet uneasily.

"That's the way I felt, too--till I happened ter think--it *would* be easier if she could find somethin', ye know. So I tried to--to remind her."

"To remind her! Of what?" John Pendleton's voice was still angrily impatient.

"Of--of how she told others ter play it--Mis' Snow, and the rest, ye know--and what she said for them ter do. But the poor little lamb just cries, an' says it don't seem the same, somehow. She says it's easy ter *tell* lifelong invalids how ter be glad, but 'tain't the same thing when you're the lifelong invalid yerself, an' have ter try ter do it. She says she's told herself over an' over again how glad she is that other folks ain't like her; but that all the time she's sayin' it, she ain't really *thinkin'* of anythin' only how she can't ever walk again."

Nancy paused, but the man did not speak. He sat with his hand over his eyes.

"Then I tried ter remind her how she used ter say the game was all the nicer ter play when--when it was hard," resumed Nancy, in a dull voice. "But she says that, too, is diff'rent--when it really *is* hard. An' I must be goin', now, sir," she broke off abruptly.

At the door she hesitated, turned, and asked timidly:

"I couldn't be tellin' Miss Pollyanna that--that you'd seen Jimmy Bean again, I s'pose, sir, could I?"

"I don't see how you could--as I haven't seen him," observed the man a little shortly. "Why?"

"Nothin', sir, only--well, ye see, that's one of the things that she was feelin' bad about, that she couldn't take him ter see you, now. She said she'd taken him once, but she didn't think he showed off very well that day, and that she was afraid you didn't think he would make a very nice child's presence, after all. Maybe you know what she means by that; but I didn't, sir."

"Yes, I know--what she means."

"All right, sir. It was only that she was wantin' ter take him again, she said, so's ter show ye he really was a lovely child's presence. And now she--can't--drat that autymobile! I begs yer pardon, sir. Good-by!" And Nancy fled precipitately.

It did not take long for the entire town of Beldingsville to learn that the great New York doctor had said Pollyanna Whittier would never walk again; and certainly never before had the town been so stirred. Everybody knew by sight now the piquant little freckled face that had always a smile of greeting; and almost everybody knew of the "game" that Pollyanna was playing. To think that now never again would that smiling face be seen on their streets--never again would that cheery little voice proclaim the gladness of some everyday experience! It seemed unbelievable, impossible, cruel.

In kitchens and sitting rooms, and over back-yard fences women talked of it, and wept openly. On street corners and in store lounging-places the men talked, too, and wept--though not so openly. And neither the talking nor the weeping grew less when fast on the heels of the news itself, came Nancy's pitiful story that Pollyanna, face to face with what had come to her, was bemoaning most of all the fact that she could not play the game; that she could not now be glad over--anything.

It was then that the same thought must have, in some way, come to Pollyanna's friends. At all events, almost at once, the mistress of the Harrington homestead, greatly to her surprise, began to receive calls: calls from people she knew, and people she did not know; calls from men, women, and children--many of whom Miss Polly had not supposed that her niece knew at all.

Some came in and sat down for a stiff five or ten minutes. Some stood awkwardly on the porch steps, fumbling with hats or hand-bags, according to their sex. Some brought a book, a bunch of flowers, or a dainty to tempt the palate. Some cried frankly. Some turned their backs and blew their noses furiously. But all inquired very anxiously for the little injured girl; and all sent to her some message--and it was these messages which, after a time, stirred Miss Polly to action.

First came Mr. John Pendleton. He came without his crutches to-day.

"I don't need to tell you how shocked I am," he began almost harshly. "But can--nothing be done?"

Miss Polly gave a gesture of despair.

"Oh, we're 'doing,' of course, all the time. Dr. Mead prescribed certain treatments and medicines that might help, and Dr. Warren is carrying them out to the letter, of course. But--Dr. Mead held out almost no hope."

John Pendleton rose abruptly--though he had but just come. His face was white, and his mouth was set into stern lines. Miss Polly, looking at him, knew very well why he felt that he could not stay longer in her presence. At the door he turned.

"I have a message for Pollyanna," he said. "Will you tell her, please, that I have seen Jimmy Bean and--that he's going to be my boy hereafter. Tell her I thought she would be--*glad* to know. I shall adopt him, probably."

For a brief moment Miss Polly lost her usual well-bred self-control.

"You will adopt Jimmy Bean!" she gasped.

The man lifted his chin a little.

"Yes. I think Pollyanna will understand. You will tell her I thought she would be--*glad*!"

"Why, of--of course," faltered Miss Polly.

"Thank you," bowed John Pendleton, as he turned to go.

In the middle of the floor Miss Polly stood, silent and amazed, still looking after the man who had just left her. Even yet she could scarcely believe what her ears had heard. John Pendleton *adopt* Jimmy Bean? John Pendleton, wealthy, independent, morose, reputed to be miserly and supremely selfish, to adopt a little boy--and such a little boy?

With a somewhat dazed face Miss Polly went up-stairs to Pollyanna's room.

"Pollyanna, I have a message for you from Mr. John Pendleton. He has just been here. He says to tell you he has taken Jimmy Bean for his little boy. He said he thought you'd be glad to know it."

Pollyanna's wistful little face flamed into sudden joy.

"Glad? *Glad?* Well, I reckon I am glad! Oh, Aunt Polly, I've so wanted to find a place for Jimmy--and that's such a lovely place! Besides, I'm so glad for Mr. Pendleton, too. You see, now he'll have the child's presence."

"The--what?"

Pollyanna colored painfully. She had forgotten that she had never told her aunt of Mr. Pendleton's desire to adopt her--and certainly she would not wish to tell her now that she had ever thought for a minute of leaving her--this dear Aunt Polly!

"The child's presence," stammered Pollyanna, hastily. "Mr. Pendleton told me once, you see, that only a woman's hand and heart or a child's presence could make a--a home. And now he's got it--the child's presence."

"Oh, I--see," said Miss Polly very gently; and she did see--more than Pollyanna realized. She saw something of the pressure that was probably brought to bear on Pollyanna herself at the time John Pendleton was asking *her* to be the "child's presence," which was to transform his great pile of gray stone into a home. "I see," she finished, her eyes stinging with sudden tears.

Pollyanna, fearful that her aunt might ask further embarrassing questions, hastened to lead the conversation away from the Pendleton house and its master.

"Dr. Chilton says so, too--that it takes a woman's hand and heart, or a child's presence, to make a home, you know," she remarked.

Miss Polly turned with a start.

"*Dr. Chilton!* How do you know--that?"

"He told me so. 'Twas when he said he lived in just rooms, you know--not a home."

Miss Polly did not answer. Her eyes were out the window.

"So I asked him why he didn't get 'em.--a woman's hand and heart, and have a home."

"Pollyanna!" Miss Polly had turned sharply. Her cheeks showed a sudden color.

"Well, I did. He looked so--so sorrowful."

"What did he--say?" Miss Polly asked the question as if in spite of some force within her that was urging her not to ask it.

"He didn't say anything for a minute; then he said very low that you couldn't always get 'em for the asking."

There was a brief silence. Miss Polly's eyes had turned again to the window. Her cheeks were still unnaturally pink.

Pollyanna sighed.

"He wants one, anyhow, I know, and I wish he could have one."

"Why, Pollyanna, *how* do you know?"

"Because, afterwards, on another day, he said something else. He said that low, too, but I heard him. He said that he'd give all the world if he did have one woman's hand and heart. Why, Aunt Polly, what's the matter?" Aunt Polly had risen hurriedly and gone to the window.

"Nothing, dear. I was changing the position of this prism," said Aunt Polly, whose whole face now was aflame.

Lesson 169

1. Read chapter 28.
2. What does Pollyanna realize she can be happy about? (hint: end of the chapter)

It was not long after John Pendleton's second visit that Milly Snow called one afternoon. Milly Snow had never before been to the Harrington homestead. She blushed and looked very embarrassed when Miss Polly entered the room.

"I--I came to inquire for the little girl," she stammered.

"You are very kind. She is about the same. How is your mother?" rejoined Miss Polly, wearily.

"That is what I came to tell you--that is, to ask you to tell Miss Pollyanna," hurried on the girl, breathlessly and incoherently. "We think it's--so awful--so perfectly awful that the little thing can't ever walk again; and after all she's done for us, too--for mother, you know, teaching her to play the game, and all that. And when we heard how now she couldn't play it herself--poor little dear! I'm sure I don't see how she *can*, either, in her condition!--but when we remembered all the things she'd said to us, we thought if she could only know what she *had* done for us, that it would *help*, you know, in her own case, about the game, because she could be glad--that is, a little glad--" Milly stopped helplessly, and seemed to be waiting for Miss Polly to speak.

Miss Polly had sat politely listening, but with a puzzled questioning in her eyes. Only about half of what had been said, had she understood. She was thinking now that she always had known that Milly Snow was "queer," but she had not supposed she was crazy. In no other way, however, could she account for this incoherent, illogical, unmeaning rush of words. When the pause came she filled it with a quiet:

"I don't think I quite understand, Milly. Just what is it that you want me to tell my niece?"

"Yes, that's it; I want you to tell her," answered the girl, feverishly. "Make her see what she's done for us. Of course she's *seen* some things, because she's been there, and she's known mother is different; but I want her to know *how* different she is--and me, too. I'm different. I've been trying to play it--the game--a little."

Miss Polly frowned. She would have asked what Milly meant by this "game," but there was no opportunity. Milly was rushing on again with nervous volubility.

"You know nothing was ever right before--for mother. She was always wanting 'em different. And, really, I don't know as one could blame her much--under the circumstances. But now she lets me keep the shades up, and she takes interest in things--how she looks, and her nightdress, and all that. And she's actually begun to knit little things--reins and baby blankets for fairs and hospitals. And she's so interested, and so *glad* to think she can do it!--and that was all Miss Pollyanna's doings, you know, 'cause she told mother she could be glad she'd got her hands and arms, anyway; and that made mother wonder right away why she didn't *do* something with her hands and arms. And so she began to do something--to knit, you know. And you can't think what a different room it is now, what with the red and blue and yellow worsteds, and the prisms in the window that *she* gave her-- why, it actually makes you feel *better* just to go in there now; and before I used to dread it awfully, it was so dark and gloomy, and mother was so--so unhappy, you know.

"And so we want you to please tell Miss Pollyanna that we understand it's all because of her. And please say we're so glad we know her, that we thought, maybe if she knew it, it would make her a little glad that she knew us. And--and that's all," sighed Milly, rising hurriedly to her feet. "You'll tell her?"

"Why, of course," murmured Miss Polly, wondering just how much of this remarkable discourse she could remember to tell.

These visits of John Pendleton and Milly Snow were only the first of many; and always there were the messages--the messages which were in some ways so curious that they caused Miss Polly more and more to puzzle over them.

One day there was the little Widow Benton. Miss Polly knew her well, though they had never called upon each other. By reputation she knew her as the saddest little woman in town--one who was always in black. To-day, however, Mrs. Benton wore a knot of pale blue at the throat, though there were tears in her eyes. She spoke of her grief and horror at the accident; then she asked diffidently if she might see Pollyanna.

Miss Polly shook her head.

"I am sorry, but she sees no one yet. A little later--perhaps."

Mrs. Benton wiped her eyes, rose, and turned to go. But after she had almost reached the hall door she came back hurriedly.

"Miss Harrington, perhaps, you'd give her--a message," she stammered.

"Certainly, Mrs. Benton; I shall be very glad to."

Still the little woman hesitated; then she spoke.

"Will you tell her, please, that--that I've put on *this*," she said, just touching the blue bow at her throat. Then, at Miss Polly's ill-concealed look of surprise, she added: "The little girl has been trying for so long to make me wear--some color, that I thought she'd be--glad to know I'd begun.

She said that Freddy would be so glad to see it, if I would. You know Freddy's *all* I have now. The others have all--" Mrs. Benton shook her head and turned away. "If you'll just tell Pollyanna--*she'll* understand." And the door closed after her.

A little later, that same day, there was the other widow--at least, she wore widow's garments. Miss Polly did not know her at all. She wondered vaguely how Pollyanna could have known her. The lady gave her name as "Mrs. Tarbell."

"I'm a stranger to you, of course," she began at once. "But I'm not a stranger to your little niece, Pollyanna. I've been at the hotel all summer, and every day I've had to take long walks for my health. It was on these walks that I've met your niece--she's such a dear little girl! I wish I could make you understand what she's been to me. I was very sad when I came up here; and her bright face and cheery ways reminded me of--my own little girl that I lost years ago. I was so shocked to hear of the accident; and then when I learned that the poor child would never walk again, and that she was so unhappy because she couldn't be glad any longer--the dear child!--I just had to come to you."

"You are very kind," murmured Miss Polly.

"But it is you who are to be kind," demurred the other. "I--I want you to give her a message from me. Will you?"

"Certainly."

"Will you just tell her, then, that Mrs. Tarbell is glad now. Yes, I know it sounds odd, and you don't understand. But--if you'll pardon me I'd rather not explain." Sad lines came to the lady's mouth, and the smile left her eyes. "Your niece will know just what I mean; and I felt that I must tell--her. Thank you; and pardon me, please, for any seeming rudeness in my call," she begged, as she took her leave.

Thoroughly mystified now, Miss Polly hurried up-stairs to Pollyanna's room.

"Pollyanna, do you know a Mrs. Tarbell?"

"Oh, yes. I love Mrs. Tarbell. She's sick, and awfully sad; and she's at the hotel, and takes long walks. We go together. I mean--we used to." Pollyanna's voice broke, and two big tears rolled down her cheeks.

Miss Polly cleared her throat hurriedly.

"We'll, she's just been here, dear. She left a message for you--but she wouldn't tell me what it meant. She said to tell you that Mrs. Tarbell is glad now."

Pollyanna clapped her hands softly.

"Did she say that--really? Oh, I'm so glad!"

"But, Pollyanna, what did she mean?"

"Why, it's the game, and--" Pollyanna stopped short, her fingers to her lips.

"What game?"

"N-nothing much, Aunt Polly; that is--I can't tell it unless I tell other things that--that I'm not to speak of."

It was on Miss Polly's tongue to question her niece further; but the obvious distress on the little girl's face stayed the words before they were uttered.

Not long after Mrs. Tarbell's visit, the climax came. It came in the shape of a call from a certain young woman with unnaturally pink cheeks and abnormally yellow hair; a young woman who wore high heels and cheap jewelry; a young woman whom Miss Polly knew very well by reputation--but whom she was angrily amazed to meet beneath the roof of the Harrington homestead.

Miss Polly did not offer her hand. She drew back, indeed, as she entered the room.

The woman rose at once. Her eyes were very red, as if she had been crying. Half defiantly she asked if she might, for a moment, see the little girl, Pollyanna.

Miss Polly said no. She began to say it very sternly; but something in the woman's pleading eyes made her add the civil explanation that no one was allowed yet to see Pollyanna.

The woman hesitated; then a little brusquely she spoke. Her chin was still at a slightly defiant tilt.

"My name is Mrs. Payson--Mrs. Tom Payson. I presume you've heard of me--most of the good people in the town have--and maybe some of the things you've heard ain't true. But never mind that. It's about the little girl I came. I heard about the accident, and--and it broke me all up. Last week I heard how she couldn't ever walk again, and--and I wished I could give up my two uselessly well legs for hers. She'd do more good trotting around on 'em one hour than I could in a hundred years. But never mind that. Legs ain't always given to the one who can make the best use of 'em, I notice."

She paused, and cleared her throat; but when she resumed her voice was still husky.

"Maybe you don't know it, but I've seen a good deal of that little girl of yours. We live on the Pendleton Hill road, and she used to go by often--only she didn't always *go by*. She came in and played with the kids and talked to me--and my man, when he was home. She seemed to like it, and to like us. She didn't know, I suspect, that her kind of folks don't generally call on my kind. Maybe if they *did* call more, Miss Harrington, there wouldn't be so many--of my kind," she added, with sudden bitterness.

"Be that as it may, she came; and she didn't do herself no harm, and she did do us good--a lot o' good. How much she won't know--nor can't know, I hope; 'cause if she did, she'd know other things-that I don't want her to know.

"But it's just this. It's been hard times with us this year, in more ways than one. We've been blue and discouraged--my man and me, and ready for--'most anything. We was reckoning on getting a divorce about now, and letting the kids well, we didn't know what we would do with the kids, Then came the accident, and what we heard about the little girl's never walking again. And we got to thinking how she used to come and sit on our doorstep and train with the kids, and laugh, and--and just be glad. She was always being glad about something; and then, one day, she told us why, and about the game, you know; and tried to coax us to play it.

"Well, we've heard now that she's fretting her poor little life out of her, because she can't play it no more--that there's nothing to be glad about. And that's what I came to tell her to-day--that maybe she can be a little glad for us, 'cause we've decided to stick to each other, and play the game ourselves. I knew she would be glad, because she used to feel kind of bad--at things we said, sometimes. Just how the game is going to help us, I can't say that I exactly see, yet; but maybe 'twill. Anyhow, we're going to try--'cause she wanted us to. Will you tell her?"

"Yes, I will tell her," promised Miss Polly, a little faintly. Then, with sudden impulse, she stepped forward and held out her hand. "And thank you for coming, Mrs. Payson," she said simply.

The defiant chin fell. The lips above it trembled visibly. With an incoherently mumbled something, Mrs. Payson blindly clutched at the outstretched hand, turned, and fled.

The door had scarcely closed behind her before Miss Polly was confronting Nancy in the kitchen.

"Nancy!"

Miss Polly spoke sharply. The series of puzzling, disconcerting visits of the last few days, culminating as they had in the extraordinary experience of the afternoon, had strained her nerves to the snapping point. Not since Miss Pollyanna's accident had Nancy heard her mistress speak so sternly.

"Nancy, *will* you tell me what this absurd 'game' is that the whole town seems to be babbling about? And what, please, has my niece to do with it? *Why* does everybody, from Milly Snow to Mrs. Tom Payson, send word to her that they're 'playing it'? As near as I can judge, half the town are putting on blue ribbons, or stopping family quarrels, or learning to like something they never liked before, and all because of Pollyanna. I tried to ask the child herself about it, but I can't seem to make much headway, and of course I don't like to worry her--now. But from something I heard her say to you last night, I should judge you were one of them, too. Now *will* you tell me what it all means?"

To Miss Polly's surprise and dismay, Nancy burst into tears.

"It means that ever since last June that blessed child has jest been makin' the whole town glad, an' now they're turnin' 'round an' tryin' ter make her a little glad, too."

"Glad of what?"

"Just glad! That's the game."

Miss Polly actually stamped her foot.

"There you go like all the rest, Nancy. What game?"

Nancy lifted her chin. She faced her mistress and looked her squarely in the eye.

"I'll tell ye, ma'am. It's a game Miss Pollyanna's father learned her ter play. She got a pair of crutches once in a missionary barrel when she was wantin' a doll; an' she cried, of course, like any child would. It seems 'twas then her father told her that there wasn't ever anythin' but what there was somethin' about it that you could be glad about; an' that she could be glad about them crutches."

"Glad for--*crutches*!" Miss Polly choked back a sob--she was thinking of the helpless little legs on the bed up-stairs.

"Yes'm. That's what I said, an' Miss Pollyanna said that's what she said, too. But he told her she *could* be glad--'cause she *didn't need 'em*."

"Oh-h!" cried Miss Polly.

"And after that she said he made a regular game of it--findin' somethin' in everythin' ter be glad about. An' she said ye could do it, too, and that ye didn't seem ter mind not havin' the doll so much, 'cause ye was so glad ye *didn't* need the crutches. An' they called it the 'jest bein' glad' game. That's the game, ma'am. She's played it ever since."

"But, how--how--" Miss Polly came to a helpless pause.

"An' you'd be surprised ter find how cute it works, ma'am, too," maintained Nancy, with almost the eagerness of Pollyanna herself. "I wish I could tell ye what a lot she's done for mother an' the folks out home. She's been ter see 'em, ye know, twice, with me. She's made me glad, too, on such a lot o' things--little things, an' big things; an' it's made 'em so much easier. For instance, I don't mind 'Nancy' for a name half as much since she told me I could be glad 'twa'n't 'Hephzibah.' An' there's Monday mornin's, too, that I used ter hate so. She's actually made me glad for Monday mornin's."

"Glad--for Monday mornings!"

Nancy laughed.

"I know it does sound nutty, ma'am. But let me tell ye. That blessed lamb found out I hated Monday mornin's somethin' awful; an' what does she up an' tell me one day but this: 'Well, anyhow, Nancy, I should think you could be gladder on Monday mornin' than on any other day in the week, because 'twould be a whole *week* before you'd have another one!' An' I'm blest if I hain't thought of it ev'ry Monday mornin' since--an' it *has* helped, ma'am. It made me laugh, anyhow, ev'ry time I thought of it; an' laughin' helps, ye know--it does, it does!"

"But why hasn't--she told me--the game?" faltered Miss Polly. "Why has she made such a mystery of it, when I asked her?"

Nancy hesitated.

"Beggin' yer pardon, ma'am, you told her not ter speak of--her father; so she couldn't tell ye. 'Twas her father's game, ye see."

Miss Polly bit her lip.

"She wanted ter tell ye, first off," continued Nancy, a little unsteadily. "She wanted somebody ter play it with, ye know. That's why I begun it, so she could have some one."

"And--and--these others?" Miss Polly's voice shook now.

"Oh, ev'rybody, 'most, knows it now, I guess. Anyhow, I should think they did from the way I'm hearin' of it ev'rywhere I go. Of course she told a lot, and they told the rest. Them things go, ye know, when they gets started. An' she was always so smilin' an' pleasant ter ev'ry one, an' so--so jest glad herself all the time, that they couldn't help knowin' it, anyhow. Now, since she's hurt, ev'rybody feels so bad--specially when they heard how bad *she* feels 'cause she can't find anythin' ter be glad about. An' so they've been comin' ev'ry day ter tell her how glad she's made *them*, hopin' that'll help some. Ye see, she's always wanted ev'rybody ter play the game with her."

"Well, I know somebody who'll play it--now," choked Miss Polly, as she turned and sped through the kitchen doorway.

Behind her, Nancy stood staring amazedly.

"Well, I'll believe anythin'--anythin' now," she muttered to herself. "Ye can't stump me with anythin' I wouldn't believe, now--o' Miss Polly!"

A little later, in Pollyanna's room, the nurse left Miss Polly and Pollyanna alone together.

"And you've had still another caller to-day, my dear," announced Miss Polly, in a voice she vainly tried to steady. "Do you remember Mrs. Payson?"

"Mrs. Payson? Why, I reckon I do! She lives on the way to Mr. Pendleton's, and she's got the prettiest little girl baby three years old, and a boy 'most five. She's awfully nice, and so's her husband--only they don't seem to know how nice each other is. Sometimes they fight--I mean, they don't quite agree. They're poor, too, they say, and of course they don't ever have barrels, 'cause he isn't a missionary minister, you know, like--well, he isn't."

A faint color stole into Pollyanna's cheeks which was duplicated suddenly in those of her aunt.

"But she wears real pretty clothes, sometimes, in spite of their being so poor," resumed Pollyanna, in some haste. "And she's got perfectly beautiful rings with diamonds and rubies and emeralds in them; but she says she's got one ring too many, and that she's going to throw it away and get a divorce instead. What is a divorce, Aunt Polly? I'm afraid it isn't very nice, because she didn't look happy when she talked about it. And she said if she did get it, they wouldn't live there any more, and that Mr. Payson would go 'way off, and maybe the children, too. But I should think they'd rather keep the ring, even if they did have so many more. Shouldn't you? Aunt Polly, what is a divorce?"

"But they aren't going 'way off, dear," evaded Aunt Polly, hurriedly. "They're going to stay right there together."

"Oh, I'm so glad! Then they'll be there when I go up to see--O dear!" broke off the little girl, miserably. "Aunt Polly, why *can't* I remember that my legs don't go any more, and that I won't ever, ever go up to see Mr. Pendleton again?"

"There, there, don't," choked her aunt. "Perhaps you'll drive up sometime. But listen! I haven't told you, yet, all that Mrs. Payson said. She wanted me to tell you that they--they were going to stay together and to play the game, just as you wanted them to."

Pollyanna smiled through tear-wet eyes.

"Did they? Did they, really? Oh, I am glad of that!"

"Yes, she said she hoped you'd be. That's why she told you, to make you--*glad*, Pollyanna."

Pollyanna looked up quickly.

"Why, Aunt Polly, you--you spoke just as if you knew--*do* you know about the game, Aunt Polly?"

"Yes, dear." Miss Polly sternly forced her voice to be cheerfully matter-of-fact. "Nancy told me. I think it's a beautiful game. I'm going to play it now--with you."

"Oh, Aunt Polly--*you*? I'm so glad! You see, I've really wanted you most of anybody, all the time."

Aunt Polly caught her breath a little sharply. It was even harder this time to keep her voice steady; but she did it.

"Yes, dear; and there are all those others, too. Why, Pollyanna, I think all the town is playing that game now with you--even to the minister! I haven't had a chance to tell you, yet, but this morning I met Mr. Ford when I was down to the village, and he told me to say to you that just as soon as you could see him, he was coming to tell you that he hadn't stopped being glad over those eight hundred rejoicing texts that you told him about. So you see, dear, it's just you that have done it. The whole town is playing the game, and the whole town is wonderfully happier--and all because of one little girl who taught the people a new game, and how to play it."

Pollyanna clapped her hands.

"Oh, I'm so glad," she cried. Then, suddenly, a wonderful light illumined her face. "Why, Aunt Polly, there *is* something I can be glad about, after all. I can be glad I've *had* my legs, anyway--else I couldn't have done--that!"

Lesson 170
1. Read chapter 29.
2. Tell someone about the chapter.

One by one the short winter days came and went--but they were not short to Pollyanna. They were long, and sometimes full of pain. Very resolutely, these days, however, Pollyanna was turning a cheerful face toward whatever came. Was she not specially bound to play the game, now that Aunt Polly was playing it, too? And Aunt Polly found so many things to be glad about! It was Aunt Polly, too, who discovered the story one day about the two poor little waifs in a snow-storm who found a blown-down door to crawl under, and who wondered what poor folks did that didn't have any door! And it was Aunt Polly who brought home the other story that she had heard about the poor old lady who had only two teeth, but who was so glad that those two teeth "hit"!

Pollyanna now, like Mrs. Snow, was knitting wonderful things out of bright colored worsteds that trailed their cheery lengths across the white spread, and made Pollyanna--again like Mrs. Snow-- so glad she had her hands and arms, anyway.

Pollyanna saw people now, occasionally, and always there were the loving messages from those she could not see; and always they brought her something new to think about--and Pollyanna needed new things to think about.

Once she had seen John Pendleton, and twice she had seen Jimmy Bean. John Pendleton had told her what a fine boy Jimmy was getting to be, and how well he was doing. Jimmy had told her what a first-rate home he had, and what bang-up "folks" Mr. Pendleton made; and both had said that it was all owing to her.

"Which makes me all the gladder, you know, that I *have* had my legs," Pollyanna confided to her aunt afterwards.

The winter passed, and spring came. The anxious watchers over Pollyanna's condition could see little change wrought by the prescribed treatment. There seemed every reason to believe, indeed, that Dr. Mead's worst fears would be realized--that Pollyanna would never walk again.

Beldingsville, of course, kept itself informed concerning Pollyanna; and of Beldingsville, one man in particular fumed and fretted himself into a fever of anxiety over the daily bulletins which he managed in some way to procure from the bed of suffering. As the days passed, however, and the news came to be no better, but rather worse, something besides anxiety began to show in the man's face: despair, and a very dogged determination, each fighting for the mastery. In the end, the dogged determination won; and it was then that Mr. John Pendleton, somewhat to his surprise, received one Saturday morning a call from Dr. Thomas Chilton.

"Pendleton," began the doctor, abruptly, "I've come to you because you, better than any one else in town, know something of my relations with Miss Polly Harrington."

John Pendleton was conscious that he must have started visibly--he did know something of the affair between Polly Harrington and Thomas Chilton, but the matter had not been mentioned between them for fifteen years, or more.

"Yes," he said, trying to make his voice sound concerned enough for sympathy, and not eager enough for curiosity. In a moment he saw that he need not have worried, however: the doctor was quite too intent on his errand to notice how that errand was received.

"Pendleton, I want to see that child. I want to make an examination. I *must* make an examination."

"Well--can't you?"

"*Can't* I! Pendleton, you know very well I haven't been inside that door for more than fifteen years. You don't know--but I will tell you--that the mistress of that house told me that the *next* time she *asked* me to enter it, I might take it that she was begging my pardon, and that all would be as before--which meant that she'd marry me. Perhaps you see her summoning me now--but I don't!"

"But couldn't you go--without a summons?"

The doctor frowned.

"Well, hardly. *I* have some pride, you know."

"But if you're so anxious--couldn't you swallow your pride and forget the quarrel--"

"Forget the quarrel!" interrupted the doctor, savagely. "I'm not talking of that kind of pride. So far as *that* is concerned, I'd go from here there on my knees--or on my head--if that would do any good. It's *professional* pride I'm talking about. It's a case of sickness, and I'm a doctor. I can't butt in and say, 'Here, take me!'can I?"

"Chilton, what was the quarrel?" demanded Pendleton.

The doctor made an impatient gesture, and got to his feet.

"What was it? What's any quarrel after it's over?" he snarled, pacing the room angrily. "A silly wrangle over the size of the moon or the depth of a river, maybe--it might as well be, so far as its having any real significance compared to the years of misery that follow them! Never mind the quarrel! So far as I am concerned, I am willing to say there was no quarrel. Pendleton, I must see that child. It may mean life or death. It will mean--I honestly believe--nine chances out of ten that Pollyanna Whittier will walk again!"

The words were spoken clearly, impressively; and they were spoken just as the one who uttered them had almost reached the open window near John Pendleton's chair. Thus it happened that very distinctly they reached the ears of a small boy kneeling beneath the window on the ground outside.

Jimmy Bean, at his Saturday morning task of pulling up the first little green weeds of the flowerbeds, sat up with ears and eyes wide open.

"Walk! Pollyanna!" John Pendleton was saying. "What do you mean?"

I mean that from what I can hear and learn--a mile from her bedside--that her case is very much like one that a college friend of mine has just helped. For years he's been making this sort of thing a special study. I've kept in touch with him, and studied, too, in a way. And from what I hear--but I want to *see* the girl!"

John Pendleton came erect in his chair.

"You must see her, man! Couldn't you--say, through Dr. Warren?"

The other shook his head.

"I'm afraid not. Warren has been very decent, though. He told me himself that he suggested consultation with me at the first, but--Miss Harrington said no so decisively that he didn't dare venture it again, even though he knew of my desire to see the child. Lately, some of his best patients have come over to me--so of course that ties my hands still more effectually. But, Pendleton, I've got to see that child! Think of what it may mean to her--if I do!"

"Yes, and think of what it will mean--if you don't!" retorted Pendleton.

"But how can I--without a direct request from her aunt?--which I'll never get!"

"She must be made to ask you!"

"How?"

"I don't know."

"No, I guess you don't--nor anybody else. She's too proud and too angry to ask me--after what she said years ago it would mean if she did ask me. But when I think of that child, doomed to lifelong misery, and when I think that maybe in my hands lies a chance of escape, but for that confounded nonsense we call pride and professional etiquette, I--" He did not finish his sentence, but with his hands thrust deep into his pockets, he turned and began to tramp up and down the room again, angrily.

"But if she could be made to see--to understand," urged John Pendleton.

"Yes; and who's going to do it?" demanded the doctor, with a savage turn.

"I don't know, I don't know," groaned the other, miserably.

Outside the window Jimmy Bean stirred suddenly. Up to now he had scarcely breathed, so intently had he listened to every word.

"Well, by Jinks, I know!" he whispered, exultingly. "I'M a-goin' ter do it!" And forthwith he rose to his feet, crept stealthily around the corner of the house, and ran with all his might down Pendleton Hill.

Lesson 171

1. Read chapter 30.
2. Tell someone about the chapter.

"It's Jimmy Bean. He wants ter see ye, ma'am," announced Nancy in the doorway.

"Me?" rejoined Miss Polly, plainly surprised. "Are you sure he did not mean Miss Pollyanna? He may see her a few minutes to-day, if he likes."

"Yes'm. I told him. But he said it was you he wanted."

"Very well, I'll come down." And Miss Polly arose from her chair a little wearily.

In the sitting room she found waiting for her a round-eyed, flushed-faced boy, who began to speak at once.

"Ma'am, I s'pose it's dreadful--what I'm doin', an' what I'm sayin'; but I can't help it. It's for Pollyanna, and I'd walk over hot coals for her, or face you, or--or anythin' like that, any time. An' I think you would, too, if you thought there was a chance for her ter walk again. An' so that's why I come ter tell ye that as long as it's only pride an' et--et-somethin' that's keepin' Pollyanna from walkin', why I knew you *would* ask Dr. Chilton here if you understood--"

"Wh-at?" interrupted Miss Polly, the look of stupefaction on her face changing to one of angry indignation.

Jimmy sighed despairingly.

"There, I didn't mean ter make ye mad. That's why I begun by tellin' ye about her walkin' again. I thought you'd listen ter that."

"Jimmy, what are you talking about?"

Jimmy sighed again.

"That's what I'm tryin' ter tell ye."

"Well, then tell me. But begin at the beginning, and be sure I understand each thing as you go. Don't plunge into the middle of it as you did before--and mix everything all up!"

Jimmy wet his lips determinedly.

"Well, ter begin with, Dr. Chilton come ter see Mr. Pendleton, an' they talked in the library. Do you understand that?"

"Yes, Jimmy." Miss Polly's voice was rather faint.

"Well, the window was open, and I was weedin' the flower-bed under it; an' I heard 'em talk."

"Oh, Jimmy! *Listening*?"

"'Twa'n't about me, an' 'twa'n't sneak listenin'," bridled Jimmy. "And I'm glad I listened. You will be when I tell ye. Why, it may make Pollyanna--walk!"

"Jimmy, what do you mean?" Miss Polly was leaning forward eagerly.

"There, I told ye so," nodded Jimmy, contentedly. "Well, Dr. Chilton knows some doctor somewhere that can cure Pollyanna, he thinks--make her walk, ye know; but he can't tell sure till he *sees* her. And he wants ter see her somethin' awful, but he told Mr. Pendleton that you wouldn't let him."

Miss Polly's face turned very red.

"But, Jimmy, I--I can't--I couldn't! That is, I didn't know!" Miss Polly was twisting her fingers together helplessly.

"Yes, an' that's what I come ter tell ye, so you *would* know," asserted Jimmy, eagerly. "They said that for some reason--I didn't rightly catch what--you wouldn't let Dr. Chilton come, an' you told Dr. Warren so; an' Dr. Chilton couldn't come himself, without you asked him, on account of pride an' professional et--et--well, et-somethin anyway. An' they was wishin' somebody could make you understand, only they didn't know who could; an' I was outside the winder, an' I says ter myself right away, 'By Jinks, I'll do it!' An' I come--an' have I made ye understand?"

"Yes; but, Jimmy, about that doctor," implored Miss Polly, feverishly. "Who was he? What did he do? Are they *sure* he could make Pollyanna walk?"

"I don't know who he was. They didn't say. Dr. Chilton knows him, an' he's just cured somebody just like her, Dr. Chilton thinks. Anyhow, they didn't seem ter be doin' no worryin' about *him*. 'Twas *you* they was worryin' about, 'cause you wouldn't let Dr. Chilton see her. An' say--you will let him come, won't you?--now you understand?"

Miss Polly turned her head from side to side. Her breath was coming in little uneven, rapid gasps. Jimmy, watching her with anxious eyes, thought she was going to cry. But she did not cry. After a minute she said brokenly:

"Yes--I'll let--Dr. Chilton--see her. Now run home, Jimmy--quick! I've got to speak to Dr. Warren. He's up-stairs now. I saw him drive in a few minutes ago."

A little later Dr. Warren was surprised to meet an agitated, flushed-faced Miss Polly in the hall. He was still more surprised to hear the lady say, a little breathlessly:

"Dr. Warren, you asked me once to allow Dr. Chilton to be called in consultation, and--I refused. Since then I have reconsidered. I very much desire that you *should* call in Dr. Chilton. Will you not ask him at once--please? Thank you."

Lesson 172

1. Read chapter 31.
2. Tell someone about the chapter.

The next time Dr. Warren entered the chamber where Pollyanna lay watching the dancing shimmer of color on the ceiling, a tall, broad-shouldered man followed close behind him.

"Dr. Chilton!--oh, Dr. Chilton, how glad I am to see *you*!" cried Pollyanna. And at the joyous rapture of the voice, more than one pair of eyes in the room brimmed hot with sudden tears. "But, of course, if Aunt Polly doesn't want--"

"It is all right, my dear; don't worry," soothed Miss Polly, agitatedly, hurrying forward. "I have told Dr. Chilton that--that I want him to look you over--with Dr. Warren, this morning."

"Oh, then you asked him to come," murmured Pollyanna, contentedly.

"Yes, dear, I asked him. That is--" But it was too late. The adoring happiness that had leaped to Dr. Chilton's eyes was unmistakable and Miss Polly had seen it. With very pink cheeks she turned and left the room hurriedly.

Over in the window the nurse and Dr. Warren were talking earnestly. Dr. Chilton held out both his hands to Pollyanna.

"Little girl, I'm thinking that one of the very gladdest jobs you ever did has been done to-day," he said in a voice shaken with emotion.

At twilight a wonderfully tremulous, wonderfully different Aunt Polly crept to Pollyanna's bedside. The nurse was at supper. They had the room to themselves.

"Pollyanna, dear, I'm going to tell you--the very first one of all. Some day I'm going to give Dr. Chilton to you for your--uncle. And it's you that have done it all. Oh, Pollyanna, I'm so--happy! And so--glad!--darling!"

Pollyanna began to clap her hands; but even as she brought her small palms together the first time, she stopped, and held them suspended.

"Aunt Polly, Aunt Polly, *were* you the woman's hand and heart he wanted so long ago? You were--I know you were! And that's what he meant by saying I'd done the gladdest job of all--to-day. I'm so glad! Why, Aunt Polly, I don't know but I'm so glad that I don't mind--even my legs, now!"

Aunt Polly swallowed a sob.

"Perhaps, some day, dear--" But Aunt Polly did not finish. Aunt Polly did not dare to tell, yet, the great hope that Dr. Chilton had put into her heart. But she did say this--and surely this was quite wonderful enough--to Pollyanna's mind:

"Pollyanna, next week you're going to take a journey. On a nice comfortable little bed you're going to be carried in cars and carriages to a great doctor who has a big house many miles from here made on purpose for just such people as you are. He's a dear friend of Dr. Chilton's, and we're going to see what he can do for you!"

Lesson 173

1. Read chapter 32.

2. The last chapter is a letter. Who is writing to whom?

3. How does the book end?

Dear Aunt Polly and Uncle Tom:--Oh, I can--I can--I *can* walk! I did to-day all the way from my bed to the window! It was six steps. My, how good it was to be on legs again!

All the doctors stood around and smiled, and all the nurses stood beside of them and cried. A lady in the next ward who walked last week first, peeked into the door, and another one who hopes she can walk next month, was invited in to the party, and she laid on my nurse's bed and clapped her hands. Even Black Tilly who washes the floor, looked through the piazza window and called me 'Honey, child' when she wasn't crying too much to call me anything.

I don't see why they cried. *I* wanted to sing and shout and yell! Oh--oh--oh! just think, I can walk--walk--*walk*! Now I don't mind being here almost ten months, and I didn't miss the wedding, anyhow. Wasn't that just like you, Aunt Polly, to come on here and get married right beside my bed, so I could see you. You always do think of the gladdest things!

Pretty soon, they say, I shall go home. I wish I could walk all the way there. I do. I don't think I shall ever want to ride anywhere any more. It will be so good just to walk. Oh, I'm so glad! I'm glad for everything. Why, I'm glad now I lost my legs for a while, for you never, never know how perfectly lovely legs are till you haven't got them--that go, I mean. I'm going to walk eight steps to-morrow.

With heaps of love to everybody,
Pollyanna.

Lesson 174

Vocabulary

1. Review your vocabulary from Lesson 15.

Spelling

1. Which word is misspelled? (I know spelling doesn't belong here, but you don't mind, do you?) Write the number and the column with the <u>misspelled</u> word on a separate piece of paper. The activity continues onto the next page. (Answers)

	A	B
1.	separate	seperate
2.	calender	calendar
3.	spaghetti	spagetti
4.	sience	science
5.	conscious	conshous

6. freindly   friendly

7. congradulate   congratulate

8. weird   wierd

9. wifes   wives

10. beutiful   beautiful

Lesson 175

1. Read the first two pages of "Even Steven" by Emma-Lindsay Squier.

Warming California sunshine, tang of December in the air, a dusty mountain road leading away from Sacramento—an old man plodding steadily, with sturdy defiance for age and the tiredness he was feeling.

He had been walking thus since early morning. The stamp of the "Old Prospector" was on him; his abundant hair was grizzled, and a dilapidated black felt hat was pushed far back from his forehead. In his eyes, crinkly and blue, was that incurable look of the adventurer who always expects something just around the curve in the road. His clothes were frayed and shabby; his dusty boots were patched in so many places that it was hard to tell where the original leather had started. His steady, plodding tread was accompanied by the jingle of pans and the clatter of a dangling short-handled pick and a miner's shovel hung above them.

He had long ago left the highway for a narrow, dusty road. Below the slope of the hill he could catch a glimpse now and then of a wide, brawling stream. He had panned for gold in it many times. But the country, though familiar, had a strangely alien feel. It was like meeting an old friend after a lapse of many years, to find that something intimate and glamorous has escaped.

The warmth of the day was gradually giving way to a wintry chill that presaged the coming of night. The old prospector stopped, shivering a little, and adjusted the knapsack on his back.

"Shanty," he said aloud after the manner of one who has lived much alone, "it's jest a plain fool ye are! With Christmas only a few days off, and goose an' trimmin's at the Poor Farm, ye had to break yer parole like, and become a fugitive! Shame be to ye, Shanty, as can't be a pauper in the proper spirit, but must be takin' to the road again!"

He sighed, and turned over a vagrant piece of quartz with the toe of his boot, scanning it with the look of one who sees in every wayside rock a potential gold mine. Then his eye caught the angle of a roof, down at the foot of the hill on the other side of the stream, almost hidden by the rusty yellowing of sycamores and cottonwood trees. The sight of it lifted his spirits suddenly.

"'Tis a shack, sure as ye're born! 'Twill have plenty o' rats infestin' it, but belike they won't mind sharin' it with ye fer one night—or maybe two ...."

He turned off the narrow road and pushed his way down through a mass of clustering bracken. The tumbling stream that barred his way for the moment was riotous, swollen by the autumn rains. There were sharp-pointed bowlders strewn across it, and he stepped warily, while the water churned close to his feet.

The cabin stood in a clearing once ample size, but now encroached on by a younger generation of cottonwood trees assuming squatters' rights. He went around to the front. The windows were dusty, and the holes in them had been stuffed with rags. The door sagged on its hinges.

But as a twig snapped under his foot, there came from within the sound of something moving. And then Shanty stood still, looking into the twin barrels of a gun poked through a broken pane of glass.

"Stand where you are." The voice was muffled, but shrill with a frightened defiance. "I'll shoot—"

The old man felt an instant of unpleasant tingling along his spine. Then he chuckled, and scratched his head under the battered brim of the hat.

"Seems as if manners ain't changed after all, even if times has! 'Scuse me, pard—I wasn't after jumpin' yer claim. It's jest a bit chilly that I was, and—"

"Aren't you from the Orphanage?" the unseen voice demanded, a little louder.

Shanty's jaw dropped.

"From the Orphanage! Do I look that young?"

There was a moment of silence. Then the gun was drawn inward. A face appeared behind the dusty window pane—a smudged young countenance, with eyes that were like great black holes, and hair that even in the waning light showed brick red.

Shanty drew in his breath sharply. "Saints above—it's only a lad! Come out, son. Are ye lost, or what?"

Again there was silence. Then a bar dropped, and the door opened cautiously, creaking on rusty hinges. Shanty was staring at a sturdy figure, at a boy who might have been a replica of himself at sixteen. The youth's square face was pinched and thin above his blue overalls. He clutched his gun with a grip that made knuckles show whitely. But as he stared into the kindly, twinkling-eyed face, some of the strain went out of his own, and a little quiver came into his lips.

"I—I guess you're all right, Mister. Sorry I pointed the gun at you." Then a grin suddenly illumined the face. "It's not really loaded," he admitted.

Shanty grinned back.

"'Twas not such a monster of a fright ye gave me. I've looked into gun barrels before—as was loaded! But what are ye doin' here, lad, miles away from anywhere?"

The boy's shadowed brown eyes took on a defiant gleam. His mouth set firmly.

"I ran away—from the Orphanage!"

Shanty burst out laughing.

Lesson 176

1. Read the next two pages of "Even Steven."
2. A pack rat is someone who doesn't like to throw things away. They save everything (and it all kind of piles up).

"Saints upon us! Two of us as has the same idee! I'm a truant meself, lad, and they're callin' me bad names this minute, I've no doubt! Well . . . could ye be givin' me the loan o' yer roof the night? Sure the climate's changed since I was out this way last, and me bones are feelin' the chill."

The boy stepped aside from the doorway.

"Sure, Mister, come on in. You're welcome to what I got—there's a bag of beans left, and apples from the tree in the yard."

The old prospector stepped inside the small, bare room and looked about. It was fairly clean, but stripped of all that goes to make a home. A pile of dried ferns with some gunny sacks over it served as a bed. A battered tin pail in the embers of the fireplace sent forth a familiar smell of cooking beans. A sluice box leaned dustily in one corner.

Shanty set down his pack, wonderingly.

"Lad, lad—it ain't much of a place ye ran away to!"

The boy answered with a fierce defiance.

"It's mine. My mother and dad and my sister Myra and me lived here, and everything was jake until Dad was killed blasting. Then Mom took sick and died in a hospital at Sacramento, and they put Myra and me in the Orphanage. I reckon they meant all right, but we just weren't used to it. Myra cried somethin' terrible—she's just a little thing, not quite ten," he explained with dignity. "I wanted 'em to let us go, but they wouldn't. So Myra and me fixed it up so I could run away. I know the place where Dad found gold, and I'm going to work that tunnel and get out enough to take care o' Myra!"

An answering light kindled in the crinkled blue eyes of the old wanderer. He looked down smiling into the earnest freckled face of the boy.

"What might yer name be, lad?" he asked gently.

"Bill Radfield."

The old prospector shook his head.

"I'm thinkin', lad, ye shouldn't have run away…."

"You did!" Bill challenged him.

Shanty sighed.

"True for ye, lad, I did—and I'm worse off than you. For when they took me for a vagrant, the judge sent me to the Poor Farm, on a parole like; but after a time the walls got to chokin' me. Well—I'll grubstake ye to bacon and coffee and the like, and to-morrow we'll have a look at yer feyther's mine. But what if the officers come seekin' ye?"

"They don't know where we lived—and Myra won't tell 'em!" the boy answered stoutly. The old prospector grinned and got to work. He opened the knapsack and spread its contents on the floor. Then, squatting before the embers, he built them into a brisk blaze; and soon the smell of frying bacon and bubbling coffee rose in a cheerful, appetizing haze in the small room.

The boy watched him approvingly.

"What's your name, Mister?"

The other grinned.

"Chauncy Wiltonshire I was born, belave it or not! But somewhere along the line I got to be called 'Shanty.' Hey!" he broke off suddenly, "there's a varmint makin' off with a piece o' bacon!"

He raised a stick of wood; but the boy sprang forward as a huge brown rat disappeared with a frightened squeak into the depths of a large hole in the broken flooring.
"Don't hurt him—that's Steven!"

448

"Oh!" Shanty put the chunk down, and looked quizzically at the boy. "So that's Steven! A pack rat, ain't he?"

"Sure!" Bill's voice was eager. He might have been talking about a faithful dog. "At first he was awful scared of us. But we kept putting out things for him to eat—and he'd always bring something in exchange. Mom called him 'Even-Steven.' And when I came back here, he remembered me. He isn't a bit scared—he'd have come right up to me if you hadn't made a pass at him!"

Shanty chuckled, and took the coffee pot from the embers.

"Seems to me his name ought to be 'Uneven-Steven.' I've known pack rats all me life, and I never seen one yet that traded anything like even for what they took away. For a chunk o' bacon, they'll bring ye a dried rabbit skull; and for a piece o' salt pork they'll leave ye a bent nail that ye can in nowise use!"

They began to eat. In the shadows beyond the firelight, there was a furtive movement. Two bright eyes peered cautiously. "Come on, Steven," Bill coaxed, "this here is my pard; he won't hurt you!"

The big pack rat slid forward, his right cheek bulging with something he was carrying. Bill extended a piece of bacon. At the appetizing odor of the long-absent luxury, Steven forgot his fear. He released what he was carrying in his mouth, snatched the meat, and whisked away into the darkness of his hole. Shanty picked up the small rock, examining it carefully.

"Well, there's plenty o' traders like him in the world! A stone for meat . . . and away they go! I had a partner like that once—'Banshee' I called him. But we'll give Steven the benefit o' the doubt—mayhap to him that pebble is a vallyable piece o' property!"

Lesson 177

1. Read the next two pages of "Even Steven."

It was morning, golden and gracious, with a warmth that denied the coldness of the preceding night. Shanty and Bill were pushing their way through a thicket of tall ferns and underbrush up the hill that rose behind the cabin.

"Gee!" panted the boy, "this sure has grown up since I was up here last! Hi!" He stopped, breathing heavily as they came out on a narrow but plainly marked trail. "Someone's been along here! See that footprint?"

Shanty nodded, sniffing. There was a perceptible odor of tobacco in the fresh mountain air.

"Did ye tell me that yer dad kep' this mine o' his a secret?" Bill hesitated.

"Well—not a dead secret! You see, there was a man who owned it, and he sold his claim to Dad. Mom didn't like him 'cause he used to drink somethin' awful, and once he tried to kill Steven for carryin' off his pipe. After he sold Dad the mine, we couldn't find gold in it anywheres; although there was plenty when he was showin' it to us. . . ."

The old prospector's eyes narrowed.

"Salted!" he said briefly. "Sech tricks ha' fooled the wisest of us!"

"But then, a few weeks later," Bill went on eagerly, "we found gold! Chunks of it!"

Shanty started. "Nuggets, ye mean, lad?" he asked eagerly.

"No, not exactly nuggets . . . little pieces of quartz like they had been broke off—and shot just full o' gold! Look, it was right here!" They had reached a ledge, set back under the sheltering brow of the hill. A rudely tunneled entrance made a rectangle of black against the gray-brown walls. Bill stooped down, his face glowing with excitement.

"Right here, it was."

Shanty, squatted down beside him, was examining the ground with attentive care. A pile of broken twigs and sticks was scattered about, a fragment or two of green glass, and a tiny piece of a mirror. He picked up a small white object and held it out to Bill.

"Was this chiny button and these pieces o' glass here when ye found the gold-bearin' quartz?" he asked.

The boy stared at him with wrinkled brows.

"Do you think we paid any attention to rubbish like that?"

The old prospector's blue eyes were squinting down at the cabin and the brawling stream below, at the foot of the hill.

"No, belike not," he said slowly, "but I'm wonderin'; ye say that yer dad found chunks o' quartz after he'd bought the mine?"

"Yes! This man came around again, and he wanted to buy it back, but Dad wouldn't sell it. Then one night he got Dad drunk, and when I went t' sleep they were playin' cards and arguin' about the mine."

Suddenly, through the low doorway, came the stooping figure of a man. He straightened up, blinking at the two on the ledge, his dark, unpleasant face streaked with grime and sweat. The boy caught his breath abruptly, and touched the old prospector's sleeve.

"That's him! That's the man I told you about!"

Shanty stood up, his eyes strange and hard.

"The top o' the mornin' to ye, Banshee Taylor! Is it saltin' the mine again that ye are, to snare some unwary devil like poor Radfield—and like mesilf when I gave ye all I had for a worthless hole in the ground?"

The man's small, heavy-lidded eyes glinted dangerously.

"You git off my property, and stay off! This here is my claim, and I got the paper to prove it!"

The boy's voice was shrill—more in anger than in fear. "You're lying! My dad never sold this mine! He knew there was gold in it—he was blastin' here when he was killed!"

Banshee Taylor grunted in derision.

"Much you know about it! He lost it to me at poker, and signed it over t' me, fair an' square. He's dead, ain't he?" A sudden thought struck him. "Say! You and yer kid sister was put in an orphanage! And you, Chauncy—I heard you was took up for vagrancy in Sacramento! The two of you is runaways, livin' in the old cabin! Now you keep yer mouths shut, or I'll make trouble! I ain't forgot, Shanty, that you took a shot at me once."

"And I ain't forgot that the bullet went through yer hat instead o' yer skull! The next time I'll aim better—kape that in mind!"

The man's face was hard and ugly. "There's another thing to remember while we're talkin' about it—Radfield was jest a squatter! He never actually registered his claim to that land down there. Even the shack don't belong to his kids."

Lesson 178

1. Read the next two pages of "Even Steven."

Down at the cabin once more, the two faced each other, breathing hard. The boy's face was white.

"Shanty, we gotta do something! I'm not goin' to let that man have my dad's mine—"

Shanty's face was grave.

"Yon's a bad un, lad, as would take the pennies off his dead mither's eyes! He has no legal claim to yer feyther's mine, for a gamblin' debt is not recognized in the Californy courts. Sure, I've had six gold mines give t' me—on paper, across the poker table—but divil a cent could I collect on 'em! He's bankin' on our position here—which ain't too good, me lad. But—I've a hunch inside o' me, churnin' around like a butter paddle. Come, lad—show me the place where yer mither used to throw out trash."

Wondering, the boy did so. Still wondering, he got pick and shovel for Shanty. But a day's steady work, grubbing in the unsightly conglomeration of broken bottles, tin cans and rusted cooking utensils, revealed nothing in the way of pay dirt.

With pan and sluice box the old prospector worked the swollen stream. The next day and the next they kept at it from early dawn until darkness. Food supplies were dwindling. Only apples were left, and a little coffee.

Of Banshee Taylor they saw nothing. But one night they heard the snapping of a twig outside the shack, and caught the flitting shadow of a face against the window pane. Instantly it was gone.

"Tis a pity," said Shanty, trying to speak lightly, "that we can't teach Steven to growl and bark when unwelcome visitors is prowlin' about!"

As if he had heard his name spoken, the big brown rat slid out of his hole in the rotten flooring, and came forward cautiously, his bright eyes fixed hopefully upon Bill.

The boy stooped down, holding out a piece of apple. The pack rat dropped what he had been carrying in his mouth, snatched the proffered morsel, and scurried back to his hole.

Shanty picked up the small white object and looked at it curiously. It was a china button, nicked at the edge.

"Now I may be crazy as a loon," he said half to himself. "but this looks like the same chiny button as I seen away up there on the ledge! Bill lad, if only that rat could talk, I'm thinkin' he could tell us somethin' we'd like to know! Was it true, lad, what Banshee said about yer feyther not registerin' his claim?"

The boy shook his head.

"Gee—I don't know! He staked it out, but mebbe he didn't get into town—"

The old prospector sighed.

"And neyther one of us dares go in—unless we want to stay put!"

It was the day before Christmas, a dark, dreary day with heavy rain clouds swirling overhead and threatening momentarily to dissolve into a torrential storm. The old prospector's heart was heavy.

"Ye're not gettin' anywheres, Shanty," he muttered, "an' ye're draggin' this lad nowheres with ye!"

He went to the door of the little cabin and looked up at the ominous gray sky. The sound of distant voices caught his ear. And then a tingling shock went through him. For from the highway at the top of the hill three men were descending—and Banshee Taylor was in the lead!

For an instant he stood helpless. The end to the brief interlude of freedom had come. Banshee had brought the authorities. It would mean jail this time!

With the thought came fierce, swift revulsion of feeling.

He slammed the door shut, and flung the heavy bar across it. He was panting as he turned around.

"Lad, lad, they're upon us!"

Bill leaped from his packing-box seat.

"I ain't going back!" he cried. "Shanty, you aren't either! You and me are pards—we're workin' for a livin'! We can get along if they just let us alone until we find that gold ...."

The old prospector's face was white.

"I'm thinkin' they won't listen to any sech talk, lad." They were at the window, crouching down together, peering out.

"Kape as quiet as a mouse, an' belike they'll go away—especially if the rain will but come!"

The sound of thrashing footsteps came nearer ... the men had paused on the other side of the swiftly racing stream to find the best place for crossing.

Suddenly, from behind the two in the cabin, came a little click. Shanty started nervously.

"It's only Steven ... he's brought something," whispered Bill.

But Shanty made a queer, strained sound in his throat. For the flicker of firelight had caught the object that the big brown pack rat had dropped on the floor—and it threw off a molten yellow gleam!

"Saints love us," he whispered, trembling, "it looks like— but it can't be. . . ."

Bill turned, staring at his friend with startled eyes. For the old prospector was crawling along the floor as if his limbs would not support him. Then he squatted in front of the fireplace, the quartz lump in his hand, and there was sweat running down his seamed face.

"Bill, Billy lad—" his voice was hoarse and shaken—"it's—it's gold! As rich and free as ever I saw it in me whole life! Bill—when first I saw that pack rat's nest up on the ledge and heard ye say that yer feyther found gold there, it came into me mind that it was carried there by a trade rat who liked shiny things! And when I glimpsed them pieces o' green glass and the chiny button—I figgered that Steven must o' packed 'em from underneath the trash pile." He paused an instant.

Lesson 179

1. Read the next two pages of "Even Steven."

"But, lad—I'm thinkin' the vein's nearer. He's been breakin' off pieces along his runway, belike! Git that pick and dig—right down that hole there, under the floorin' where Steven comes up!"

There were voices outside—the men had crossed the stream. Shanty got to his feet. His eyes were blazing.

"I'll hold 'em off, lad! If we can prove we ain't paupers—"

There was a peremptory knock on the barred door. Then a crisp, authoritative voice.

"Open up! We know you're in there, Shanty—"

For a terrified second, Bill hesitated. Then he leaped for the short-handled pick. He swung it above his head, and it came crashing down into the rotten flooring.

"That's it, lad—dig! Straight along Steven's burrow—" He had the double-barreled shotgun in his hands, and was poking it through the broken pane.

"Stand where ye are," he called out sharply. "Banshee, kape yer hands well above yer head; and you, Mister Sheriff, and you, Mister Deputy, take the same positions! I'm in no argyfyin' mood, and Banshee will tell ye whether I can shoot straight."

The three men outside, startled at the unexpected menace of the steady gun, lifted their arms involuntarily. Banshee Taylor's face had turned a mottled bluish white.

"D-d-on't shoot—" he stammered. "We—we don't mean you no harm, Shanty—"

The voice from within was pricked with sarcasm.

"Ye don't need to be tellin' me, Banshee! Sure, I've had plenty of experience in the past with yer dove-like kindness . . . . (Go on, lad, dig!)"

The sheriff frowned. He was a short, gray-eyed man with a deeply tanned face.

"Shanty, you're just making things harder for yourself and the boy. You deliberately became a fugitive. Defying the law with a weapon is another serious offense. And you're crazy if you think you can dig out of the shack. It's hopeless, Shanty. Put that gun down, and let us in!"

The deputy spoke softly, out of the corner of his mouth.

"Mebbe I can sneak around the corner and stick a gun through one o' the side windows!"

The gathering storm was nearer. The clouds were heavy and black. A white swish of lightning was followed by a crackling rattle of thunder.

"I'll not let ye in unless ye agree to give us a chance! (Dig, lad! Tear up that board yonder!)"

The sheriff's voice was stern.

"You're spoiling every chance for yourself and the boy. Open that door and surrender peaceably!"

Again came the white gnashing of the lightning's teeth, and the snarling roar of the thunder. The air was murky black….

"Beat it!" rasped out the sheriff to his deputy, and the man slipped like a phantom around the corner of the shack.

"Open the door, Shanty. You're covered from the other side!"

Suddenly, from within, there came an inarticulate cry. Then the gun barrel wavered, and the sheriff sprang forward and seized it, and dragged it through the broken window pane. Banshee, like a coyote, had turned tail and fled to the edge of the clearing. He came slowly back when he saw the gun safely in the hands of the sheriff.

"Be careful o' that old cuss," he said fearfully. "He shoots awful straight!"
The sheriff flung him a look of disgust.

The rain came down suddenly, in a vicious, breath-taking deluge. The three men hunched themselves against it.

"Let's get back to the car until this is over!" shouted Banshee Taylor above the smashing fury of the storm.

"Shut up, you!" the sheriff roared at him.

Then the cabin door opened abruptly, with the sound of falling bar and creaking hinges. The old prospector stood there, a strange, wild look in his eyes. His gray hair was disheveled by the driving wind.

"Come in!" he cried out to them, "come in and take shelter! Mister Sheriff, it's trustin' to yer honor that I am ...."

They stumbled inside, gasping for breath. Shanty shut the door behind them. The sheriff shook from his hat a shower of rain drops. "I've told you, Shanty, I can't promise anything except the law."

The bent figure straightened. There was an electric quality to his voice that seemed a part of the unleashed storm outside.

"It's justice of the law that I'm askin'! Justice fer an orphaned lad and his wee sister—fer them as has no feyther, and is hounded by a black devil in human form! You, Banshee Taylor—" he pointed a shaking hand at the dark, belligerent face—"you tricked William Radfield once by saltin' a worthless mine—and then, when ye thought gold was truly there, ye tricked him into gettin' it back again! But there's a justice above all yer dirty schemin's—and the instrument of it was a humble one! Jest a pack rat it was that fooled ye, Banshee Taylor, with his cache o' shinin' rocks! The vein is not up on the hill—it's here, under our very feet !"

The three men followed his pointing finger with hypnotized eyes. They saw a boy's bowed form, bent over something on the floor beside him—and there was tragedy in his figure.

Lesson 180

1. Finish "Even Steven."

"What the ..." muttered the sheriff, and lit a match. Then he drew his breath in a sharp, gasping sound. In the hollow space uncovered was a pack rat's cache; a litter of rusted nails, bits of glass, a bottle stopper—and a handful of quartz chunks, each one sparkling up into the flickering light.

But that was not all. Along the burrowed passage, ran a broad rusty yellow band—an outcropping vein of purest gold!

The boy looked up with dimmed eyes.

"I—I killed Steven!" he choked out. "He gave us all this—and I killed him! The pick went into him as he was runnin' out—"

The limp, inert body of a pack rat lay in his lap. Steven had made his greatest trade.

Suddenly there was a furtive movement in the room. Banshee Taylor was at the open door and in his hands was the double-barreled shotgun covering them.

"Hey! What are you doing?" The sheriff wheeled about and spoke sharply. In the man's face there was triumph.

"You all stay right where you are! I'll blow the head off of anyone that moves! This claim ain't never been registered . . . but it's going to be—today! I'm goin' to take the car!"

The sheriff's voice was hoarse with rage.

"You—you scoundrel! You'd try to take a strike like this away from a kid an' an old man. . . ."

He moved forward, but the gun halted him. "Stand back—or I'll shoot—"

Then Shanty's voice came, clear as a ringing bell. "Fooled again, Banshee—the gun ain't loaded!"

The man hesitated, his jaw sagging. In that instant, the sheriff and his deputy whipped out their revolvers.

With an oath Banshee Taylor flung his useless weapon from him and stumbled through the driving fury of the rain toward the stream. A bullet cracked past him. He swerved, and plunged into the water. The turbulent, muddy current caught at him. He leaped for a bowlder, missed his foothold— and crashed face downward on the sharp point. The three men and the boy upon the bank saw him throw out his arms, thrashing wildly. Then the rushing eddy and whirl of the maddened torrent dragged him down, rolling him over and over like a log. .

The sheriff and his deputy plunged in and battled with the fierce current. The rain beat at them with frenzied, stinging fury. The inert body avoided them, was swirled away, pushed under, battered against jutting logs and bowlders—but at last they dragged it up on the bank. The sheriff straightened up, shivering in the downpour.

"He's done for," he said briefly. "Skull's smashed in. Well, he had it coming to him. Shanty, I'll stand by you and the kid—we'll register that claim in his name today!"

"It's half Shanty's!" cried out the sober-faced boy. "He's goin' to be my adopted father!"

In Sacramento the next day, freshly clothed, and entertained by the sheriff at the most bountiful dinner either of them had known for many days, the question arose as to a name for the claim that was to prove one of the greatest finds since the old days of the Gold Rush.

On one side of Shanty sat Bill; on the other side, a demure, red-headed little girl whose adoring brown eyes never left the kindly, weather-beaten face.

"I think, lad," Shanty said solemnly across the remnants of turkey and cranberry sauce, "that in honor o' the day it oughta be called 'Christmas Mine,' for—"

But Bill shook his head.

"Nope—it's goin' to be called 'The Even-Steven'! You wouldn't find many pals who would give their lives for you!"

The sheriff and the old prospector looked at each other.

Shanty nodded gravely.

"I reckon that's so; 'The Even-Steven' it shall be! An' don't ye be takin' yer pal's death too much to heart, lad. For if Steven is the b'y I think he was, he'd be glad that he could trade his life fer the happiness o' two sech as yerself and the wee lass !"

"And you too, Shanty," Bill said quickly.

The old man smiled. Tears of complete happiness were smarting behind his own eyelids. Then the sheriff lifted his big white coffee cup.

"Here's to you all!" he said heartily. "A merry Christmas, and many of 'em!"

Congratulations on finishing the EP Fifth Reader!

Answers

Lesson 91

1. alphabetize, conflagration, congratulations, congregate, polite, political

Lesson 92

Vocabulary 1S 2S 3A 4H 5A 6H 7S 8A

Lesson 93

2. Answers will vary. These are just examples.
   - big-humungous, small-miniscule, loud-clamorous
   - vigilant-watchful, subside-calm, venerable-respected

Lesson 97

Vocabulary 1.D, 2.F, 3.E, 4.B, 5.G, 6.H, 7.A, 8.C

Lesson 98

6. Plumfield is a school and Jo is the woman in charge.

7. There are rules and guidance, but it's a fun place. Did you read about the pillow fight?

Lesson 100

4. They learned about God's love and miracles from looking at nature. Sermon in stones means that they can learn about God just from looking at and learning about the stones…how God formed them, placed them, uses them…

Lesson 101

2. She says they can **cultivate** self-denial and then they will learn to deny themselves and not stuff themselves full of Christmas-time goodies. Cultivate is a word you use for gardens, you tend the plants, take care of them, to help them grow. You can also cultivate a character trait or a skill by working on it or by encouraging it.

Lesson 116

4. The first is in the third person. The second is in the first person.

Lesson 117

4. There is an omniscient narrator who can see what everyone is doing at all times.

Lesson 121

5. Mrs. Joe is referring to Dan as the "colt." She feels like she if finally beginning to tame him.

Lesson 126

Vocabulary 1.F, 2.D, 3.C, 4.A, 5.G, 6.H, 7.B, 8.E

Lesson 128

3. They wanted more stories.

Lesson 131

3. The Gypsy grandmother. I lived with Gypsies for more than seven years. I can picture the cackler and her horse. Yes, I've known people with just four teeth. I can hear her cackle. People use the word gypsy to mean someone who doesn't settle anywhere, just keeps moving. But I capitalized Gypsy because they are an ethnic group. Their real, official, name is the Roma. In the village where I lived, they called me the white Roma. Their skin is darker because they are originally from India.

Lesson 132
2. The main character tries to make a plane; it crashed. Then the character tries to make a car; it crashes. Then the character flies through the sky on a pogo stick. What happens in the air? When the plane lands?
3. The lost pencil is the one you had a minute ago and now can't find.

Lesson 134
5. "I learned that from…" also lots of figures of speech, idioms, expressions

Lesson 137
2. the best, be in charge for awhile, get organized, in a bad situation, frozen in place not knowing what to do, go to bed, yell at someone, be patient

Lesson 141
5. It sounds like her parents die and she is sent to live with her aunt.
6. Will she be able to stay cheerful when everyone else is sour (or will she be able to make the sour town cheerful)?
7. She breaks her legs and doesn't think she can be glad anymore.
9. She finds a way to be glad and everyone can have a happy ending!

Lesson 143
2. 11

Lesson 146
2. To find something about everything to be glad about.

Lesson 174
Spelling 1B 2A 3B 4A 5B 6A 7A 8B 9A 10A

ABOUT

Easy Peasy All-in-One Homeschool

Easy Peasy All-in-One Homeschool is a free, complete online homeschool curriculum. There are 180 days of ready-to-go assignments for every level and every subject. It's created for your children to work as independently as you want them to. Preschool through high school is available and courses ranging from English, math, science and history to art, music, computer, physical education and health. A daily Bible lesson is offered as well. The mission of Easy Peasy is to enable those to homeschool who otherwise thought they couldn't.

Made in the USA
Monee, IL
20 July 2023

39641131R00256